THE
GLORIOUS
GRACE
OF
GOD
Unveiled

Dr. Glenn E. Clifton

WESTBOW
PRESS®
A DIVISION OF THOMAS NELSON
& ZONDERVAN

Scripture taken from the King James Version of the Bible.

Scripture taken from the New King James Version®. Copyright © 1982 by Thomas Nelson. Used by permission. All rights reserved.

THE HOLY BIBLE, NEW INTERNATIONAL VERSION®, NIV® Copyright © 1973, 1978, 1984, 2011 by Biblica, Inc.® Used by permission. All rights reserved worldwide.

The Authorized (King James) Version of the Bible ('the KJV'), the rights in which are vested in the Crown in the United Kingdom, is reproduced here by permission of the Crown's patentee, Cambridge University Press.

Scriptures marked ASV are taken from the American Standard Version (ASV): American Standard Version, public domain.

Scripture quotations are from the ESV® Bible (The Holy Bible, English Standard Version®), copyright © 2001 by Crossway, a publishing ministry of Good News Publishers. Used by permission. All rights reserved.

Scripture quotations marked (NLT) are taken from the Holy Bible, New Living Translation, copyright © 1996, 2004, 2007 by Tyndale House Foundation. Used by permission of Tyndale House Publishers, Inc., Carol Stream, Illinois 60188. All rights reserved.

Scripture taken from the NEW AMERICAN STANDARD BIBLE®, Copyright © 1960,1962,19 63,1968,1971,1972,1973,1975,1977,1995 by The Lockman Foundation. Used by permission.

The Holy Bible, Berean Study Bible, BSB Copyright ©2016 by Bible Hub Used by Permission. All Rights Reserved Worldwide.

Scripture taken from the Darby Translation Version of the Bible.

Scripture taken from the Webster's version of the Bible.
WestBow Press books may be ordered through booksellers or by contacting:

WestBow Press
A Division of Thomas Nelson & Zondervan
1663 Liberty Drive
Bloomington, IN 47403
www.westbowpress.com
1 (866) 928-1240

ISBN: 978-1-973-60047-3 (sc)
ISBN: 978-1-973-60048-0 (hc)
ISBN: 978-1-973-60046-6 (e)

Library of Congress Control Number: 2017913208

Print information available on the last page.

WestBow Press rev. date: 09/29/2017

Contents

Foreword
By Dr. Jim Richards

ANYONE WHO HAS experienced the saving power of the Lord Jesus Christ knows what grace is: A recipient of grace may not be able to articulate in theological terms the supernatural event that transpired in their life. There will be no doubt that something outside of them is responsible for the reality of God translating them from darkness to light. Grace is the work of God alone. Salvation in Christ is impossible through human effort.

Personally, I am amazed that God keeps me saved. What Jesus did to cleanse me from my sin at Calvary is incomprehensible. God knows when he saves us that we are incapable to live sinless lives. Yet He applies His keeping grace to us on a daily basis. We could not save ourselves. We cannot keep ourselves saved. It is equally remarkable to me that God keeps me by His grace as it is that He saved me by His grace.

What little God does through me is because He has enabled me by grace. Grace guards me when I am vulnerable. Grace produces righteousness in me when I am unrighteous. Grace is the sine qua non of the Christian life. I am what I am by the grace of God. Everything else is my effort.

Dr. Glen Clifton takes the subject of grace and extensively reveals for us the marvelous work of God. He mines the riches of God's supply for every aspect of life. I was reminded and deeply encouraged as I read the explanations of God's grace.

Throughout the book you will find abundant scripture references. Dr. Clifton is a man who believes the Bible is the inerrant, infallible Word of God. Any teaching he would set forth is grounded in Scripture. From beginning to end the Bible is expounded. Every point, every position is supported by chapter and verse. When you read this book you will find yourself immersed in God's Word. When you finish you will have journeyed through references that express, "Thus saith the Lord!"

Spurgeon liked a sermon to a house. He said that it was necessary to have windows to let the light shine in. Illustrations are the windows in a sermon. Once again, Dr. Clifton uses abundant light on the narrative. His illustrations are drawn from history. He refers to numerous events familiar to his readers. Real live experiences are intertwined to bring to life points of view. Humor is interspersed throughout the writing. The Grace of God Unveiled is not a dry theological treatise. It is a warm personal expression from the heart of the man of God.

Dr. Clifton clearly demonstrates that he believes salvation is a work of sovereign grace. He is not argumentative. He states his view without being negative toward others. His desire is to uplift the grace of God.

Glen Clifton is a man who poured his life out for the gospel. He has expressed his biblical conviction in this volume. It is the testimony of a life given over to the glory of God. I am honored to have the privilege to write the Foreword.

Dr. Jim Richards
Executive Director Southern Baptist of Texas
Convention Grapevine, Texas May 2017

Acknowledgements

I WOULD LIKE to say thank-you to several individuals who helped make this study book possible. From the original manuscript much was done ... spelling, duplicate passages, grammar, and clarification of certain paragraphs.

First, I would like to thank Dr. Jim Richards, Executive Director of the Southern Baptist of Texas Convention, for sharing in this book, and for writing the FORWARD of this book. He is a wonderful Bible Teacher and Expositor of the Word of God, as well as being a leader doing a marvelous work in directing this one-time fledgling Convention from almost infancy to hundreds of cooperating churches and thousands of souls in serving our Lord.

Tom Lancaster, my brother in Christ, a former church member and adult Bible teacher in the F.B.C., in East Texas helped correct and made some great suggestions from the first manuscript.

Rev. Paul McKinney, Pastor of the First Baptist Church in Eustace, Texas where I served as Senior Pastor for eight and a half years. A big thank you to him for his corrections, recommendations and helpful suggestions.

Carolyn Carter, former Church Secretary and Minister of Education at the F.B.C. of Eustace. Her positive proposals were great encouragement to me.

Salvatore "Sal" Franco, former professor of languages in Long Island, N.Y., and more recently at Indian River Community College in Port St. Lucie, FL., for his assistance in corrections from the original manuscript. Sal, with a Catholic background, I had the privilege of leading him to a new relationship with Christ and baptizing him off the beach of the Atlantic Ocean, with six other seniors.

Dedication

"Jehovah Rapha – the Lord Who Heals Thee (Me)"

I WOULD LIKE to **dedicate this book** to a **lady originally** from **Israel.** After graduating from High School, as a teen-ager, she served two years in the **Israeli Defense Forces,** as **all youth do,** (boys and girls). In fact, even as I write this, **her daughter** is now serving in the **Special Forces** in the **Israeli Armed Forces.**

Today, she is **Director of Minimal Invasive Surgery** and the **Director of Surgical Endoscopy** in the **Department of Surgery** at **University of South Florida,** and **Florida Hospital** in **Tampa. Dr. Ross** was **one** of the **first surgeons** in the United States to undertake **Laparo-Endoscopic Single Site Surgery,** and continues to **develop new techniques** and **instrumentation** to improve its **safety** and **application. She treats** many **abdominal conditions, one of which** is **cancer.**

This is how **I met her.** After **losing 35 lbs. in 3 months from internal bleeding** of a **stomach cancer tumor,** finally found by an **endoscopy,** I drove across Florida for a **consultation.** After looking at **pictures, scans** and **notes** from the Doctors where I lived, **Dr. Ross said,** "Mr. Clifton, you are **not** going home! **I'll find you a bed today."** After three days and many more scans and tests, **she operated on my cancer tumor. Dr. Ross saw me** every day to **fully explain** the **surgery she was** going to **perform** on my **abdomen** and **stomach,** as well as **afterward until my release.** I came home three days later, and **"Praise the Lord,"** I'm **doing fine now,** except for a **few pills.**

Dr. Sharona Ross was used of God to save my life and give me a little more time of ministry for our Lord. I thank God for sending her into my life.

I lived through about four or five months of miracles ... one day after another, with my internal tumor bleeding, physical weakness, loss of weight, tests of all sorts, hospitalizations, seeking a cancer surgeon across the state who was away ... then I was given Dr. Sharona Ross.

I also thank God daily for His grace which He provided my wife and boys who had to take care of the 'ole man' during this time of Doctors, Hospitals and home care.

Disclaimer

THESE EXAMINATIONS OF the word 'grace' in this book are offered for your **personal edification** and **enrichment**. It will **lead us** to follow the challenge by **Paul** to, "**Study** to show **yourself** approved to God, a **workman** that needs not to be ashamed, **rightly dividing** the **Word of truth**" (II Timothy 2:15 - KJV).

I make no personal legal copyright on this material. **In my endeavor to write** this book **I have gleaned** from **many sources.** I have **attempted to cite exact quotations, and** give credit. **Where I have failed to give credit** is because many of the studies in this book are **given from materials** (books, sermons, papers, research, lectures, and articles, etc.), while **teaching** and **preaching for more than 60 years,** and many times **I failed to copy the name** of those in a particular quote. This was simply an **oversight on my part.**

Today I have noticed, in writings, music, and message, **many Christians are turning back** to the **old time Puritans** to, "**walk in the old paths,**" of **God's Word,** and to **continue to proclaim** old **truth** that **glorifies Jesus,** the Christ.

I am a student, not only of the **Word of God, but also the old "Master Preachers," their "Commentaries,"** sermons, and writings. **They** were **great** teachers, Bible expositors, and theologians, **Bereans** of the **Word** of **God,** who were **not ashamed** to **preach** and **write of it.** Today, few **Christians have turned their back on liberal theology** - to "**walk in the old paths,**" of **God's Word,** and to **continue to proclaim** old **truth** that **glorifies Jesus,** the Christ.

Many of their **books and writings I found** years ago (in the '50's and '60's) **upstairs** in a musty, dusty **used Book Store** in **San Francisco while pastor** in California.

If you are a student, preacher or teacher, I encourage you to use this material **to stimulate your own Spirit-driven imagination.** Additional **study** beyond this material **will benefit both you and your listeners.** You have **my full permission to use any of this material** as long as you **cite the source** for any substantial amount used in your message.

Should you desire to **use** any of the **studies** in your **message or article,** it is **okay with me.** This **simple reference** may prevent any criticism or question that may be directed toward you.

To put this into **my country boy's Texas terms:** "You're mighty **welcome to use any and all** of my **ingredients** for **your stew** ... just **use your own beef!**"

Preface

GOD CALLS HIS people to be transformed by the renewing of their minds" (Romans 12:2). **This transformation of thinking God's thoughts** after Him should be the **daily pursuit of the Christian.** This book exposits **the glories of the grace of God revealed** in the **Bible** against the **backdrop of** culture, philosophy, apologetics, ethics, and church history. As you **read** and **study, think** of it as **bridging the gap between Sunday school** and **seminary - equipping you** for the **Christian walk.**

I have discovered that **many of those in the church** do not comprehend the **'doctrine' of 'grace'** … while others just **do not believe** in **"grace."** Many **cheapen** grace. Some (most) **do not take grace** as it is - **pure merciful grace -** but desire to **overshadow** that **'grace'** with their **own faint hearted utterances, or their own anemic clichés, platitudes and weak opuses.** Man's **work** many times **gets in the way** of grace and **rob God** of His **glory.**

My longing is to **gracefully demonstrate,** with this book, that **grace** is the **most important declaration** and **doctrinal teaching** in the **Bible, Christianity,** and the **World. Grace** is most **clearly articulated** in the **promises of God** revealed in Scripture. **The true teaching** of grace is **always faithfully personified in Jesus Christ.** Grace is many things, but it **is honestly** the **love of Almighty God shown** to **despicable, unlovely, vile sinners.** May these pages **help bring** the **peace of God** to the restless, the **unmerited favor of God.**

Grace must **remain grace, true** grace **if grace is to be totally understood, praised** and **loved. God is gracious.** Everyone would admit that, but **most do not stand** up to the **Scriptural definitions and truths** of grace. **How gracious is YOUR God?**

The following **study is an overview** of what we **call the doctrine (s) of grace. This study** is a **happy reminder** that **one cannot get to heaven by works,** and that **God alone** is the **Savior** through **His beloved,** the **Lord Jesus Christ.**

I have no fantasies that this is **'the' profound book on grace,** or anything close to it, **or on the wonderful subject of 'grace,'** or **"the works of grace."** As you read this book, **my prayer** is that you would **find** the **means of grace** to be **practical** and **proficient** in your spiritual pursuit **of joy you have in Christ. Are In this study** the **message I will attack** again and again, **without** any apology, the **definitions** or **works of grace. In them you will** find **greater**

understanding and the means of discernment of the 'grace' of our Eternal, Almighty God.

In II Timothy 1:9, Paul writes, "(God, Who has saved us and called us to a holy life, not because of anything we have done but because of His own purpose and grace. This grace was given us in Christ Jesus before the beginning of time" (NIV).

> "The very center and core of the whole Bible is the
> doctrine of the grace of God." – J. Gresham Machen

My desire for this book is to exalt the grace of God from salvation to sanctification; to proclaim salvation alone through the grace of Jesus Christ; to humble the pride of mankind by declaring the sinfulness, helplessness and hopelessness of man outside the grace of God; and to describe the living experiences of the children of God who through the grace of God overcome their trials, temptations, sorrows, consolations to receive the blessings and holiness of God in their hearts and lives.

In our world, there are millions in need of the grace of God, just as we once were. It is a desperate hour in our world. Grace, through Christs' church, needs to take its stand among the lost world and proclaim Who God is! We are the lighthouse of His grace. The silent killer of our day is the silence of grace in the lives of God's children. I want to challenge you to be a lighthouse of grace. True grace givers know that they have been recipients of grace when they did not deserve it.

For a brief testimony ... several years ago, when my wife became ill with several physical problems, and then on-set dementia, I had to quit all my outside activities (except teaching/preaching), to become a 24/7 caregiver. I did have more time to study my Bible. It seemed as if the Lord told me one day, "Glen, quit, stop 'reading' your Bible ... and start 'studying' it." It changed my life. Since then, I have written and published several other books. So, this book is the result of my studies on the study of "grace" while she slept.

> "Life is hard, God is good, Glory is coming,
> therefore, stand firm in His grace." - John Piper

A neglected subject, 'grace' must be absolutely understood and practiced if we are going to have a right relationship with God. He is Creator and

Sovereign Ruler, and we are His servants that He has chosen out of the good pleasure of His will. While He honors His covenant with us, He also retains the right to use us as He wills. The position He has put us in is an humbling honor, awesome privilege and place of nobility, which carries with it an awesome responsibility. The value of this graciously tendered gift is so great we in no way want it to be misused in our grasp. God's grace has made us heirs of God and joint heirs of Jesus Christ (Romans 8:17).

My desire here is to bring out of Scriptures given, and not to force what I think might be there. I have a great safeguard on my head; never to share more or less than I believe to be the mind of the Spirit, in a passage I am translating and interpreting. I take Deuteronomy 4:2 seriously!

Word searches are important for deep study of the Bible to conduct one, search for a particular word throughout the Bible to help clarify meaning and make connections to other Scriptures, and learn how it's used in the context of the story.

If I were to say, "Hands up, everyone who has a Bible!" Everybody's hands here would go up, as I suppose that nobody here is without a Bible. But if I were to ask, "How many here, as a habit and a delight, daily meditate (study – not just read) upon the Scriptures?" - I wondered how many hands would be lifted to my question. Well, I will not ask you that question, but let everybody reading this book, ask it for yourself and judge yourself concerning it in the sight of God.

> My personal mission with this book (Lord willing),
> is to make the life-changing grace and wisdom of
> the Bible understandable and accessible to all.

My longing is that you know the important characteristics about this wonderful word ... 'grace' ... because everything God has for you revolves around this word! Grace was planned before it was exercised, purposed before it was imparted. (II Timothy 1:9).

My purpose is that the Holy Spirit, Who is the Heavenly Revealer, Convictor and Interpreter of Christ and His truth, may impart to your hearts a sober, spiritual and sanctifying receptivity to His grace, through His Word which exalts Christ!

My intention is to magnify the Lord Jesus Christ and His grace to His people - to unveil His glory, beauty, and fullness - to define the close bond that unites to Him all His people - and to bring you into a more personal

realization of **what Christ is to you,** and of **what you are to Christ, because of Grace.**

> **"...God has chosen the foolish things** of the world to **confound** the **wise;** and God hath **chosen the weak things** of the world **to confound** the things **which are mighty"** (I Corinthians 1:27 AKJV).

As believers in Christ, **we claim to understand grace.** From Sunday school to adulthood we've **been taught** that **we're saved by grace through faith. We know** the **Bible verses** and the **sinner's prayer,** but **have we** really **taken hold** of it ... or rightfully, **of Him?** Or rather, **'has He taken hold of us'?**

As you **devote time** to **studying 'The Glorious Grace of God Unveiled', I pray** your **knowledge** will be **transformed** into the **wisdom** of a **Spirit-filled soldier** of Christ. This will **not** be easy. It **will** involve **change.** The **people around you** may **not** understand you **stepping out** in this **new wisdom** for your **walk with Him. They** (like you, at first) **may be uncomfortable.**

"I can flip a switch, but I don't provide the electricity. **I can turn on a faucet,** but I don't make the water flow. **There can be no light** and **no liquid refreshment** without someone else providing it. And **so it is** for the **Christian with** the **ongoing grace of God.** His **grace is essential** for **building** our **spiritual** lives, but **we don't control the supply. We can't make the favor of God flow,** but **He** has **given us circuits** to **connect** and **pipes** to open expectantly. **There are paths** along which **He has promised His favor."** –David Mathis

Christian, for **your information: Grace is not** just a **nice idea.** It's **not** a **sweet song lyric,** a **romantic mystery,** a **poetic expression** or some **warm, emotional, fuzzy feeling.** It is the **'radical-change' of life that Christ** now **lives in** you. **Grace gives you** the **freedom to love** the unlovable, and **forgive the** unforgivable, **because you know** how much **you're loved,** and **know** how much **you've been forgiven.**

> **Marvelous, infinite, matchless grace, freely bestowed on all who believe!**
> **You that are longing to see His face,**
> **Will you this moment His grace receive?** (J. Johnson)

Some of you may be tasting the sweetness of this grace for the first time as a new child of God. Some who may have delayed their obedience toward the will of God in their life may now be yielding to the Holy Spirit's wooing conviction. That is the work of the Holy Spirit in your life, and I urge you to yield to Him and be mastered by His sovereign grace.

Some of you have lived in this sweet assurance for decades and simply join me today in rejoicing over this glorious reality in our lives. I invite you all to sing with me, to bless the Father and the Son and the Holy Spirit for the sovereign, sustaining grace that has kept us as a church (Gr. = ekklesia = called-out ones) for centuries and will keep God's elect in the faith till Jesus comes or Jesus calls us home to himself.

> "Grace may be free to us, but it is so only because God
> has borne all the cost Himself in Jesus" - Iain Duguid

My mission with this book is to make the life-changing knowledge of the doctrine of "grace," as found in the Bible, understandable and accessible to all. While we can know something to be true, sometimes we don't know it in actual fact and personal experience. We may know it intellectually, but are yet to accept it as a part of our daily walk factually. We may know about something without ever practicing it.

As never before, we as Christians need to know the major teachings about the "Doctrine of Grace." We live in uncertain times ... with global economic problems, the threat of terrorism, natural disasters and violence around the world. But as I pray this study will offer peace of mind by revealing God's plan for our times ... and how it applies to our life today. It is my prayer that these studies will empower you to live victoriously ... even in these uncertain days!

Not only do we need a knowledge concerning grace, we must turn this knowledge into the practice of grace, and live this grace in our daily walk. The author of Hebrews wrote us a real challenge: Hebrews states, "See to it that no one misses (falls short of) the grace of God," (Hebrews 12:15 (NIV).

Nothing is as hard to explain as the grace of God. Sometimes it doesn't seem to make sense. It's not fair. The doubters and critics say that grace can't possibly cover over what I've done and the sins I have committed. The best way, (and probably the only real way) to understand grace is to experience it. Too often pastors, teachers and churches may be taught about grace, but God's grace is not experienced.

In these pages, I ask you to consider **trading your ordinary, everyday, unexciting Christian life,** for an **indescribable** and **powerful adventure** with **God** as **He convicts** and **leads you by His** grace into **unknown territory spiritually.** I urge you to **start your journey today.** Let **God change** your **life** and **destiny from** the **natural to the supernatural! The Lord says,** "Call to Me and I will answer you, and **I will tell you unsearchable things, you do not know"** (Jeremiah 33:3 NIV).

I earnestly **pray this book** will be found valuable in **assisting** you in your **personal devotion** to **Jesus Christ** and the **ministry He has committed** to your care. Though **nothing can replace or supplant** your primary **commitment to the Holy Scriptures,** I trust this book, **"The Glorious Grace of God Unveiled,"** will help **complete what** the Lord is **teaching** you through **His** Word. **Pray, study, meditate, re-read, absorb, mark-the-book, pray again ... and experience the joy. Then, share** with your **friends, relatives, S.S. Class, and pastor.**

Introduction

"This is the true grace of God, wherein
you stand" (I Peter 5:12 AKJV).

GOD IS CALLED "the **God of all grace**" in this Scripture. Sometimes when we are **away from the grace of God,** as if we have **lost it all,** remember, **we cannot** find it of ourselves. We, **like the sheep,** can wander from the fold, and **cannot return without the help** and **leadership** of the **shepherd.** We must go to the God of all grace. **God is the first planter,** the **promoter,** and the **perfector** of grace. God is the **Father of lights** (James 1:17). **He must light up this candle of grace** in the soul. **Grace is in His gift.**

Grace is the most central concept in the Bible, Christianity, and the world. It is most **clearly expressed** in the **promises of God revealed in Christian Scriptures** and **embodied in Jesus** Christ. **Grace is** the **love of God** shown to the unlovely; **the peace of God** given to the distraught; and the **unmerited favor of God** to the **outcast.**

It is **my hope** that "**The Glorious GRACE OF GOD
Unfolded,**" will **encourage, stimulate,** and **assist you** to
grasp onto Grace, so that Grace may get a **grasp** on you."

Grace is the most extravagant gift ever **given** to the **believer** and it was the **most expensive one too,** yet it is **given completely free; without concerns** to merit or works or status. **Without grace** there is **no Jesus. That's why grace is so very amazing.**

Dear Christian it is imperative that God's people **comprehend the meaning and significance of grace.** This is **essential** to fully understanding the **gospel message.** Now as children of God, **we are recipients of grace as a gift** and are **able to understand it** when we know **God's character.**

"Except for "Jesus," the teaching of "Grace" is the most
important doctrine in the Bible, and the world. It is most
clearly expressed in the promises of God revealed in
Scripture and incarnated in Jesus Christ." - G. Clifton

Our sovereign God is gracious! In His grace **He has spoken** to me **through His Word,** informing me that **I was a sinner.** I was **warned** of the **wrath** that **is to come.** In **His grace,** I was **taught** that a **loving Almighty God sent His Son Jesus,** to the **cross of Calvary,** in order **to satisfy** the **requirements of His Justice** by punishing **His Son in my place.** "If you will but **admit your sin** and your **sinful state** and **call upon Jesus** for salvation, you will **be saved."** God's **grace is for sinners** like you and like me. **He will either deal with you in grace, or** you must **face the consequences** of **rejecting** His **gracious offer of salvation.**

We are unable to comprehend the **incomprehensible personage, pardons** and **mercies** of God. **He is,** after all, **an unfathomable, incomprehensible, majestic Almighty God.** It is **written,** "For as the heavens are higher than the earth, so are My ways higher than your ways, And My thoughts than your thoughts" (Isaiah 55:9 AKJV).

In I Corinthians 1:27-28, He tells us whom He has chosen the weak, the **foolish,** and the **despised!** "**God has chosen** the **foolish** things of the world … **God has chosen** the **weak** things of the world … **God has chosen** the base things of the world, and the things which are **despised** … the things **which are not!" Can you understand what God is saying here?** Often **we delude ourselves** by **thinking** that because **we are 'far better'** than others, **we have** been **chosen by God.** But if we have **been truly called, chosen** and **saved** by God, we will **realize that we are 'no better'** than **others; perhaps** we are **worse, except** for **His eternal grace!**

Our Christian life shows us **how wretched,** how **mean,** how **selfish we were before accepting redemption** - deep within ourselves. It **is high time** we learn that **there is nothing good in us!** (Romans 3:10; 7:18). I can **boast of nothing** in myself. **I had no merit,** I was **not worthy. It is by** the **sheer sovereign grace of God** that **I was chosen,** I was **called,** and **I was saved.**

I Peter 5:12 states, "By Silvanus, our faithful brother - **true grace of God in wherein you stand."**

God's grace turns rebels into citizens, **orphans** into children, **an adulteress** into a sinless bride, **an alcoholic** becomes a sober, loving mother, **a thief** that grace turns into a **minister** of the gospel, **a liar** who now tells the truth. **We receive the grace,** our **God receives the glory.**

**As soon as grace infiltrates into the depth of a sinning
soul, joy in the Lord secures a lasting faith.**

We were chosen in Christ **before the foundation** of the world (Ephesians
1.4). **God said to Jeremiah,** "Before I formed you in the womb **I knew you,
And before** you were born **I sanctified you;** I **have ordained** you a prophet
to the nations." (Jeremiah 1:5 NKJV). **This is one** of the **mysteries of God's
ways,** the mystery of **God's sovereign grace. Paul says,** He **called me by His
grace.** (Galatians 1.6). **He chooses, He calls.** Sometimes **we think** that when
we have **made a decision** for Christ, that **we have chosen Him.** But **actually it
is His Spirit working in us.** Otherwise, we would **never have come** to Christ
for **His pardon** and **salvation.**

All of us were 'lost' in sin – utterly **cut off from God. God sent Christ**
into this world, and He **sent Christ to me. I** was that lost sheep! **I didn't even
have the strength** to come to Him. **He came** into the wilderness of the world,
He found me and He **carried me** on His shoulders, **like a Shepherd** holding
a small lamb. (Luke 15.4-6).

What did the Lord Jesus tell His **disciples?** "You have not chosen Me,
but I have chosen you." (John 15.16). **What does God say there?** "I will have
mercy on whom I will have mercy; and I will have compassion on whom I will
have compassion."

Jesus is the beginning (Colossians 1:18), **before** ever **the world was.** He
is the **Source** of all things (Colossians 1:16). He is the **One Who** is over all
(Ephesians 1:22). **All that has stained creation is by the sin** of **men** and of
angels. Our **sin** and theirs, but by **His amazing grace,** would send us to
Hell. **His active, undeserved love** and **favor removes** that **stain** and **blemish
by** the **redemption of His chosen ones.** He has removed us from the **final
destruction** of all that **offends.** So **all that is,** will in the end **bring the praise
of His glorious grace.**

No one understands like Jesus!

In fact, it is **difficult,** if not impossible, **to truly understand grace** without
knowing the **character of God. Grace** is often **defined** in the **dictionary as
"the free and unmerited favor of God."** This is true, however, **grace is much
more than that.** Grace is **similar to other qualities of God** that **we can seek
to understand and embody,** such as love, forgiveness, mercy, benevolence. **We**

can understand grace better by seeking to understand how God is willing to bless and forgive us, although we do not deserve such generosity.

This world is longing for hope, in a world of hype, not realizing that the Gospel of Jesus Christ is the news we have been waiting for all our lives. Jesus came to liberate us from the weight of having to make it on our own, from the demand to measure up. He came to emancipate us from the burden to get it all right, from the obligation to fix ourselves, find ourselves, and free ourselves. Jesus came to release us from the unquestioning need to be right, rewarded, regarded, and respected. Jesus came to set the captives free and give us hope. Life does not have to be a tireless effort to establish ourselves, justify ourselves, and validate ourselves as humans.

Have your ever tried to define "Grace?" In today's religious world we find many very clichéd and superficial definitions given to this word. This book is all about the meaning and the message of grace. When you finish this book, you will have read scores of various definitions, descriptions, and designations of grace.

> "The very center and core of the whole Bible is the
> doctrine of the grace of God." - J. Gresham Machen

One dictionary defines grace as, "unmerited help given to people by God." However, grace is much more than that! Look at this definition, "the merciful kindness by which God, exerting his holy influence upon souls, turns them to Christ, keeps, strengthens, increases them in Christian faith, knowledge, affection, and kindles them to the exercise of the Christian virtues. Grace is one of those special words that belongs to the child of God. God has given us some words that the world just doesn't know. Unfortunately, many Christians don't know enough about it to properly appreciate.

> Here's a Biblical truth that we must remember:
> God has already done everything necessary for
> our salvation, past, present and future!

There are basically two ways to spell salvation: One is "D-O." Some people believe Jesus Christ died on the cross for their sins, but they still think there is something for them to DO to be saved. The other way to spell salvation is: "D-O-N-E." The Bible says, "He is the atoning sacrifice for our sins, and not only for ours but also for the sins of the whole world" (1 John 2:2).

For the sake of this study, **if you think God** has **already done 99.999%** of what's **necessary** for you to be saved and then **it's up to you to do** the remaining **.0001%** then you **don't grasp the truth about grace.** For the **Bible teaches** that there are **two kinds of righteousness** - the righteousness that **we** try **to establish ourselves** - and the **Bible says that** "all our righteous acts are like filthy rags." (Isaiah 64:6) **The other kind** of righteousness is **the righteousness God gives us** as a **gift** - the **righteousness of Jesus** (Ephesians 2:8, 9).

Let me just give you **a few words about grace** to **start this book.** Someone once said, **Grace is One-Way Love. Grace is love** that **seeks you out** when you have **nothing to give** in return. **Grace is love** coming at you that has nothing to do with you. **Grace is being loved** when **you are unlovable! Grace is the love of God shown to the unlovely; the peace of God given to the restless; the unmerited favor of God.**

One cliché definition of grace is **"unconditional love."** It is a true statement, for it is a **good description** of the thing. **Let's go a** little **further,** though. **Grace is a love** that has **nothing** to do **with you. Grace is everything. Grace is irrational** in the sense that it has nothing to do with weights and measures. **Grace has nothing to do** with **my inherent qualities** or so-called "gifts" (whatever they may be). **Grace reflects a decision** on the **part of the giver,** the **One Who loves,** in relation to the receiver, the one who is loved, that **negates any qualifications** the receiver may personally hold … **As stated: Grace is one-way love, from the Everlasting Father, to you and me!**

It is important that we **know** that we **can't understand** the **truth of** the **wooing** (call) **of the cross,** if **we don't understand grace.** It's **inside** and **around the truth of the cross** that we **find God's grace** most fully given and experienced. **Grace is one of the hardest things** for us to **grasp** and **live** out. In fact, it is **impossible apart** from the **redemption of Jesus** on the cross.

> **"May the Lord grant you grace as you study**
> **to understand the Holy Scriptures."**

The grace of God is a **subject** which, of all others, **demands** our **most serious attention.** God's **grace is nothing less,** than the **free, sovereign, and eternal favor of God** toward poor sinners in Christ! (II Timothy 1:9) **When a Christian** comes to **understand** the **full meaning** of this word, we consider **grace** the **most majestic word** in Scripture: **omitting the name of our adorable Master - Jesus -** where will you find one word to equal grace?

Grace is a magnificent word, truly a great Bible truth is resident in this word. In fact, grace is a word and concept without which man's salvation would be impossible. The gospel (good news) is a result of God's grace (Galatians 1: 6-9). Grace is presented as sufficient and Christians are called by grace (II Corinthians 12: 7-10; Galatians 1: 15).

God's grace is, unfortunately, an unappreciated word, which is misused and misunderstood by most people, even many Christians. Grace isn't limited to gold cross necklaces that hang on the necks of little old ladies, priests and pastors. Grace doesn't only decorate in the multicolored glow of stained glass windows or on the ends of creaky wooden pews. Grace is available every second of every minute for every human being who will ever live. Grace is given to bind our wounds, heal our hearts, and accept us just as we are. Thank You Lord!

The doctrine of the grace of God is the dominant theme of the Bible. In musical terms, the grace of God is like the melody line of a beautiful song. As a rule, only one note carries the melody, and all of the other notes serve to compliment that note with a harmony. Grace is the dominant note in God's dealings with man. His justice, His holiness, His omnipotence, and His omniscience are all an integral part of the music of His character and activities, but grace stands apart and above them all.

Christians live every day by the grace of God. We receive forgiveness according to the riches of God's grace, and grace drives our sanctification. Paul tells us, the grace of God has appeared, bringing salvation for all people, training us to renounce ungodliness and worldly passions, and to live self-controlled, upright, and godly lives (Titus 2:11). Spiritual growth doesn't just happen; we "grow in grace and knowledge of our Lord and Savior Jesus Christ" (II Peter 3:18). Grace transforms our desires, motivations, and behavior. Grace definitely and permanently changes us for good forever!

Grace is defined in Scripture as that which teaches us how to live! It is the Scriptural definition. Titus 2:11-12 states, "For the grace of God that brings salvation has appeared to all men, teaching us that, denying ungodliness and worldly lusts, we should live soberly, righteously, and godly, in this present world" (NKJV).

As I write this introduction, I hear Christmas Carols coming from my wife Dee's radio … so pretty. I'm reminded that from the very first Christmas until today God's goodness has not changed. The grace of God appeared on that wondrous evening in the form of an infant. That child was born in humble circumstances, but nevertheless that child, who was not recognized by most, was the **King of kings and Lord of lords.** Most Christians **celebrate the birth of the Savior** and **Great Redeemer of humanity** and learn how to fully **abide in His wonderful grace** in your daily life.

Again, **can you answer** this question? **What is grace?** In the **New Testament grace means God's love in action** towards men who **merited the opposite** of love. **Grace** means **God moving heaven and earth to save** sinners who could not lift a finger to save themselves. **Grace** means **God sending His only Son** to **descend into hell on the cross** so that **we guilty ones** as **He keeps on giving!**

The Bible teaches us that we **cannot earn God's grace** apart from **His free gift.** But God **positions us** to **go on getting** might **be reconciled** to God and **received** into heaven.

> "(God) hath made Him to be sin for us, who knew no
> sin, that we might be made the righteousness of God in
> Him." (II Corinthians 5:21).as **He keeps on giving!**

As an idiom, **"saving grace"** refers to a **"redeeming quality"** that **makes a person** or a **thing acceptable.** But that **is not the biblical meaning.** The **word grace in the Bible means** "unmerited divine assistance given humans for their regeneration or sanctification" **or** "God's benevolence to the undeserving." **"Saving grace"** is **the grace of God that saves a person.**

In day-to-day conversation, the **word 'grace'** means that someone **moves fluidly** and **beautifully.** We admire a **dancer's graceful steps** or a **figure skater's graceful twirls.** Or, it can be a **woman's name,** like my **aunt Grace.** It can mean **a prayer of thanks** before you eat: to **"say grace."**

But when you study it in the **New Testament,** and you will see it a lot, it **means something else entirely.** It means **nothing less** than **that God chooses** to **love the unlovable,** just because. "God demonstrates his own love for us in this: while we were still sinners, Christ died for us" (Romans 5:8 NKJV). **Grace means that God came to us first to rescue us.** Grace means **that the purchase of our freedom was 100 percent God's doing.** Grace **means** that the **pressure is off you to perform,** that you can always **find a resting place in your Savior.**

Scripture says that grace, the unearned favor of the Lord, is **necessary "because by the works of the Law no flesh will be justified in His sight"** (Romans 3:20). The **only way to receive** God's saving grace **is through faith in Christ:** "But now apart from the Law the righteousness of God has been manifested … the righteousness of God through faith in Jesus Christ for all those who believe" (Romans 3:21-22).

For He (Jesus) Himself has said, "I will never leave
you nor forsake you." (Hebrews 13:5, ESV)

Grace is the goodness of God on behalf of sinners who humbly **acknowledge** their **own deficiency** and thus their **dependence upon God's grace** for forgiveness and salvation: **He gives a greater grace. Therefore God says,** "God is opposed to the proud, but **gives grace to the humble" (**I Peter 5:5, NASB).

Grace is a truth atypical to divine revelation. It is a concept to which the **unaided powers of man's mind** never rises. **Proof of this** is in the fact that **where the Bible has never gone "grace" is unknown.** Very often **missionaries** have found, when **translating the Scriptures** into native tongues of the heathen, they are **unable to discover a word** which in any way **corresponds to the Bible word "grace." Grace is absent** from all the **great heathen religions** - Brahmanism, Buddhism, Islam (Mohammedanism), Confucianism, Zoroastrianism. **Even nature or culture or religion does not teach grace:** break her laws and you must suffer the penalty.

"Grace be unto you, and peace from God the Father,
and from the Lord Jesus Christ" (I Corinthians 1:3).

As a Christian, we must know how grace fits into Gods plan for and in our lives. It is **the chosen instrument** which God uses in **freeing** and **delivering** His people from error, ignorance, darkness, and the power of Satan. **It is by and through the Gospel of grace, applied by the Holy Spirit,** that His elect are **liberated** from the **guilt** and **power of sin.** "For the preaching of the cross is to those who perish foolishness; but unto us who are saved it is the power of God … But **we preach Christ** crucified, unto the **Jews** a stumbling block, and unto the **Greeks** (Gentiles) foolishness; but unto **those who are called,** both Jews and Greeks, **Christ the power of God, and the wisdom of God"** (I Corinthians 1:18, 23).

Each of us were created to **experience God's grace. Angels cannot** experience God's grace like we can. **We are the only living creatures** who are able to **experience God's grace** in such intimate ways. **God's grace** is **everything.** We are alive only by the **grace of God.** It is **by His grace** that we

are even able to have a personal **relationship with Him,** and **by His grace** that **His presence** is manifest **in our lives.**

That makes the **honest seeker for truth to ask, "How does grace work?"** The **grace of God** is something **more than** a good-natured smile, or a sentiment of pity. **It redeems, conquers, saves, matures, secures and sanctifies.** The **New Testament interprets grace** as **power.** By it, redemption comes, for it was by "the **grace** of God" that **Christ tasted death** "for everyone" of the sons (Hebrews 2:9 NKJV).

> **The precedence in my studies is not about grades. My**
> **desire is for understanding, insight and wisdom in this**
> **most important 'word' in Scripture.** - G. Clifton

Forgiveness of sins is proclaimed through **Jesus blood** "**according to the riches of his grace**" (Ephesians 1:7). **Grace not only** makes **salvation possible** but also **efficacious** (valuable). **Grace is omnipotent, (all-powerful).** "**My grace** is sufficient for you" (II Corinthians 12:9 NKJV). **Grace is sufficient to overcome unbelief,** the **infirmities** of the flesh, the **oppositions** of men, and the **attacks** of Satan. **Hallelujah!**

Years ago a young black woman was put up for **auction** at a slave-market. **She was distressed** lest she might be **sold to a cruel master. A godly man bought** her and **immediately set her free.** But she **would not leave him** who had set her free - **and insisted upon going into his household** and working for him. Now that **she could do** what she pleased - **she would not go anywhere** but to him. **She would say:** "He saved me! He saved me, **He has set me free,** and **I want to serve Him!"** This is how **we ought to feel toward Jesus** Who **died to set us free.**

> **The Psalmist states,** "For the LORD God is a sun
> and shield; the LORD will give **grace and glory;**
> no good thing does he withhold from those whose
> walk is blameless. O LORD Almighty, **blessed is**
> **the man who trusts in you!"** (84:11-12 NKJV).

As we study the **Holy Scriptures,** we find **the fullest exposition** of the **amazing grace of God** is to be **found in the Epistles of the Apostle Paul.** In his writings **"grace" is the teaching that** stands in **direct opposition to works and our own personal worthiness,** all works and merit, of whatever kind or degree. **This is abundantly clear** from Romans 11:6, "And if by grace, then it is no longer by works; if it were, grace would no longer be grace." (You may want to read that again! – G.C.).

We will study deeper how **grace and works** will **no more unite,** than **oil and water.** "By **grace** are you saved through faith; and that **not** of yourselves; it is the **gift** of God: **not** of works, lest anyone should boast" (Ephesians 2:8, 9). **The absolute favor of God** can no more consist with **human merit** than oil and water will fuse into one (Romans 4:4, 5).

> **Grace can neither be bought, earned, or won by the creature. If it could be - it would cease to be grace.**

Grace, faith, and works are **three terms** which we must understand to **comprehend God's system of redemption. Misconceptions** and **misinterpretations** of these words have **produced much confusion** about **how God saves** men from sin. **Major errors** have arisen because of the **failure** to "**correctly** handle the **Word of truth**," with teaching "**faith only.**" "**Grace excludes all law,**" and "**grace and faith exclude all works.**"

I once heard the argument from one well-known preacher on T.V., "But **Jesus wasn't** just a grace guy! **He was the perfect balance of grace and truth** and those **two things** are at the **opposite ends** of the **spectrum!**" **Partially true! Grace is Truth, and Jesus is Truth! The two are not** mutually exclusive, **any more** than **Grace is Peace, or Grace is Love.**

In the original Greek text the word "**grace**" (charis) **means "unmerited favor."** But, **what** does that mean? **It is God's doing of beneficent love and benevolence** for someone who does **not** deserve it. **Nothing in us merits salvation.** God is **gracious,** full of **mercy, love, and kindness** for man; therefore, **He has reached out** through His Son Jesus Christ to save man.

Grace is defined as the "**underserved love and favor of God toward fallen man.**" When you **take a moment** and consider all that means, **it is an awesome thought!** It means that **any sinner** can be saved! **Any storm** can be weathered. **Any situation** can be faced. **When we sing Amazing Grace,** we are telling the truth. **This passage in** Titus 2:11-16 is one of the clearest in the Bible **on grace and its results.**

The theological definition of grace from **The Merriman-Webster Dictionary,** brief and **to the point:** "The unmerited divine assistance given humans for their regeneration or sanctification." This **meaning covers literally scores of different** applications **in both Old and New Testaments. Key** to this definition **is "unmerited,"** meaning that grace, the divine assistance, **is in no way earned.** In terms of our spiritual well-being, **this is vital to understand.**

In other words, **now, as a child of God** because of the second birth, **I am a product of God and His grace.** It is **a gift** of God. **Paul is telling the Gentile believers** that they are what they are **because of the grace** of God. If somebody gets up **to testify** of their salvation experience, **they have not one right under heaven** to **say** they had anything to do with it.

Grace is what only God can do **to** a man, **for** a man, **in** a man and **through** a man, things that **a man could never do** on this earth and will **never deserve. It will never be deserved** in any way. It is **what God has done** for you and me. **A believer cannot take any credit whatsoever** for his salvation.

In the Bible, the word "saved" (Greek: **sozo**) is a passive verb. **It emphasizes what has been done to us.** We do **not save ourselves** by numerous **catechisms, confessions, prayers,** and **meritorious works** (Ephesians 2:9); **God saves us by His grace, through faith!**

The first step to receiving God's grace and forgiveness is to admit that we need it!

The **salvation that comes to us by grace** comes through the channel of our "faith" (Greek: pistis). **We must have faith to receive God's gracious offer** of salvation. **God expects us** to **trust in** and **act on** His Word.

Grace abounding, grace **reigning,** grace **conquering,** grace **justifying,** grace **comforting,** grace **purifying,** grace **sanctifying** – and such is the **foundation** of the history of the church. **Grace is the history** of **Christ's expansive love toward undeserving sinners.** The **Scriptures** are emphatic that **for everything pertaining to the sinner's deliverance** and **eternal life** comes down **to us from God. Man is** simply the **receiver** and the **enjoyer** of a love as **boundless** as it is **unbought!**

"Faith is a living, daring confidence in God's grace, so sure and certain that a man could stake his life on it a thousand times." (Martin Luther)

The Gospel of God's grace is for **sinners** in whom there is no hope. **Grace is implemented by God** "without respect of persons," **without regard** to merit, **without requirement** of any return. Listen, **the Gospel is not good advice, but** the "Good News!" It does **not speak of what man is to do, but tells what**

Christ has done. Grace is **not sent to good men,** but **to evil,** immoral men. **Grace alone is something that is worthy of the sacrificial love** and **death of Jesus.**

It is necessary to have true belief or **trust,** or **reliance upon** the Lord **for receiving salvation** from the **Redeemer.** When the gospel is presented, **revealed to** the human heart by the Holy Spirit, **there has got to be a response of faith,** of receiving **of** trusting **in,** of being willing **to obey what the gospel has said.** There is one thing **we are inclined to overlook,** lest **anybody think you did anything** to get saved: **it is all God's idea!**

When a diamond is mined from the ground, it is dirty, muddy, rough and ugly. But when **placed in the hands of a master diamond cutter,** that rough, ugly **stone is cut and cleaned and transformed into a thing of tremendous value and beauty.** It may **adorn a queen** or someone **familiar to us all**.

That is a **similar thing the Lord does in our lives!** He **takes old dirty, rough sinners** and **transforms** them by **His love and grace** and **His patient work** in their lives. He **then puts them on display** where **they bring glory and honor to His name!**

Man's obedient faith does **not cancel grace.** The **fact is** that **an obedient faith allows initial grace** (Acts 2:38) and **permits continual grace** (1 John 1:7). Since belief, repentance, confession, and baptism **are all works of faith** (Romans 1:5; 16:26), yet **they are not works of merit** which result in **boasting and bragging** (Luke 17:10). **It follows** that **they are necessary** in **order to be obedient to our new redeemer.**

The wonder of salvation is that God, in **His grace, saves** sinners by **giving them the faith** to believe in Jesus Christ. **Do you remember when the scales fell away from your eyes** and you were allowed **to see yourself as you were** and **Jesus Christ** as **your only** hope? **Do you remember** the glory of believing on Him for salvation? **If you do, then you know the wonder** of salvation. **If you don't know anything about that,** I invite you to **come to Jesus Christ right now, today.** You need to be saved, **and Jesus is the only way** for you to be saved, (John 14:6)! **The only way** you will ever **come to Him** is **through** the 'Amazing Grace' of God.

Because of God's grace, God has said, "I will never leave thee nor forsake you" - (Hebrews 13:5 NKJV)

Remember the story of the old man who lived in a broken-down shack on a **corner lot** that was **very valuable.** He had secured this property before the area was developed, now **it was the section of the city** where **millionaires built their homes.**

One afternoon on his porch, he **was roused by a man who wanted to purchase his land.** "**What's your price?**" he inquired. "**A hundred thousand**" came the reply. "**Fine, I'll buy it,**" said the stranger without hesitation. Before leaving, he **handed the owner a check for $10,000 as earnest money to bind the contract.**

In the weeks that followed, **the old gentleman felt guilty** about **asking so much for his worthless shack.** Thinking he could make it more presentable, he **began fixing it up.** On the day of the closing, the **new buyer came** to complete the transaction. After the **final payment** had been made, the **old fellow turned** to the **rich man** and said, "**Don't you think** you've got a nice little place here? See, I've **painted** it, **patched** the roof, and put **new boards** on the floor. You can sure be proud of it."

The new owner responded bluntly, "Sorry, I can't use it. It **must come down.** It will be **bulldozed next week,** for I'm going **to build a brand new house!**"

Friend: God doesn't want you fixing up your old house, He wants to **tear you down** and **rebuild you** in **His image!** He wants **to start you over!** "If anyone be in Christ, he is a new creature, (creation), old things are passed away (done away with), and behold, all things are made new" (II Corinthians 5:17 KJV, with my emphasis). **That's grace!**

The grace of Jesus brings hope and light
in the darkest of circumstances!

Once this gospel of grace grips your heart, it **changes everything.** Grace **frees you** from **having to** be perfect. **Grace frees you** from **having to** hold it all together. **The Gospel of grace is not too good** to be true. **It is true!** It's the **truest truth** in the entire universe. **God loves each of us independently** of what we may or may not bring to the table. **There are no strings attached!** No ifs, ands, or buts. **No qualifiers** or **conditions.** No need for balance. **Grace is the most dangerous, expectation** - wrecking, **smile** - creating reality there is.

The grace of God - the **most amazing theme in all the Bible.** The **most astounding truth** ever proclaimed is that **God is** and remains **absolutely just** and at the same time **He justifies** - **He makes just and** right - one who, being unjust, unrighteous, defiled, and guilty, **puts his faith and life in Jesus** (Rom. 3:26).

"For by **grace** you are saved through faith; and that not of
yourselves, it is the **gift of God;** not as a result of works,
lest any man should boast." (Ephesians 2:8-9 KJV)

When we understand grace, we come to know **it is a gift from God.**
Many places **throughout the Bible** refer to **grace as a gift,** which is the **perfect
analogy** for our understanding of how we come by grace. **Nothing is owed** in
return (Ephesians 4:7). **A gift is free** to the recipient (Romans 5:15). **A gift is
generous** and voluntary (II Corinthians 8:9). **We become the owners** of the
gift (II Corinthians 6:1). **A gift has nothing to do** with our merit or qualities
(Ephesians 2:8–9, above).

Please understand that a gift is much **different from a loan,** which we
must pay back. **The gift of grace** that **God freely gives us** is done through His
love, and **He does not require** payment in return. **Grace, is not valueless,** and
God paid dearly to give it to us. **Jesus paid with His own life** our ability to
receive grace!

Because the nature of a gift is that once it is given, **it belongs to the
recipient.** Those who have **received salvation** through Jesus **are owners of
that gift.** We **do not have to worry** about **God revoking** this gift of grace after
we receive it. **The Bible emphasizes again and again** that **we do not have to
count on our works to receive grace** - either to **earn** salvation or to **maintain**
it (Romans 4:4; 11:5–6; II Timothy 1:9–10).

With your studies in this book, you will **quickly find** that **God's thoughts
and ways** are far above those of man-kind. This is **immediately recognized**
when you turn your thoughts toward God. **He is infinite** in **knowledge,**
and **perfect** in all His ways, **whereas man** not only has **limited knowledge,**
his ways are **characteristically evil.** That is, **man and God** are **distinctly
antithetical** in these matters.

And yet, **in His infinite grace and mercy,** God has been **pleased** to **reveal
Himself,** and in some measure His ways. **In His good pleasure** God has **given
us His written Word,** and in a manner **beyond our understanding,** the **Living
Word.** Thus, **men are enabled to embrace God** in His revelation, and to think
thoughts after Him.

Moreover, through this encounter, **men are brought into what is deemed**
"newness of life" (Romans 6:4), and to have "passed from death unto life" (John
5:24). **This experience is described in these words,** "Therefore, if any man be
in Christ, he is a new creature: old things are passed away; behold, all things
are become new" (II Corinthians 5:17). **This emphasis is upon the dramatic**

and radical miracle which every believer undergoes, and which is called the "new birth."

Grace, as stated, is a constant theme in the Bible, and it climaxes in the New Testament with the coming of Jesus (John 1:17). We can all extend grace to others; but when the word grace is used in connection with God, it takes on a more powerful meaning. Grace is God choosing to bless us rather than curse us as our sin deserves. Grace is God's compassion and kindness to the undeserving.

Question: What can arise from the eternal infusion of divine relationship with the human heart? What happens when a person runs out of themselves and desperately hangs onto an invisible thread of faith, provided by God's grace, bringing you to your personal relationship with God?

This is not a call to unattainable greatness. This is not a teaching on doctrinal secrets that must be unlocked in order to experience the extraordinary. This book, I pray, is what can happen when normal, ordinary people, like you and me, truly meet Jesus and surrender their lives to Him.

It doesn't matter what stage of spiritual maturity, or lack of it, you find yourself in right now. Listen: when you start to engage with Jesus on a regular basis, you will be astonished and amazed with what God does both in and through you! Get ready to be and blessed.

Christians can to some extent understand the phenomena about grace, and yet most totally underestimate the magnitude, the preeminence, and the total significance of grace in their own lives."

For two-thirds of a Century, I've heard about grace, I've sung about grace, I've taught about grace, I've preached about grace, but I confess ... most of it was from the outside, not from the inside experience. I had the facts, but did not have the many experiences that God promises, and grace provides for His children. Oh, I had been redeemed, but I had failed to experience the continuous grace that leads to spiritual growth.

Examining my own spiritual life, in study, meditation and prayer, I found what kept me from experiencing the full victory and joy of God's grace and kind-heartedness in my life was (and is sometimes today) a refusal to be honest with myself about struggles, illnesses, deaths, about failures, about ways that I have fallen short."

I found that to truly encounter and receive His grace daily, I had to be in a place that is secure (like a prayer closet) to be vulnerable. And the real test for a lot of Christian leaders is we don't feel like we can be vulnerable with each other in front of a church that we're leading." When I allow myself to be in a place of **humility, weakness** and **vulnerability, I can receive grace** and **other people** can **find and experience grace."**

Whatever circumstances you are facing today - in your **marriage,** your **home,** your **work** - your **relationships, know this:** The **more you knock** on the **door of heaven** in **prayer,** and began to **receive** His **grace promises,** the more **you will find God ready** and **willing** to **carry** the **burden you bear.**

Let us pray: Dear Father, please **use this study** to **teach us** about this important doctrine - **grace! Father, give me the grace** to **understand that Your purposes** are far above what I can see with my human eyes. **I ask Your blessing,** and Your **guidance** in every way upon what is accomplished in me, **that it would honor** and **please** you, **glorify Your name Your Son.** I commit myself into Your hands, **asking** Your blessing, not only now, **and for those** who will be **reading this study** at a later date, **that the words written here,** taught, would **have a positive impact** in the lives of all who seek You. **I pray** and **ask all** of this, and **commit it into Your hands,** in the **name of Jesus Christ, and for His sake, AMEN!**

The grace of our Lord Jesus Christ be with you all. Amen" (Revelation 22:21).

Chapter 1

God 'SAVES' Me by His Grace

"BUT GOD, BEING rich in mercy, because of **His great love** with which **He loved us,** even when we **were dead** in our **transgressions,** made us alive together with Christ **(by grace you have been saved),** and raised us up with Him, and seated us with Him in the heavenly places, **in Christ Jesus,** in order that in the ages to come He might **show the incomparable riches of His grace** expressed in His kindness toward us in Christ Jesus. **For by grace** you have been saved through faith; and that **not** of yourselves, it is the **gift** of God; **not** as a **result of works,** so that no one can boast. (Ephesians 2:4–9 NIV)

> **Let me give** you **my Texas transliteration** of the **verse** above: "For it is by God's unconditional free grace (**God's absolute favor** you don't deserve) that **you are saved** (made **partakers of Christ's salvation** here and now, and delivered from judgment to come) **through your belief,** (trust, and faith). And **this salvation** or **redemption** is **not** of **ourselves** (of your own doing or accomplishments, and it came not through our own striving or works), **but it is** the **gift of God** - or you would be able to **brag** about it (boast, as your own accomplishment)."

In these six verses above, God twice asserts that we **were saved by grace.** It is **written in the past tense** because the period of time Paul is writing about is that **time immediately following justification.** His **audience** was **within the sanctification process. Salvation occurs because** of what God freely gives.

Have you ever heard someone **preach** or say the phrase **"saving faith?"** There's no such thing! **You are saved by grace** through faith. You're **not saved by faith alone.** Only **Jesus saves.** Only **He can change** you; it's **not something you have or can do.**

> For **by grace are ye saved** through faith; and that **not**
> of yourselves: it is the **gift of God: Not** of **works,**
> lest any man should **boast** (Ephesians 2:8–9).

The deceiver - Lucifer, **the devil** - is very **clever** when it **comes to our faith. Here is a scheme** he may use on you. **First,** he will start agreeing with you so he can **trip you up.** He'll try to **persuade** with **cunning thoughts:** "Sure, you're saved by faith in Christ." **Sounds good!** "But **how** do you **know** that your faith is **good enough** or **strong** enough to **save you** and **keep you** saved?" (More doubt.) "**What if** your **faith is too weak? What if** you don't make it?" **The tempter** will try to **cause you** to **put your faith in your faith rather** than in Christ.

> A church has no right to make anything a
> condition of membership which Christ has not
> made a condition of salvation. - A. A. Hodge

If anyone ever insists that Paul is saying that **faith is the gift of God** - **but** that we **must** do or **keep certain works** that are **commanded (for our salvation)** - then **this person's biblical understanding** is clearly **missing** a central fact. **Paul** immediately **adds** in Ephesians 2:9–10 that "**not** of works, lest anyone should **boast.** For we are **His workmanship, created** in Christ Jesus **for** good works, which **God prepared** beforehand that we **should walk** in them."

> Amazing Grace, how sweet the sound, that saved a
> wretch [sinner] like me. I once was lost, but now am
> found, was blind, but now I see. - John Newton

Grace was (and is) the most **elaborate** and **extravagant gift ever given** to the unbeliever and believer. It was the most costly one too, yet it is **given completely free** and **without regard** to **merit** or **works** or **status.** That's **why grace** is so very **amazing.**

The expensive price tag for us **showed God's great love** for us: "Greater love has no one than this: to lay down his life for his friends" (John 15:13). **Jesus** "was **delivered** over to death for our sins and was **raised** to life for our justification" (Romans 4:25 NIV), so we know that "Christ died for the ungodly" (Romans 5:6).

Someone once said, "Grace, this grandiose word, is an enchanting sound - harmonious to the ear!" **Grace comforted, yet challenged us** in our guilty, helpless, sinful, condemned condition—and **provided a Savior** for us. **Grace introduced** us to the **jurisdiction** of gospel **reconciliation** - and brought the glad tidings of divine mercy to our ears. **Grace opened** our blinded eyes - and **led us** to observe and envision **our need** for the precious **blood of Christ.**

Grace is the active expression of God's love for humanity. **Grace is** what every **person** desperately **needs** and what every heart **secretly longs for.** Often we **fail to understand** the **depth of grace** or to gain from its embrace.

> **The cross** is the lightning **rod of grace** that short-
> circuits **God's wrath** to Christ so that only the **light**
> **of His love** remains for believers. - A. W. Tozer

God's sovereign grace is the intensity of **our Creator's love shed** abroad in our hearts. **It is God's reality** enveloping our own. **Grace is a divine** touch from the Almighty - **a divine opening** and **empowering** to do what is good in His sight. **Grace** is **God directing** someone **like a father directing** his son on the right path. **God's grace** is His **embrace** - even when we don't deserve it.

I caution you: I fear that there are **huge numbers** in many **churches** across this country who **only imagine** and **sincerely believe** that they are **among the saved,** yet they are entirely **strangers** to a work of **God's grace** in their lives. **One thing I do know** is that **God demands repentance.** It is quite another matter to experimentally mourn and groan over our vileness.

In my studies, I find that **we are living in a day** where practically all of the **historical Bible doctrines** are being **attacked** from within by **unbelief** and **biblical liberalism.** Many **Christians** and **churches today** have **already succumbed** and **surrendered** to seducing spirits (heresy) and doctrines of demons (profane doctrines; I Timothy 4:1). **I am persuaded** that **the future of biblical Christianity** is bound up with a system of unbelieving, **liberal universalism** that, with no revival to God's truth, **will quickly lead** to the **demise of evangelical growth** as we have known it. With the **departure from biblical theology,** there has been a **strong downward tendency** into the depths of an **anthropocentric** (humanistic) philosophy of naturalism or secularism.

Let me articulate further. There is **very little thunder** from our **pulpits,** very **little preaching** that creates an **atmosphere of holy reverence** (what the Bible calls "the fear of the Lord"), very **little that challenges** us and **confronts** us and **stirs** us and **awakens** us, and **very little** that **equips** us to endure hardship, to be **courageous,** or to **confront the culture** and **live a sacrificial life** out of love for our neighbor. And unless you live in a little country town, you know very little about your neighbors.

> **Only when God gives us** a new beginning,
> may we find **irrefutable victory** that is
> never terminating. - Glenn Clifton

Today, in many of our churches, it's all about making people **feel-good** about themselves, it's **all about the coming** breakthrough (probably financial), and it's all **about fulfilling our personal dreams.**

Many of today's **preachers preach** a **toothless pep-talk** gospel that **fits** in **perfectly** with our **convenience-store, quick-fix** Christianity, **promising all kinds** of **benefits without** any **requirements.** What a deal! Who could refuse it? **No wonder** we are producing consumers rather than **disciples.** What else can we expect when we so **studiously bypass the cross** to **preach** about the **comforts and personal riches** in so much of our preaching? **What else can we expect** when we preach **God the genie** rather than **God the judge?"**

In an 1883 sermon, Charles Finney said, "Brethren, **our preaching** will bear its legitimate fruits. **If immorality prevails** in **the land,** the fault is ours in a great degree. **If there is a decay of conscience,** the pulpit is responsible for it. **If the public press lacks moral discrimination,** the pulpit is responsible for it. **If the church is degenerate and worldly,** the pulpit is responsible for it. If the world loses its interest in religion (Christianity), the pulpit is responsible for it. **If Satan rules in our halls of legislation,** the pulpit is responsible for it. **If our politics become so corrupt** that the **very foundations** of our **government** are **ready to fall away,** the pulpit is responsible for it. **Let us not ignore this fact,** my dear **friend; and Pastors:** let us lay it to heart, and be **thoroughly awake** to **our responsibility** in respect to the **moral and spiritual values** of this nation."

Although **the pulpit** was **more influential then** than today, what he said **was largely true!** If America is seriously in moral and **spiritual decline, many of our preachers are partly to blame. I say its past time** that we restore **more thunder to our pulpits.** (My thanks to Michael Brown for his thoughts.)

It is one thing to believe that **Christ is the only Savior** for sinners, but it is **quite another** matter to **really trust Him** from the heart enough **to commit our lives** to Jesus as Lord. **It is one thing** to intellectually **believe** that God is the great and holy one, but it is **quite another** matter to truly revere and fear Him. **It is one thing** to believe that salvation is of the Lord, but it is quite another matter to **become an actual partaker** of it through His gracious workings. **As someone once said,** "There are too many **talkers and not enough walkers in our churches."**

Today in this book, you are starting a **new series of studies on the subject of grace. Grace is** one of the **most important** and **enlightening principles** in Holy Scripture, and **it is imperative** that we have an **accurate understanding.**

When we truly understand God's grace, it will change our lives. But to **understand his grace,** we must **first comprehend** the **depth of our sin** and our complete **spiritual deadness prior** to receiving it. **Only then can we appreciate** that being made **alive with Christ is** an act of **pure grace.** It is the sheer **gift of God** that he **raises** the dead and **gives** us new life. We have **been made anew,** no longer **trapped** by the world and the **devil** to **mindlessly walk** in **rebellion** against God. We now **belong to him,** having been **seated in His** very presence in the **heavenly realms.**

Now that we **have been made alive** with Christ, we are **able to walk** in a **way** that **pleases God.** We have been **created for good works.** We can **walk in the deeds** He has prepared for us to do—**not to gain our salvation,** but **because we are saved by grace.** If we **truly understand** this, **nothing can remain the same.** The **burden of sin** and guilt has been **lifted.** Our feelings of **inadequacy are now quenched.**

> **We may rest secure** in the **overwhelming love of God and in** His **abundant mercy. We know** the true **freedom of God's grace.**

Bible students first **realize** that **God's grace is revealed** by His **love.** We **should not be surprised** that **motivation for grace** is the **love of God.** Everything that **God does flows from His love and grace.** Every **blessing God gives is an act of His love.** All **that God is** and **all that God does flows** out of His **divine love.**

The grace of God is an **extension of His love** for humanity. **God loves everyone** totally and without condition. **God loves us in spite of our faults,** failures and weaknesses. **God loves and cares** for every person the same. **God may not love** our **behavior (sins),** but **He will always love the sinner in spite of their sins.**

The grace that God gives **allows us** to **have a life** that is **full and abundant. God's grace is revealed by His gifts. God loves the world** to such a **degree** that **it is beyond our ability to comprehend. God sacrificed His own Son** on our behalf. We never asked Him to do it. **God's grace is so vast** that He did it without being asked. **God sent Jesus** because **He knew the depth of our need.**

> **God's salvation is infinitely costly, but because**
> **of God's grace, it is absolutely free!**

Grace is most needed and **best understood** in the **midst of sin, suffering, and brokenness.** We **live in a world of earning,** deserving, and merit, and these result in judgment. **That is why everyone wants** and needs **grace. Judgment** kills. Only **grace makes alive.**

Listen: A shorthand for what **grace is** - "**mercy, not merit.**" Grace **is** the **opposite of karma,** which is all about **getting what you deserve.** Grace **is getting what you don't deserve. Christianity teaches** that what we **deserve is death** with **no hope** of **resurrection.**

> **Grace is the love of God shown to the unlovely; the peace**
> **of God given to the agitated; the unmerited favor of God**
> **to those who deserve none!**

Ephesians 1:1-2 "Paul, an apostle of Jesus Christ by the will of God, **to the saints** who are in Ephesus, and **faithful in** Christ Jesus: **Grace to you** and **peace** from God our Father and the Lord Jesus Christ" (KJV).

In Paul's various **letters** to people or churches, **grace always comes first** in his greetings. It is **always grace followed by peace. In his letters to Timothy and Titus he added mercy;** "Grace, mercy, and peace, from God our Father and Jesus Christ our Lord." **This is a beautiful lesson for us.** You see friend, **we need God's grace** to **have peace with Him.** By **His grace,** we are invited to believe in Jesus as our Savior and **through our faith in Him** we are saved. Now **we are forgiven** and **at peace** with God! **Grace and then peace!** God shows us **great mercy and love** in this.

> **"He offers peace 'from' God** (Romans 1:7) **to all who**
> **are the recipients of His grace. He makes peace 'with'**
> **God** (Romans 5:1) **for those who surrender to Him in**
> **faith. And He brings the peace 'of' God** (Philippians
> 4:7) **to those who walk with Him."** - John MacArthur

The study of the grace of God reminds me of the goodness of God in His dealings with mankind in general, and with me in particular. Whatever comes into my life, it has come from the God of all grace, who has purposed to enrich my life by His gift, whether it be in what He gives or what He denies me.

Man does not like to think of God showing grace. Grace - which means the full and free forgiveness of every sin, without God demanding or expecting anything, except total allegiance, from the one so forgiven - is a principle so opposed to all man's thoughts and ways, so far above man, that he dislikes it. Man's own heart often secretly calls it injustice. He does not deal in this way and he does not like to think of God doing so.

Our choices have led us down some wrong roads from time to time. Every person reading this has done something they have known to be wrong. Like sheep we have all gone astray. Those mistakes have a name: sin. The result is that we have become estranged with God but God acted to mend the rift and stop the estrangement. God sent Jesus to be the payment (atonement) for sin. God sent Jesus to be the ultimate act of grace. God gave us what we needed and not what we deserved.

> "A man is not saved against his will, but he is made
> willing by the operation of the Holy Ghost. A
> mighty grace which He does not wish to resist enters
> into the man, disarms him, makes a new creature
> of him, and he is saved." - C.H. Spurgeon

Sovereign grace: means God moving heaven and earth to save sinners who could not lift a finger to save themselves. Grace means God sending His only Son to descend into hell on the cross so that we guilty ones might be reconciled to God and received into heaven. Paul wrote, "(God) has made Him (Jesus) to be sin for us, Who knew no sin, that we might be made the righteousness of God in Him" (II Corinthians 5:21).

We must fight our battles with Satan in humble submission to God and His grace, not according to Satan's terms. When we say, "The Lord rebuke you!" We are not saying "I rebuke you!" We have no power to rebuke Satan, and so we must call upon the power of God in humility, in obedience, and in submission to God, realizing that our own human power cannot fight against spiritual principalities without the power of the Holy Spirit. It gets back to seeing ourselves realistically, being dressed in the "whole armor of God" (Ephesians 6:10-16).

> "Faith is the radar that sees through the fog."
> - Corrie ten Boom

Faith is simply receiving God's grace. We can't even exercise faith on our own; it is a gift from God. Faith is not just believing God exists, and faith is not just believing facts about Jesus. Faith is trusting God with a commitment to Him. Faith is receiving the truth that God is full of goodness, mercy, and grace. Faith is not just believing God CAN do something—it is believing God WILL do something.

Our salvation (most literally: God's salvation in us), is not of works - not of any works, including the works of faith. God, the real Author, would not contradict Himself by suddenly giving approval of any work of faith as a means of salvation. Grace, a merciful gift, preceded our having faith in Him. Without His gift of grace, we would never have godly faith, the faith, in the first place. Faith, our reliance in God, is a fruit of the grace God freely gives.

God gives us the free gift of grace, which gives us the free gift of eternal life. All have sinned and come short of the glory of God (Romans 3:23), and the only wages we've earned is death but the free gift of God is eternal life (Romans 6:23). It is all about and all from God and not one bit from us and in this way, God receives all the glory.

> "In Whom (Jesus) we have redemption through
> His blood, the forgiveness of sins, according
> to the riches of His grace" (Ephesians 1:7).

Grace led us to cast away the filthy rags of our own self-righteousness - and to receive with thankfulness and joy, the spotless robe that Jesus voluntarily paid for us. Grace brought us to the footstool of mercy, with the cry of the publican, "God be merciful to me a sinner!" Grace enables us to live a life of dependence on Jesus alone, for all spiritual supplies. The Grace that began a good work within us - is that same grace that will perform it until the day of Jesus Christ.

> Hallelujah, by grace we are saved! "We are justified
> freely by His grace through the redemption
> that is in Christ Jesus!" (Romans 3:24).

When God truly **saves** us, He also **spiritually transforms** us. The **only payment for sins** that will ever **be sufficient is the blood of Christ,** including **His laid down life** on the cross as a **substitutionary atonement** for our sins. The **wages** (earnings) **of sin is death,** a price that **if paid by a sinner,** would **conclude** in **eternal damnation.** But the **sinless Son of God died for us:** "For Christ also hath once suffered for sins, the just for the unjust, that he might bring us to God, being put to death in the flesh, but quickened by the Spirit" (I Peter 3:18).

It is **imperative that we know that we cannot cause our own salvation,** we can **only receive it as a gift** of God's grace. **Ephesians 2:4 quoted** at the beginning of this article shows that **we were dead** (in our sins), and that **God made us alive** (spiritually). **Corpses cannot resuscitate themselves.**

Faith is simply receiving God's grace. We can't even exercise faith on our own; **faith is a gift from God.** Faith **is not just believing** God exists, and faith **isn't just believing facts** about Jesus. **Faith is trusting God.** It is receiving the truth that God is full of goodness, mercy, and grace. **Faith is not just believing God can** do something, it **is believing God will do** something.

When we become a Christian, we have **received His saving grace:** "For by **grace** are ye saved" (Ephesians 2:8).

We **also receive justifying grace,** because we are **"justified freely by His grace"** (Romans 3:24), **having the very righteousness of Christ credited** to our account. **It is then standing grace, enabling us** to stand confidently **in our grace-given salvation.** "By whom also we have access by faith into this grace wherein we stand, and rejoice in hope of the glory of God" (Romans 5:2).

The heart is not redeemed by facts and knowledge, the heart is transformed by divine intervention through the grace of God in Jesus Christ!

When God **truly saves** us, He also **spiritually transforms** us. The **only payment for sins** that will ever **be sufficient is the blood of Christ,** which includes **His laid down life** on the cross as a **substitutionary atonement** for our sins. The **wages** (earnings) **of sin is death,** a price that **if paid by a sinner,** would **conclude** in **eternal damnation.** But the **sinless Son of God died for us:** "For Christ also hath once suffered for sins, the just for the unjust, that he might bring us to God, being put to death in the flesh, but quickened by the Spirit" (I Peter 3:18).

It is imperative that we know that we cannot cause our own salvation, we can only receive it as a gift of God's grace. Ephesians 2:4 quoted at the beginning of this article shows that we were dead (in our sins), and that God made us alive (spiritually). Corpses cannot resuscitate themselves.

Faith is simply receiving God's grace. We can't even exercise faith on our own; faith is a gift from God. Faith is not just believing God exists, and faith isn't just believing facts about Jesus. Faith is trusting God. It is receiving the truth that God is full of goodness, mercy, and grace. Faith is not just believing God CAN do something, it is believing God WILL do something.

When we become a Christian, we have received His
saving grace: "For by grace are ye saved" (Ephesians 2:8)

We also receive justifying grace, because we are "justified freely by His grace" (Romans 3:24), having the very righteousness of Christ credited to our account. It is then standing grace, enabling us to stand confidently in our grace-given salvation. "We have access by faith into this grace wherein we stand" (Romans 5:2).

The heart is not redeemed by facts and knowledge,
the heart is transformed by divine intervention
through the grace of God in Jesus Christ!

Salvation is not given to us out of expectation, or as a reward for all our goodness, quite the opposite. It is not exchanged for something else. It is pure gift. Why does God give us salvation? spiritual law-breakers, God loved us. Yes, loved (loves) us. Paul says in Ephesians 2:4 - 5, "But because of His great love for us, God, who is rich in mercy, made us alive with Christ even when we were dead in transgressions - it is by grace you have been saved" (NIV).

Paul writes about the true riches in his second letter to the Corinthians, (8:9, NIV), "For you know the grace of our Lord Jesus Christ, that though He was rich, yet for your sake He became poor, so that you by his poverty might become rich" because Jesus, "Who, being in very nature God, did not consider equality with God something to be used to His own advantage, rather, He made Himself nothing by taking the very nature of a servant, being made in human likeness. And being found in appearance as a man, he

humbled himself by **becoming obedient** to death– even **death on a cross"** (Philippians 2:6-8 NIV)! **Jesus, as God, divested Himself** by becoming a Man and **gave** His own **life for our sake.**

> The Apostle **John wrote** in I John 5:13, "These things have
> I **written unto you** that **believe (trust)** on the name of the
> Son of God; that **ye may know** that ye **have** eternal life, and
> that ye may **believe (trust)** on the name of the Son of God."

When we are **reading** the **Gospel of John, remember: John was interested** in **helping people believe** in the Son of God so that they **would be saved** but **to know** that they **were saved.** He wrote as **if salvation** was **something** "knowable," and it is. We **can know** that **we possess eternal life now. Paul** wrote, "The **Spirit Himself** bears **witness** with **our spirit** that we **are children of God,** and **if children, then heirs - heirs of God** and **joint heirs** with Christ, if indeed **we suffer** with Him that **we may** also be **glorified together"** (Romans 8:16-17 NKJV).

The **Holy Scripture** affirms that **grace** is the sinner's only hope. **Unless we are saved by grace** we **cannot** be saved at all. **To reject a gratuitous salvation** is to spurn the only One that is available for lost sinners. **Grace is God's provision** for those who are **so corrupt (so sinful),** that they cannot change their own natures; **so averse** to God, they cannot turn to Him; **so blind** they cannot see Him; **so deaf** they cannot hear Him; in a word, **so dead** in sin that He must open their hearts if ever they are to be saved. **Grace,** then, **implies that the sinner's case is desperate,** but that God is merciful.

We can never **exhaust the riches of the grace** of our Lord Jesus Christ. **When we receive Him as Savior,** we receive **"grace for grace"** - that is, **one grace** after another, **grace upon grace.** The **Apostle John said** it like this: "And of His fullness have all we received, and **grace for grace"** (John 1:16).

> **"For the grace of God** that brings salvation has appeared
> to all men. **It teaches us to say 'No'** to ungodliness and
> worldly passions, and to live self-controlled, upright and
> godly lives in this present age" (Titus 2:11-12 NIV)!

> "The **goodness of God** satisfies our 'emptiness,'
> the **mercy of God** satisfies our 'sinfulness,'
> and the **grace of God** satisfies our 'unworthiness.'

The grace of God is proclaimed in the Gospel (Acts 20:24), which is **to the self-righteous Jew a** "stumbling block," and to the conceited and **philosophizing Greek** "foolishness." **And why?** Because **there is nothing whatever** in it that is adapted to the **gratifying** of the **pride of man.**

God's grace announces that **unless we are saved by grace, we cannot be saved at all. It declares that apart from Christ,** the unspeakable Gift of **God's grace,** the **Gospel addresses men as** guilty, condemned, perishing criminals. It declares that the **most virtuous moralist** is in the **same terrible plight** as is the most **decadent criminal** and **reprobate.** God's **grace declares** that the **zealous professor,** with all his **religious performances,** is **no better off** than the most **profane infidel** and **unbeliever.**

Religion can be an attempt to impress or to **placate** a 'higher power' with the 'fact' that **we really aren't so bad.** Human history indicates otherwise. That's why **Jesus is so vital to all of us.** When He came to earth, **He was** "full of grace and truth," **as John phrased it** (John 1:14 NIV). **And He made some pretty bold claims about Himself.** "I am the way, the truth, and the life." **He said,** "No one comes to the Father but by me" (John 14:6). **That's an exclusive claim,** yet it's **drenched** in **hope** and **love.**

There is an **unfortunate attitude** that **assumes** there is something **we can do** to be saved. This is a **humanistic, legalistic** lie **propagated** by Satan in this unbelieving world – that we **must do something ourselves** for salvation, **God does His part** and **I do my part!** What an unbelieving world fails to recognize is that - **God has already done everything necessary** for my **salvation!**

At salvation, we become God's workmanship. That means, as Christians, that **God has made** us what we are … **"In Christ!"** Just as **when God created** Adam and Eve - they were what they were because God created them. **So it is with the new creation,** when we are born-again, we are God's work. **We are what we are because of God's grace.**

He has made us for noble purposes. In all this Paul is not just referring to our initial salvation - but also of our progress. That's what **Paul writes in 1 Corinthians 15:10,** our text. **Ephesians 2:10** said that we **have been created in Christ Jesus to do good works,** which God has prepared in advance for us to do.

> **Let me, in plain terms, tell you what grace really is!** We **deserve punishment** and **get forgiveness;** we **deserve God's wrath** and **get God's love, because of God's grace!** (Glenn Clifton)

Salvation is indeed a free gift. It **cannot be earned** by anyone's works. But **that does not mean Christianity has no works!** Why would **Christ say,** "I know your works," **if He did not expect people** to have works as part of their way of life, **as part of Christianity,** and if He was not, in most cases, disappointed at the way that the people were working? **Christianity does have works** as a **major part** of its **makeup** and **doctrine.**

That's an incredible statement. The **good works** that you have done - you **only did them** because **God prepared them** for you to do. The **reason you did them** because God made you what you are - **you are His workmanship.** Paul attributed his work **all to grace.** In I Corinthians 3:10, **Paul wrote,** "According to the grace of God which is given unto me, as a wise master-builder, I have laid the foundation, and another buildeth thereon. But let every man take heed how he buildeth thereupon." **Grace to us is free!**

That's why grace is free **because no one could afford it anyway.** The **irony to the world** is that they **couldn't ever earn it** by all the good works **in the world because,** "God so loved the world that **He gave** His only begotten Son so that whosoever believes on Him should not perish, but have eternal life" (John 3:16). **We are saved,** not by anything we do (thankfully), **but by God's goodness;** His **free gift of grace** and **eternal life. Amazing grace!**

The glorious grace of God, (under the leadership of Holy Spirit inspiration) is the central **obsession** of the Apostle Paul and the **great theme** of his letter to **the church in Ephesus. God is at work,** working all things in accordance with 'the **purpose** of his will' (Ephesians 1:5) and 'to the **praise** of his **glorious grace'** (Ephesians 1:6 NIV).

Grace is a gift freely given, irrespective of any **merit or worth** within ourselves. **Paul shows us** this by setting out clearly what grace is not. **God demonstrates to us that salvation,** "…is not your own doing." (v. 8). And, "not a result of works (deeds)." (v. 9). **This classic gospel verse** stresses that **even the faith** through which **we receive God's salvation** is the **free gift of God.** We have nothing of which to boast (Ephesians 2:9, emphasis – G.C.).

You say, "Now, wait a minute, pastor, **are you saying** I'm like a robot and God just saves me and **I have no part in** the transaction? **Don't I choose Him?**" Sure, but **He chose you before you chose Him. "Don't I have to accept Jesus?"** Sure, but **before you ever accepted Him, He accepted you and Jesus came to** "seek and to save you."

Do you want to know what **our part in salvation is?** Visualize this **book I hold** in my hand. I'm **going to drop it. Gravity** is going to **do its part** and the **book is going to do** its part. **What did the book do? Nothing!!!** It just

dropped, because of the power of **gravity. It didn't** have to **DO anything.** Just as **gravity drew the book** downward, **Jesus said,** "No man comes to Me unless the Father who sent Me draws them" (John 6:44 NIV).

In Christian discussions, **the phrase "saving grace"** is generally used to refer **to God's grace** to **lead a person to salvation.** This is based on a variety of biblical principles that **emphasize salvation as a free gift** of **God's grace rather** than something that a person **earns through good deeds** or **actions.**

The heart is not changed by argument, the heart is changed by divine intervention through the grace of God!

Salvation requires saving grace. "Therefore by the deeds of the law there shall no flesh be justified in his sight: for by the law is the knowledge of sin" (Romans 3:20). **No amount or level of human accomplishments is good enough** to obtain salvation.

Isaiah 64:6 teaches "all our righteousness (righteous acts) are like a filthy rags (polluted garments NIV)." **Instead,** "But **now** the righteousness of God has been manifested **apart from the law,** although the Law and the Prophets **bear witness** to it - the righteousness of God **through faith** in **Jesus Christ** for all who believe. For there is no distinction" (Romans 3:21-22 ESV).

Although the **world's philosophies and religions can never accept** this, **grace is a gift, pure and simple.** We might be adamant on **trying to pay,** but **the balance has been settled** (and our money's no good!). Of course, **even if we're able to** accept true grace, **we have trouble when** it reaches other people, **especially those who've done us wrong.** Why? **Grace offends our sense of justice** by being both **implausible** and **unfair. We are uncomfortable because grace** turns the **tables** on us, **relieving us** of our precious **sense of control. We try to tame the message** of **God's grace,** after all, **who could trust in** or **believe something so radically unbelievable?**

From Genesis to Revelation our salvation is **by means** of divine benevolence, **gifting by God.** In **no way is grace given because God is obligated,** compelled, forced, or duty bound to us to do so. **God gives grace freely,** not by constraint. **All He truthfully owes us** is the **death** we have earned through sin (Romans 6:23). **He gives grace because** that is the way He is; it is His character. **He gives grace because of what He is** working out in His purpose, **not because He owes us** for what we think we have earned **or for what our pride** is demanding in the **mistaken belief** that we are entitled to what we desire.

Paul's conversion was pure grace, as is ours. Paul gave **all the credit to God,** as should we. **Paul traced his conversion** from **before** eternal times, to his birth, to his calling on the Damascus road. **We see this in Galatians 1:15-16** where **he wrote,** "But when it pleased God, Who separated me from my mother's womb, and **called me** by His grace, to reveal His Son in me, that I might preach Him among the heathen."

In II Timothy 1:9 Paul speaks of God, "who has **saved us** and **called us** to a **holy life** - not because of anything we have done but because of His own purpose and grace. **This grace was given us in Christ Jesus**" (NIV).

Friend, **God's greatest demonstration of grace** is **seen in Jesus Christ!** Without **Jesus** there is **no grace! Jesus is** the **very personification of God's grace!** And **His death** on **the cross** was the **"greatest show on earth" of God's grace!**

This is the heart of what **God wants us to know.** Undeserved, unmerited "grace" (Greek - charis) which **springs from the free, sovereign love of God** alone and **becomes operative** in **human life** not only **determines Paul's life** and apostolic vocation, and **characterizes all Christian experience,** not (only) the promise of resurrection and **the reality of the activity of Christ as Lord.**

O, my dear friend, **the truth that this gift is unmerited** and **undeserved** magnifies the **glory of grace** and the **generosity of the Giver.** In truth, **all of us should instinctively understand this to be true.** God's **grace** is the **single most important aspect** of our spiritual and **eternal** salvation. **His giving of grace** to us is completely and **totally unmerited.** There are no automatic entitlements. **Every sin we have committed** is personally **against Him** and His Son, **and still He gives grace.** He is **our Creator;** He has **given us life.** He has **given us the hope** of something far, far better than we now have. **Without what He freely gives, we are nothing** - we would not even exist.

Imagine now that it is **Christmas day** and you **hand your love** this **perfect gift,** immaculately wrapped. **Envision the look** of **wonder on her face** as the gift is opened. This special, much-wanted and much sought **gift is finally revealed.**

In gratefulness, they thank you with love and hugs. **Now they reach for their wallet** or purse. They **now write out a check** for the **full amount as payment** and give it to you. **Do you see the problem?** You see, the **moment the check** is received the **gift is no longer a gift. Payment nullifies grace!**

Paul makes this very point in his letter to the church at Rome, "But if it is by grace, it is no longer on the basis of works; otherwise grace would no longer be grace" (Romans 11:6 NKJV).

> Ephesians 1:7, "In Him" (Jesus) we have redemption
> through His blood, the forgiveness of sins,
> according to the riches of His grace" (NIV).

Then Paul adds, "according to the riches of His grace which He lavished on us," to show that there are no sins too great for God to forgive through the blood of Christ. This has always been God's appeal to repentant sinners.

In Isaiah 55:6-7, the prophet calls, "Seek the Lord while He may be found; call upon Him while He is near. Let the wicked forsake his way and the unrighteous man his thoughts; and let him return to the Lord, and He will have compassion on him, and to our God, for He will abundantly pardon." Abundantly pardon! Rich grace lavished on us!

Even in the Old Testament we see grace at work. Now Joshua was standing before the angel, clothed with filthy garments. And the angel said to those who were standing before him, Remove the filthy garments from him. And to him he said, I have taken your iniquity away from you, and I will clothe you with pure vestments (Zechariah 3:3-4, my paraphrase).

Joshua was not a wicked man. This was the best religion had to offer ... the high priest! And yet, as Joshua stood in the presence of God, he was viewed as wearing filthy clothes. He needed God's forgiveness just as much as you and me.

It's important to remember that you are saved and sustained by grace alone. At times you may feel like you are doing okay in your Christian life. You may serve, witness, give, perform acts of kindness, and have admirable character. But don't be mistaken. You are not saved by any of that! And to the degree that you are clinging to your self-righteousness or any merit that you have, you are missing the blessing of grace.

> "Our values determine our expectations. If we value
> comfort more than character, then trials will upset us. If we
> value the material and physical more than the spiritual, we
> will not be able to 'consider it all joy!'

If we live only for the present and forget the future, the
trials will make us bitter, not better." - Warren Wiersbe

The grace of God means that you and I come **without anything to offer.**
We come into the Kingdom **helpless and hopeless** and empty. **And He invites
us there,** not on the basis of our merit or money, **but on the basis of His grace.**
Never forget, eternal life is a gift ... a gift of God, therefore it **cannot
be earned** by **good works,** or **claimed as a right.** Seeing that **salvation is a
"gift,"** who has any right to tell God on whom He ought to bestow it? **It is
not** that the **Giver ever refuses this gift** to any who seek it **wholeheartedly,**
and **according** to the rules **which He has prescribed.** No! **He refuses** none
who come to Him **empty-handed,** and in the way of His appointing. But **if
out of a world of impenitent** and **unbelieving rebels,** God is determined to
exercise His sovereign right by choosing a **limited number to be saved, who
is wronged? Is God obliged** to **force His gift** on those who value it not? **Is God
compelled to save** those who are determined to go their own way?
We are saved and sustained by grace alone! So today, **remember that your
salvation is a gift of grace** through and through. **It doesn't depend** on what
you do ... **it is based entirely on what Jesus did for you!**

"**For by grace are ye saved through faith; and that not
of yourselves: it is the gift of God; Not of works, lest
any man should boast (brag)**" (Ephesians 2:8-9).

You're not saved by grace and works ... but **by grace alone.** According
to the Word of God, **grace is not God making up the difference** in your
shortfall. **It does not mean** that **you do a little bit** and **then God does the rest.**
That's **not grace! Once you have faith, as James urged,** you **will have works!
With no works, your faith is fraudulent** (14-24).
If you think you're going to heaven **because you are a good person,** or **by
your good works, I guarantee you** that **you** will always **wonder if you've done
enough.** You do **not have a "know-so"** salvation. You will **have a "hope-so"**
salvation. Rather than standing up straight in confidence **like an exclamation
point,** you will be bent over and wondering **like a question mark.** That is, until
you **understand** that **it's all by grace.**
Moreover, through this encounter, **men are brought into what is deemed**
"newness of life" (Romans 6:4), **and to have** "passed from death unto life" (John
5:24). **This experience is described in these words,** "Therefore, if any man be

in Christ, he is a new creature (or creation): old things are passed away; behold, all things are become new" (II Corinthians 5:17). **This emphasis is upon the dramatic and radical miracle** which **every believer** undergoes, and which **is called the** "new birth."

> **"The Lord will give grace and glory: no good thing will He withhold from them that walk uprightly."** Psalm 84:11 (KJV).

J. Vernon McGee writes about a country boy down South years ago who **wanted to join the church.** In this church, the **deacons examined everyone** before they could join. **They asked** him, **"How did you get saved?"** His **answer** was, **"God did his part, and I did my part."** They were a little **concerned** with this answer, so they asked him, **"What was God's part** and what was **your part?"** His answer is classic. **He said, "God's part** was the **saving, and my part was the sinning.** I **done run from Him** as fast as **my sinful heart** and **rebellious legs** could take me. **But God done took out** after me **till He run me down."** That's the way all of us are saved. If it **is by works,** then it is **not of grace—but** if it **is of grace,** then **none** of it is by works.

Did you know that grace has to chase us down? If God didn't **run faster** than us, **we would never be saved! Grace seeks** to **give to vile** and **wicked people** that **which they don't deserve** and can **never deserve. God convicts** us and **calls us** by **the Holy Spirit to Jesus** (John 6:44; 14:6).

> "For if by one man's offence **death reigned** by one,
> much more they which **receive abundance of grace**
> and of the **gift of righteousness** shall reign in life
> by one, **Jesus Christ"** (Romans 5:17 KJV).

Please **don't be confused** by all the **terms** in this verse. Simply put, **the goal** of the **gospel** is **redemption** - and **God's grace** includes **everything He has done** for us **through Christ** to **redeem us** from the **power** the **devil** and bring us into the **kingdom** of his **glorious light!**

Justification is the **cornerstone of grace.** To be 'justified' **by God** means to be 'acquitted' - **forgiven of all sin** and **guilt** - and to be **considered holy** and **righteous** before Him.

No one is justified - that is, he **cannot become holy** or **righteous** - by his **own works, obedience** or **faithfulness.** Rather, these things are all **the result**

of a **justifying faith** in the power of **Christ's blood** to make us **acceptable in God's sight:** "For by **grace are ye saved** through faith; and that **not of yourselves:** it is the **gift of God: not** of **works,** lest any man should boast" (Ephesians 2:8-9).

The price tag for us showed God's great love for us as "Greater love has no one than this: to lay down one's life for one's friends" (John 15:13 NIV). **Jesus** "was delivered over to death for our sins and was **raised** to life **for our justification**" (Romans 4:25 NIV), **so we know that** "Christ died for the ungodly" (Romans 5:6 NIV).

The theological definition of GRACE is "the unearned pardon, **mercy** and **favor** of God." **Scripture says:** "But of him are ye in Christ Jesus, who of God is made unto us wisdom, and righteousness (which is justification), and sanctification, and redemption" (I Corinthians 1:30 KJV).

If we were to describe 'grace' to the **chemist,** we would say that **grace is an element**, not a compound. In more **biblical terms, grace is never a mixture** of divine **benevolence** and **human effort. Grace** is **entirely the work of God,** unprompted by man, **undeserved** by man, and without regard to anything that the **object of grace** will later accomplish.

> "And **if by grace,** then it **cannot** be based on works; **if it
> were grace would no longer be grace**" (Romans 11:6, NIV).

In God's Word **grace means God's love in action towards men** who merited the opposite of love. **Grace means God moving heaven and earth** to save sinners **who could not** lift a finger to save themselves. **Grace means God sending His only Son** to descend into hell on the cross so that we guilty ones might be **reconciled** to God and **received** into heaven. "(God) hath made him to be sin for us, who knew no sin, that we might be made the righteousness of God in him" (II Corinthians 5:21).

Suppose everybody who wanted to be saved **had to run around the block.** Some can't run. What if you **had to read a chapter in the Bible** to be saved? Some can't read. But **there is one thing** that can **make the promise sure, and that is grace.**

Do you know what a "legalist" is? A legalist is **someone whose list** of **rules** are **more** numerous **than God's.** Many **Christians embrace** the **idea** of **grace** for salvation, **but then they fall into the trap** of thinking that after they **become a Christian** there are **things left to "do"** (or not do), **to keep their salvation** in effect. **They say,** "If I obey God, I'll earn more of His love!"

Since I've found the truth in grace, I say, "**I want to obey** God **because I am so greatly loved, by my Creator and Lover of my soul!**"

There are **many sincere church members and attenders** today **who** have **not yet submitted** to the **righteousness of Christ.** They **still go** about **trying to please God** by their **good efforts and deeds.** They **accept salvation by faith** but then they **want to take over from there!**

There is **something in our flesh** that rebels **against a faith-walk.** We want to **earn our salvation** - to **help God out!** We **don't mind** being saved by grace through faith; but we **don't want to live by His grace** and **continue** in **His faith.** Our **flesh cries out,** "All my **obedience,** all my hard work to **please God** - it has to **count for something!**" Yes, it **is worth something** - but **not** for **meriting forgiveness, pardon and complete redemption!**

We **don't want to accept** that we are **made right** before God simply **by believing/trusting/committing.** We would **rather "bite the bullet"** - and when **temptation overwhelms us,** we say through gritted teeth, **"Bless God, I'll get victory if it kills me!"** (And it will kill you!). Your **flesh cannot keep** you!

The **Bible emphasizes** repeatedly that our **relationship with God** is **not based** upon what **we do, but on WHO HE IS!** "For the kingdom of God is not a matter of eating and drinking, but of righteousness, peace, and joy in the Holy Spirit" (Romans 14:17 NIV). In other words, **faith has nothing to do** with what goes into your body: **It has everything to do with Who lives in your heart.** For the Christian, **Jesus is my righteousness,** because I could **never be good enough** on my own. **Jesus is my peace,** because **I could never have security** without Him. **Jesus is** my **joy unspeakable** and **full of glory.**

Paul wrote this of a certain people: "They have a zeal of God, but not according to knowledge. For **they, being ignorant** of God's righteousness, and **going about** to establish **their own** righteousness, **have not submitted themselves** unto the righteousness of God. For **Christ is the end of the law** for **righteousness** to everyone that **believeth**" (Romans10:2-4 KJV). **They were trying** "to establish their own righteousness." We know **that process** by another name: **legalism!**

> "(God) who has **saved us,** and **called us** with a holy
> calling, **not** according to our works, **but** according to
> **His own purpose and grace** which was **granted us in
> Christ Jesus** from all eternity" (II Timothy 1:9 NKJV).

Paul's life is a powerful example of God's transforming grace. In Philippians chapter 3, **Paul describes** how **he once depended on his good works,** nature, and conduct to gain acceptance before God. **He did not originally understand** there is only **one way** to be made **acceptable in God's sight** by **His grace.**

The difference between legalism and grace is in the **"motive"** behind your obedience. **If you obey God with the belief** it will **improve your standing** with God, **or** that He will **love you less** if you don't, then you're sliding into the **gloom of frozen legalism.** But **if you obey God because you love Him and** know you are deeply loved, then **you are basking** in the **warmth** of light of His grace.

> **Jesus said,** "Whoever has my commands and obeys them, he is the one who loves Me. He who loves Me will be loved by My Father, and I too will love him, and show Myself to them" (John 14:21 NIV).

There are **millions of people who sincerely but wrongly believe** they will be **acceptable** to God based on **how good they are.** It **grieves my heart** to think **they will die in ignorance, deceived by** the false doctrine of **working to earn** the Lord's approval. **By grace,** Paul's thinking was corrected - **he learned that everything** he had counted as valuable **was worthless.** In this way, **Christianity's worst enemy became its greatest asset,** chief proponent, and dearest friend.

Grace makes men of the harshest, sourest, crabbiest natures - **to be of a sweet,** lovely, amiable, pleasing temper. **Grace turns lions** into lambs, **wolves** into sheep, **monsters** into men, **and men** into angels - as you may see in Manasseh, Paul, Mary Magdalene, Zacchaeus, Rahab, and others.

How does this change come about? Saul, the "Hebrew of Hebrews" **committed to destroying anything related to Jesus** Christ, was approaching Damascus. **Blinded** after a sudden flash of light, **he fell to the ground and** heard **Jesus say,** "Saul, why are you persecuting Me" (Acts 22:7-9 NKJV)? **The future apostle learned** that **being critical of the church** or **Christians** was **equivalent** to **opposing Jesus Himself** (Matthew 25:40), and that **to attack the body of Christ** meant putting oneself under condemnation and judgment. **But God's grace** was **about to transform Saul** by giving him a **new nature** and a fresh start. **His hostile, vengeful heart** would abruptly be **changed,** and he would become the **church's most powerful preacher.**

The grace that saves and transforms today is the **same grace that changed Saul,** the sinner, into Paul, the saint. And he became an example to those around him as well as to future generations. **God wanted all of us to know** that if He can come out of nowhere, knock Paul down, blind him, and transform him completely, then He can save anyone. **Witnessing Paul's conversion makes us ask,** "Who among us cannot be transformed by the grace of God?"

No 'born-again' Bible believing Christian would ever want to **assert that Christians cause** their own salvation. That would be **tantamount to denying that salvation is a gift of God** and a work of God. **Grace that saves** and **faith that saves** are **gifts from God.** This is not declaring that **grace was a gift** and **faith was a meritorious work** that we did. The whole of it, **grace and faith is not** of ourselves and **are gifts of God.**

Nowhere in the Bible does it teach that **human effort** can bring salvation. We are **saved by grace** alone **through faith alone in Christ alone.** When we **relinquish all hope except faith in Christ** and **His finished work** on **our** behalf, we are **acting by** the **faith that God in His grace supplies.**

Believing is therefore the first act of an **awakened spiritual corpse. God alone** is the **cause** of salvation. He uses the agency of the gospel message which is to be preached to all nations. **The preached gospel** is to **include the facts** about Christ's **atoning work,** including His **resurrection,** and a call **to repent** and **believe.**

Let me review: Legalism is the attitude that **I** can try to establish, **to improve my** standing before God **by my activities, keeping rules and laws. That attitude is a vindictive grace-robber.** Maybe it would help to **leave you with a definition of grace,** too. **You might want to write this down in your Bible,** or at **least burn it into your brain.**

II Timothy 1:9 Paul speaks of God "who has **saved us** and **called us to a holy life - not** because of anything **we have done** but **because of His own purpose** and **grace. This grace** was **given us** in **Christ Jesus before** the **beginning of time"** (NIV).

Grace is ... JESUS. Grace is **not just a power** or a **force** – it is that **catalyst** that, through the Holy Spirit, **brings us** to Jesus ... **a Person ... Grace Incarnate.** God loves you so much He sent His only Son into the world to suffer and die so He could enjoy a love relationship with you. **That's Grace! The Bible says of Jesus,** "The Word became flesh ... **full of grace** and truth." (John 1:14) **In Jesus was all the fullness of God's grace,** and **when we**

allow Jesus to fill us then we **are filled with God's grace.** Don't let anyone or anything rob you of the blessing of **God's amazing grace!**

Brethren, **God's greatest demonstration of grace is seen in Jesus Christ!** According to the Bible, **WITHOUT JESUS THERE IS NO GRACE! Jesus is** the very **personification of God's grace!** And **His death** on the cross **was** the "**greatest presentation of God on earth**" of **God's grace! The salvation of my soul** (and yours), **cost God a huge price!**

Do you remember as the **Nazi's began** to **advance** in Europe **before** and **during World War II?** German **theologian, pastor/teacher Dietrich Bonhoeffer** was **arrested** and put in Concentration Camp (s) until **he was executed** by hanging in 1945. One of his **books, "The Cost of Discipleship"** (1948 in English). **Bonhoeffer's most widely read book begins, "Cheap grace** is the **mortal enemy** of our church. **Our struggle today** is for **costly grace."** That was a sharp **warning to his own church,** which was engaged in **bitter conflict** with the **official Nazified state church.**

Bonhoeffer condemned "cheap grace" and **promoted "costly grace"** - **not that grace costs us** something, but that it **cost God everything,** and **we cheapen it** by **being ungrateful,** by **living lives** of **lazy spirituality,** or **by sinning** so **that grace may abound.** He said that **cheap grace** is the **preaching** of **forgiveness** without requiring repentance, **baptism** without church discipline. **Cheap grace** is **grace** without discipleship, **grace** without the cross, and **grace** without Jesus Christ, **living** and **incarnate.**

Costly grace is the treasure hidden in the **field;** for the sake of it a **man** will gladly go and **sell all** that he has. **It is the pearl of great price** to buy which the **merchant** will **sell all** his goods. **It is the kingly rule of Christ,** for whose sake a **man will pluck** out the **eye** which **causes** him to **stumble. It is the call of Jesus** Christ at which the **disciple leaves** his **nets** and **follows him.**

The price tag **for us** showed **God's great love for us** as "Greater love has no one than this: to lay down one's life for one's friends" (John 15:13). Jesus **"was delivered** over to **death** for our sins and was **raised** to life for our justification" (Romans 4:25 NIV), **so we know** that **"Christ died for the ungodly"** (Romans 5:6).

Such grace is costly because it **calls us** to follow, and **it is grace because** it **calls us** to follow Jesus Christ. **It is costly because** it **costs** a man his life, **and it is grace because** it **gives** a man the only true life. **It is costly because** it **condemns** sin. **It is God's grace because** it **justifies** the sinner. And above all, **it is grace because** God did not **reckon His Son too dear a price to** pay for our life, **but delivered Him up for us all** how will He not also, along with

Him, **freely give us all things? Costly grace** is the **Incarnation of God in Jesus. Hallelujah!**

The measure of God's forgiveness is not according to how much we **punish ourselves,** or how many **prayers we mimic,** or how much **money we give,** or **mourn over our sin,** although we should mourn when we realize how **we have spurned God's** great **love,** as Jesus taught (Matthew 5:4).

Forgiveness of our sin is the **divine miracle of grace.** The **cost to God** was the **Cross of Christ.** To forgive sin, while remaining a holy God, **this price had to be paid. Never accept a view of the fatherhood of God** if it **blots out** the **atonement of Jesus.**

Jesus said His mission was **not** to be **a diplomat, not** to be a **peacemaker,** but **to bring death** to hatred, strife, and sin through His **reconciling blood.** What does this mean? There is **no other way** to a **holy God,** but **through the cross.** Are you **living like a child of God** and **telling others about Jesus?**

The revealed truth of God is that **without the atonement He cannot forgive** - He would contradict His nature if He did. **The only way** we can be forgiven is by being **brought back to God** through **the 'atonement'** of the Cross. **'Atonement' is being made one with Christ which equals 'at-one-ment.' God's grace and forgiveness:** possible only in the supernatural realm.

Rather, the measure of God's forgiveness is "according to the **riches of His grace,"** lavished on us on God's riches, (Ephesians 1:7, 18; 2:4, 7; 3:8, 16). **Paul does not say,** "out of the riches of His grace," **but** "according to the riches of His grace." **What is the difference?**

Let me illustrate. If you **go to a multi-millionaire** and ask for a **contribution** for a worthy cause and he **gives you $100,** he has **given 'out'** of his riches. **But,** if he **hands you a blank check** and **says,** "Fill in what you need," he **has given 'according' to his riches.**

Grace goes down into the gutter, and brings up a jewel!

One night in a church service God opened the heart of a young woman to **respond to His call and believe on Christ as her Lord and Savior.** She had a very **rough past,** involving alcohol, drugs, and prostitution. **The change in her was evident.** She experienced God's forgiveness. In **time,** she became a **faithful member** of the church, and **served by teaching** young children.

It was not long until **she caught the eye and heart of the pastor's son.** The **relationship grew** and they **began making wedding plans.** But then the **problems began.** Many in the church did not think that a **woman with a past** such as hers was suitable for a pastor's son. The church began to gossip and argue about this matter. So, they decided to have a meeting.

Emotions heated up, tension increased, and the meeting was getting out of hand. The young woman became very upset about all of the things being brought up about her past. As she began to cry, the pastor's son stood to speak. He said, "My fiancé's past is not what is on trial here. What you are questioning is the ability of the blood of Jesus to wash away sin as He guaranteed.

"Today," the young man stated ... "You have put the blood of Jesus on trial. So, does it wash away sin or not?" The whole church began to weep as they realized that they had been slandering the blood of the Lord Jesus Christ.

Christian! The only thing that makes you different from the vilest being that pollutes the earth, or from the darkest fiend that gnaws his chains in hell, is the free grace of God!

POINT TO PONDER: UNLESS GRACE has radically altered MY BEHAVIOR, it CANNOT possibly alter MY DESTINY!

If you think grace means there are no rules, you've missed the point by a country mile. And if you think grace means you can sin all you want, you've turned it into what Dietrich Bonhoeffer called "Cheap grace." When you really understand grace, you will want to obey God's commands. And Jesus said all the commands of the Old Testament can be summarized in these two: Love the Lord your God with all of your being, and Love your neighbor as yourself.

"The riches of God's grace" was proven in the fact that God loves you and me ... and He gave His all through His Son Jesus. To us who deserve nothing spiritually, having broken all the laws of God, and deserve nothing but judgment.

Flimsy, careless, un-Biblical views of human depravity (our sinfulness) always lead to very indistinct and unclear ideas of the grace of God. Someone has rightly said, "Whatever begins with God's grace will always lead to glory ..."

We need to remember that we have nothing in ourselves that will commend us to God (Romans 3:10-11) - we have no "saving grace" on our own. Being fundamentally unacceptable to God, we ask, along with Jesus' disciples, **"How can we be saved?"** Jesus' answer is **reassuring**: "What is impossible with men is possible with God" (Luke 18:26-27 NIV). **Salvation is the work of God.** He **gives the grace** we need. Our **"saving grace" is Christ Himself.** His work on **the cross** is what **saves us, not** our own merit, virtue, or religious quality.

Unfortunately, **many in the church** have been **led to think** that, **by our faith, we contribute** in some small way to our salvation. **After all, Christ's merit** must be applied to us **by faith,** and it seems our faith is coming from us. But **Romans 3:10-12 says** that **none of us seek after God. And** Ephesians 2:8 says, "For **by grace** you have been saved through faith; and that **not** of yourselves, it is the **gift** of God." Hebrews 12:2 tells us that **Jesus is the author and finisher** of our faith. **God's saving grace is completely His gift.** Even our ability to accept His saving grace is **just another gift from God.**

Christian, always remember: **grace is God's dynamic force,** a **dynamic** and **benevolent power** that applies the goodness of God and the resources of God to our lives **to save us,** to **keep** us, to **enable** us, to **deliver** us, to **sanctify** us, and to **glorify** us. **All of God's good favors** to His children **are given** through the means of this **benevolent goodness called grace.**

Christian, you need to know that **you** are **precious and invaluable to God Almighty and His Kingdom's work!** Having said that, "what do you think you are worth to Jesus?

> **"It was not with perishable things such as silver or gold that you were redeemed, but with the precious blood of Christ"** (I Peter 1:18–19 NIV).

There is a **story** that **in 75 B.C.,** a young **Roman nobleman** named **Julius Caesar** was **kidnapped** by pirates and **held for ransom.** When they **demanded 20 talents of silver** in ransom **(about $600,000 today),** Caesar **laughed** and said they obviously **had no idea who he was.** He insisted they **raise the ransom to 50 talents!** Why? Because **he believed he was worth far more than 20 talents.**

> **Our worth is measured by what God paid to rescue us, not by what you or others think of us!**

What a difference we see between **Caesar's arrogant measure** of his own worth and **the value God places on each of us.** Our worth is **not measured in terms of monetary** value but by **what our heavenly Father has done on**

our behalf. What a **ransom He paid to save us?** He did for us, **what we could never do** for ourselves. Through the **death of His only Son** on the cross, the **Father paid the price** to ransom and rescue **us from our sin. God loved us so much** that He gave up His **Son to die** on the cross and **rise from the dead** to ransom and **rescue** us. **That is what you are worth to Him!**

Peter tells his readers that Christ has redeemed them from an empty way of life. In the original language, **the word translated "redeemed"** (I Peter 1:18) means **"to set free."** It is **often used** when **talking about slaves** who have **been liberated from their bondage.** They had been **set free** from the bondage of a futile and **useless way of life** that has been handed down to them from their ancestors. **And this redeeming love of Christ** was present **even before sin entered** the equation (vv. 18-20). Have you ever thought about the **fact that Christ loves you knowing everything about you, even your sin?** How does it make you feel that you have been or can be set free from the slavery of sin and death? **I want to shout, "I'm FREE!"**

In Ephesians, Paul writes, "God being rich in mercy because of His great love with which He loved us, even when we were dead in our transgressions, has made us alive together with Christ. **By grace you have been saved.** And God raised us up with Him, and **seated us** with **Him in the heavenlies** in Christ Jesus, in order that in the ages to come **He might show** the **exceeding riches of His grace** in kindness **toward us** through Christ Jesus" (2:4-7).

> **Sin is sovereign, until sovereign grace dethrones it!** (Charles Spurgeon)

Paul may have been a mess when **Jesus found** him, but Christ **didn't leave him that way.** Because of **God's mercy and grace** Paul became a great missionary, preacher, and theologian. **It is only the one who has experienced** the **power** of the **resurrection** in his life **who can experience** such a thorough **transformation** in character and **then give the credit to God.**

The purpose for a gracious salvation is that God might be **unendingly gracious** to us and **bestow on us** the surpassing **riches of His grace** forever. **Every benefit given by God** to you and to me **is by grace.** And always and only **this grace comes through Jesus Christ.**

> **"Grace be with you, mercy, and peace, from God the Father, and from the Lord Jesus Christ, the Son of the Father, in truth and love"** (II John 3 KJV).

G. Campbell Morgan was approached by **a miner,** who said he had **trouble believing** that he could just **receive forgiveness so easy.** "**It's too cheap.**" Dr. Morgan **asked him if he worked** in the mine today. "**How'd you get out of the pit**" "The way I usually **do in the cage.**" "How much **did you pay** to come out of pit?" "**Well nothing**" "Weren't you afraid to trust the cage if you'd paid nothing." "Oh, no **it wasn't cheap. In fact,** it **cost the company a lot of money** to sink that shaft." It was then **he saw the light,** and **realized how much it had cost Christ for the grace** to set us free.

Jesus paid the sin debt of all who live. **He offers the free gift of Grace** that **brought and paid for our sins** and many have **committed their lives to Him** and **received salvation** and the cure for our sins. **Yet many will never receive the gift of eternal** life simply **because** they would **not in faith** just take Jesus as their Lord and Savior.

The preached gospel is to include the **facts about Christ's atoning work,** including His **resurrection,** and a call to **repent** and **believe.** God uses this call **to draw His elect to Himself. Some may mock** and **ridicule** this message, but **those who are being saved** will respond as the **Holy Spirit convicts them and draws** them to the Lord.

> **Paul wrote: "For the preaching of the cross is to them**
> **that perish foolishness; but unto us which are saved**
> **it is the power of God"** (I Corinthians 1:18 KJV).

If we start to think pride-fully that **we merited** this **salvation** or **received** it because of **some activity of our own** that made us **acceptable to God, think again:** "It is because of him that you are in Christ Jesus, who has become for us wisdom from God-that is, our righteousness, holiness and redemption. Therefore, as it is written: **Let the one who boasts,** boast in the LORD." (I Corinthians 1:30-31 NIV).

Notice that **the apostle includes many aspects** or **conditions** that are true of those who are saved, such as, "wisdom, righteousness, redemption, and sanctification," as part of what Christ has become to us. **Clearly all that is provided us in Christ** is **God's gracious provision** for everyone that is called.

> **"We believe it is through the grace of our Lord**
> **Jesus that we are saved"** (Acts 15:11 NIV).

Be honest with yourself before the God who made you. **You are a sinner** and **your sin if not cured** will bring **eternal death** and **separation. Today,** right now, why not **put aside any excuse you have. Repent** of your sins, and **give your life** to Christ.

The Bible emphasizes repeatedly that **our relationship with God** is **not based** upon **what we do,** but on **Who He is.** "For the kingdom of God is not a matter of eating and drinking, but of righteousness, peace, and joy in the Holy Spirit" (Romans 14:17, ESV). **In other words, faith has nothing to do** with what goes into your body: It has **everything to do with Who lives in your heart. When Paul said,** "Set your minds on things above, not on earthly things. For you died, and your life is now hidden with Christ in God" (Colossians 3:2, 3 NIV).

He was not writing to some elite saints who had decided to pay more **for the super-charged version of Christianity,** but to the whole church. **For every Christian has died** (to sin and self) and now **has new life in Christ.** We may **need to be reminded of it** and **urged to earnestly seek to live** up to all of the implications of this, but **it is nevertheless true or** we are **not** Christians.

Jesus is my righteousness, because **I could never be good enough** on my own. **Jesus is my peace,** because I could never have security without Him. **Jesus is my joy,** because **without Him,** I would be of all men, most **miserable.**

Did you go to church Sunday because you **were afraid** if you didn't, God wouldn't love you quite as much? **That's legalism (and not Biblical grace)!** The **truth is, God would still love you every bit** as much right now if you had chosen to stay home, or go to the lake, or go to the boats on the ocean! **Absolutely, the Bible speaks** about the **importance of gathering to worship,** but **grace says God loves us** even **while** we are yet **sinners.**

Phillip Yancey tells the story of **Ernest Hemingway.** Hemingway **grew up** in a very **devout Christian family,** and yet there **he never experienced the grace of Christ.** He **lived a wild sin-filled life** but since there was no father, no parent waiting for him, **he sank into the mire of a graceless depression.** A short **story he wrote** perhaps **reveals the grace that he hoped for.**

It is the **story of a Spanish father** who **decided to reconcile with his son** who had run away to Madrid. The **father, in a moment of remorse,** takes out this ad in the town's **newspaper. "Paco, meet me at Hotel Montana, Noon, Tuesday ... All is forgiven ... Papa."** When the father **arrived at the square** in hopes of meeting his son, **he found 300 Pacos waiting to be reunited** with their father. **It is the Father's forgiveness** which we yearn for and seek in our life. **God's grace is available to all. Why?** Because **Jesus died for all** on the cross and **the call of the cross** is to **extend that grace to all.**

The key to that story **is the Father - Son relationship.** It is **imperative that we become a child of God by means** of the **New-Birth** as described in John, **when Nichodemus came to Jesus** by night to **find out who Jesus really was. Is Jesus your Lord and Savior? Are we His true children** (sons and daughters) **by birth …** a **spiritual birth** (John 3)?

Grace tells us God has done it all and **God will do it all,** therefore, there is **no longer any pressure** to **"work hard" in hopes God** will toss us a few more favors! **For true Christians,** we are **enjoying the full riches of God's grace.**

A Roman emperor, after a **successful military campaign,** was returning **in triumph** to Rome. Great throngs of people filled the city to **welcome the mighty hero.** While passing through one of the crowded thoroughfares, **a little girl,** wild with joy, **dashed toward his chariot.**

The **officer stopped her** and said: "That is **the chariot of the emperor,** and you must not attempt to reach him." **The little one** replied: **"He may be your emperor - but he is my father!"** In a moment she was **not only in the chariot,** but **also in the arms of her father.**

It is even so with true believers. While **God is the Emperor/Creator** of all men - **He is that,** and infinitely **more, to us who** are **His. He is our Father, and we are His children!**

Concluding Question: Are you embracing the grace that God offers you? **His grace is seeking you. If you are lost, without Jesus** as your **Lord and Savior,** you can **know his grace** right now. But you have to receive it. **If you** are a **believer** and found yourself in a place where you need his grace, **His grace is available for you** as well. Come today, this could be **your day of grace.**

My unsaved friend, if you have never realized it before, God is gracious. **In His grace** He has **spoken to mankind** through **His Word, informing them** that they are sinners and **warning them of** the wrath that is to come. **In His grace** God has **sent His Son** to the cross of **Calvary** in order to satisfy the requirements of His justice by punishing His Son in their place.

If you will but admit your sin and your helpless state and **call upon Him for salvation, you** will be saved. **God's grace is for sinners like you and like me.** He will either deal with you in grace, or you must face the consequences of rejecting **His gracious offer of salvation.**

As beautiful and lifesaving as grace can be, **we often run from it.** By nature, **we are suspicious** of **promises** that seem too good to be true. **We wonder** about the **ulterior motives** of the excessively generous. **We long ago**

stopped opening those emails and letters that tell us what we've "already won." What's the catch? What's the fine print? What's in it for them? Are you skeptical or just dubious? OR, are you just still unconvinced and just have more questions?

In 1987, all of America stopped to watch a real-life drama unfolding in Midland, Texas. Eighteen month old Jessica McClure fell down an abandoned well and was trapped. Millions of Americans watched the story of Baby Jessica unfold. To the relief of everyone, Jessica came out of the well on October 16, 1987.

In case you don't remember the details of the story, let me give you a summary of what happened: "After 55 grueling hours trapped at the bottom of a 22-foot well, eighteen-month-old Jessica clawed her way out of the bottom of the pit, inch by inch, digging her little toes and fingers into the side of the well. What a hero, that Jessica!"

You may be thinking, "Whoa! That's not what happened! The baby didn't climb out! She was totally helpless down there; she was powerless to save herself. If she hadn't been rescued, she would have perished." You are exactly right! Listen, you and I were both in exactly the same situation spiritually.

The Bible says, "At just the right time, when we were still powerless, Christ died for the ungodly" (Romans 5:6 NIV). We deserve no more applause for our salvation than baby Jessica got for being rescued. God alone deserves the credit. There is no act we can perform that deserves the applause of others.

To end this Chapter, let me give you a simple, clear definition of grace. Grace is not a power or a force - (it's a type) of a Person. Grace is the personification of - JESUS. The Bible says of Jesus, "The Word became flesh ... full of grace and truth" (John 1:14). In Jesus was all the fullness of God's grace, and when we allow Jesus to fill us then we are filled with God's grace. Never let anyone or anything rob you of the blessings of "Amazing Grace!"

Friend, the idea that there is an unconditional love that relieves the pressure, forgives our failures, and replaces our fear with a faith in Jesus seems too good to be true ... but millions through the centuries can attest that it is. For you or me to make even the slightest contribution to our salvation is to rule out the possibility of grace. For one thing, any contribution on our part would be exaggerated in our own minds.

You may have heard the story of a man in England who was condemned to death for embezzlement. The royal family took pity on the man, however, and determined to **help him.** The king contributed $2000 from the royal treasury, while the **queen gave $1000** and the **crown prince $980.** The **people in the gallery passed the plate** and collected another contribution **of $19.90.** The **total amount of $3999.90 was only a dime short** of that which **was required,** but it was not enough. **The king reluctantly said that the man had to die.** The crowd in the gallery sighed. **Suddenly the condemned man reached into his pocket** and found a **dime,** just **what he needed. He was free!**

The point of this story is: that **no matter how small** the **contribution of** the condemned man, it would become, in his mind, of too great importance. **God is demonstrating His grace to the world** and the **angelic hosts** (Ephesians 1:3-12), and **He will not share His glory with sinful man.** Worse yet, **our efforts to contribute to Almighty God's saving grace are an affront to Him.**

It is either all of grace, or it is not grace at all!

Suppose that the **President** of the **United States invites you** to a **magnificent banquet.** It is **an evening** that you will **never forget.** But **as you leave that evening** you **greet the President** at the door and **wish to show your appreciation.** You **say to him,** "**Mr. President,** I want to **thank you** so much for the **wonderful evening.** I know this must have been a **very great expense,** so I would like **to make a small contribution** to **help cover the cost." You** then **press a dollar into his hand and go home.** That **is no compliment!** That **is an insult! God's grace** does **not require, nor** will it **accept,** any **contributions from** its **recipients.**

Be aware: that **we** do **not deserve to live in heaven with Christ,** but **we can** because **we participate with Him through the conviction** of **the Holy Spirit,** and **commitment to the Lord Jesus Christ.** We **are drawn** in to share in his achievements.

As Christians, we have been invited to **share** in the **achievements of Christ.** We have **no natural right** to share in them, **except that through the grace of God we have been invited** to do so. That is **participation with Christ.**

Have you received the life transforming grace of Almighty God in your life? Today is the day of your salvation!

To sum up this Chapter, let me share ... We are **saved by grace** as we **exercise** faith. We **are to live our lives by faith relying** on **this grace** as we walk in Him. This is **how we started** and this is how **we are to continue. We are to exercise faith,** but we are **saved by grace. Paul's instruction** to us that we are **saved by grace,** but we are **not to stop there,** we are **to keep walking by faith in grace.** We are **saved by grace,** we are **kept** by grace, and we **live** by grace to good works.

> "all are justified freely by his grace through the redemption that came by Christ Jesus. God presented Christ as a sacrifice of atonement, through the shedding of his blood-to be received by faith. He did this to demonstrate his righteousness, because in his forbearance he had left the sins committed beforehand unpunished" (Romans 3:24, 25 NIV).

Did you see the **News Broadcast on T.V.** where a **police officer rescued a deer** whose **head** got **stuck** in a **discarded light globe?** The **officer's first attempt** to pull the **plastic object** off the frightened **animal's head failed,** but it **came free** on the **second try.** The **deer paused** a second, **looked at** the officer, before **bolting into the woods.**

Similar to the **deer's helpless predicament, Paul says** that **we** are poor, sinful, lost creatures, **incapable of getting ourselves out of** our **sin dilemma.** He notes that **our hearts are trapped in sin** - **all of us** are **born under sin's power** and "fallen short of the glory of God" (Romans 3:23 NIV/KJV).

In Romans 3:10-18, the **apostle quotes** from **six Old Testament passages** revealing that **we're born alienated** from God, **don't naturally seek Him,** have **turned away from Him,** and **don't have a true view** of His greatness. **Without God,** we're **utterly helpless** and can't **rescue ourselves.**

In view of **our helplessness, God stepped in** and **provided** a **perfect rescue by His grace** through our **faith in Jesus His Son** (Romans 3:24). **Jesus alone provided** the perfect **sacrifice** God required, and **His death for us** on the cross **satisfied the demands** of sin—**freeing us** from the **grip of sin** and making a **restored relationship with God possible (**Romans 3:25).

My friend, pastor David Dykes in Tyler, Texas shared this **story** that should help us **understand 'grace' better.** "I love the **testimony of Iris Blue,** who for **over twenty years** was a **prostitute on the streets** of Houston, Texas. **All her life was abusive. She just wanted to be a lady,** but nobody would treat her like one. She didn't look very feminine - **she had been hurt** and **rejected** her entire life. **When she was 40, she looked 60.** She was no longer even attractive enough to be a prostitute. She was **running girls on the streets of Houston,** but some **men from** a Baptist Church there **went onto the streets**

in that part **of the city and began to tell people about the grace of God...
in Jesus.** She said, **"No, I can't take that.** I've been **too bad!** I've made **too
many mistakes.** God cannot love me." They said, **"Yes, God can love you ...
He does love you."** So, **one night, Iris Blue knelt down** on the **sidewalk** in
downtown Houston, and by **her own testimony said, "I knelt down a tramp
and I stood up a lady!"**

One day God's going to look at Iris Blue and say, **"Look** at **My grace.**
It was **nothing she did.** She **didn't deserve it.** This is **what God did!"** God's
going to look at you if you are a **child of God** and **He's** going **to say, "Look
at this. It's nothing they did. It's all by my grace."** Hallelujah to the Lord!

God opened the door for **brother Blue and Iris to** come to our **church**
in North East Texas, after that, **to give their testimony** about the **wonderful
transformation both their lives. When Iris finished testifying** about what
the **Lord had done in her life, there wasn't a dry eye in the building. I'm
happy** to say that **some who heard** her that day, **experienced** the **call of God,**
and **gave their life to Jesus as their Lord and Savior.**

Friend, we should be eternally thankful for **God's love and grace** and
display it in our life **for God freely gave us His grace;** that which we **received**
but did not deserve. That's **why grace is free** because **no one could afford** it
anyway. The **irony** to the world **is that we couldn't ever earn** it by all our good
works. So, "God so loved the world that He gave His only begotten Son so that
l life" (John 3:16). **That's amazing grace!**

GOD'S GRACE AND FORGIVENESS
NOT ONLY COVERS YOUR SIN, IT
REDEEMS YOUR LIFE AS A SINNER.

My friend, **it is grace** from **beginning to end** for the child of God. **In light
of this,** we **should see our problems** and **ourselves** from **God's viewpoint.**
God has an **eternal viewpoint** and **His viewpoint** is one **of grace.** He sees
all **of us from** the **beginning to the end** under His **matchless grace** and His
great love for us.

Here's the **great news about the grace** of the Lord Jesus. **It covers every
sin, including** the **physical or mental act of murder.** And it **doesn't just
cover the sin, it redeems the sinner. Think about Moses. Or David.** Or the
Apostle Paul. In the **world's eyes, each** of these men was **a murderer.**

Because of God's forgiveness, Moses wasn't a murderer ... he was a
liberator. Because of **God's forgiveness, David wasn't** a killer or adulterer ...

he was a man after God's own heart. And **because of God's forgiveness, Paul wasn't** a persecutor … he was a missionary.

I find from the **Word of God** (through the **grace of God**) that **two roads** lie **through** the **wilderness of this world.** The **one,** at its **beginning, is pleasant** to carnal nature, **being strewed** with **forbidden** pleasures, **sensual** delights and **materialistic** gratifications, **but growing** darker and **more** crooked and **thorny** as it advances, **it ends abruptly** in eternal **misery.**

The other, difficult at the entrance, **requires** many sacrifices and **much** self-denial; but **gradually increasing** in light and beauty, **it terminates** in the **blissful** regions of **immortal glory.** Ask yourself now: "In which of these roads am I now walking?" Story from: **"The Two Roads of Life" by Thomas Reade.** (Edited by Glenn Clifton).

Let me tell you a story that may give you **more insight into the doctrine of the grace of God.** In 1964 a **young man** had just **returned from Viet Nam** where he had served in the Navy. Upon his release **he had sufficient funds** to fulfill a long-time desire to **own a new Jaguar.** He returned **to Oklahoma** and one morning he **was driving** in a remotely **populated part** of the State which, he reasoned, was the **perfect place** to find out **how fast the car could go.** The speedometer was easing its way **past 160** as the powerful sports car **reached the top** of a small rise. Just beyond, **a highway patrolman** was waiting. A law-abiding citizen, my friend **slammed on the brakes,** slid past the officer at **150 miles per hour,** and came to a halt some distance down the road.

The officer caught up and stood beside the sleek convertible. **"Do you have any idea how fast you were going?"** he inquired. **"Well, roughly,"** was the deliberately evasive reply. **"One hundred sixty-three miles per hour!"** the officer specified. "That's about what I thought," my friend confessed, somewhat sheepishly. **Guilt was obvious,** and there **was no possible excuse** to be offered. My friend could **only wait** to discover what this fiasco was going to cost. He **meekly waited for the officer** to proceed. **To his amazement the patrolman queried,** "Would you mind if I took a look at that engine?"

The **fine points of high performance automobiles cannot** be discussed quickly, so **both went on to a coffee shop** where they could talk further. **A while later,** both of the **men shook hands** and **went their separate ways.** My friend was elated, for the officer had **not given him a citation.**

Listen: that is about as close to grace as one can come on this earth, **but it is still not quite up** to the **standard of biblical** grace. (I say that because **biblical grace** would be demonstrated **only if the patrolman had paid for the coffee**).

Have you ever experienced grace in your life? Perhaps a **policeman** stopping you for speeding and **just giving** you a **warning** when you deserved a ticket. **Perhaps** a time when **you said hurting words** to a friend or spouse **and they forgave you.**

The gifts or **abilities** are **given by God's grace.** Romans 12:6 states, "We have different gifts, **according to the grace given us." God's grace is everything.** We cannot boast in anything. **In** faith, **in** who we are, **in** our gifts, **in** our good works, **in** our blessings, **God's grace is unique and incomparable!** How wonderful He is! **Do you experience His grace in** your life? If so, **give thanks** and **show forth His grace** by **being gracious to one another.** Think of what He has done for you and give thanks. **The principle of grace is as fundamental to Christianity** as that of **justice** is to Law, or **love** is to marriage. **The Bible cannot be understood** apart from Grace. **Christianity itself cannot be understood** apart from an adequate **grasp of grace.**

The doctrine of grace distinguishes the **Christian faith** from every **other religion in the world,** as well as from the **cults. Rightly understood** and **applied,** the **doctrine of grace** can **revolutionize one's Christian life.** That is **the reason for this book,** that you will never be the same after this study.

Someone once asked a former great **statesman** named **Daniel Webster** a question. **He asked,** "You have a **colossal mind. What is the greatest thought** that you have ever had?" **Webster replied, "I've thought** about **many things,** but the **most awesome,** the most **terrifying,** the most **shattering thought** I've ever had, **is my personal accountability to God one day."**

Since **we must all stand** and **give account** of **our lives** someday, just remember, it will **not be done,** with **positive results without grace. Please allow this book** to **lead you to the teachings** of God's Word on **Grace. It will change your life!**

Let us pray ... "Heavenly Father, thank Lord You** for the **love You** have **shown to me** and for the **price You paid** for my forgiveness – all by your eternal grace. **Lord, I admit** that the **language** of **grace** and **faith** are not as familiar to me as they should be, **I am willing** to learn, because **I want to live** a life **pleasing** to You. **Thank You Jesus** for **loving** me and **saving** me. **Help me live** to be an **ongoing expression of gratitude,** for **You are the One** whose **worth** is **beyond measure. In Jesus name, AMEN!**

**For the grace of God that brings salvation
has appeared to all men,** - (Titus 2:11)

Chapter 2

God 'HUMBLES' Me With His Grace

"YOUNG MEN, IN the same way **be submissive** to those who are older. All of you, **clothe yourselves with humility** toward one another, because, **"God opposes the proud** but **gives grace to the humble. Humble yourselves,** therefore, under God's mighty hand, **that He may lift you up** in due time. **Cast all your care** (anxiety) **on Him** because He cares for you" (I Peter 5:5-7)

According to God's Word, one of the main characteristics of God's children **is an un-assuming nature,** one that is **not arrogant or reveling in the glow of his accomplishments**. We **call it "humility!"** This **is one** of the **proofs** of **God's special love**. It is God that makes us humble, and then, **approving** of our humility, **gives many great and precious promises** to us in that character.

The Apostle used an expression here of a remarkable kind, and which **never occurs again in Scripture**. The **word** rendered in the Authorized Version, **"be clothed,"** or better in the Revised Version as **"gird yourselves with,"** really **implies** a **little more than either** of these renderings suggests. **It describes a kind of garment** as well as the **act of putting it on,** and the sort of **garment** which it describes was a **remarkable one**. It was a part of a **slave's uniform**. When **Peter wrote** this sentence, **was he thinking of his Master's act,** as recorded **in John 13:4-5** – **"(Jesus) rose** from supper. He **laid aside** his outer **garments,** and taking a **towel,** tied it around his waist. Then **He poured water** into a basin and began to **wash the disciples' feet** and to **wipe them** with the **towel** that was wrapped around Him" (ESV).

> **Christ is the humility of God embodied in human nature; the Eternal Love humbling itself, clothing itself in the garb of meekness and gentleness, to win and serve and save us.** – Andrew Murray

The humble Christian, is an **honored personality.** He is **a blessing** to all about him (both saved and lost), and is an **honor to Christ** of a changed life. He has **great fellowship** with God, and **receives** much from God, **so becomes** increasingly **like God.**

I have always hesitated to speak/preach **(now write)** at all on the **subject of humility** because of **not wanting to come across** in any way that would make me **seem superior,** better or **greater** than others, or as one **who has attained.** So, **I do feel like I should qualify this teaching** by saying that **this subject is given first** to me, and **second** to you. As **I sometimes say** when I am preaching, **when I point** … there are **three fingers pointing back at me and one at you.**

I am many times **more to blame** of **prideful attitudes** as you, and this is **the method** I will take in writing this chapter. **Dear reader:** I believe the **chief-sin** of my **life's ministry** has been that of the **lack of humility** … because of **my pride.** After all these years, **I realize** that during **many times** in my life the **Lord blessed me** or the **church I served.** Sometimes **I took the credit,** and for that **I failed both God, myself and His church.**

Humility is perhaps one of the most elusive of all **Godly characteristics listed in God's Word.** Yes, most of us **easily notice pride in other people,** but genuine **humility is not easy to see** because **humility, like love,** does not parade itself and is offered in a spirit of respect, submission and obedience. **In this brazen and insolent world in which we live,** humility, like humbleness or meekness is **viewed as weakness by the un-Christian world.** Since **humility is a condition of the heart,** it can be **faked,** or **imitated** outwardly.

> **Paul states** in **Colossians 2:21-23** "Do not touch, do not taste, do not handle (i.e.-stay-away from), **certain 'things' which perish** with the using - according to the commandments and doctrines of men? **These 'things'** indeed have **an appearance** of in **self-imposed** religion, **false humility,** and neglect of the body, but they are of no value against the **indulgence of the flesh**" (ESV).

Let me give you **another version** of these **verses,** "Don't handle! Don't taste! Don't touch!? **Such rules are mere human teachings** about **things that deteriorate** as we use them. These **rules may seem wise** because **they require strong devotion,** pious self-denial, and **severe bodily discipline.** But **they provide no help** in conquering **a person's evil desires.**"

You can see that 'grace' is an 'inside' job. God wants our humility to be inward and genuine, not a performance just to be seen by others. Once coming from the heart, humility's fruits will become outwardly evident, but it is not something that we have to work on showing.

The culture in which we live sometimes influences us to feel guilty if we enjoy ourselves in a lawful way; that there is some guilty feeling that we should feel from that. Religion has been seen in such a way through the centuries, and it is often associated with the practice of strictness, or denial of oneself or one's body, and other man-made rules of fleshly strictness.

> The Holy Bible flourishes in promises to the humble, then
> makes them available to those who qualify! - G. Clifton.

The humble Christian, because of the grace of humility, avoids many temptations and snares of the tempter. He escapes many dangers into which others fall. He obtains many blessings, and enjoys many comforts, to which the boastful and proud are strangers. This precious grace is a distinguishing mark of the Lord's people! May I grow downward in humility before God. Oh, to be like Jesus, rooted in humility.

Question: Have you ever been humbled by one of your children? I have! One afternoon after I got home from my church office in downtown Long Beach, CA, and my oldest son Stephen ran up to me shouting, "Daddy, daddy, look what I did at school." His eyes glistened with excitement as he showed me a paper he had brought home from school. It was an arithmetic test, marked with a big star and a grade of 100 percent. As we looked at the exam, he said he had three questions left to answer when the teacher said time was up. Confused, I asked how he could have received a perfect score. He replied, "My teacher gave me grace. She let me finish the test although I had run out of time."

Wow! What a teaching opportunity! First, I was amazed at his young son's use of the word "grace" in his explanation. Perhaps he did listen, from the front row, more than I thought. So, my little son and I sat down and discussed the meaning of grace, I pointed out that God has given us more than we deserve through Jesus. We deserve punishment and death because of our sin (Romans 3:23). Yet, because He loved us, "while we were still sinners, Christ died for us" to forgive us (Romans 5:8). We were unworthy, yet Jesus - sinless and holy - gave up His life so we could escape the penalty for our sin and one day live forever in heaven.

> Eternal life is a gift from God. It's not something
> we earn by working for it. We are saved by God's
> grace, through faith in Christ (Ephesians 2:8-9).

Remember, **it is only God Who can see pride or humility** of the heart whereas, in contrast, we **human beings see mainly what appears on the surface.** It **makes it easy for any of us to give an impression** that we are **something that we are not,** and this is why a person of a prideful heart **can appear humble** outwardly. **God wants our humility to be inward** and **genuine, not** a performance just to be seen by others. **Once coming from the heart,** humility's fruits will become **outwardly evident.** It is not something that we have to work on showing.

> **A man can counterfeit love, he can counterfeit faith, he
> can counterfeit hope and all the other graces, but it is
> very difficult to counterfeit humility** - D.L. Moody.

Some people think of themselves as humble, but **in actuality,** are full of **envy and jealousy.** Some **become depressed** because they see **their own callousness** and **unimportance,** and some may be **rebellious** against their responsibilities and realize their negative tendencies. **Low-mindedness** is not **lowly-mindedness. Depression is not humility.** Sometimes I think that people misunderstand those different emotions. **God requires all true Christians** to esteem others above themselves, or better than themselves.

> **"The best definition of humility I ever heard was
> this – to think rightly of ourselves. Humility is the
> proper estimate of oneself"** - C.H. Spurgeon.

True humility cannot be faked for very long. It **will always be revealed** even to other people by whether one consistently submits to God. However, our **Heavenly Father,** Who looks on the heart **knows immediately.** It is a quality of great value. **God openly expresses His pleasure** in those **who humble** themselves before Him. **Why?** Because it not **only glorifies Him** through the way that they live, but it is also very rewarding to those who do so. **God requires all true Christians** to **esteem others** (regard) above themselves, **or better** than themselves.

**"Let nothing be done through selfish ambition or
conceit, but in lowliness of mind let each esteem others
better than themselves. "** Philippians 2:3 (KJV).

Paul did not mean that he, **as an apostle,** should look on the members
of the church **as being above** his apostolic office, or that a **pastor should
consider** his position **less important** than that **of an usher.** We are **not to
have feelings of inferiority** about ourselves. **We should not act** like we have
humility over our abilities when we are **better skilled** or **more qualified** than
others to do a task, **or hold an office.** This is **an area** that I think we commonly
misunderstand about humility.

This is the awareness that Paul is conveying. Philippians 2:3 expresses **the
idea of being lowly in mind,** unassuming, **humbling ourselves in preference
to others.** This is **critical to understand.** In preference to others is **giving the
preference** of whatever **we are doing to others,** rather than **taking it upon
ourselves** and **fulfilling our own desires.** Humility **is putting** the interests,
cares, and **comforts of others above our own,** and **forgetting ourselves** in
sacrifice and service. Two **key words in humility** are "sacrifice" and "service."

Grace demands humility, the **humility** that **constrains us** to be **debtors**
all along the line of salvation from its **fount in election** to its **consummation
in glory. Salvation** is **from the Lord,** and it is **only of Him** if it is all of him.
This is the **doctrine of grace** and **it is its glory."**

Did you know that **Almighty God** is **attracted toward a person who
is humble.** In Isaiah 66:1-2, **God plainly states** that humility attracts His
attention: **Thus says the Lord:** "Heaven is My throne, and earth is My
footstool. Where is the house that you will build Me? And where is the place
of My rest? For all those things My hand has made, and all those things exist,
says the Lord. But on this one will I look: On him who is poor and of a contrite
spirit, and who trembles at My word"

**"Let nothing be done through strife (selfish ambition)
or vainglory (conceit), but in lowliness of mind, let each
esteem others better than himself"** (Philippians 2:3).

Another transliteration/rendering of **Philippians 2:3 reads,** "Do nothing
from **factional motives** (selfish ambition, or for unworthy ends) or **prompted**
by **conceit** and empty **arrogance.** Instead, **in the true spirit of humility**

(lowliness of mind) **let each regard the others as better than** and **superior to himself** (thinking more highly of one another than you do of yourselves)."

Paul did not mean that he, **as an apostle,** should look on the **members** of the church as being above his apostolic office, **or that a pastor** should consider his position less important than that of an usher. We are **not to have feelings of inferiority** about ourselves. We should not **act like we have humility** over our abilities when we are **better skilled** or **more qualified** than others to do a task, or hold an office. This **is an area** that I think we **commonly misunderstand** about **humility.**

Humility expresses the idea of being lowly in mind, unassuming, humbling ourselves in preference to others. **This is critical to understand.** In preference to others is giving the preference of whatever we are doing to others, **rather** than taking it upon ourselves and fulfilling **our own desires. Humility is putting** the interests, cares, and comforts of **others above our own,** and **forgetting ourselves** in sacrifice and service. **Two key words in humility** are "sacrifice" and "service." Earlier Paul had admonished the Roman members to do the same.

> **Romans 12:10, 16 states,** "Be kindly affectioned one
> to another with brotherly love; in honour preferring
> one another. Be of the same mind one toward another.
> Mind not high things, but condescend to men of low
> estate. Be not wise in your own conceits" (KJV).

Genuine true humility is found in the alliance between **realistic self-respect based on truth** and **dedicated self-sacrifice in service. A person who knows his own gifts and abilities,** and yet **is willing to serve those who have nothing** with which to offer in return, **shows a humble attitude.** Esteeming others above ourselves **describes the attitude God wants us to develop** as an essential approach to life—whether **toward each other,** or toward **the world.**

Since humility reflects godly character - Jesus is the epitome of humility. He not only strongly **impressed upon His disciples** the need **to have humility,** but was in Himself its personification. **Jesus knew that the Father** had given all things into His hands, and **that He came forth from God** and **would go back** again to God, and **still His incomparable superiority** over human beings **did not influence His desire to serve. Mark 10:45 states,** "For even the Son of Man did not come to be served, but to serve, and to give His life as a ransom for many" (KJV).

Oh, how we soon forget that **Jesus was so meek and lowly in heart, so humble in spirit** and **ready for service,** that He **girded Himself** with a towel and **washed the disciples' dirty, dusty, feet.** Genuine **humility leads the strong to serve the weak.** It never underestimates its own worth, but **in unreserved unselfishness** it is **ready to sacrifice** its own needs at any moment for the good of others ... **exactly what we see Christ doing** in this example that John recorded in John 13:3-15.

> **The higher a man is in grace. The lower he will be in his own esteem.** - C.H. Spurgeon

Jesus taught them the meaning of **true humility** by **washing the feet** of His disciples. **The Pharisees** and the **teachers** of the **Law saw** leadership as an opportunity to **serve themselves rather** than as an opportunity to **serve others. We** should **not make** the **same mistakes they** did by not letting our **love for positions** come **before our loyalty to God.**

Our humility puts God first and when we do so we will do His will. **Jesus always put the Father's will first.** He taught, suffered and died that **we might be saved. Service to others** is **rewarding** and is very easy when we put God first. **Everyone has something to offer.**

According to D. L. Moody "The **measure of a man** is **not** how **many servants** he has, but **how many men he serves.**" We **all have something to offer.** Let us **humble ourselves** and **serve God** by meeting the **needs of others** with our talents, our time and our tithe. **We cannot serve everyone but** we **can** serve **someone.** And **if everybody** is **serving somebody,** everyone **will be served. Amen!**

> **Humility is not thinking less of yourself, but thinking of yourself less.** - C.S. Lewis

Jesus acknowledged that He was their Teacher and their **Lord,** but He was **still a humble man.** He **demonstrated His humility** by His action of lowering himself to washing their feet. This task was usually **the work of the household slaves. If He instructs and commands you and me to do this as well,** would we be obedient to His command?

As we see in this example, **genuine humility loses all its self-conceit,** but **never loses** all its **self-respect.** This is consistent with upholding one's personal dignity and integrity of character. **Christ was, and is, of the greatest dignity.**

Yet, more importantly, He humbled Himself to become a man. He "made Himself of no reputation." Jesus "did not come to be ministered to, but to minister." He was the servant of all. He never forgot that He was a servant and He never forgot His dignity at the same time. Jesus was "made in the likeness of man, and was found in manner as a servant" after being divine and powerful. In sharp contrast, this is something that Satan would never do.

> "Humble yourselves in the sight of the Lord,
> and He shall lift you up" (James 4:10).

Have you ever wondered what humility is all about? True humility is not thinking negatively about yourself. It is agreeing with what God knows about you. The grace of God will exalt a person without inflating him and humble a person without debasing him. When I exude humility, I am what I am because of Christ. In this life, you are not going to be sinless, but as you deal with sin in your life, you can come closer to being free from sin. Sinless? No. Blameless? Yes!

The Holy Spirit led Paul to write, "Let this mind be in you which was also in Christ Jesus, who, being in the form of God, did not consider it robbery to be equal with God, but made Himself of no reputation, taking the form of a bondservant, and coming in the likeness of men. And being found in appearance as a man, He humbled Himself and became obedient to the point of death, even the death of the cross" (Philippians 2:5-8).

Paul was a man who displayed a lot of humility, but he also realized that he had a lot of pride. He was constantly working to rid his life of that pride. He realized, from a spiritual standpoint and the desires of his heart, that the things that he wanted to do he did not, and the things that he did not want to do he did (Romans 7:15).

Jesus' perfect example throughout His life is what Paul admonishes the Philippian members to develop within themselves, and by extension to us. Christ did not attempt to please Himself, but put the needs and feelings of others above His own, and He did it for His entire life.

The word for 'proud' in James 4:6, is (Greek - 'huperephanos'), which literally means "one who shows himself above other people." Its real problem is that it is a thing of the heart. It means haughtiness. But a person suffering from it might appear to be walking in downcast humility, while all the time there is, in his heart, a vast contempt for all others.

> **"Oh, love the LORD, all you His saints!**
> **For the LORD preserves the faithful, And fully**
> **repays the proud person"** (Psalm 31:23 NKJV).

God hates pride! The apostle **Peter said,** "Clothe yourselves, all of you, **with humility** toward one another, for **God opposes the proud** but **gives grace** to the **humble"** (I Peter 5:5 NKJV). For the sake of **God's glory** and for the sake of **your soul's satisfaction, never** let up in **killing every vestige of pride** in your heart.

The most important thing that we can take from Peters' verses is the **understanding** and the **knowledge,** the **belief and the conviction,** that **humility is a choice. Peter says,** "Humble yourself!" **We** can **choose to go the right way,** and when we do, we **have humbled ourselves. Humility is not a feeling** but a **state of mind** wherein **a person sets his course** to submit to God - **regardless** of **his feelings.** This is a terribly **hard** thing **to do.**

> **The most powerful position on earth is kneeling**
> **before the Lord of the universe.** - Bill Crowder

The determining factor of whether someone receives grace or not is given by **James who wrote that** "God opposes the proud, but gives grace to the humble" (James 4:6, NKJV). **The point is that God gives His grace** only to those who **are humble** and He **"opposes ("at war with"** in the Greek) **the proud"** of heart. **We receive God's grace** when we **acknowledge the greatness of God, who humbled Himself at the cross** (Philippians 2:5–11).

Many times the proud have an undue self-esteem. They have a **high and unreasonable conceit** of their **own excellence** or importance. **This may extend to anything;** to beauty, or strength, or accomplishments, or family, or country, or clothing, or position, or religion. We can be **proud of anything that belongs to us,** or **which can in** any way be construed as a part of or regarding ourselves.

It is amazing the things that we have noticed people around the world becoming proud over. **People can be proud over how violent** they are, **or how good they are at stealing or lying.** We find that **today in commercials,** it is amazing to find a commercial that does not **glorify lying** in some way, and **many times the commercial itself is a lie.** It is **amazing what people** can **find to glorify themselves** with, or **glorify their products with.**

Although very difficult, it is **possible** to have a **correct estimate of ourselves,** and attach no undue importance to ourselves because of it.

Remember this: every human being on earth has some pride. The mind that is set on the flesh is hostile toward God, because it does not submit to God's law; and in reality it cannot. Those who are in the flesh cannot please God. But, when we are true members of God's church we are not in the flesh but in the Spirit if, in fact, the Spirit of God dwells in us.

By continually working to overcome pride, we work toward the goal of having a heart that is not lifted up, that claims no undue regard for itself, that concedes to all others what is their due, and that is humble before God. It is obviously a very tough thing to develop and we really cannot do it without God's Holy Spirit. A person who has this heart feels that all he has, and is, is nothing in God's sight. The humble person is willing to occupy his appropriate place in the sight of God and his fellow human beings, and be esteemed just as he is, even though they may see him as "weak" instead of "meek" and humble.

> It was through Pride that the devil became the devil: Pride leads to every other vice: it is the completely anti-God state of mind. - C.S. Lewis

Committing our lives to God in righteous acts in doing good things does not come from a proud heart. We have a faithful Lord and Savior Who understands how hard it is to develop humility. Nevertheless, we must treat others righteously even while we suffer.

God can save, but He can also punish. Hope is held out to the repentant, humble, and submissive person, but the way is not guaranteed to be easy. For even the most devout are among those who have broken God's laws, and God calls them back. So God's decision to save is ultimately, and finally, and always His decision of grace.

The doctrine of redemption of Jesus magnifies and motivates the Christian to humility. If I recognize that all my salvation (actually, God's salvation imparted to me), is a gift of God, that if God had not touched me, if God had not convicted me of my sin, if God had not send someone to tell me the "good news," of Jesus, if God had not done things in my life, I would have certainly gone to hell. That's the work of grace!

God's salvation drives me down on my face before God. It strips me of my pride because I realize that I don't deserve salvation any more than anyone else does. I don't know why God has allowed the people in China to go without hearing the Gospel. I know that I don't deserve it any more than they do, **and yet God for some reason unknown to me has chosen that I** should hear the Gospel **and in His providence** be drawn to Jesus Christ, and in **His omniscience called me** to be a **servant** and a **minister** of His Gospel. **I tell you that humbles me,** and it **puts me on my face before God** in **true humility** and **praise.**

Jesus had an encounter with a Samaritan woman and told His disciples of the meeting to. **This** very **simple account of Jesus' interaction with an outcast woman** on a hot day can be found in **John Chapter Four,** so please read it to see how it turns out.

Remember, the Jews didn't talk to Samaritans, and the **Samaritans didn't talk to Jews.** This meant she could get her water and move on. But **she could feel the stranger's burning gaze** as she drew the water. **"Give me a drink."** (John 4:7). **His words** had **no bite** or **judgment,** but simply. "Give me a drink." It is **easy to overlook** the personal element of the story - **the one-on-one encounter** of the **Creator** of the Universe **with one** of His most **damaged children.**

Men had always wanted something from her. **The polite ones** often turned out to be the worst, so **without averting her gaze, she handed him** the dripping vessel. **She watched him drink,** and after a very long draught, he looked content, **so she spoke. "How is it that you,** being a Jew, **ask a drink from me, a Samaritan woman?"** (v. 4:9)

No 'proper' woman would have been **so brazen as to talk to a stranger** in that day and age, **much less a lowly Samaritan woman to a Jewish man,** but this was not brazenness. She had been **married five times** and was **currently shacked up with someone** in a **small town** where everyone harshly judged everyone's business. This was brokenness. **And in that naked humility,** she managed to **ask the essential question** we all struggle with: **Why would You, Jesus,** reach out to me, much less **ask me** for something?

The only thing more revealing than the humility of her question is the **warmth of Jesus' response.** Not just His words, but His embrace. **He embraced her with all her flaws,** her **past,** and her **baggage. Jesus responded to her humility,** and as a result, **she became His messenger** to the very people who had rejected her: **"many** of the **Samaritans** of that city **believed** in Him **because of the word** of the woman" (v. 39).

"Humility is terribly elusive, because if focused on too much it will turn into pride, it's very opposite. Humility

is a virtue to be highly sought but never claimed, because
once claimed it is forfeited" - John MacArthur.

One immutable personality trait of God Almighty is His responsiveness
to humility: "God resists the proud but gives grace to the humble" (James
4:6). But it is important to recognize that humility is not humiliation, it is
simply openness, honesty, and sincerity. It is the recognition of who we are in
light of Who He is.

Jesus imparted grace to the Samaritan woman because that is the type
of leader He is. The Bible says that "a bruised reed He will not break, and
smoking flax He will not quench." (Matthew 12:20). So even when the acrid
smoke of our faults sting others' eyes, and even when the lightest touch would
break us, we can be confident that Jesus will embrace us, too. As a leader,
Jesus brought out the gifts in a woman everyone else had given up on. He
had the wisdom to realize that her past mistakes had finally brought her to a
point of great potential. He saw her for not only who she had been, but who
she would become.

We know that Jesus was willing to break the rules, simply by talking to
this woman, but we can also be assured of something He would never do - and
that is to reject the humble.

Dear brothers and sisters, always remember that our spiritual provision
is from exactly the same source. The necessities that sustain spiritual life and
produce the kind of strength that we want to have - the sense of well-being
that we desire, along with a clear conscience - all of these vital "nutrients"
come from God.

Pride manifests itself in many ways such as: praising ourselves, adoring
our own physical appearance, giving a false superior impression, and contempt.
It also manifests itself with slander of others, envy at the talents and skills of
others, anxiety to gain applause, distress and rage when slighted, impatience
of contradiction, and opposition to God Himself.

Pride is a devastating sin and is complex. Most sins
turn us away from God, but pride directly attacks
God. It lifts us above and against God, seeking to
dethrone Him by enthroning ourselves. - Joel Beeke

A proud heart cannot receive help, because it does not know that it needs
help, and, therefore, it cannot ask. In contrast, the humble heart that James is

encouraging us to develop is not a weak-kneed thing. **It has two advantages** with regard to Satan and help in time of need.

It is not at all unusual for men to desire and build beautiful and costly edifices **to honor God and to worship within them.** However, **God makes clear** that He **prefers to be revered** and **communed with within the hearts** of men. **This gets His positive attention,** motivating Him to respond in loving kindness. **When this occurs,** it cannot be anything but **good for those who humbly seek Him.**

Has This Sneaky Sin Of Pride Wormed It's Way Into Your Daily Life?

Is any statement regarding **humility's value** more clearly rewarding than **James 4:6-7, 10?** "But **He gives more grace.** Therefore He says: '**God resists** the proud, but **gives grace** to the **humble.**' Therefore **submit** to God. **Resist** the devil and he will flee from you ... **Humble yourselves** in the sight of the Lord, and He will lift you up."

Salvation is by grace through faith. It is **also the key** to all **obedience** and **growth** in God's way of life. Can anything be more valuable? **Humility is a key** to **obtaining it as a gift** from God.

There seems to be **a lot of teaching** on the **grace of God these days. Some** of it is **extreme,** but **much** of it **is actually good. Most Christians** enjoy good **Scriptural teaching** on the **empowering grace of God** and want **to learn to walk** and **live in** more of it. But **how do we increase our capacity to receive more of God's grace in our lives? The Word is clear** on this. **Here it is again:** "God resists the proud, but gives grace to the humble" (James 4:6 NKJV).

The measure of grace that you **receive from God** in your life **is in proportion** to the measure of **humility you walk in.** More **grace operating in your life** means more **fruitfulness,** more **power,** and more **wisdom to know** and **do** the will of God. **Who wouldn't want that?** The **key is to humble yourself.** Without **cultivating true humility** in your life, you **cannot receive additional grace.**

In order to cultivate true humility in your life, you must **identify pride** and learn to **resist it.** There is **always more pride** in us **than we think.** Pride is a **hindrance** and a **barrier** to **walking** with the Lord and **receiving** from the Lord. **Christians cannot operate** in any kind of **falsehood** and **pretension if** you **want to walk closely** with God.

Warning: One of the worse and more subtle kinds of pride in the church today is spiritual pride. For example, when Christians try to be spiritual, put on airs and constantly argue doctrinal points, it is usually a sure sign of this most subtle and worse kind of pride working in their lives. Know this: God hates pride, and it blocks Him from releasing more grace and spiritual understanding and power into your life. Pride is the nature of the devil, and that is enough reason for every Christian it, too.

> "But the natural man receives not the things of
> the Spirit of God, for they are foolishness to him;
> nor can he know them, because they are spiritually
> discerned" (I Corinthians 2:14 KJV).

The natural man is the person who does not know Christ. They have never been born-again by the Holy Spirit and therefore the Spirit does not live within them. Because the Spirit does not live within them, they neither desire spiritual things, nor can they understand them. Paul says that the things of God are foolishness to such men. To them, salvation and surrender to Christ are a waste of time. Rather than living for God, they would rather live for self. Ultimately such men will stand before God and be judged for their sin (Revelation 20:11-15).

We have no humility by nature. There may be a softness of disposition, and a readiness to yield to others - but there is no true humility. That is a fruit of the Spirit, a new covenant blessing. True repentance of the heart must be manifested in works: seeking the Lord and doing what He commands. The "humble" are to "seek the Lord," which is defined in the same verse as seeking righteousness and humility. Only the "meek" (or humble) are exhorted because nothing can be done at this point with the rest.

Committing our lives to God in righteous acts in doing good things does not come from a proud heart. We have a faithful Lord and Savior Who understands how hard it is to develop humility. Nevertheless, we must treat others righteously even while we suffer.

We learn in II Timothy 1:12, "For this reason I also suffer these things; nevertheless I am not ashamed, for I know Whom I have believed and am persuaded that He is able to keep what I have committed to Him until that Day" (NKJV). There is no exception clause in a contract that says we only have to do good when we feel good. The actions of a humble and contrite heart are not thwarted by suffering.

God can save, but He can also punish. Hope is held out to the repentant, humble, and submissive person, but the way **is not guaranteed to be easy.** For **even the most devout** are among those who **have broken God's laws,** and God calls them back. **So God's decision to save is** ultimately and finally **His decision of grace.**

The doctrine of redemption of Jesus **magnifies** and **motivates the Christian to humility.** If I recognize that all **my salvation** (actually, God's salvation given to me)**, is a gift of God,** that **if God had not** touched me, **if God had not** convicted me of my sin, **if God had not** send some to tell me the "good news," of Jesus, **if God had not** done things in my life, **I would certainly be in hell;** it doesn't puff me up. **It drives me down on my face** before God. **It strips me of my pride** because I realize that **I don't deserve salvation** any more than anyone else does.

Who are those who seek to be humble? Simply put, the humble are **those who willingly obey and submit to God's pleasure and will for them,** rather than proudly insisting on satisfying their own desires for pleasure. Like Jesus Christ, **the humble are not here to be served, but to serve. One of the most wonderful aspects of His grace** is that **He will never leave** the **humble** nor forsake them.

> **James wrote: "Humble yourselves in the sight of the Lord, and He will lift you up."** (James 4:10, NIV)

> **"Therefore humble yourselves under the mighty hand of God, that He may exalt you in due time, casting all your care upon Him, for He cares for you"** (I Peter 5:6 NKJV).

When we are called by God to do a task, we often begin to **look at what resources** we have to perform it. This **can be the beginning of our fall** from the faith that will be required to do the true works of God. It is at the point **when we see our resources running out** that we will **experience the power** of God. **What we need** to do the true works of God **will not be found in our own resources,** or our **own wisdom,** but in **the limitless resources of God.**

The more 'holy' a man is - the more 'humble' he is!

How great would the miracle have been to **feed the five thousand if the disciples** had hundreds of fishes and loaves, and just needed a little more? **It**

was a great miracle because they had so little in their own hands with which to do what they were asked by God to do.

Christian friend, when we are called by God to do a task, we often **begin to look at what resources** we have to perform it. This **can be the beginning of our** fall from the faith that will be required **to do the true works** of God. It is at the point that **we see our resources running out** that we will experience the power of God. **What we need to do** the true **works of God** will **not be found** in our **own resources,** or our own **wisdom,** but in the **limitless resources of God.**

We know that **"God is opposed** to the **proud,** but **gives grace to the humble" (James 4:6).** This verse **is a quotation** from **Proverbs 3:34:** "Surely **He scorns** the scornful, But **gives grace to the humble"** (NKJV).

Humility is the highway for spiritual growth, but too many **counterfeits** are in action. In fact, there **is a false humility** on the loose that **is giving people** the **wrong model** of what it looks like **to walk in true humility.**

I once read a **Bible Study** entitled, **"The Hidden Jewel of Humility."** Humility, though of **great value, like a jewel,** is something **rarely discovered,** but **when found, becomes** a **prized possession** to its **owner.**

Someone said, "Humility is found in a **vast ocean of still waters** which **run very deep.** At **the bottom lies self-esteem.** At first, **going within the ocean** is like **journeying into** an unknown **area of immense darkness.** But, just as **exploration** can **lead to buried treasures,** one **searching his or her inner world** can find **jewels buried** in the **depths.** And the **jewel buried deepest -** which **shines the brightest** and **gives the most light** - is **humility.**

> **Augustine** once **commented: "Should you ask** me
> what is the **first thing of importance** in Christianity,
> I should **reply** that the **first is humility,** the **second**
> is **humility** and **third thing** is **humility."**

Real humility is **not** something you **can fabricate.** It only **comes** through **an authentic process with God.** When you carry it, **the humble heart shines** through because of **the journey** you have been on. **As the Scripture states** in Proverbs 22:4, **"By humility** and the **fear** of the **Lord** are **riches,** and **honor, and life."**

Biblical humility is simply the **opposite of selfishness** and empty **conceit,** Philippians 2:3-4, Romans 12:3. **Biblical humility** is something **we do,** not something **we feel,**

Philippians 2:8 and Matthew 26:39. Ephesians 4:2, John 13:1-17. **Biblical humility flows out** of our **strength** and **security,** John 13:2-5 and 12-17. If you **want to get to the top** and stay there, **humbly serve** those above, below and around you, (Philippians 2:8-11, Matt. 20:26-28, James 4:10, 1 Peter 5:5-6.

Sometimes we see **so few examples** of **true humility** we **don't know** what it **looks like** when it manifests. Because of this, **most people think** that just **rejecting** and **hating on themselves** with contempt is **a spiritual attribute.** We **often think** the more someone **demeans** themselves, the **humbler they are. Not so!** This is a **false humility. Self-rejection** or **self-denunciation** has **nothing to do** with **humility.** And it **will work** overtime to remain hidden, using **religious practices** or **Scriptures** out of **context** to **keep** from exposing **the fact** that millions are **believing its lies. Humility is an inside job!**

However, **there is a false-self-effacement** that is an **offense to God,** and can **keep us** from being **useful to Him. It** was **this kind of false humility that Moses displayed** when **God** first **called** him at the **burning bush.**

> **"I will praise You, for You made me with fear**
> **and wonder; marvelous are Your works, and**
> **You know me completely"** (Psalm 139:14).

We all have experiences of being **around people** who were genuinely **filled with pride** and **arrogance.** We then **sought** to avoid being **prideful at all costs,** but it often **landed** in a **pit of self-rejection. As we were growing** up, the **common phrases** to **spiritualize** this **dysfunction** was, "He must increase, but I must decrease" (John 3:30 NKJV), as a way to **never truly accept encouragement** from others. "It wasn't me; it was the Lord" is **another classic way** to **deflect genuine** relational connection **from others.**

I thought that for years. When **people encouraged** me, I deflected it back, **thinking** I was being humble. I never saw that **I was uncomfortable** with **loving interaction** because **I didn't like myself.** When **I knelt before God,** the more I painfully **held myself in contempt, the** more I thought it **would get God's attention.** I actually thought **beating myself up** was a great spiritual exercise.

When the Lord told Moses that He was sending him back **to release His people from bondage,** Moses **responded by saying** that he was **not adequate** for this great task. **This seemed humble,** but it **caused the anger of the Lord** to burn against Moses. The **Lord was angry** because **this seeming humility**

was actually an ultimate form of pride, and an affront to God. What does this mean? **Moses was saying that his inadequacy was greater than God's adequacy.** He was **focusing on himself instead of the Lord.** This is the **one thing** that **may have caused more people to fail** to fulfill their calling than any other single factor.

If we are waiting for a 'feeling' to come along **before** we **submit** to God, we **will be waiting a long time.** It may come; it may not. However, **we may use** 'feeling' in the sense of a **decision** that is **reached.** When **we say that we 'felt'** we **had to go in a certain direction for the Lord, we may not** be **speaking of an emotion** at all. In **that case, our 'feeling' is correct** and would be a right **understanding** of **God's conviction** and **leadership.**

We will never 'feel' adequate within ourselves for what the Lord calls us to do. In our flesh, which is our natural strength, we cannot accomplish one thing for the Lord. That is why Paul the Apostle told the men of Athens that the Lord is not served by human hands.

One of the greatest statements in the Bible is said by Jonathan, the son of King Saul. In I Samuel 23:17 he said to David who had been his father's enemy; "I will be second to you." The rarest man in the orchestra of God is the saint who knows how to play second fiddle well! (Forgive me Lord!).

It is the humble man who can recognize who God really is and who he himself really is! Instead of just being discontent all the time for where God has you the humble man recognizes God's leading and is content where ever he is led, even if it means being second fiddle!

Only the Holy Spirit can create that which is spirit. We are utterly dependent on the Lord to do His work. We will never be adequate within ourselves for His work, and when we ever start to feel adequate we will almost certainly be in the midst of a fall from what and where we ought to be.

> "A man can counterfeit love, he can counterfeit
> faith, he can counterfeit hope and all the other
> graces, but it is very difficult to counterfeit
> humility" - Dwight Lyman Moody (1837-1899).

True faith is not a feeling of adequacy in ourselves, but rather of our focus on the adequacy of God. True faith is not having faith in our faith, but a faith in Him. The greatest faith is that which can see and believe in His provision in the time of the most pressing need. We need to see every circumstance that is beyond ourselves as an opportunity to see a miracle. If we are faithful in the **little opportunities,** He will **bless us** with greater ones. And yes, **those blessings are trials.**

Grace sweetens all your **services** and **duties. Your best religious performances** are but stinking sacrifices - **if they are not attended** with the **exercise of grace. Grace is that heavenly salt** which makes **all** our **services savory and sweet** in the **nostrils of God.**

We are about to see great miracles, because He is going to **allow us to come into places** where we are going to need them. **Let us determine now** that we are **not** going **to focus** on the need, or ourselves, **but on Him.** Let us **prepare for these opportunities by focusing on Him today.**

> "For we have **become partakers** of Christ, if we **hold fast**
> the beginning of **our assurance** firm until the end; while
> it is said, **"Today, if you hear his voice do not harden your
> heart as you did in the rebellion"** (Hebrews 3:15 NIV).

Grace is given only to the humble. When our **Lord came** to the earth, **He came to minister** to the poor, the suffering, and the needy. To the "poor in spirit" **Jesus offered** the **riches of the kingdom** of heaven. **Jesus had come** to this earth in order to **minister to those** who were in need and knew it. When **Jesus chose to associate with the needy** rather than with the elite of His day, it greatly **offended the Jewish religious leaders.**

And **when** the **scribes of the Pharisees saw** that Jesus **was eating** with the **sinners** and tax-gatherers, they began **saying to His disciples,** "Why is He eating and drinking with tax-gatherers and sinners?" **Upon hearing** this, **Jesus said to them, The Scripture is resolute,** "It is not those who are healthy who need a physician, but those who are sick; I did not come to call the righteous, but sinners" (Mark 2:16-17 NKJV).

Pride offended, turned to jealousy (Mark 15:10), **so that** if the **religious leaders** of Israel couldn't persuade Jesus to endorse their ideology, **they concluded** that He must **be done away** with (John 11:47-50).

> **"There is none so empty of grace as he that
> thinks he is full."** - Thomas Watson

Jesus put His finger on this **matter of pride** when He told the **parable of the Pharisee** and the tax-gatherer in Luke 18. The **Pharisee had no appreciation** for **his own sinfulness,** and thus **he prayed,** "God, I thank

Thee that **I am not like** other people, swindlers, unjust, adulterers, or even like this tax-gatherer. **I fast** twice a week; **I pay** tithes of all that I get" (Luke 18:11-12 NKJV).

The tax-gatherer, however, was humbled by the awareness of his sinful condition and so **petitioned a gracious God for mercy: "God, be merciful** to me, the sinner!" (Luke 18:13, NKJV). **Jesus said** it was this **humble sinner** who went home **justified** (v. 14).

Grace is the goodness of God on **behalf of sinners** who humbly acknowledge their own deficiency and thus their dependence upon **God's grace for forgiveness** and **salvation. But He gives a greater grace.**

> **Peter writes, "clothe yourselves with humility toward**
> **one another, for God is opposed to the proud, but**
> **gives grace to the humble"** (James 4:6 NKJV).

To be "clothed" means to **tie a knot** or **put on a "servant's apron." Basically** this verse tells us to **tie on the apron of a slave and be humble** while **serving others.**

Why did Peter use that figure of speech? It was **because Jesus laid aside His garments,** girded Himself with a **towel,** and **washed** the **disciple's dirty feet. Peter** would **never forget** that moment. **The Scripture** records, **"Peter said unto Him,** "Thou **shalt never wash** my feet." **Jesus answered him,** "Unless I wash you, you have no part with **Me,"** (John 13:8 NIV). **Washing their feet** was **not** a mere **ritual. It could also be seen as a picture** of our need of **Christ's cleansing - a cleansing that will never be realized** unless **we are willing to be humble** before the Savior.

This is hard for **most** of this **Western world to understand** and **accept. We** are a **proud, arrogant, conceited, ego-driven society,** and it's sometimes **hard to learn** that **we must** be **clothed in humility.** Remember, **you can't look down** on somebody **when you're washing their feet. Even though we are saved,** we **walk** in a **dirty world.** We **need to come to Jesus daily for cleansing** from our sins, and to **restore** and **refresh** our **fellowship** with Him.

> **Boasting is the outward form of the inner**
> **condition of pride. Boasting is the voice of pride**
> **in the heart of the strong. Self-pity is the voice of**
> **pride in the heart of the weak.** - John Piper

Remember this: While sin is an **occasion for grace, grace is never** to be **an occasion for sin.** Many of the objections to the **biblical doctrine of grace** originate from **the abuses of this** doctrine in the lives of Christians. **Any biblical doctrine** can be **misapplied** in such a way **as to justify sin** in our lives. **In Romans 5, Paul taught that** "where sin abounded, **grace** abounded more" (verse 20 NKJV), **but he quickly went on** to say that **this is no incentive** to **careless living** (sin). "What shall we say then? Are we to continue in sin that grace may abound? By no means! (God forbid! KJV). How can we who died to sin still live in it?" (Romans 6:1-2 ESV).

We ('real' Christians) **who have died to sin** cannot **casually** and **carelessly persist** in sin, for **it is inconsistent** with our new life in Christ. **Grace must never** be used as **an excuse** for sin: "Live as free people, but do not use your freedom as a cover-up for evil; live as God's slaves" (I Peter 2:16 NIV).

Proverbs 22:4 also promises riches and honor, as well as life, **to the humble** individual, **but II Chronicles 7:14 promises two additional** and immensely **important benefits** to everyone **seeking a humble relationship** with God: **forgiveness** and **the hearing** of our **prayers.** "**If My people** who are called by My name will **humble themselves, and pray** and **seek** My face, and **turn** from their wicked ways, **then I will hear from heaven,** and will **forgive** their sin and **heal** their land."

Godly humility is **not difficult to understand,** but it **is difficult** to **accomplish** because of **human nature's ever-present confrontation** to our Lord and Savior. This quality requires us to be **constantly aware of the need to glorify God,** and **the fear of God is a necessary** and complementary element to help keep us aware. Nevertheless, **our part** in **settling our discrepancies with God** is to **be humble before Him.** The **separation** will not be **spanned until we do - what Adam and Eve did not: humbly submit!**

All Christians must learn to understand the **difference** between **true and false humility. False** humility is another very deceptive from of pride. **False** humility poses itself as beggarly, self-degrading, inferior and unworthy. **It will be-little itself** while **acting pious.** It **refuses to say** anything **good about itself.**

Those with false humility will even **refuse to say** what the **Word says about them.** That's **not** being **humble.** That's **actually being proud.** The **balance is to not** to have a **lofty estimation of ourselves** while still maintaining truth, reality and soberness in our lives. **It is not pride** to say what is **true** and **what is scriptural.** It is **not pride** to **believe** and to **say** the **good things the**

Bible says about you as a **new creation in Christ Jesus** (II Corinthians 5:17). We are to **acknowledge every good thing** that is **in us.**

All in the church need the leadership of the Holy
Spirit to perceive pride in your life. Here are some
indicators of pride that I have posed in question form.

Are you always **talking about yourself?** Are you **seeking for others** to be **impressed** with you? **Why do you feel** it is **important to tell others** your **status,** your **accomplishments, important places** you've been and **important people** you may know? **Are you unhappy** when you are **not the center of attention?** Do you **enjoy being seen** and **noticed?** How **do you handle being ignored?**

Does it **bother you** when **others don't recognize you** and **acknowledge you? Why?** How **do you handle it** when **someone else gets the credit** for what you did? Does **your pride negatively express itself?** When you are **accused of wrongdoing,** do you **have the faith** and **humility** to leave your defense and **justification** in **God's hands?**

Do you show genuine interest in **people** and in what **others are saying?** Are you a **good listener? Ask yourself** occasionally, **"Why am I doing this?** Why **am I saying this?** Why **do I feel this way? Why** am I hurt? **Why** did that bother me? **Why** did that **hurt me** or **make me angry?"**

"A man's pride shall bring him low: but honor shall
uphold the humble in spirit" (Proverbs 29:23).

Have you ever **taught someone to drive?** What was the **first thing** you **showed him?** If you're like me, even **before I showed my children** the ignition switch, the accelerator, or the blinker, I **showed them the brakes!**

Suppose your child said, "I **don't want** to know **anything** about **the brakes.** I just want to know **how to make this thing go!"** You would **probably reply,** "You **aren't ready yet** to learn to drive! **Forget the accelerator.** Before you can go, **you've got to learn to stop."**

When Florence Nightingale had reached the **age of ninety,** and could **no longer** follow **sustained reading,** she still **liked to hear familiar hymns.** Her **biographer says:** "A favorite, if one may judge by the frequency with which verses from it appear one of **her last written meditations was:** "O, Lord, how happy should we be, **If we** could cast our care on Thee, **If we** from self could rest.?"

LET US PRAY ... "Father, help us today, this **very moment, to allow the Holy Spirit** to **guide us** into this **truth** of **spiritual might** and **power through humility. Lead us** to a **humility** that will **give us triumph over pride** or any **appearance of arrogance,** or any **braggadocios spirit** of the **flesh** that would **draw us away** from a **humble attitude** and **Godly character. We do love you Lord!** As we **seek you daily** for a **closer walk, give us needed leadership,** through **conviction** and **guidance to be effective in our daily lives, for Jesus sake, Amen!**

And the grace of our Lord was exceeding abundant with faith and love which is in Christ" (1 Timothy 1:14).

hapter 3

God 'SAFEGUARDS' Me With His Grace

"BUT **BY THE grace of God I AM WHAT I AM:** and **His grace** which was **bestowed upon me** was not in vain; but **I labored more** abundantly than they all: yet not I, **but the grace** of God which **was with me**" (I Corinthians 15:10).

As stated, grace is one of those special words that **belongs to the child of God.** God has given us **some words that the world** just doesn't know **how to properly appreciate**. For instance, there are words like glory, amen, hallelujah, faith, etc.

The verse above states, "**BY THE GRACE OF GOD, I AM.**" Again, let me urge you to **answer** this **question. "What is Biblical grace?"** Before we go any **further into "works,"** I must spend another study (or more) **on "grace."** **Without a proper discernment of "grace"** in the Bible, we certainly will **have improper knowledge of "works."**

> Grace, grace, God's grace,
> Grace that will pardon and cleanse within;
> Grace, grace, God's grace,
> Grace that is greater than all our sin. (Julia Johnson)

Whatever he became, according to his own statement, **Paul owed** it all **to "the grace of God."** When I **consider** the words from that **magnificent apostle,** I come up with what we might call **his doctrine.** Occasionally, **it helps** to take a profound, **multi-dimensional theological truth** and **define it** in **simple, spiritual terms.**

God does what He does **by His grace. Paul's first claim for being allowed to live,** to say nothing of **being used** as a **spokesman** and **leader,** was "**by the grace of God.**" The Apostle **Paul deserved** the **severest kind of judgment,** but

God gave the man **His grace instead. Humanly speaking, Paul should** have been **made to endure incredible suffering** for all the **pain and heartache he had caused others.** But he didn't, because **God exhibited His grace.**

> **There is a God we desire, and there is a God**
> **Who IS, 'I AM WHAT I AM,' and they are**
> **not the same God** (I Corinthians 15:10).

In our day of **high-powered self-achievement, personal successes,** and an **overemphasis** on the **importance** of building **self-esteem, individual achievements,** and one's own **ego-centered kingdom,** this **idea** of **giving grace** the **credit** is a **much-needed message.**

How many **people** who reach the **pinnacle** of their career **say** to the **Wall Street Journal reporter,** or in an **interview in Business Week,** "I am what I am by the grace of God?" **How many athletes** would say that kind of thing at a **banquet in his or her honor? What a shocker it would be today** if **someone** were to say, **"Don't be impressed** at all with **me.** My **only claim** to fame is the **undeserved grace of God."**

> **"The Christian life is not a constant high. I have**
> **my moments of deep discouragement. I have to go**
> **to God in prayer with tears in my eyes, and say, 'O**
> **God, forgive me,' or 'Help me.'"** - Billy Graham

Far too many Christians (?) (or Church Members) **want a manageable, domesticated sweet** mild **Jesus** who **makes no demands** on their time, money, words, social life and sexuality. In the **middle of this great** and **growing dishonesty, God is looking** for **uncompromising believers** who are **committed** to **proclaiming the truth** of the **gospel** and **not** the **counterfeit Jesus of** 'Western Culture' - Anonymous.

As I **observe** the **teaching/preaching in our nation,** I believe **many** of our **churches are experiencing** a **scarcity** of the **truths of grace.** Everything **seems focused** on **God's blessings on personal experiences.** So many **people want to hear** about **their** upcoming **monetary promotion, the fulfillment of their dreams,** their **visions,** and their **next big financial** or **relational blessing.** They get **so involved** in the **hype** of the **"positive-minded"** services that they **don't** seem to **want to hear about** the **holiness of God,** the **consequences of** sin, **repentance** and **confession** of sin, the **suffering** that comes **from following Christ,** the **reality of hell,** and **what is morally right** and **morally wrong.**

Many people today don't want to hear **vibrant, doctrinal Bible preaching and teaching,** so the **preacher appeases and pacifies. Many** come in **pretense,** and are **placated. Many** don't want **sound doctrine,** so they are **entertained** and **amused** with **'Religious Pablum'.** Far **too many** Church **Members** have **constructed a 'god in a box,'** a **god** whose **job** is merely to **pander to our** desires, wants, physical lusts, and ambitions. And **we are both content** and **comfortable** to **attend the box** (the four walls of the building) once a week or month **trying to appease** this 'god' **with some formal, attempt to pacify ourselves** even with a **Hollywood worship style** that is so far away from the **New Testament gathering** that makes **Almighty God sick.** Sinful and nefarious individuals have **fashioned their own 'little-god,' of sweetness,** (both in pulpit and pew) who will **not hold them responsible or punishable.**

"**As a child, I received instruction** both in the **Bible** and in the **Talmud.** I am a Jew, **but I am enthralled** by the **luminous figure of the Nazarene.** No one can **read the gospels** without feeling the **actual presence of Jesus. His personality pulsates** in **every word.** No myth is filled **with such life.**" - **Albert Einstein,** Saturday Evening Post, Oct. 26, 1929.

Far too many pastor/teachers offer an enthusiastic, inspirational, stimulating pep-talk, feel-good, personal-empowerment, self-help, Jesus. **Different from the Jesus of the Word of God,** and, in doing so, they are **damning** their **hearers rather** than **releasing** them **from sin** for **their redemption** and the **work of Christ.**

I **even dare say, if** Yeshua HaMashiach (Jesus) **physically visited** most **American churches,** He would **not recognize what** was being **taught and advocated** as being **remotely** like **what He articulated and lived.**

And to the prophets, "**Do not prophesy to us right things.**

Speak to us smooth things, prophesy deceits. Get out of the way, Turn aside from the path, Cause the Holy One of Israel to cease from before us" (Isaiah 30:10-11 NKJV).

Unfortunately, many **churches** are **suffering** a **famine** because many **pulpits** are **not feeding** their **flocks** the heavenly **bread.** If you are **not feeding** on the Bible daily, **you are either not saved** or you are **dying** of **spiritual malnutrition.** The **only strength** we have is found when we **feed upon the Word of God.**

**"He (Jesus) answered and said, It is written, Man
shall not live by bread alone, but by every word that
proceeds out of the mouth of God"** (Matthew 4:4 NIV)

Many churches are **suffering a famine** because so many pulpits are **not feeding their flocks** the **heavenly bread.** If you are **not feeding on the Bible daily,** you are either **not saved** or you are **dying of spiritual malnutrition.** The **only strength** we have is found **when** we **feed upon the Word of God.**

Job said, "I have esteemed the words of His mouth more than my necessary food" (Job 23:12). In other words, **Job was saying** that if he **had to choose** between **eating physical bread or spiritual bread,** he would **rather** have the **Word of God.**

How **I pray that everyone** will **commit to a daily** routine **study** of the **Word** of God … **(not just reading** some little **devotional booklet** or just some **quick scanning of the Bible)** on their knees in prayer.

Paul said in the last days people will **not endure sound doctrine.** They will **come to church** to **have their ears tickled** so they **can feel good** as they **continue in sin.** If **they are confronted by truth,** they will **decry it** as **judgmental, despicable, indifferent,** and **outdated** (II Timothy 3:1-5).

When Christians **curtail, minimize** or **make light** of **God's grace,** the **world** will never **find hope** through **salvation.** When we **minimize truth,** the world **sees no need** for salvation. To **present the pure gospel** to the world with **Jesus as Lord** and **Savior,** we must **offer unabridged grace** and **truth,** emphasizing both, **apologizing for neither** (Romans 1:9-17).

Paul's closing statement: I let you be what you are by the grace of God. **Grace is not** something simply **to be claimed;** it is **meant to be demonstrated.** It is to **be shared,** used as **a basis for friendships,** and drawn upon for **sustained relationships.**

Jesus spoke of an abundant life that we enter into when we claim the **freedom He provides by His grace. Wouldn't it be wonderful** if people cooperated with **His game plan?** There is **nothing to be compared to grace** when it comes to **freeing others from bondage. Grace is one of those special words** that **only belongs** to the **child of God.** God has **given us** some **words** that the world just **doesn't know how to properly appreciate.** For instance, there are **words like** glory, amen, hallelujah, faith.

This book will give you **many descriptions** and **definitions** of 'grace.' **The reason for this is:** Before you finish this book, **I want you** to be able **to**

recognize, identify, and understand this **wonderful gift from God** that we all have **come to know** as the **grace of God.**

I have **my own simple definition** of God's 'grace.' - The 'Grace of God' **is the unmerited, undeserved, unwarranted, unearned, unjustified grace, favor, approval, gift, and kindness, of Almighty God.** This **grace is given** to **those who do not merit,** deserve, earn, warrant or justify it. That's **why it's called grace.** If **earned or worked for,** it **wouldn't be grace anymore since,** "If by grace, then it cannot be based on works; if it were, grace would no longer be grace" (Romans 11:6 NIV).

When you receive a birthday present, did you really **earn it?** Were you **responsible for earning it?** Could you **have cause** the reason **for you to receive it?** Of course not. **A birthday gift is a gift** that was **never earned** nor was it something that you worked for to gain. **It was simply a gift.** That is **what grace is** … it **is given** to those who **did not earn it** and really, **don't deserve it.** That's why **it's called grace.**

The double 'eimi' ("I AM") is firmly assertive - '**I am what I am**' is the **favor,** utterly **undeserved,** that summoned Saul of Tarsus - (Galatians 1:13, 14, 15). The verb "**I am**" is in the **present tense** which signifies **Paul was continually** what he was **by virtue of the grace of God.** He **never lost sight** of this **foundational truth** that undergirded and enabled all aspects of his (and our) **Christian life** and his (our) **Christ honoring service. It is as if he were admitting,** "If there is any goodness now found in me, I deserve none of the glory; grace gets the credit." **Read** the **first stanza** of "Grace Greater than Our Sin."

> **"Marvelous grace of our loving Lord, Grace**
> **that exceeds our sin and our guilt, yonder on**
> **Calvary's Mount outpoured, there where the**
> **blood of the Lamb was spilt."** (J. Johnston)

Whatever Grace is, Paul says, "I am what I am" by it. **Meditate on that a moment.** What a **Christian he was,** what **a giant** for God. **Paul has gone down** in **Christian history** as probably the greatest **heroes of faith** the world has ever known. Let me **ask you** again, "**What is Grace?**" It is **God doing for us** what **we could not do** for ourselves, and **giving us** what **we do not deserve.**

By the grace of God, **the salvation I possess, never depended on my righteousness,** and now the **assurance I have in this salvation, does not depend** on **my attitude** or **righteousness.** The **late John Jasper,** when asked,

"What right do you have to be in heaven?" **replied,** "I am not here on my righteousness but on the righteousness of the Lord Jesus Christ." **Paul said,** "By the grace of God I am what I am."

As Christians, **we must remember that God's ultimate will is for every believer to be conformed to the likeness of His Son.** His grace is responsible for our rebirth, and from that point it directs, moves, and **influences us to become increasingly Christ-like.**

In I Corinthians 15:10 Paul wrote, "By the grace of God I am what I am, and **His grace** toward me was not in vain but I worked harder than any of them. Nevertheless **it was not I but the grace of God** which is with me." **Grace is not only the pardon** that passes over our badness; it is also **the power that produces** our goodness. If **God says that it's necessary for grace to do that,** it is **not a nullifying of grace** when we agree with him.

Our little "I am" always sulks and pouts when God says do. **Let your little "I am"** be shriveled up in God's wrath and indignation, **"I AM WHO I AM,** has sent me to you" (Exodus 3:14 NIV). He must dominate. **Isn't it piercing to realize that God not only knows where we live,** but also knows the **gutters** into which we crawl! **He will hunt us down** as fast as a flash of lightning. **No human being knows** human beings **as God does.**

"By the Grace of God I am what I am." **This is the believer's eternal confession. Grace found him a rebel - it leaves him a son. Grace found him wandering** at the gates of hell- it leaves him at the gates of heaven. **Grace devised the stratagem** of Redemption, as **Justice** never would; and **Reason** never could. **And it is Grace which carries out** that scheme. No sinner would ever **have sought** his God **but "by grace." - Read slowly!**

> **"But by the grace of God I am what I am, and His grace toward me was not in vain; but I labored more abundantly than they all, yet not I, but the grace of God which was with me"** (I Corinthians 15:10 NKJV).

Grace is not simply leniency when we have sinned. **Grace is the enabling gift** and **power of God** not to sin. **Grace** is **power, not just pardon.** This is plain, for example, in I Corinthians 15:10. Paul describes **grace as the enabling power** of his work. It is **not simply the pardon** of his sins; it is the **power to press on in obedience.** "**I worked harder** than any of them, though it was not I, but the grace of God that is with me."

Therefore, **the effort we make to obey God** is **not** an effort done **in our own strength,** but "by the strength that God supplies - in order that in everything God may be glorified" (I Peter 4:11). It is the obedience of faith. **Faith in God's ever-arriving gracious power** to **enable us** to do **what we should.**

Paul confirms this in II Thessalonians 1:11–12 by calling **each** of our **acts of goodness** a **"work of faith,"** and by saying that the glory this **brings to Jesus** is **"according** to the **grace** of our **God"** because it happens **"by his power."** As you study the Word - **listen** for all **those phrases:**

"Therefore **we** also **pray** always **for you** that our God would **count you worthy of this calling,** and fulfill all the good pleasure of **His goodness** and the work of faith with power, that the **name** of our **Lord Jesus Christ** may be **glorified in you,** and you **in Him** (Jesus), **according to the grace of our God** and the Lord Jesus Christ" (vs. 11-12 NKJV).

The obedience that **gives God pleasure** is produced by the **power of God's grace** through faith. The **same dynamic** is at **work at every stage** of the **Christian life.** The **power of God's grace** that **saves** through faith (Ephesians 2:8) is the **same power** of **God's grace that sanctifies** through faith.

The thickets of Eden would have proved Adam's grave **had not grace called** him out. **Saul would have lived and died** the haughty self-righteous persecutor, **had not grace** laid him low. **The thief on the cross would have continued breathing out his blasphemies, had not grace** arrested his tongue and tuned it for glory. **"Out of the knottiest timber,"** says Samuel Rutherford, **"He can make vessels of mercy and grace** for **service** in the **high palace of glory!"**

> **"Our values determine our expectations. If we value comfort more than character, then trials will upset us. If we value the material and physical more than the spiritual, we will not be able to '[consider] it all joy!' If we live only for the present and forget the future, the trials will make us bitter, not better."** - Warren Wiersbe

Christian please remember that all (eternally worthwhile) **good works** are **God works!** Why? Because they are **grace works.** According to the **grace of God** which was **given to me** (**It is not** "which **was earned** by me because I worked so hard and I deserved it!)" (1Corinthians 3:10) From this we see that **the grace that saves the greatest, saves the least as well.** I believe it was **D. L. Moody,** who once said, **"from the 'gutter-most' to the 'uttermost'."**

As a Pastor/Teacher/Evangelist for over 60 years, I have counseled **all types** of people, from **all walks** of life, with **all kinds** of **successes** and **sins. I have heard** every **type of sin** confessed … **from Christians** and **non-believers. With some,** there was **shame** and **repentance,** and a few to **salvation** in Christ, **while others,** some who **came at the request** of a family member or friend (or a policeman or judge), **remained arrogant, uncaring** and **unrepentant.** Some **responded to God's grace** … most did not, at least while I was there. **I just pray** that **God's** good **seed** was planted for a later harvest.

> There is only one safeguard against error, and that is
> to be established in the faith; and for that, there has to
> be prayerful and diligent study, and a receiving with
> meekness the engrafted Word of God. - A.W. Pink

What we **need** is grace! **More grace from God** and more **grace working through us** to bless the lives of others! **When people** are **touched by the grace of God** they become **gracious people.** They **become an actual extension of the grace** of God. **They do things** they would not otherwise do. They **become God's grace** in action. **Here** are some **examples …**

- **To the woman** caught in **adultery, Jesus said,** "Neither do I condemn you. Go and sin no more."
- **For the crowd** who **crucified** Him, **Jesus prayed,** "Father, forgive them for they know not what they do."
- **To the thief** crucified alongside, **Jesus said,** "Today, thou shalt be with me in paradise."

That's grace in action. And it's exactly **what we all need. Paul attributed everything good** in him **to God's grace.** Talking about **his apostleship** and **comparing himself** to the other apostles, **Paul wrote in** I Corinthians 15:10, "But **by the grace of God** I am what I am, and **his grace to** me was not without effect. No, **I worked harder** than all of them, **yet not I,** but the **grace of God** that was with me."

That is a tremendous statement. **If** it were the **only verse** in the **Bible about grace,** it would be enough to give us a good understanding of it. For this reason, we should **pay close attention** to it. **All the good** that was in him, **Paul gave credit to God's grace.** This **verse, we should memorize,** we should **take**

to heart, that we should **bring to mind** every day of our lives. This is a **verse that will help us to live** as we should.

> "I do not frustrate the grace of God; for
> if righteousness come by the law, then is
> Christ dead in vain." - (Galatians 2:21)

As we consider Paul's life, it was all about grace. In II Timothy 1:9 where **Paul told us** that we were **given the grace of salvation** before the "eternal ages" began. **Under the inspiration of the Holy Spirit,** he wrote, "(Jesus), Who has **saved us** and **called us** with a **Holy Calling, not according** to our **works,** (because of anything we have done) but according to **His own purpose and grace.** This grace was given us **in Christ** Jesus **before the beginning of time**" (NKJV).

This is the voice of humility. We are aware that **were it not for God's unearned favor toward us,** we would **still be in our sin,** aliens from God, still lost, without hope, uncaring.

We can now say along with Paul, "If there is anything good in me, anything praiseworthy, anything commendable, it is only **because God's grace is at work in me.**"

It is not surprising, in the light of **Paul's background,** that he regarded himself as the least of the apostles, unfit to be called an apostle. **Only the grace of God** could overcome such **demerits:** but **because God's grace** had been lavished on such an unworthy person, Paul was not going to let anyone take either his position or his vocation away from him. **To let that happen would be to treat God's grace frivolously.** The only proper **response to grace** is **total commitment** with every fiber of our being.

Friend, **if you will honestly admit** you are **not a Christian,** or you are **just not sure,** the **lesson for you here** is that **you need the grace of Jesus.**

You may think that you're a pretty good person. According to God's Word, **if you are,** it's **because of God's grace.** It's part of **God's common grace** which is shown to everyone. **What you are is because of grace.** But, you could have and **you need** much more. **If you are without the saving knowledge of Jesus, you need God's saving grace** ... now! You can be much more than what you are now - **instead of being** by nature an object of God's wrath, **you can be** a shining star of God's grace. Go to Jesus **now!**

Before his death, John Newton, read the verse, "**By the grace of God I am what I am.**" **After the reading** of this text, **he uttered** this moving declaration:

"I am not what I ought to be – ah, how imperfect and deficient! I am not what I wish to be. I abhor what is evil, and I would cleave to what is good. I am not what I hope to be. Soon, soon, shall I put off mortality, and, with mortality, all sin and imperfection. Yet though I am not what I ought to be, nor what I wish to be, nor what I hope to be, I can truly say I am not what I once was - a slave to sin and Satan; and I can heartily join with the apostle, and acknowledge, "By the grace of God I am what I am.'"

John Newton's tombstone reads: "John Newton, once an infidel and libertine, a servant of slaves in Africa, was, by the rich mercy of our Lord and Savior Jesus Christ, preserved, restored, pardoned, and appointed to preach the faith he had long labored to destroy!"

Let us look at this word 'grace' and its meaning again. Grace: this is one of those special words that belongs only to the child of God. God has given us some words that the world just doesn't know or how to properly appreciate, for example, words like glory, amen, hallelujah, faith, redemption and sanctification, etc.

> "I would not have you think that I understand
> all about the mystery of grace - only that it meets
> us where we are, but it never leaves us where we
> were when it found us." - Glenn Clifton

A close friend of mine in Texas, who has been reading these Bible studies, this week sent me this quote from the late pastor/teacher, A.W. Pink who wrote, "Grace is much more than unmerited favor. Example: If a beggar came to my door and asked for food and I gave it to him, that would be unmerited favor, but if that same beggar came in and robbed me, and I still gave him food ... that would be grace." WOW! Let that sink in! When I heard that, I had to pause and have a 'self-check.'

> I Timothy 1:15 states, "This is a faithful saying and
> worthy of all acceptation, that Christ Jesus came into
> the world to save sinners; of whom I am chief."

Paul considered himself the chief of sinners. Someone has said, "The beginning of greatness is to be little; it increases as we become less, and is perfect when we become nothing."

Paul was a monument of what God's grace can do. Look at Paul's life **before God's grace saved him** (v13)! He was a **Blasphemer** - Paul was a **blasphemer of Jesus,** not knowing He was God. **A Pharisee** couldn't slander God. **He** "did it ignorantly in unbelief" and thus obtained mercy. A **Persecutor** - the idea is of pursuing **as one chasing an animal. Injurious** - One whose **contempt** breaks forth into **outrageous acts of harm.** But Paul **obtained mercy because of God's loving grace. That's** what Jesus **did for us, and more (Isaiah 53:5-6)!**

Yes, **Paul was a monument of God's saving grace.** And **SO ARE YOU if** you are saved today! **The same grace** that saved Paul will receive you! **(Revelation 22:17)**

God's saving grace cuts out the flesh, and lays all the **glory for saving a soul,** at the **feet of Jesus (1 Corinthians 1:18, 21, 27-31)! Every born-again believer** in Christ Jesus **is a testimony of what God's Grace** can do.

At a time **when the church needs** a **fresh encounter** with **Jesus,** the **easy-grace proclamation** in the church has **deceived many** with **a message** that is **not God's message.** Meanwhile the **hyper-grace message** is **pacifying sinners** in the church **to sleep. It is my intention to present** what the **Bible teaches** about God's grace, man's sin, redemption, sanctification, and God's Sovereignty. It is **my prayer** that our **God will** empower **readers** to **steer clear of compromise** and live **holy, consecrated, sanctified, victorious lives in Christ.**

Paul tells his readers that because of his **sins** and **attacks** against the church, that **he was the least of the apostles and** is **not even worthy** to be named among them. However, **Paul goes on** to say that **he knows God has used** him and that anything he has, is, or ever will be, **is because of the precious grace of God.**

> "For from **His fullness** we have all received, **grace upon grace** For the **law** was given through Moses; **grace and truth** came through Jesus Christ" (John 1:16-17 KJV).

I would like to remind you today that the **same is true for you and me.** Because of **our sinfulness** we **deserve nothing** less than an **eternity in Hell apart** from the presence of the Almighty. **However, because His grace** has **been revealed** unto us in the **Person of His Son the Lord Jesus,** we **can be saved** and **used** by the Lord in a wonderful fashion.

Dear friend, **truths** about the **transforming power of grace** beg **the question,** "can you say," **like Paul,** "by the **grace** of God I am what I am?"

Dear believer you can truly say you are **living each day "by the grace of God?"** If not, **consider surrendering** your rights, your self-efforts, your "good" (but God-less) works, etc., **to the God of all grace** that you might come to **genuinely experience** the **grace of God** as your sole source of strength to live a supernatural life. **Through His grace others** may see your "abundant" life **in Christ** (John 10:10) and **glorify** our otherwise invisible Father Who is in **heaven** (Matthew 5:16).

The Holy Spirit is the **Orator and Author** of **grace,** therefore as He articulated, "And I **will pour** on the house of David and on the inhabitants of Jerusalem the **Spirit of grace and supplication;** then they will look on Me whom they pierced. Yes, they will **mourn for Him** as one mourns for his only son, and **grieve for Him** as one grieves for a firstborn" (Zechariah 12:10 NKJV).

The contrast is between the **law** with **all its regulations** and the **new era of salvation by grace** through faith **apart from** the **works of the law** that has come with Jesus Christ. It is a great contrast. **Under the law, God demands righteousness** from people; **under grace, He gives it to people to work it out.**

Keep in mind that **grace and truth** were still **present in the Old Testament,** but just **not as fully and finally understood** as they were **in Jesus Christ.** And so **in the midst of great spiritual darkness and sin on earth** we read that **"Noah found favor** (grace) **in the eyes** of the Lord." (Addendum at ending of book)

The Old Testament equivalent of grace and truth is lovingkindness and truth and is **found 19 times** in the **Old Testament,** especially in the Psalms.

Under law, righteousness is based on Moses and good works; **under grace,** it is based on Christ and Christ's character. **Under law,** blessings accompany obedience; **under grace,** God bestows his blessings as a free gift. **The law is powerless** to secure righteousness and life for a sinful race. **Grace came in its fullness with Christ's death** and resurrection to make sinners righteous before God.

Moses was known for **giving** God's people **the Law.** That was his deal, his special role in the story of God. **Jesus, however, is now known as the Grace-and-Truth Giver.** That's his deal. **Jesus brings grace and truth** because **He** is **full of grace and truth.** That's **His conditional gift. His main thing!**

"Grace finds you a rebel - it leaves you a son."

God the Father is the **Fountainhead Source of all grace** to **all His people,** for He purposed in Himself the everlasting covenant of redemption. **God the Son** is the only **Conduit or Avenue** of grace to the elect who believe. **The Gospel of the Word** is the **Publisher and Editor** of grace.

The Holy Spirit is the **Giver** and **Bequeather** of grace. The **Holy Spirit is** the **One** who **applies the Gospel** in saving power to the soul: **quickening the elect** while spiritually dead, **conquering** their rebellious wills, **melting** their hard hearts, **opening** their blind eyes, **cleansing** them from the leprosy of sin.

Grace is a provision for mankind who are so **fallen** that they cannot lift the axe of justice, **so corrupt** that they cannot change their own natures, **so averse** to God that they cannot turn to Him, **so blind** that they cannot see Him, **so deaf** that they cannot hear Him, **and so dead** that **He Himself must open their graves** and **lift them** into resurrection.

In John 1:18, John says that the life of Jesus provides detailed information in a systematic manner regarding the **character of God.** In a sense, **Jesus is the "exegesis"** (the explanation, interpretation, and exposition) **of God! Jesus "narrates"** or **"relates"** the **full story about God!** He is the **Word of God** and the **Word about God. Jesus is the grace** of God in the flesh (John 1:14).

Jesus is God in human form. In coming into our world, **He revealed the heavenly Father to us** (He **exposed, revealed and explained** God to us in a new and different way). That's **what John meant** when he said that **"the Word became flesh"** (John 1:1-12). **We call** this the **doctrine** of the **incarnation.**

> **"God will meet you where you are in order to take you where He wants you to go."** - Tony Evans

Many things in life will fail us. Friendships will blossom and then die. **Our wellbeing** will sometimes come and go, and can be an elusive thing. **Earthly possessions and prosperity** will often remain just beyond the reach of our outstretched hands. **Those we adore** and **love will pass** from the scene leaving a void in our hearts hard to be filled. However, **there is one thing** that **every child of God** possesses that can **never fail,** never **end,** never **run out,** never **run dry** and that will **never be found** to be **insufficient,** and **that is the 'Glorious Grace of God'!**

> "In Him (Jesus) **we have redemption** through His **blood,** the **forgiveness** of our **trespasses,** according to **the riches of his grace"** (Ephesians 1:7 KJV).

Yes, **the road** of **your life may be long and dreary,** the **days** may be filled with difficulties and struggles, **but rest assured** that **there will be grace sufficient** for **every need** and **every trial.** That is the **promise of God** and the **hope of the saints!**

Today, in this book, **with the help of the Lord,** I would like to **show you** some of the **possessions that belong** to the **child of God because of grace.** Join me for a **few moments** as we consider together **the thought, "By The grace Of God, I Am!"**

The evidence of God's grace in the **early church** was the **simple fact** that **everyone had enough,** and were **turning** the **"world upside down" spiritually** (Acts 17:6). And **as we are increasingly filled** with **grace and truth,** we can then **become instruments** of building **communities of grace and truth,** which I'll share later in this book. As **we live and work in grace and truth,** we become **agents of grace and truth. Jesus, through his grace** toward us **is our protection.**

Let us pray ... "Blessed Jesus! Pardon me, **correct** me - but **never leave me** to myself! **Draw me - or drive me;** but **never allow me** to live long at a distance from You! **Gracious Lord, keep me** near You, **looking to** You, **living for** You, **leaning on** You, **believing in** You, and **expecting from** You, **all that I need!** Surely this is a sweet life - leaning on Jesus alone, making Him all in all! **O bring me to Your sacred feet, And let me stray no more!"** Amen!

> **"That the name of our Lord Jesus Christ may be glorified
> in you, and ye in him, according to the grace of our God
> and the Lord Jesus Christ"** (II Thessalonians 1:12).

hapter 4

God 'SECURES' Me With His Grace

"(BELIEVERS) ... BEING **JUSTIFIED** freely **by His grace** through the **redemption** that is **in Christ Jesus**" Romans 3:24.

For many, this is possibly the greatest single verse in the entire Bible on the **manner** of **justification by faith.** I implore you, to **study** and **re-study** this verse. **I have witnessed** many a soul, upon understanding it, **come into God's perfect peace. God develops,** in this verse, **His teaching** about salvation.

> **Securing grace** is the **demonstration of God's love, compassion** and **kindness,** by which **the redeemed** are **kept secure in spite of sin.**

"...**having been justified** by faith, we have peace with God through our Lord Jesus Christ, through whom also we have obtained our introduction **by faith into this grace in which we stand;** and we exult in hope of the glory of God (Romans 5:1-2).

> **Peter stated,** "Through Silvanus, our faithful brother (for so I regard him), I have written to you briefly, exhorting and testifying that this is the true grace of God. Stand firm in it! (1 Peter 5:12).

Listen: Just as a lost man (a man without Christ as Lord) **cannot obtain salvation** through any good work of his own, **neither can the Christian maintain his** salvation by doing good works. **Salvation is obtained** and **maintained** by **grace alone.**

> **"Amazing Grace,"** (one verse **not normally sung**), "The Lord has promised good to me,

His Word **my hope secures;**
He will my shield and portion be, ... **As long as life
endures."** (John Newton)

In Alfred Hitchcock's famous movie, "The Man Who Knew Too Much,"
Doris Day croons, "When I was just a little girl, I asked my mother, what
would I be? Would I be pretty; would I be rich? Here's what she said to me..."
The answer of this **supposedly wise mother,** designed somehow to bring
comfort is, **"Que sera, sera; whatever will be, will be," OR, "It is all** in the
hands of **blind fate."** This **is a lie** because it **is unscriptural** and **against** the
teachings of the **Almighty!**

The hope of the **believer** is **not,** "Que sera, sera," but it is "**What God
has said will be.**" He has said that all whom **he has given to Jesus,** all who
truly come to him, **he will never cast out.** That **is a promise** on which we can
construct all our hopes and expectations.

For the serious Christian, of all the **questions that might cause us
concern,** none is **so important as the question,** "What will the outcome of
my Christian life be? **Will God be pleased with me** to the end of my days and
so finally save me?" Needless to say, "whatever will be, will be" **is not adequate**
for most of us **as an answer to that question.**

"Therefore, having been **justified by faith,** we **have peace**
with God through our Lord Jesus Christ, **by Whom** also we
have access by faith into **this grace wherein we stand,** and
rejoice in hope of the glory of God" (Romans 5:1-2 KJV)

This Bible verse teaches us the truth that **through Jesus Christ,** we
have **direct access to God Himself.** The word **"access"** means **"to enter the
presence of the king."** This teaches us that, **through Jesus,** we have the **right
to enter** into the very **presence of the God** of Heaven without fear! We have
access to the Heavenly Father!

When we are sure, this is real assurance! Here (Notice the phrase),
"grace wherein we now stand." The **Greek** word **"stand"** carries the idea of
**"permanence," of being firmly fixed and immovable. Basically, this verse
teaches us** that **we are absolutely secure in the Lord Jesus Christ.** In other
words, **this verse** is all about our **eternal ability** to be in **God's presence,** as
well as our **eternal security** in God **as believers.**

I thank you **for giving us Your unlimited grace which** leads us to **salvation, sanctification,** and finally **glorification. I praise your name, AMEN! Those receiving blood covenant righteousness** through faith brings **God's grace into our lives.** This **grace enables** and **empowers us to live** in fellowship with God and **to do the works** that He has given us to do. These are **deeds that cannot be done** in our own ability; they are **done through our faith in God's ability (His grace)** working through us. So **faith righteousness** unleashes **God's grace** into our lives.

Sometimes we talk about, or **sing about** "grace being greater than our sin." **But, when you experience** that ever-flowing, sin- destroying, power-giving, **life-changing grace personally, rather than** trying to **explain it, you continue to experience it.** Could you or would you let that happen to you?

Redemption: is an **image** from the **slave market. Propitiation**: is an image from the world of religion, appeasing God through sacrifice. **Justification:** solves the problem of man's guilt before a righteous Judge. **Redemption:** solves the problem of man's slavery to sin. **Propitiation** solves the problem of offending God (**Propitiation means** the turning away of **wrath by an offering.** It **means placating** or **satisfying** the wrath of God **by the atoning sacrifice of Christ and** carries the **basic idea** of **appeasement,** or **satisfaction,** specifically **towards God).** This is **what grace,** through Jesus Christ, **brings to you.**

Justification is God's **declaration** that **all the demands** of the **law are fulfilled** on behalf of the **believing sinner** through the **righteousness of** Jesus Christ. In **justification, God imputes** (places on one's "account") the **perfect righteousness of Christ** to the believer's account, then **declares the redeemed one fully righteous.**

Justification, (a legal term that is - when **a person** is being seen and **proclaimed as perfectly righteous), even in spite of past sins** - must of course **be authorized by God the Creator.** "It is God that justifies" (Romans 8:33). **That God can indeed be both** "just, and the justifier of him which believeth in Jesus" (Romans 3:26) **is based entirely** on the **substitutionary death** and **bodily resurrection of Christ** who conquered death. "Being now justified by His blood," **the Lord Jesus Christ** "was delivered for our offenses, and was **raised again** for our **justification**" (Romans 5:9; 4:25).

> **"Ah, dear child of God - Remember who you are.**
> **Don't compromise for anyone, for any reason. You**
> **are a child of Almighty God. Live that truth!"**

Securing grace is the dimension of **divine activity** that enables God to confront human **indifference, apathy** and **rebellion** with an inexhaustible capacity to forgive and to bless. **Grace** is the good that **you get** from someone when he **owes you nothing.** So what **Paul means** when he says that we are **"justified as a gift by his grace"** is that **we can't work for justification.** The phrase **"as a gift"** means you can't **pay** for it, or **work** for it. And the phrase **"by his grace"** means you can't **work** for it.

As a boy, I grew up in **South Texas** in the **Rio Grande valley** just north of the Mexican border. Several times a year, especially **at Christmas we would go to Mama and Papa's** (my grandparents) **home** in **Northeast** Texas, a full day's drive.

After these 81+ years, **I still remember my Papa** sitting on his East Texas front porch, and **singing a song** entitled, **"The Old Gray Mare."** I am not sure of all the words, but a portion of that song says, **"The old gray mare, she ain't what she used to be."** Well, friends, **when you are saved** (really **knowing and possessing** the Lord Jesus as your **Savior** and **Lord**), **the very same things** can be said about you. **Paul wrote** in II Corinthians 5:17, **that when anyone** is **"in Christ,** he is **a new creation!" In other words, "you ain't what you used to be** ... as far as **sin** and **Almighty God is concerned."**

> **"I'm not perfect. And who knows how many times**
> **I've fallen short. We all fall short. That's the amazing**
> **thing about the grace of God"** - Tim Tebow.

Today, I know God wants you to see **the greatest question in the world - "How can a man be right with God?"** It is the **supreme question** of life. No more important question could ever be asked. **God's Word states** in Ephesians 1:7, "In Him **(Jesus),** we have **redemption** through His blood, the **forgiveness** of our trespasses, according to the **riches of His grace." And, again Paul writes in** Colossians 1:14, "in Whom we have **redemption,** the forgiveness of sins."

A dignified looking lady approached the **great preacher** Dr. G. Campbell Morgan and said, **"Dr. Morgan, I don't like** to **hear about the blood.** It is **repulsive** to me and **offends** my **esthetic nature." Dr. Morgan** replied, "I agree with you that **it is repulsive,** but the only thing **repulsive** about it is **your sin and mine."** It is **repulsive to man,** but it is **through His blood** that we have **redemption.**

Christian, Say to yourself: "God has **declared me righteous** without any basis in me, **by His grace, through** the **redemption** from sin's penalty that is **in Christ Jesus." Listen:** It is the **bold believing use** for ourselves of the **Scripture we learn,** that God desires; and **not merely the knowledge** of Scripture.

May we find grace to walk in the Master's steps!

Every living person must ask this question. **Every sincere Methodist asks,** "How can a man be right with God?" Every sincere **Presbyterian asks,** "How can a man be right with God?" Every sincere **Catholic asks,** "How can a man be right with God?" Every sincere **Lutheran asks,** "How can a man be right with God?" **Every person from every denomination in the world** asks this question.

Do you realize that **somewhere in the world** today, someone is **offering a child** upon a burning altar, hoping to appease his angry god. **Somewhere in the world** a man is **cutting and slashing himself** with a knife, hoping by his pain to win the approval of his deity. **Somewhere in the world** a man lies on a **bed of nails,** proving by his **mastery of pain** to prove his worthiness of eternal life.

In the Middle East, millions of **Islamic believers** pray toward Mecca this morning, following the dictates of their religion. **In Haiti** followers of **Voodoo kill chickens** and place the carcass before a makeshift altar, hoping to cause their god to smile upon them with good fortune. **Why?**

The answer is always the same. The men and women who **do these things desperately want** to be **right with their god.** They do what they **do** because **they hope to appease their god** or to **please god** or to **pacify their god** or to somehow **manipulate their god** into favoring them, **because of what they've done.**

We all want to stand before God someday and have him **declare us righteous** in his sight. That one fact **explains most of the religious activity** in the world around us. **From killing chickens** to **bowing to Mecca,** from resting on a **bed of nails** to **praying the rosary,** from **going to Sunday School** to saying the **Lord's Prayer,** we do what we do because **we want to be right with God** ... and we **don't know how!**

What is the answer to this **great question?** How **can** a man **be right with God?** To that **all-important** question, **no answer is more satisfying** than the answer given in **Romans 3.** It is the **essence of the gospel** and **the heart** of the Christian message.

God tells us in His Word, the Bible, that **as sinners** (rebels, law-breakers), **we all fall short of the "glory of God."** What precisely is the **glory of God?**

In a theological sense, **God's glory is the perfection of all his attributes.** But where do we see **His attributes clearly displayed?** We see them in the **person of his Son,** the Lord Jesus Christ, which is why Hebrews 1:3 **calls Jesus the "radiance of God's glory."**

> **Christ was not made sin by any sin inborn in Him, neither are we made righteous by any righteousness inherent in us, but by the righteousness of Christ imputed to us.**

The **redemption** of a sinner is **only possible** by **payment** of the **ransom** price, the blood of Christ. **Peter writes that believers** "were not **redeemed** with perishable things like silver or gold **from your futile** (a lifestyle that is without purpose, unfruitful, and useless) **way of life** inherited from your forefathers, but **with precious blood,** as of a **lamb unblemished** and **spotless,** the **blood** of Christ (I Peter 1:18-19).

Think about this! Do you realize that **it cost more to redeem us** than to **create us? In creation** it was but **speaking a word. In redemption** the Word became **flesh and blood** (John 1:1, 14) and **shed** of His **precious blood** (I Peter 1:19). **Creation** was the work of **God's fingers** (Psalms 8:3). **Redemption** was the work of **His arm** (Luke 1:51). **In creation,** God gave us **ourselves;** in the redemption He gave us **Himself.** With **creation,** we have life in **Adam;** in **redemption,** we have eternal life **in Christ (**Colossians 3:3).

All right, then, **let's apply that to Romans 3:23.** "All have sinned and fall short of God's glory in Jesus Christ." **How does your life measure up** when it is **compared to Jesus Christ?**

Let us consider Him. He lived 33 years and **never committed a sin. He never had an evil thought,** never **said an evil word,** never **committed even one evil deed.** He never **cheated,** never **lied,** never **procrastinated,** never got **bitter,** never **lost His temper,** never **lusted,** never **sought an easy way out** of a hard situation, never **bent the truth** to make himself look good, never **cursed,** never **turned his back** on his friends.

On top of all that, He **lived a life of perfect holiness,** perfect **purity,** perfect **kindness,** perfect **truth** and perfect **goodness. He was in every way the one perfect person** ever to live on the earth. **How do you stack up against Him? My stack had fallen** down because **of my sin.**

In the Christian life, grace is everything. How good to us Jesus has been. **Grace is based on the work of Jesus.** Because of the **work of Jesus, and His grace, we have a new standing before God.** This new standing is **from grace.**

As **Paul wrote** in **Romans 3:24,** "we are **justified freely by His grace** through the **redemption** that came by Christ Jesus."

Verse 24 tells us how God begins the salvation process. "And are **justified freely by his grace." The Greek word "freely"** literally means **"without a cause."** Salvation **comes "without a cause" in us.** That is, **God saves us despite** the **fact** that **He can't find a reason** within us to save us.

Salvation is a "free gift" to the human race. **There is nothing good within us** that causes God to want to save us. **No good works,** no **inner beauty,** no **great moral attainment,** no **intellectual merit** of any kind. **When God saves, forgives, cleanses and redeems,** he does it **despite the fact** that we **don't deserve it.**

> **God's grace is free, for none did ever purchase it:**
> **"Being justified freely by His grace"** (Romans 3:24).

In Verse 24, this verse introduces us to **two great theological** words and they are the words **"justify"** and **"redemption."** The word **"justify"** is a **legal word** and **means to "To declare one not guilty, or to make one as he ought to be."** In the **biblical sense,** it means that **God, in His power** and in **His grace declares us** to be **righteous and worthy** of a relationship with Him. The word **"redemption"** means **"to set at liberty after the payment of a ransom price."** These **words are "legal terms"** used in a **court of law** – in this case – **God's legal system.**

HALLELUJAH! That's what the grace of God is all about. What you **need** but **do not deserve! God declares us righteous** when **we have nothing but the sewage of sin** in us!

This is the doctrine of God's free grace. God **saves people who don't deserve it!** God saves people who **actually deserve condemnation!** God saves people **in spite of themselves** and **contrary** to their record. **It is "pure, abounding, astounding grace!"**

Saved, Sealed and Secure!

Let's look one more time at two words. "Justify." This word **comes from the courtrooms** of ancient Greece. As noted above, **"justify" means** to **declare "not guilty."** More than that, **'justify'** means: to **'wipe away'** the **record of sin** and **to 'declare a sinner righteous'** in God's eyes. It's what happens **when God alters our "permanent record"** in heaven. When a sinner trusts Christ, **God**

declares him righteous (and remember, this is not because he is good, or sweet, or nice, or pays his bills, or treats others nicely, or gives to the poor, etc.), and that declaration never changes!

Through God's grace we are never out of God's sight and His loving care.

God's grace secures us - Grace not only sought us out when we were lost in sin; **grace keeps us** in our saved condition. **In this flesh, we are prone** to failure. **We are prone** to spiritual wandering. **If our salvation** rested **upon our own ability** to be faithful to the Lord, **none of us would ever be forgiven of sin.** Thankfully, **salvation is the Lord's Courtroom** and not ours! Understand, it is **not our salvation** … it is **God's salvation given to us.** We are **saved by His grace** and we are **kept by that same grace.**

The **Apostle Paul affirms,** "…if by grace, then **is it no more of works:** otherwise grace is no more grace. But **if it be of works,** then is it **no more grace,** otherwise work is no more work" (Romans 11:6). **Salvation cannot be partly by works** and partly by grace … **Works have zero** to do with salvation. **The Bible clearly states,** "For by grace are ye saved … **not** of works …" (Ephesians 2:8, 9).

The **Almighty God is not looking** for **skilled and talented people or** people who **are self-sufficient** (abundantly adequate). He is **looking** for **inadequate people** who will **give their weakness** (limitations and vulnerabilities) to Him and **open** (expose) **themselves** to the **ministry of the Holy Spirit** and the **transforming grace** of the **new covenant** as it is **ministered by Christ Jesus Himself.**

True to such scriptures, for centuries, Christians have **firmly declared** that we **cannot earn or merit** salvation in any way. **Eternal life must be received** as a **free gift of God's grace,** or we cannot have it. **Salvation cannot be purchased** even in part by us, because **it requires payment** of the penalty for sin - a payment we can't make. **If salvation from the penalty** of breaking God's laws **cannot be earned** by good deeds, then it **cannot be lost** by **bad deeds.**

Friend, the dirtiest thieves this side of hell are the teachers and **preachers** who tell you that **your works** and **deeds are the things** that will get you into **heaven.** Listen: **If you can work your way to salvation** by your **works** … **then you** can **lose your salvation with bad** or **evil works** and **go straight to Hell, even on the same day.**

"The doctrine of assurance looks into eternity past to
the eternal purposes of God, looks into history to the
accomplished work of Christ, and looks to the future
toward the perfect fulfillment of God's purpose to
redeem a people through His Son. - Albert Mohler

The **Word of God states,** "In Whom (Jesus) you also trusted, after that
you heard the Word of Truth, the gospel of your salvation: in Whom also **after
you believed, you were sealed** with that **Holy Spirit of promise."** (Ephesians
1:13). **What does it mean** that you **are sealed with the Holy Spirit?**

Gods 'seal' is a **mark of 'authenticity'.** If the **Holy Spirit is not in you,**
then you are a fake. **I John 3:24 says,** "And he that keeps His commandments
dwells in Him, and He in him. And hereby we know that He abides in us, by
the Spirit which He hath given us."

**The One who holds the universe together
will not let go of His bride!**

The 'seal' is a **mark of 'ownership',** like the **branding** of a cow. You are His.
Romans 8:9 says, "if any man have not the Spirit of Christ, he is none of His."

The 'seal' is a **mark of your 'security' protecting.** Esther 8:8 tells about
this type of seal, which **"no man can reverse." The way I am kept saved - is -**
because **God sealed me.** The way you are **kept saved,** is because **God saved
you, and has sealed you.** You **may not fully understand it,** but since **God
promised and supplied it … you can accept and trust it** (Ephesians 1:13-14;
Ephesians 4:30; 2 Corinthians 1:21-22; Revelation 7:3-4).

When you are redeemed, justified and **sanctified by** the **Holy Spirit,
is it** too **far-fetched** to **believe God's Word,** and **accept the fact that** we are
also kept (sealed) by Jesus Christ? Do you **believe you are secure?** You **are
preserved by Jesus Christ. Nothing can separate you** from the **Love of God**
(Romans 8:35-39). **Nothing you can do** will **make Him love** you **more** or love
you **less. You are** "in the beloved," **or** "in Christ" (II Corinthians 5:21), **and
Jesus is your wonderful, eternal security blanket** (covering). **Since salvation
is by grace, it is impossible** for any **true believer** to **lose his salvation.**

**"By redeeming us, the Lord secured us in His
hand, from which we cannot be snatched and from**

which we ourselves cannot escape, even on days
when we feel like running away." - Burk Parsons

In John 10:27-29, **Jesus states:** "My sheep hear My voice, and I know them, and they follow Me. **And I give them eternal life,** and they shall **never perish;** neither shall anyone **snatch (steal/seize) them out of My hand. My Father,** who has given them to Me, is greater than all; and **no one is able to snatch them out of My Father's hand."**

The Christian life isn't just a matter of **you** and me **holding on** and **hoping** for the best. **No, the Christian life** is actually about **God holding you** and **me in his grip,** and **us trusting Him** to **not let go.**

You see, as believers in the Lord Jesus Christ, **you and I are still** going **to stumble** and **fall into sin** as long as we are **in this flesh.** God **understands** our **humanity.** And **He knows** our **possibilities for greatness as well** as our **possibilities** for **failure.**

The **Savior's preservation of His people** is in **obedience** to the **Father. Jesus said,** "This is **the will of Him** who sent Me: that I should **lose none** of those He has given Me but should raise them up on the last day" (John 6:39). Thus, **the security of the saint** depends **not only** upon the **Savior's love** unto His own, **or His all-mighty power,** but is as well **His act of subjection to God.**

In Ephesians 1:13, 14, **Paul writes:** "In Whom **(Jesus)** you also trusted, after **you heard the word of truth,** the gospel of your salvation; in whom also, **having believed,** you were **sealed with the Holy Spirit of promise,** who is the **guarantee** of our inheritance until the **redemption** of the **purchased possession,** to the praise of His glory" (Emphasis mine – G.C.).

These two verses in Ephesians **extols the uniqueness** of the **church,** which **Paul refers** to as **"the purchased possession." God chose Israel** and **Israel became God's** personal possession through the **destruction of Egypt,** and more importantly, with the killing of Egypt's firstborn as the **price** for Israel's liberty. **God "purchased" Israel** and its liberties by this means.

Notice, **what we discern** here is **a separate and unique people.** Although **all mankind owes its existence to God** as their **Creator, Israel and the church** are **both separate** and **unique** because **they belong to God in a way** other **people** and **nations do not. Amos 3:2 declares,** "You only have I known of all the families of the earth." **God purchased these people** at awesome **cost** and thus **came into possession** of them.

It's the **same with the church,** but **we receive more besides.** Among other things regarding the **uniqueness of the church, Paul explains** that its members **have** been **set apart** (redeemed and freed from the rest of mankind and its ways) **and sealed through the gift of the Holy Spirit.**

The **word 'sealed'** is important because **it embraces,** not only **the sense of ownership,** but **also security** and **guarantee. Individual seals were unique,** used on **documents** for the **identification** the sender and to **render the content secure** from **prying eyes** and **theft,** and so **they were a guarantee** that the contents would **reach the intended destination safely.**

The church (ekklesia = called out ones) **may look no different** on the **outside,** but they have been **given something inside,** something **spiritual,** that **makes them different** from others and **special to God.** They **are different** only because of **something God has done,** which also **makes them His personal, treasured possession.**

In 1Peter 1:3-5, **Peter writes,** "Blessed be the God and Father of our Lord Jesus Christ, who according to **His abundant mercy** has **begotten us again** (born-again/redeemed) to a **living hope** through the resurrection of Jesus Christ from the dead, to **an inheritance incorruptible** and **undefiled** and that does not fade away, reserved in heaven for you, **who are kept by** the **power of God** through **faith for salvation ready to be revealed in the last time.**

Peter had even experienced the **'forgiving,' 'holding' power** of the Almighty **after He had become a child of God** and **follower** of Jesus. **Think about Peter** and **Jesus** at the **time just before the crucifixion.** Peter **told Jesus** there was **no way** that **he would ever deny him.** And **yet, he did** just as **Jesus said** he would.

Jesus knew in advance about the shame, regret, and the complete **sense of failure** that **Peter would experience.** He **knew all about it!** Yet **God was holding onto Peter** every step of the way, and **restored him** in a **mighty** and **extraordinary way** to **build His church.**

Although our salvation is secure, Paul **alerts** us to the possibility that **we can be spoiled** (Colossians 2:8), **our faith** can **be shipwrecked** (1 Timothy 1:19), and **we can fall** from our own "steadfastness" (II Peter 3:17). These are **not idle threats.** There are **those who are the** "enemies of the cross of Christ" (vs. 18), thus **these startling descriptions** in today's verse.

Face it, for all the blessings of God, the **Tempter never sleeps.** "Be sober-minded and alert. Your adversary the **devil prowls around** like a **roaring lion,** seeking someone to devour." (I Peter 5:8). **Even in your victories,** the **Devil** will come and **try to make you doubt** the Scriptural **truths of the power** of the Almighty.

A mystery in the Bible is a previously unrevealed truth that was not fully revealed until the New Testament. The mystery that is revealed in 1 Timothy 3:16 is that Jesus Christ was wholly man, and wholly God, or God of very God.

"And without controversy great is the **mystery of godliness:** God was **manifest** in the flesh, **justified** in the Spirit, **seen** of angels, **preached** unto the Gentiles, **believed on** in the world, **received up** into glory" (1 Timothy 3:16). The **"Security of Almighty God"** over sinful mankind who **have been redeemed - is a "mystery."**

The **"Security of the Saints,"** is one the **great doctrines** that **rises** to the **surface** in the **Word of God.** God **expresses** Himself in many ways. If you **have a hard time understanding** this, **don't worry** about it because you **never** will **completely figure** it all out. **Elsewhere, the apostle, Paul, says,** "Great is the **mystery of godliness** that was **manifested** in the flesh, was **justified** in the spirit, **appeared** unto angels, hath **been preached** unto the Gentiles, **is believed** in the world, is taken up in glory. (I Timothy 3:16)" **You never will completely understand it.** Just **believe** it. Just **accept** it. Just **enjoy it!**

The late **Leonard Ravenhill** once said, "When **God opens the windows of heaven to bless us, the devil is going to open** the **doors of hell to blast us."** Have you **had a wonderful spiritual experience recently?** Then you **better not start coasting.** If the **devil tempted Jesus,** be sure **he will tempt you as well.**

But there is more! **Not only are we accepted,** we are **"sealed with the Holy Spirit** of promise" (Ephesians 1:13), **an "earnest (down payment, deposit)** of our inheritance" (v. 14). We are **"established - anointed - sealed"** (II Corinthians 1:21-22).

We are "confirmed" in everything (1 Corinthians 1:6-8), **consecrated (set apart), and sanctified** to serve (Exodus 28:41; 1 John 2:27), and **given the "earnest"** (down payment) **of the Spirit** (II Corinthians 5:5), **to empower our ministry. And Jesus, our attorney** Who has **adjudicated** our **sin.**

"My little children, these things write I unto you, that ye sin not. And if any man sin, we have an advocate with the Father, Jesus Christ the righteous" (1 John 2:1).

There may come times in your **Christian walk** when it seems like your faith is **slipping away.** You see the **hardships in your own life** and the **evil**

in the world around you and wonder if God is truly good. **You ask yourself,** "Have I followed Jesus for nothing?"

In Psalm 73, Asaph faced a similar crisis of faith. It wasn't until he "entered the sanctuary of the Lord" that his **hope was restored. God compassionately heals the brokenhearted** by revealing his glory and majesty. This **doesn't happen** in a **church service** or during **flashes of intimacy** with Him, but when we **make a choice to continually seek Him.**

A personal failure (sin) is a painful thing to the true child of God. It can **send you reeling** on a **detour** from the **path that God** has for you. **It's easy to feel so lost** that you **wonder if God even knows** where you are. **But I assure you** that **the Lord knows exactly** where **you are** and he **knows exactly what's going on** in your life. **So live your life** with the **great joy that comes** with **knowing Christ** and the **cleansing power** of **His redemption.** When you fall, **get** back **up, confess** and **accept His forgiveness** and **move on!**

The way to deal with your sins is for you to **confess** - that **means,** you are to **begin by agreeing with God** as to what He says about your sin. You need to also **confidently deal with your sin.** Now, what do I mean by that?

Christian, you **have your own attorney** when you **go into the judge's chambers** for **adjudication.** According to God's Word, **you have an Advocate, (another name** for **attorney)** Who **pleads your case in the courtroom of eternal justice** before the **Throne of grace.**

Remember, **the devil** is the **prosecuting attorney** who **points** the **accusing finger** at you and me. **He then says,** "Look at him!" **Then Jesus,** our **defense attorney,** stands by your side and says, "But Father, look at Me. I shed My blood for him." **Because Jesus died,** our **debt is paid. Hallelujah!** Though **our sins are** as bright **as scarlet,** He **washes us as white as snow!** "Come now, let us (reason together) settle the matter," **says the LORD.** "Though your sins are like scarlet, they shall be as white as snow; though they are red as crimson, they shall be like wool" (Isaiah 1:18). **Also remember, Praise God,** today that **our defense attorney** is the **Judge's Son!**

The Holy Spirit does His work through **a threefold ministry** in our lives. 1) **He will work** on **Christ's behalf,** through our witness, 2) **to bring conviction** to those not yet in Christ (John 16:7-11). He will **also** 3) **minister to us as the teacher** of our spirits to **guide us into all truth** (John 16:13; 14:17, 26; 15:26).

You may call this eternal security or "once saved, always saved," **or even** "perseverance of the saints," (although this phrase is not in the Bible), but we **might better call it "the perseverance of God,"** since **He is the one who saves**

and **keeps us by His power, and in His hand** unto **final salvation** and eternal **glory.**

> **"And you, that were sometime alienated and enemies**
> **in your mind by wicked works, yet now He (Jesus)**
> **has reconciled in the body of His flesh through**
> **death, to present you holy and un-blameable and un-**
> **reproveable in His sight"** - (Colossians 1:21-22).

I'm afraid that most **Christians** really **don't understand what the perseverance of the saints** is all about. **Our perseverance with God - is a gift from God.** In **our salvation, God blesses us** with **assurance** through **His gift of perseverance** (II Thessalonians 3:5). However, **many Christians lack** full **assurance of their salvation** because their **understanding of assurance is founded** on the constantly **changing emotions** of their hearts **rather** than **on the eternal Word of God.**

The question of the eternal security of **the believer** is often raised in questions I receive. **This subject** has been **the cause of much controversy in the church** for centuries, and **still creates** confusion and **distress** for many Christians. **Volumes** of books, **studies,** and **sermons** have filled **thousands of libraries** around the world on this subject. It is **too much to expect** to **completely banish** this **difficult** and **problematic subject completely** for everyone in a **brief chapter** of this book, **but perhaps** we can at least **lend some scriptural light** to help in that direction.

> **"Whereby are given unto us exceeding great and**
> **precious promises: that by these ye might be partakers**
> **of the divine nature, having escaped the corruption**
> **that is in the world through lust"** (II Peter 1:4).

Some people distort the doctrine that **"when a man is saved** he **is always saved."** They **get the idea** that if this is true, then he **will sin all he wants to. The thing is, I don't want to! If the only thing** that keeps you from **sinning is fear of losing your salvation,** I wonder **if you have really surrendered yourself to God** or **asked Him** to **save you.**

When a believer claims to have no sin (sinless perfection), then **they are disagreeing with Scripture** and **with God** (I John 1:8, 10) because the **context of this chapter** is referring **to believers,** but even **after** a **person is saved,** they will **still sin,** in time, they will **sin less** ... and **less,** but **never reaching sinlessness** this side of the kingdom, **but on the other hand,** "let no one **deceive you. Whoever practices righteousness** is righteous, as he is righteous. **Whoever makes a practice of sinning** is of the devil, for the **devil has been sinning** from the beginning. **The reason** the **Son of God (Jesus) appeared** was to **destroy the works** of the devil" (I John 3:7-8).

When you practice something, it **means you** are **doing** it **fairly often,** and **when you practice it often** enough, you might get **good at it** (even sinning!), so **practicing sin means** an **ongoing participation** in **sinful activities,** and when you're **practicing** it, you **must be enjoying it.** It **isn't just an occasional falling** into **temptation** which **leads into sin** that **John is writing about.**

The Apostle Paul describes some of these **sins as** "when the **works of the flesh** (the old/lower side of human nature) **are evident, these are** sexual immorality, impurity, sensuality, idolatry (debauchery), sorcery (witchcraft; enmity (hatred), strife (discord), jealousy, fits of anger (rage), rivalries (selfish orgies, and things like these. **I warn you,** as I warned you before, that **those who do such things** will **not inherit** the kingdom of God" (Galatians 5:19-21, emphasis mine - G.C.).

This list is **not "fun"** to **write** an **explanation/commentary** on, and is **in some ways very "painful,"** as it is **like picking up a mirror and looking at my own face.** It seems to me that although we **certainly should not "major"** on these **negatives, neither should we skim** over them as **"dirty sins"** (which they **are**), but that **we should do what God calls us to do** with **all of Scripture** ... we should **meditate on these painful passages** ... we should **seek to grasp their wicked heinousness** ... we should **seek to recognize** how **offensive and scandalous** they are to **God's holiness, and armed with God's truth,** we can instead **choose the will** of God, and **praise Him** for His **enabling grace to walk** in the **power of His Spirit,** Who **gives us the victory** in Christ **Jesus our Lord. Amen!**

Peter tells us that we have now become **"partakers of divine nature."** Does that **mean** that **you don't sin anymore? No!** Before I was saved, I was **running to sin.** Now, **I'm running from it. I may slip, but I'm saved.** I have a **desire to live pure** and **clean** to the glory of God.

What about you? **Do you have a desire to be holy?** Or do you **treat** the doctrine of assurance as a **license** to **live** a **sinful life of shamelessness, wickedness, or other transgressions?**

In the Greek, Christ's cry from the **cross, "It is finished!" (Greek** is **Tetelestai)** is an **accounting term, meaning** that the **debt had been paid in**

full! Justice had been satisfied by full payment of its penalty, and thus God could "be just, and the justifier of him which believes in Jesus" (Romans 3:26).

On that basis, God offers pardon and eternal life as a free gift. He cannot force it upon anyone or it would not be a gift. Nor would it be just to pardon a person who rejects the righteous basis for pardon and offers a hopelessly inadequate payment instead - or offers his works even as "partial payment."

God's salvation in us is the full pardon by grace from the penalty of all sin, past, present or future. Eternal life is the bonus thrown in with that redemption. Denying this cardinal truth, all cultists, reject salvation by grace and insist that it must be earned by one's good works.

They accuse evangelical churches of teaching that all we need to do is to say we believe in Christ and then we can live as we please, even in the grossest of sins, yet be sure of heaven. Listen, evangelicals don't teach that at all, yet a similar complaint is made by those who believe in "falling away." They say that "once saved, always saved" encourages one to live in sin because if we know we cannot be lost then we have no incentive for living a holy life.

Scripturally, on the contrary, love for the One who saved us is the greatest and only acceptable motive for living a holy life; and surely the greater the salvation one has received, the more love and gratitude there will be. So, to no one is secure for eternity gives a higher motive for living a good life, rather than the fear of losing one's salvation if one sins!

While those who believe in "falling from grace, or losing their salvation," are clear that good works cannot earn salvation, they teach, knowingly or not, that salvation is kept by good works. Thus one gets saved by grace, but thereafter salvation can be lost by works. To teach that good works keep salvation is almost the same error as to say that good works earn salvation. It denies grace to say that once I have been saved by grace I must thereafter keep myself saved by works. I have learned, according to God's Word that ...

> I cannot sin beyond God's grace, because as wicked and
> extensive as my sins might be or become, my sins will
> never come close to the greatness of His grace and love.

Take note, if those who are saved could lose their salvation, then they must by their own actions and religious works, keep themselves saved. If that is true, then those who stay saved and get to heaven will be able to boast that they played the key role in their own salvation: What? Christ saved them but they kept themselves saved. On the contrary, no man can take any credit for his salvation. **We are "kept** by the power of God" (I Peter 1:5), **not by our faith** or **efforts.**

Read this information slowly. This **"Falling Away" teaching,** says in **Hebrews 6:4-9,** rather than glorifying Christ, **once again holds Him up to shame** and **ridicule** before the world for **two reasons: if we could lose our** salvation, then **(1) Christ would have to be crucified again** to save us again; and **(2) He would be ridiculed for dying** to **purchase a salvation** but not **making adequate provision to preserve it** - for **giving** a **priceless gift** to those who would **inevitably lose it.**

If **Christ's death** in our place for our sins and **His resurrection were not sufficient** to **keep us saved,** then He has foolishly **wasted His time. If** we could not live a good enough life **to earn salvation, it is certain** we cannot **live a good enough life to keep it!** To make the salvation He procured ultimately **dependent upon our faltering works** would be the utmost folly.

The "Falling away" doctrine makes us **worse off** after **we are saved than before.** At least **before conversion** we **can get saved.** But after we are saved and have **lost our salvation** (if we could), we **can't get saved again,** but **are lost forever.** Hebrews 6:6 declares, **"If (not when) they shall fall away,** it is **impossible ...** to **renew** them **again unto repentance." That** "falling away" is **hypothetical is clear** (v 9): "But, **beloved,** we are **persuaded** better things of you, and things that accompany salvation, though we thus speak." So **"falling away" does not** "accompany salvation." **The writer is showing us** that if we could lose our salvation, **we could never get it back** without **Christ dying again** upon the cross. This is folly! **He would have to die** an **infinite number of times (every time every person** who **was once saved sinned** and was **lost** and **wanted to be "saved again"). Caution:** in this, as in others **do not listen** to your own **human knowledge** and **logic!** Listen **to the Scriptures** and **to the Holy Spirit** Who will **teach you** this.

John assures us, "These things have I written unto **you** that **believe** on the name of the Son of God; **that ye may know (present tense knowledge)** that ye **have (present possession)** eternal life ..." (1 John 5:13). **To call it eternal life,** if the person **who had it could lose it** and **suffer** eternal death, **would be a mockery. Eternal life** is linked with the promise that **one cannot perish** - a clear **assurance of** "eternal security."

John 3:16 promises those who **believe/trust** in Jesus Christ that they **"shall not perish,** but **have everlasting life." John 5:24** again says, **"has everlasting life,** and **shall not come into condemnation"** One **could not ask** for **clearer**

or greater assurance than the **words of Jesus:** "I give unto them (My sheep) **eternal** life and they shall **never perish**" (**John 10:28**).

If, having **received eternal life,** we could **lose it and perish, it would make Christ a liar.** Yet this is the teaching of many churches today. **The idea that a person once saved** could **be lost** also **denies the sufficiency of Christ's death** upon the cross.

> **"The eternal God is your refuge, and underneath**
> **the everlasting arms!"** (Deuteronomy 33:27).

The **image** of that **verse suggests,** is that **of a little child,** lying on the **strong hands and arms of a father** who is **able to withstand** all **storms** and **dangers. We see two extremes** of life, **childhood** and **old age,** this **promise comes** with **special pledge. "He shall gather the lambs in His arms, and carry them in His bosom"** (Isaiah 40:11), is **a word for** the **children.**

"Even to your old age and **gray hairs** I am He; **I am He who will sustain you.** I have **made you** and **I will carry you;** I will **sustain you** and I will **rescue you!"** (Isaiah 46:4 NIV), **brings** its blessed **comfort to the aged.**

This thought **of God's embracing arms** is very **expressive. What** does an **arm represent?** What is the **thought suggested** by the **arm of God** enfolded **around His child?**

One insinuation, is **protection. As a father puts his arms** about his **child** when the **child is in danger** - accordingly **God protects His children. Life** itself is **filled with danger.** There **are temptations** on every hand! **Enemies lurk** in every shadow -**enemies** strong and swift! **Yet we are assured** that **nothing can separate us from the love of God.** "Underneath are the everlasting arms" (Deuteronomy 33:27)!

Another consideration, is **affection. The father's arms drawn** around **a child,** is a **token of love.** The child is held in the **father's bosom,** near his heart. The **shepherd carries the lambs** in his bosom. **John lay on Jesus' bosom.** The **mother holds** the child **in her bosom,** because **she loves it. This picture of God embracing,** protecting, and securing **His children in His arms,** tells of **His love** for them. **His love is** tender, close, intimate.

Another thought suggested by **an arm, is strength.** The arm is a **symbol of strength. His arm is omnipotence.** "In the Lord Jehovah is everlasting strength" (Isaiah 26:4). **His is an arm** that can **never be broken! Out of this clasp, we can never be taken.** Jesus - I give them **eternal life,** and **they will never perish, ever! No one** will **grab/steal them out of My hand!** (John 10:28).

Another proposal is **endurance**. The **arms of God** are **"everlasting."** **Human arms grow weary** even in love's embrace; they cannot forever press the child to the bosom.

Many years ago a husband stood by the coffin of his **beloved wife** after only **one short year** of **wedded happiness**. The **clasp of that love** was very **sweet** but how **brief a time** it lasted, and **how desolate was the life** that had **lost the precious company!**

A little baby two weeks old was left motherless. **The mother embraced her child** to her bosom and **drew her feeble arms** about it in **a loving embrace; the little one will never** more have a mother's arm around it.

So **pathetic is time** we **realize** the **waters of trouble are very deep - like great floods** they roll over us. But **still and forever notice,** underneath the **deepest floods - are** these **everlasting arms!** We **cannot sink below** them - **or out of their clasp!**

When death comes, and **every earthly thing is gone** from beneath us, and **we sink away** into what **seems abysmal darkness** - out of all **human love,** out of **warmth and gladness and life - into** the **gloom** and **strange mystery of death - still** it will **only be** - into the **everlasting arms!**

This assessment of God's divine care is **full of inspiration** and comfort. We are not saving ourselves. **A strong One,** the **mighty God** - holds us in **His omnipotent clasp!** We are **not tossed like a toy boat on life's wild sea** - driven at the **mercy of wind** and **wave.** We are **in divine keeping.** Our **security** does **not depend** upon **our own feeble, wavering faith** - but **upon the omnipotence,** the **love,** and **the faithfulness** of the **unchanging,** the **eternal God!**

No power in the universe can **snatch us out** of **His hands!** Neither **death nor life,** nor **things present,** nor things **to come - can separate us** from His **everlasting arms!** (Romans 8:31, 39).

I like the way **Sam Storms teaches God's security. He writes, "Is there anyone among you** who truly **thinks their salvation hangs suspended** on the thin **thread of your own will-power** and **commitment to righteousness?** I know **my own soul** all too well. Were it not for **God's preserving grace I would** have **lost my salvation** the day after **I was born again.** If ever it should come to pass, that **sheep of Christ** might fall away, my fickle, feeble soul, alas, would fall a thousand times a day!"

If you do not believe in the security of your soul in Christ, tomorrow should **hold little but fear** and **misery** and perhaps despair for you. For it **may well be the day you commit** that sin that will **forever sever you** from the

Savior's love. **I can face tomorrow** and **the day after and the day after** that with confidence, because **I know that He will never leave me nor forsake me** (Hebrews 13:5).

One more time: **if sin causes the loss of salvation,** what **kind or amount** of **sin does it take?** There is **not one verse in the Bible** that **tells us we can be lost again** after making Jesus the Lord of our life. **The Bible teaches** that **if we confess our sins He is faithful** and just to **forgive us** and to **cleanse** us from **all unrighteousness (1 John 1:9),** so apparently **any sin can be forgiven.** Even **those who teach falling away** rarely if ever say **they got "saved again."** **Rather,** they **confessed their sin** and were forgiven.

Listen to my urgent request here…
Ask God's forgiveness for hidden faults. You don't need to
remember them all. His grace is sufficient!

Hebrews 12:3-11 tells us that **every Christian sins,** and that **instead of causing a loss of salvation,** sin **brings God's chastening upon us** as His children. **If when we sinned** we ceased to **be God's children,** He would have **no one to chastise - yet he "scourges** (disciplines) every son whom he receives." Indeed, **chastening is a sign** that **we are God's children,** 'not' that we have **lost** salvation: **"if you** be **without chastisement,** whereof all are partakers, then are **you are bastards** (illegitimate), and **not sons"** (Hebrews 12:8).

Some teach that one **"must be baptized"** to be **saved;** others that one **must "speak in tongues."** Both are forms of **salvation by works** (doing something). **Some** people **lack assurance of salvation** because they haven't "spoken in tongues," **others** are **confident they are saved** because **they think** they have. Both are like **those who say,** "Lord, Lord, **have we not … in thy name done** many **wonderful works?"** (Matthew 7:21-23). They are **relying on their works to prove** they are saved, **instead of upon God's grace. Jesus does not say,** "You were once saved but lost your salvation." **He says, "I never 'knew' you!"** (Matthew 7:23).

There is an important distinction. Those who **believe in falling away** would say of a **professing Christian who has denied the faith** and is living in **unrepentant sin** that he has "fallen from grace" and has "lost his salvation." In contrast, **those who believe in eternal security,** while no more tolerant of such conduct, would say of the same person that probably Christ "never knew him" - **he was never a Christian.** We must give the **comfort and assurance of Scripture to those who are saved; but** at the same time we must **not give**

false and unbiblical comfort to those who merely say they are saved but deny with their lives what they profess with their lips.

Are we not then saved by our works? Absolutely not! We must not use our human reasoning and human logic, or our humanistic analytical minds to understand truths of the Almighty. For a Christian, who possesses the Holy Spirit, using the philosophy of this present world - asserting human dignity and man's capacity for fulfillment through reason and scientific methods and often rejecting religion. We must know and fully trust in what God has said in His Word.

In I Corinthians 3:13-15, every Christian's works are tried by fire at the "judgment seat of Christ" before which "we (Christians) must all appear" (II Corinthians 5:10). Good works bring rewards; a lack of them does not cause loss of salvation. The person who hasn't even one good work (all of his works are burned up) is still "saved; yet so as by fire" (v 15). We would not think such a person was saved at all. Yet one who may seem outwardly not to be a Christian, who has no good works as evidence - if he truly ever received the Lord Jesus Christ as his Savior, is then "saved as by fire" and shall never perish in spite of his lack of works.

Do we then, on the basis of "once saved, always saved," encourage Christians to "sin that grace may abound?" With Paul we say, "God forbid!" (Romans 6:1, 2). We offer no comfort or assurance to those living in sin. We don't say, you're okay because you once "made a decision for Christ." Instead, we warn: "If you are not willing right now to live fully for Christ as Lord of your life, how can you say that you were really sincere when you supposedly committed yourself to Him at some time in the past?" And to all, we declare with Paul, "Examine yourselves, whether you be in the faith; prove your own selves" (II Corinthians 13:5).

To repeat, some say that "once saved, always saved" (a phrase which is not found in the Bible), inspires one to live in sin because if we know we cannot be lost then we have no incentive for living a holy life. On the contrary, love for the one who saved us is the greatest and only acceptable motive for living a holy life; and surely the greater the salvation one has received, the more love and gratitude there will be. So to know one is secure for eternity gives a higher motive for living a good life than the fear of losing one's salvation if one sins!

We cannot sin beyond God's grace, because as wicked and extensive as our sins might be or become, they will never approach the greatness of His grace. - John MacArthur

Our confidence for eternity always rests in His **unchanging love** and grace and the **sufficiency of God's provision in Christ** - not in **our worth or performance.** Only **when this is clear** do we have **real peace** with God. Only then **can we truly love Him** and **live for Him** out of gratitude for the **eternal life** He has **given to us** as a free gift of **His grace** - **a gift He will not take back and** which He makes certain **can never be lost!**

Do you know what a "repo-man" is? He is **someone** who comes **for your car or your boat, or** (whatever), **to re-possess them** when you **get behind in your payments** or just **stop making payments.**

The "repo-man" **is a sad reality** for many Americans **struggling in a difficult economy.** But, **I want to share** with you **one gift that, once accepted,** can **never be repossessed** or **rescinded.** It is, **Scripture says, "irrevocable," the gift of eternal life through the grace of God** and the Lord Jesus Christ. In truth, it is **the only gift that matters. Satan, the evil one,** is the **repo-man** who is **in charge** of the **unsaved** (not the saved), in this **evil world. The genuine Christian** can **never be repossessed,** because he is **not** in a place that **is well fortified** and **secure.**

The Psalmist wrote, "For in the time of trouble **He shall hide me** in his **pavilion: in the secret** of His tabernacle **shall He hide me;** He shall **set me** up **upon a rock." Christian, Gibraltar** is a secure fortress - like **the Christian is spiritually free from danger** as far as his/her **eternal salvation** is concerned; - **safe!**

Psalms 32:7 states, "Thou art my **hiding place;** thou shalt **preserve me** from trouble; thou **shalt compass me** about with songs of deliverance. Selah." **The child of God is 'Free'** from **fear** or **apprehension of danger. We should not** be alarmed; **not disturbed** by **fear;** and always **confident of safety** through our Lord. **Men** are **often most in danger** when **they feel most secure.**

Harry Ironside stated that **salvation was** like **Noah inviting** a **pagan** in his day to **place his trust in God's Word** and **come into the ark. Some view salvation** like **Noah offering** to put a **peg on the outside** of the ark. "If **you just hang** on through the storm, **you'll be saved."** Salvation is **not dependent** on our **holding on** to God, but **on our being securely held by Christ.**

Grace has a soul-securing Excellency. Grace brings security along with it. **You all desire to be safe** in dangerous times; **if sword** or **pestilence** comes, **if death peeps** in at your windows, would you be safe? **Nothing will secure you in Christ during times of danger** - but grace. **Grace is the best lifeguard;** it **frees them** from the power of **hell** and **damnation.**

> "Blessed be the God and Father of our Lord Jesus
> Christ, Who according to His abundant mercy hath
> begotten us again unto a lively hope by the resurrection
> of Jesus Christ from the dead" (1 Peter 1:3).

There are **some people who think** you can **lose your salvation** once you have it. You know: **One day you are saved, then** you **sin** the next day and are **lost again.** You now **ask forgiveness** and are saved again. The **next day you sin** … etc." **I have one truth** that will **dispel that idea. Whether or not** you can **lose** your salvation **depends upon how you got it.**

Listen: if you were saved by your good works, then you **can lose** your salvation **by your bad works or our sin. God's Word is clear** on this point. **Titus 3:5 says, "Not by works** of **righteousness** which we have done, but **according** to **His mercy** He **saved us,** by the washing of **regeneration,** and **renewing** of the Holy Spirit."

Once again: **our works play no part in either earning or keeping salvation. Redemption** for sinners **can only be given to us** as a **free gift,** since the penalty for our sin has been **fully paid. We** have **violated infinite Justice,** requiring an infinite penalty. **We are finite beings** and could not pay it: we would be **separated** from God for eternity. **God is infinite** and could pay an infinite penalty, but it wouldn't be just, because He is not a member of our race.

Therefore God, in love and grace, through the **virgin birth, became a man** so that He could **pay the debt** of sin **for the entire human race!** In the Greek, Christ's cry from the cross, **"It is finished,** is an **accounting term, meaning** that the debt had been **paid in full. Justice** had **been satisfied** by full **payment** of its penalty, and thus God could "be just, and the justifier of him which believeth in Jesus" (Romans 3:16).

> **"God is totally committed to the eternal security**
> **of his blood-bought children"** -John Piper

The everlasting covenant - the new covenant — includes the **unbreakable promise,** "I will put the fear of me in their hearts, **that they may not turn from me."** They may not. They will not. **Christ sealed this covenant with his blood.** He **purchased your perseverance.**

If you are persevering in faith today, **you owe it** to the grace of God. For you see, **because of God's grace,** God the **Father sent Jesus** to this earth **to shed His blood** for the **eternal covenant** through His own blood. **The Holy**

Spirit, Who is **working in you** to **preserve your faith,** honors the purchase of Jesus. **God the Spirit works** in us **what God the Son obtained for us.** The **Father** planned it. **Jesus** bought it. **The Spirit** applies it - **all of them infallibly.**

God offers pardon and eternal life as a free gift. He **cannot force it** upon anyone **or** it **would not be a gift.** Nor **would it be just** to **pardon** a person who **rejects the righteous basis** for pardon and offers a hopelessly inadequate payment instead - or **offers his works** even as **"partial payment."**

So, how is someone saved? By **grace.** And **if it is by grace,** then you're **kept by grace. Salvation** is **not rooted** in the **merit or goodness or works** of man, **but in** the **love** and **mercy** and **grace** and the **forgiveness** of our Almighty God.

> **But now, O Lord, you are our Father;**
> **we are the clay, and you are our potter; we are all the work**
> **of your hand** (Isaiah 64:8).

"'O house of Israel, cannot **I do with you as this potter?'** says the LORD, 'Behold, as **the clay** is **in** the **potter's hand,** so are ye in Mine hand, O house of Israel'"** (Jeremiah 18:6). **The potter's wheel represents a place** of **transformation** for something as **useless as (mud) clay. God used this illustration** here in the book of Jeremiah **to show us** what **He can do with us, and for us.**

The beauty of this passage is that it is **not** the **value of the clay,** but the **life-changing power** of the **hands** that **mold it!** If **God can use** a lump of clay, He can certainly use the things **you and I have to give Him** today! **We** are far **more valuable** than a lump of clay! **God did not send His Son** to buy back clay. **God sent His Son** into this world because we are sinners! **He sent His Son** into this world **to rescue us** from our sinfulness, and our sinful behavior! **He loves us** ... a **true miracle!**

The vessel the **potter** was making of **clay** was **marred** (damaged or wasted) v. 4, in the potters hand, and the **potter reworked** (remolded) it **into another vessel,** as **seemed good** to the potter. **This verse gives us some important information** to note.

First, the **vessel** was a **work in progress,** it was **not complete. Secondly,** the **vessel** was **in the potter's hand,** although it **was changed** in the potter's hand. **And third** it **was remade** into a vessel that the **potter was pleased** with. From the text, **it's OK to be marred, or messed up** if you will, but you are still in the potter's hands. **By the time you reach verse six, it might appear to be a**

message of doom - but in verse four, I found a message of hope. Hope for the future, hope for our churches, and hope for our nation.

Don't resist the hand of the Master Potter today. Remember, there is plenty of clay in creek beds today that will never resemble a work of art, because they have remained in the creek bed. There are multitudes of people beyond number, who have tremendous potential, but will never amount to what God wanted them to be, because they never allowed God to put them on the potter's wheel. Don't make that mistake today.

Please rest assured, in the biblical knowledge, that the Potter has the pottery safe in His hands, just like Jesus and the Father has you in His hands, and He's not about to drop you. Jesus said in John 10:28-30, "I give them eternal life, and they shall never perish; no one will snatch (uproot) them out of My hand. My Father, Who has given them to Me, is greater than all; no one is able to snatch them out of my Father's hand. I and the Father are one" (NAS).

Proverbs 10:2: "Righteousness delivers from death." Don't righteous men die? Yes - but righteousness delivers from the sting of the first death, and the fear of the second death" (I Corinthians 15). Someone once said, "I am not afraid to die - but to be damned." But here is a believer's comfort - the fire of God's wrath can never kindle upon him! Grace is God's own image stamped on the soul - and God will not destroy His own image!

Xerxes the Persian (486 B.C), when he destroyed all the temples in Greece, caused the temple of Diana to be preserved for its beautiful structure. Just so, that soul which has the beauty of holiness shining in it, shall be preserved for the glory of the structure. God will not allow His own temple to be destroyed. Would you be secured in evil times? Get grace and fortify this garrison; a good conscience is a Christian's royal fort. When David's enemies lay round about him; yet, he said, "I lay down and slept. I woke up in safety, for the Lord was watching over me" (Psalm 3:5 NLT).

Someone once said, "A good conscience can sleep in the mouth of a cannon." Grace is a Christian's coat of armor, which fears neither the arrow nor the bullet. True grace may be shot at - but can never be shot through. Grace puts the redeemed soul into Christ, and there it is safe - as the bee is safe in the hive, and as the dove is safe in the ark. Romans 8:1 states, "There is no condemnation to those who are in Christ Jesus."

It is tragic, but many will never accept their position in Christ - sainthood. A while back, it was in vogue for believers to make comments like

"I'm saved, but I'm not a Christian." **Then the person would explain,** "Well, I'm **not worthy to call myself** a **Christian** because I'm **not living** like one."

Let me nail this down for you. Have you **personally committed yourself** to the **name** and **person** of the **Lord Jesus** Christ, **repented** of your sins, and **asked Him** to be **Lord** and **Savior** of your life? Have you **called upon Him to save you** from the judgment of hell? **If so, then you are the next of kin to the Trinity.** You are a **child of the King!** Since you **are part of God's family,** Jesus is **not only your Lord and Savior,** but He is your **Friend and Elder Brother.**

What a treasured truth! That the **Creator** of the universe, the **Son** of God, the **King** of kings, **would not only call us His brothers and sisters,** but would actually **make the sacrifice necessary** "to redeem them that were under the law, **that we might receive the adoption of sons**" (Galatians 4:5).

Two marvelous chapters (Romans 8 and Hebrews 2) **provide insights** into this **increase in the size of the family of God,** initially **consisting of God** the **Father** and God the **Son,** through the ministry of God the **Spirit. Please read slowly** to **let the Word of God speak to you in these Scriptures,** "For as many as are led by the Spirit of God are the children of God. **The Spirit Himself bears witness with our spirit,** that **we are** the **children of God.** And **if children,** then heirs; **heirs of God,** and **joint-heirs** with **Christ;** if so be that we **suffer with Him,** that we may be **also glorified together** (Romans 14-17).

We were **foreknown** by God, **predestined** to be "conformed to the image of His Son" **(v.29), called, justified,** and **glorified (v.30). Why?** "That He might be the **firstborn** among many brethren" **(v.29). He is our elder brother,** in a favored position in God's eyes, **but we are also** "**heirs** of God, and **joint-heirs** with Christ" **(v.17)** (Romans 8).

Christ paid dearly to allow us the **privilege of Sonship.** He was "made like unto His brethren" **(Hebrews 2:17),** "a little lower than the angels for the suffering of death - **that He by the grace of God** should **taste death for every man" (v.9),** and is "not ashamed to call (us) brethren" **(v.11).** Yet, in all, He praised and honored His Father, even proclaiming from the cross, "I will declare thy name unto my brethren" **(v.12).**

Think of it! **Our elder brother set aside aspects of His deity,** became like one of us, **suffered and substituted** in **full payment for our sins** to make our salvation complete, and even now aids us **(Hebrews 2:18)** and intercedes for us **(Romans 8:34). All this because of God's grace toward us! What amazing security that is!**

> "For ye have not received the spirit of bondage again
> to fear; but ye have received the Spirit of adoption,
> whereby we cry, Abba, Father" (Romans 8:15).

So great a salvation: When we consider something **great**, we will **naturally pay attention** to it and not **neglect** it. If we do not consider something great, we leave it to convenience rather than to commitment. **Therefore, if we neglect something**, we probably do not consider it great. **Yet our salvation is great,** because: We are **saved by** a **great** Savior. We are **saved at** a **great** cost. We are **saved from** a **great** penalty.

Have you felt like you couldn't call yourself a Christian **because of your sin**? Then get on your knees and **repent of the sin of unbelief** that keeps you from **knowing you are a child of the King!** It is time we quit using human equations and human logic ... and **listen to God's Word.**

Remember this story in Matthew, "Immediately **He** [Jesus] made the **disciples get into the boat** and go before him to the other side, while he dismissed the crowds." - (Matthew 14:22). **Yet Jesus did not send His disciples** into the **teeth of a storm** to be malicious or uncaring. **He did it to help build the disciples' faith!** And by doing this, **Jesus also showed that He was in complete control.**

The captain of their salvation (and ours). Jesus is the **captain** - the **leader**, the **advance** - of the salvation He provided for us! What are the wonderful implications of that statement? **A captain makes all the arrangements** for the march, and Jesus makes the arrangements for our progress as Christians. **A captain gives the commands** to the troops – "Go" or "Stay" or "Do this." Jesus commands us as our captain. **A captain leads the way** and is **an example** to his men, and Jesus does this for us. **A captain encourages** his men, and Jesus encourages us. **A captain rewards** his troops, **and Jesus rewards His followers.**

You know, for the Christian, outside of salvation itself, the most liberating, life-producing, joy-producing, **peace-giving truth** is the fact that **Jesus Christ is sovereignly in control** of your life. **This means no matter what storm** you're in or what storm you're going to be in (because you'll always be in one of those two places), **God has you there for a reason.**

So you can give Him thanks ... not necessarily for the circumstance or the crisis itself ... but **for the Christ who reigns and rules** in your heart **and** in your daily experiences. **And you can thank God** for loving you enough to be willing to send storms into your life to either perfect you or correct you.

**Understand: that it's not 'me trying' to live for God but
it's really now 'God living' in and through me as me.**

There's a song by Babbie Mason that says, "God is too wise to be mistaken, God is too good to be unkind. So when you don't understand, when you don't see His plan, **when you can't trace His hand, trust His heart.**" Listen: **the same God who took you into the storm** is the **same God** who **will bring you out of it!** So trust His heart ... and His love for you ... today.

"**Who are kept** by the **power of God** through **faith** unto salvation ready to be revealed in the last time" (I Peter 1:5).

This word "kept" in 1 Peter 1:5 is a '**military term**'. It literally **means** to be '**garrisoned about**' as soldiers **around a fort. While our inheritance is being kept guarded** in heaven under the watchful eye of God, **we are being garrisoned** about by **God's protecting care** for it. **Think of the power of God** as a **fortress** and **you are on the inside.** Now how do you feel? **Pretty secure,** right? **Many people have the idea** that **we keep ourselves safe, which we don't.** Friend, **He keeps us safe! The Almighty God stands sentry** over us all our days **guarding our** "going out and our coming in from this day forth and forever."

This is like the father who was **crossing a street** with his **son. The son had hold** of his **daddy's hand,** then the light changed and the **cars** surged forward. The **father grabbed his son's** chubby **little hand** and almost lifted his son across the street **to escape** the oncoming traffic. That is the way **God holds us from** our **sinful indulgences.** The **Psalmist penned it** like this:

"**Though he fall, he shall not be utterly cast down: for
the Lord upholds him with His hand. As you carry
me across this day You have given me**" (37:24).

What is the certainty of this future? That is, how certain **can we be that we will be a part of God's eternal home in heaven?** The **answer to that** can be found in the phrase **"kept by the power of God."** Listen, if I was to be **kept by my own power,** then I would not have any certainty at all. But **because I am kept by the power of God, I have total certainty** because, of course, **God's power is unlimited.** God will **overcome any failure** on my part. **God will overcome any sin** on my part. God will **overcome any ruse** by the devil or his minions.

Almighty God, our Guard, has never changed. He is **on duty "24/7"**, year in and year out until we arrive safely home. **Believers are not kept** by their **own power,** but by **the power of God.** Our faith in Christ has **so united us to Him** that His power now **secures us, guards us and guides us**. We are **not kept by our strength,** but by His faithfulness. **How long** will He guard us? Until Jesus Christ returns. **We are in His hands,** and as **John 10:29 states,** "no one (nothing) is able to pluck us out of the Father's hand." **Thank God for** His unfailing, unchanging, **faithful grace!**

One New Testament word which **reveals the truth of "security of the believer"** is **"Redeem" or "Redemption."** This historical word **comes as part of the description of the slave market.** To redeem **means to "set free by the payment of a price."** When **we were slaves to sin, because of His grace, God paid the price** and **set us free from our slavery.** The **price was the blood of his Son.** When a **sinner trusts Christ,** God **releases him from the chains of sin** and sets him free forever!

Everyone needs redemption. **Everyone** needs to be set free from the "sin that does so easily beset us." **During World War II,** an **Imperial Japanese Army** soldier, **Hiroo Onoda, was** assigned to a **secret mission** on the Philippine island of **Lubang.** He was to **lead his men in guerilla warfare** to secure the island, and he was **told not to surrender, no matter what.** His commander promised to return for him.

When the Allied forces conquered the **island in 1945, Onoda retreated into the jungle** - and **remained there** for the **next 29** years, **unaware the war had ended** and still **following** his **original orders.** He only emerged after being **found by a college student** who brought his original **commanding officer to assure him** he could surrender. **Onoda remained committed** to his **cause** and spent a **significant portion of his life honoring his** superior **officer's commands.**

Our verse today stresses the importance of **following God's commands.** It **assures** that if you do, **you will live** – not just victoriously in **this lifetime,** but also **for all eternity. Are you following orders** and remaining united with God's cause? **Pray today to stay focused** through obstacles and hardships. **Only surrender when Christ,** your **commanding officer, returns** for you. Then **pray for your nation's leaders** to **seek** and **follow God's orders.**

A story told by Paul Lee Tan illustrates the **meaning of redemption:** When **A. J. Gordon** was pastor of a **church in Boston,** he **met a young boy** in front of the **sanctuary carrying** a **rusty cage** in which **several birds** fluttered nervously. **Gordon inquired,** "Son, where did you get those birds?" **The boy replied,** "I trapped them out in the field." "What are you going to do with them?" **"I'm going to play** with them, and then I guess I'll just **feed them** to an **old cat** we have at home."

Gordon offered to buy them, and the lad exclaimed, "Mister, you don't want them, they're **just little old wild birds** and can't sing very well." **Gordon replied,** "I'll give you $2 for the cage and birds." **"Okay, it's a deal,** but you're making a bad bargain."

The exchange was made and the boy went away whistling, happy with his shiny coins. **Gordon walked** around to the back of the church property, **opened the door** of the small wire coop, and **let the struggling creatures soar** into the blue.

The next Sunday he took the empty cage into the pulpit and used it to **illustrate his sermon** about Christ's coming to **seek and to save the lost -** **paying for them** with His **own precious blood. "That boy told me the birds were not songsters,"** said Gordon, "but **when I released them** and they **winged their way heavenward,** it seemed to me they **were singing,** 'Redeemed, redeemed, redeemed!

We all have been captive to sin** and it's **damning** process in our lives. Now, **through the grace of God** in Jesus Christ, **God has liberated** us and **set us free. Romans 8:1 states,** "There is **no condemnation to those** who are in Christ Jesus" (1:12).

You and I have been held captive to sin, but **our security was established** when **Christ purchased our pardon and set us at liberty.** When a person has this **life-changing experience,** he will want to sing, **"Redeemed, how I love to proclaim it!"**

Remember: the story of the Potter and the Clay? I don't know about you, but I'll admit that **I have been messed up,** but **I am in** the Master's hands. **I may be a work in progress,** but **I am in** the Master's hands. I may **be marginalized** but I am in the Master's hands. I may **be sometimes misunderstood,** but **I am in** the Master's hands. I may **trapped by un-mitigating circumstances,** but I am in the Master's Hands. I may **sometimes under misconceptions,** but in the Master's hands. **Messed, up,** messed **on,** messed **over, marred,** but in the Master's hands. **Question: Are you in** the Master's hands?

> **"Lord, mold me and make me after Your will,**
> **while I am waiting, yielded and still."**

A Roman emperor, after a **successful military campaign**, was **returning** in triumph to Rome. **Great throngs filled the city** to welcome the mighty hero. While **passing through** one of the **crowded thoroughfares, a little girl,** wild with joy, **dashed** toward his chariot.

The officer stopped her and **said:** "That is the **chariot of the emperor,** and you must not attempt to reach him." **The little one replied:** "He may be **your emperor - but he is my father!"** In a moment she was **not only in the chariot,** but also in the **arms of her father.**

It is even so with true believers. While **God** is the **Emperor of all men -** He is that, and **infinitely more to us - He is our Father!** This then, because of **God's grace,** is **how you should pray:** "**Our Father in Heaven.**" (Matthew 6:9)

And **Christian, never forget - Nothing can separate you from the love of Christ.** "For I am sure **that neither** death nor life, nor **angels,** nor **rulers,** nor **things present** nor **things to come,** nor **powers,** nor **height** nor **depth,** nor **anything else** in all creation, **will be able to separate us from** the love of God in Christ Jesus our Lord" (Romans 8:38-39 NIV).

Many people have been **led to believe** that self-doubt, self-condemnation, feelings of unworthiness, and conviction for individual sins **are the work of the Holy Spirit.** But it's **just not true!** In John 16:7, **Jesus speaks of the Holy Spirit,** "Nevertheless I tell you the truth; it is **expedient for you** that I go away: for if I go not away, **the Comforter** will not come unto you; but if I depart, I will send him unto you." The **word "expedient"** means **"to your advantage."** Jesus is saying that it's **better to have** the **Holy Spirit ministering** to you **than** it is to **have Him** present in His physical body. What a declaration!

And He (Holy Spirit), **when He is come,** will **reprove** (convict) the world in respect of **sin,** and of **righteousness,** and of **judgment:** of **sin, because** they **believe not on me;** of **righteousness,** because I go to the Father, and ye behold me no more; of **judgment,** because **the prince** of this world **hath been judged** (John 16:8-11. The **coming of the Spirit,** at the day of "Pentecost," as the **things ascribed to Him,** and which **were** then **done** by Him, **clearly show;** though it may also include his coming along with, and **by the ministration of the Gospel,** into the **hearts of his people** at conversion, in all after ages of time.

This verse **teaches that the whole world** that **lies in wickedness;** and **must be** "reproved." This "reproving," as it may respect **different persons,** may intend **both such reproofs** and **convictions,** as are **not attended with conversion,** and issue **in salvation;** and such as **are powerful, spiritual, and to saving purposes:** the several things **the Spirit of God is said to reprove of,** being **repeated** in the following verses (9-11) **with reasons or specifications** annexed to them.

Question: Do you ever worry that you could **lose your salvation?** That you could **do something so awful or sinful** that you would **no longer be saved?** Remember, you could not have even been saved without the Holy Spirit.

The fact is, when you **make a decision to accept Christ** as your Lord and Savior, **your eternal future** is made **secure,** for no one **nor anything is able to take them** from **Jesus** or the **Father** (John 10:27-30); because this union has been **sealed with the Holy Spirit** (Ephesians 1:13). **And, "The Spirit Himself testifies** with our spirit that **we are God's children"** (Romans 8:16 NIV). **God's work is finished because of Christ** as far as a **Christian's security** is concerned!

> And **do not grieve the Holy Spirit** of God, with whom **you
> were sealed** for the day of redemption (Ephesians 4:30).

Thanks to what Jesus did on the cross, **God has wiped away any sin** that separates you from Him. **In fact, Psalm 103:12 tells us,** "As far as the east is from the west, so far does he remove our transgressions from us."

I encourage you to claim this promise **from God today** ... and **commit Romans 8:38-39 to memory. It states,** "For I am **sure** that neither death nor life, nor angels nor rulers, nor things present nor things to come, nor powers, nor height nor depth, nor anything else in all creation, **will be able to separate** us from the **love** of God **in Christ Jesus** our Lord."

The **next time Satan tempts you to doubt** your standing in Christ, **say** these verses out loud ... **and stand on God's promises!** And the next time **some person poses a hypothetical** or **theoretical narrative** about **someone** who claimed to be **a Christian,** and **committed a sin, (and for the sake of this story), he was hit** by a **truck** and **was killed** before he could **confess his sin to God** ... **could he still** be a **child of God** ... or **is he lost again, and gone to Hell? Remember:** it is **not what I think or say,** or even **what you think or say** or have been taught, **it is Who God is** and **what He has said in His Word.**

> **"I will sing praises to you, for you, O God, are my fortress,
> the God who shows me steadfast love"** (Psalm 59:17).

The Ozama Fortress, was **built in** the early **1500's.** It is the **oldest known military construction** of European origin **in the Americas.** At the port of

Santo Domingo in the Dominican Republic, it was built to protect the country from its enemies. The fortress was constructed so well it was later used as a prison and still stands today for visitors to tour.

The Ozama Fortress is one of many such structures around the world. For thousands of years, people have searched for ways to provide protection. Psalm 51 speaks of the security that comes from God. When the ordeals, trials and sufferings of the world seem to come against you, you don't have to hide behind the walls of any castle. Instead, run to God and praise Him for His never-ending love and protection.

Knowing God and accepting the refuge that His shelter provides brings freedom from fear. The Lord is your strong tower. Rest today in God's steadfast love for you. "The LORD is my rock and my fortress and my deliverer, My God, my rock, in whom I take refuge; My shield and the horn of my salvation, my stronghold" (Psalm 18:2 NASB).

Unfortunately, there seems to be a growing trend among Christians to deny that Christians can be sure whether they are saved - or will remain so - until they die. Is it true, "once saved always saved" is not in the Bible, or "can we lose our salvation through disobedience or unbelief?" Theologically, this doctrine has been referred to as the perseverance of the saints or security of the believer.

My concern for the eternal security skeptic is that at least some of them give the impression that they believe they have to earn or maintain their salvation through some form of conformity to the law. Paul makes it clear in Galatians 5:4 that those who seek to be justified by the law have "fallen from grace" and "have been severed from Christ." In other words, they are not even saved! My advice to them is to trust in God's promises and believe that Jesus died for all your sins, regardless of your ability to live up to the standards of the law.

> While sin is an occasion for grace, grace is never
> to be an occasion for sin. - Bob Deffinbaugh

The security of the believer is a core doctrine in biblical Christianity. The doctrine is not just based upon a few verses in the New Testament. As shown here, there are over 400 verses that espouse this doctrine in one way or another. Skeptics of eternal security selectively cite a few dozen verses out-of-context or that aren't really addressing the topic of salvation, but usually of rewards.

You Christian's who are "in Christ," because you **have committed** your life to the **Lord,** and **believe** that **Jesus died** on the **cross** and **rose** from the dead so that **your sin can be forgiven.** Because **you done that, God says** you are **clean** and **pure** in **His sight** because **He sees you as** "in Christ."

God has **promised** to **protect us.** This **does not mean** that you will **never get hurt, be tempted or sin,** but it does mean that **God is always able to care for you. Remember,** sometimes **God allows things** to happen to us that **we think are bad,** but God **uses them** for our **good.**

It's like **taking a piece of paper** all **covered** with **marks** and **drawings,** then **placing it inside your Bible.** Now **all you can see** is your **Bible.** You **can't see the dirty piece of paper.** In the same way, **you accept that Jesus took** your **punishment on the cross. What Jesus did** on the cross **satisfied God's need to punish all sin** – then **God no longer sees you as guilty** before Him. He only **sees Jesus' righteousness** because **you are** "in Christ" (II Corinthians 5:17; Hebrews 13:5-6). **He is our place of shelter** and **safety** from the wrath of God against sin.

Before we close this Chapter, let me share this story ... When **my son** was **young** and **willingly disobeyed** me by **not taking the gum out** of his **mouth before bed,** he **paid the consequences** the **next morning** when **I had to use ice to freeze** most of **it out.** It had become a **tangled web overnight** and **I couldn't get it all out,** and **he** was **not happy** about that, mostly **at himself** because **my little boy knew he was paying the consequences** for **not listening** to **his dad. I never told** him, "I told you so," but rather **I said,** "I'm sorry it happened,** but now **it's over.** You've **learned a valuable lesson.** Let's **leave it at that. It's forgiven."**

The next day my boy came to me again and **said,** "Dad, I'm sorry** about yesterday and **I promise not to do it again."** I said, **"What do you mean? Sorry for what?"** When he **reminded me of the gum,** I said, **"Oh that! That's all over son. Don't worry about it.** It's been forgiven, like I told you yesterday. **You don't have to keep bringing it up."**

In the same way, some **people just cannot forgive themselves.** They **keep asking for forgiveness** over the same thing, but if **they've already confessed it,** my **question is,** "Why do you keep bringing up what God has forgiven?"

If **my little son** came back **day after day** and **asked for forgiveness,** after a while I'd say, **"Son, don't you believe me? I forgave you** and it's over. Now **you must forget it too." That's** the **way God may feel** about our **continually coming before Him** for the very **same sin, no matter how grievous it is.** The **children of God** are **promised** that if **they ask for forgiveness, God will** grant it (1 John 1:9). **Once it's done,** there is **no cause** to go back and **ask for forgiveness again** is there? - (Jack Wellman).

> Paul told the Colossian Christians, **"For you have died and your life is hidden with Christ in God"** (3:3 NIV).

Wow! **Can you believe that statement?** This is **perhaps one of the most startling,** liberating, and 'take your breath away' **passages** in the **entire New Testament. Colossians 3:1-4 expands** on 1:27, "Christ in you, the hope of glory." It is equally an ongoing thought that began in 2:12-15. **For Paul, the essence of the Christian life** is **who we are in Christ** and **what He is for us. Paul's conclusions** are **based on immutable** (absolute, irreversible) **truths.**

When you have **trusted Jesus for your salvation,** your **name has already been written** in the **Lamb's book of life** (Revelation 20:11-15; 21:27), and **you will go to heaven.** However, **if you are pretending to be a Christian,** going through the **motions,** and **don't** really **believe,** no amount of **pretending** will get you into heaven. **Do you feel guilty** about the sin in your life? If so, **this is the work of the Holy Spirit to conform you** to the **image of Jesus.** Follow Him!

> **Notwithstanding in this rejoice not, that the spirits are subject unto you; but rather rejoice, because your names are written in heaven** (Luke 10:20).

Let me end this Chapter with **this story** … **Watchman Nee** tells about a **new convert** who came in **deep distress** to see him. **"No matter how much I pray,** no matter how **hard I try,** I simply **cannot seem to be faithful to my Lord. I think I'm losing my salvation."** Nee said, **"Do you see this dog** here? He is **my dog.** He is **house-trained;** he **never makes a mess;** he is **obedient;** he is a **pure delight** to me. **Out in the kitchen** I have a son, a **baby son.** He **makes a mess,** he **throws his food** around, he **fouls his clothes,** he is a **total mess.** But **who is going to inherit my kingdom? Not my dog;** my **son is my heir.** You are **Jesus Christ's heir** because **it is for you that He died." We are Christ's heirs, not through** our perfection but **by means of His perfection and grace.**

These truths are **sourced solely** in **who God is and what God does.** May this **truth fortify us** for the **journey ahead** and may **our lives be lived giving Him all the glory,** Amen.

I write these things to you who believe in the
name of the Son of God so that you may know
that you have eternal life" (1 John 5:13).

"Dear Jesus, open my ears to hear Your Words clearly. Give me hunger
to feed on Your heavenly manna, and health to follow Your will and do the
work that You lead me to do. Help my heart to see and understand the eternal
'security' which I now possess in You.

LET US PRAY TOGETHER ... "Jesus, pardon me, correct me – but
never leave me to myself! Draw me – or drive me; but never allow me to
live long as a distance from you. O, bring me to Your sacred feet, and let me
wander no more! I thank you for giving us Your unlimited grace which leads
us to salvation, sanctification, and finally glorification. In Jesus name ...
Amen!"

"Grace be with all them who love our Lord Jesus Chris n
sincerity" – Ephesians 6:24
"Brethren, may the grace of our Jesus Christ be with your
spirit. Amen" – Galatians 6:18

hapter 5

God 'STRENGTHENS'
Me With His Grace

"AND HE SAID unto me, **My grace** is sufficient for thee: **for my strength** is made perfect **in weakness.** Most gladly therefore will I rather **glory in my infirmities,** that the power of Christ may rest upon me" (II Corinthians 12:9).

> **"Now to Him who is able to do far more abundantly**
> **beyond all that we ask or think, according to the power**
> **that works within us"** (Ephesians 3:20 NASB).

"God is able!" Only **He has all power** for this life or the next. **Our being able** to give away what you have can **appear fool hardy** if you **don't understand the grace and power of God** and understand that: **"He is able."**

> **"And God is able** to make **all grace** abound toward you, that
> you, always having **all sufficiency** in **all things,** may have an
> abundance for **every good work"** II Corinthians 9:8 (NKJV).

This verse is full of **so much seeming hyperbole** it's inescapable. **In fact,** in the **original Greek** language **the "all's" here just go on and on** in **almost every form** that you could put them, you have <u>pason</u>, <u>panti</u>, <u>pantiti</u>, <u>pasonpon</u> (?), all of **those forms** of the **word "all."**

It could be read, "And **God is able** to make **all grace** abound to you that **always** having **all sufficiency** in **all things,** that you may have **all abundance** for **all good deeds."** This is so grandiose, so immense, and magnanimous that it has **no limitation.** And **that was the intent** of the **Apostle Paul** in throwing in all the superlatives.

God's Word shows us that **God's power** is **exhibited** in creation, in providence, in miracles, in the resurrection of Christ, the resurrection of saints, **the transforming power of the gospel** and the **ultimate destruction** of the wicked. **God is able!**

"**Through many dangers, toils and snares,
I have already come;
'Tis grace hath brought me safe thus far,
And grace will lead me home.**" (John Newton)

Your faith says in I Corinthians 2:5 that we **must rest not** on **our own strength** and **wisdom of men but** on the **power of God.** When **your faith** rests on the **wisdom of men,** you're **not** going to **give your time, talents or tithe** away because men will tell you that's how you have less, **but God says** that's how you have more, **so your faith** must rest on the power of God **and not** the wisdom of men. That has been tested **throughout redemptive history,** throughout the **pages of Scripture,** men who put their **life on the line** with regard to the power of God.

For example, just think of Daniel 3:17, the **three young men** in the **fiery furnace,** "If it be so, **our God** whom we serve **is able** to **deliver us** from the furnace of **blazing fire**" (NASB).We're going in that **fiery furnace** because **we believe He is able** to keep us from frying. **God is powerful** enough to do it. **He is able.**

While God's infallible Word often **speaks** of the **grace** of God **as saving grace,** it also makes mention of it **in a broader sense,** as in **Isaiah 26:10,** "Though the wicked is shown **favor (grace), He does not learn righteousness;** He **deals unjustly** in the land of uprightness, and **does not perceive the majesty** of the LORD" (NASB).

The **grace of God is** of the greatest **practical significance for sinful men.** It was **by grace** that **the way of redemption** was opened for them, **Romans 3:24** states, "being **justified freely by His grace** through the redemption that is in Christ Jesus." **II Corinthians 8:9** says "For **you know the grace** of our Lord Jesus Christ, that though he was rich, yet for your sakes he became poor, that you through his poverty might be rich." and that the **message of redemption** went out into the world."

Acts 14:3 says, "So **Paul and Barnabas spent** considerable time there, speaking boldly for the Lord, **who affirmed the message of His grace** by enabling them to perform signs and wonders" (BSB). **By grace sinners receive the gift** of God in Jesus Christ, Acts 18:27; Ephesians 2:8.

By grace they are justified, Romans 3:24; 4:16; Titus 3:7, they **are enriched** with spiritual blessings, John 1:16; and **II Corinthians 8:9 which states,** "For **you know the grace of our Lord Jesus Christ,** that though he was rich, yet for your sakes he became poor, that you through his poverty might be rich (ESV; and in II Thessalonians 2:16-17 says, "**Now may our Lord** Jesus Christ Himself, **and our God** and Father, who has loved us and **given us everlasting consolation and good hope by grace,** comfort your hearts and **establish you** in every good word and work" (DBT). And Ephesians 2:8; and Titus 2:11 which state, For **the grace of God** has **appeared, bringing salvation** to **all men ...**

All mankind has **absolutely no merits of their own,** they are altogether **dependent on the grace of God** in Christ. **In today's modern theology, with** its belief in the **intrinsic 'goodness' of man** and his ability to **perfect himself,** the **doctrine of salvation by grace** has practically **become a "lost chord,"** and even **the word "grace"** was **emptied of all spiritual meaning** and **banished from sacred discussions.** Today in **many Theological Schools** and **Church's,** a **new type** of grace, that has been **labeled "cheap –grace."**

Cheap grace (which is not true grace) **cries out for expression** in the **church today. Human** decisions, **crowd** manipulations, and **fleshly altar calls** does **not** produce genuine converts. **Only the old-fashioned gospel** of **sovereign grace** will **capture** and **transform sinners** by the **power of the Word** and **Spirit of God.**

"**Cheap Grace is the deadly enemy** of the **Redeemed** of the **Church.** We are **fighting to-day** for costly grace. **Cheap grace means grace sold** on the **market** like **cheapjack's wares.** (a **peddler/dealer of cheap goods),**" said Dietrich Bonhoeffer.

Cheap grace means grace as a doctrine, a principle, a system. **It means forgiveness of sins** proclaimed as a general truth, the love of God taught as the Christian "**conception**" of God. **Cheap grace** means the **justification of sin without** the **justification of the sinner.**

An intellectual assent to that **idea** is held **to be of itself sufficient** to secure **remission of sins.** The Church which holds the **correct doctrine of grace has,** it is supposed, '**ipso facto' a part in that grace.** In such a Church **the world finds a cheap covering** for its sins; no **contrition is required,** still less any real desire to be delivered from sin. **Cheap grace** therefore **amounts to a denial** of the **living Word of God,** in fact, a **denial of the Incarnation** of the **Word of God ... Jesus!**

Under Cheap Grace the Christian life comes to mean **nothing more than living in** the world and **as the world,** and being **no different from** the world. **I no longer need to try to follow Christ,** for cheap grace. **The most effective foe** of true discipleship, has **freed me from that.** Has **cheap grace led you** to the place **of a deceptive conclusion** that **self-sacrifice, and surrender** of personal desires and **laying down your life** for the brethren and the church are just **leftovers of a bygone times?** Is it a **grace that has set you free to seek your own purposes** at the **sacrifice** of our **Lord's call to true discipleship?**

Many Christian's and church's today have gathered around the **remains** of **cheap grace** like a **vulture** gathers to **eat the flesh which has destroyed the life** out of following Christ. **Cheap grace hungers** more for **quick forgiveness without commitment** to **His Lordship** and **Leadership** because we **see the first** as making **less demands upon** our **personal lives. Cheap grace is preaches forgiveness without demanding repentance, baptism** without discipline, **communion** without confession. **Cheap grace** is grace **without discipleship,** the **cross,** and **the incarnate living Jesus Christ.**

Costly Grace, on the other hand, **is like the treasure hidden in a field.** For the sake of it **a man will gladly go and sell all that he has.** It is a **pearl of great price to buy** which will **cost us everything.** It's the **kingly rule of Christ,** for whose sake a man will **pluck out the eye** which **causes him to stumble.** It is the **call of Jesus** at which a **disciple leaves his nets** and follows. It **is grace which** must be **sought again and again,** the gift which **must be asked for,** the **door at which** a **man must knock.**

Such grace is costly because **it calls us** to follow, and **it is grace** because it **calls us** to **follow Jesus Christ.** Costly because it costs a man his life, it is grace because it gives a man the only true life. **Costly** because it **condemns sin,** and **grace** because it **justifies the sinner.** Above all, **costly because** it cost God **the life of His Son: "You** have been **bought with a price"** and what has **cost God** so much **can't be cheap** for us. It is grace because God did not regard his Son too **dear a price to pay** for our life, **but delivered him up for us.** It is **costly because** it **compels a man** to **submit** to the burden of Christ, but **is grace because** "My yoke is easy and my burden light."

Low cost, discount grace closes the way to Christ and **hardens men's hearts** in **their disobedience. I often see new believers** take the **first few steps down** the path of discipleship, and **inevitably some disciple** of the **humanistic church** introduces them to a **cheaper way of grace** and) **their growth just stops.**

They have discovered a grace (which truly is **not** God's grace) that **relieves them of** all response to **committed discipleship** and the body. We **must rediscover** and **rekindle** the mutual **relationship between grace and discipleship.**

In our Western World, the church is littered with the **disciples of cheap grace** and **many are in so-called** very evangelistic churches. **Our most urgent need** today is learning **how to live the Christian life** in this modern, aggressive, **sinful world?** Very, **very happy are those** who have **discovered the true grace of God. Those who have truly left all,** like Peter and John leaving their nets, or Levi his job, **realize at once** that they are **still incapable of answering** the **call** of God upon their lives **by their own strength.** They **do not see their success** as a **personal achievement** accomplished **by their great sacrifice.** Instead, **they see and know** that only by **the costly grace** of God have their **efforts brought forth any fruit** of lasting value.

Which kind of grace have you embraced? What does **your answer** to the call of discipleship reveal? **Does Sunday morning** find **you and your family gathering** around the **Tele-evangelists, unwilling** to **lay down your life** for a body of believers who need you? **Maybe you should trade** in that **sorry excuse of a Christian life** for the **New Life** offered in the **true grace of God.**

We need to be like Abraham of whom **Scripture says** in Romans 4:21, **"able also to perform."** "He was **fully persuaded** that **what God had promised** He was able to perform." **God's ability** is so great He is able to **make all grace abound** to you. **God possesses all grace,** all the grace there is in the infinity of God is available and **He gives it in abundance.** God doesn't hold anything back.

The Scripture has to remind us "that not many wise men after the flesh, not many mighty, not many noble, are called: ... That no flesh should glory in His presence" (I Corinthians 1:26, 29, ASV). **We should,** indeed, **desire wisdom,** might, and riches, but not as measured by the world. "The fear of the Lord is the beginning of wisdom" (Proverbs 9:10). **"My grace is sufficient** for thee: for **My strength** is made perfect in weakness" (II Corinthians 12:9).

Observe the **word "sufficiency."** That **word** is a word **loaded with meaning** in the **Greek culture.** It was a word that was bandied around in ethical **discussions by philosophers** from **Socrates clear** on to the **time of Paul. It meant contentment.** It **meant literally** to the philosophers, particularly to the Stoics, like Seneca who was a contemporary of Paul, they understood as **the proud independence of self-sufficiency** which, they thought, makes for true happiness. They said: you **find your true happiness** when you are **self-sufficient,** when you are **proudly independent.**

> Our strength for living: **"Be strong by the grace that is in Christ Jesus" (II Timothy 2:1),** for **"it is good for the heart to be strengthened by grace"** (Hebrews 13:9 NASB).

Wow, nothing's changed, has it? All the **self-esteem stuff,** all the **ego building stuff** that is in the **current philosophy** of our time which is **called psychology,** all of that stuff is **intended to produce** independent, self-sufficient, proud people. **It's not like,** "my God shall supply all your need according to His riches in glory by Christ Jesus, (Philippians 4:19). And **there's no stinginess.**

Humankind typically despises weakness. We have a **tendency throughout history** to **shun the simplicity of faith,** and **gravitate to** something more **visual,** more **hands-on,** more **self-satisfying.** Do **we live our** whole life **trying to get out of** the very things that **God has sent to make us strong?**

Years ago, during a large Bible conference a debate began about, **"what is it that sets Christianity apart** from other religions?" **Some argued** that it was God coming in the flesh that set Christianity apart from other religions. **Some argued** that it was love, or sacrifice, or the resurrection, or one thing or another. **Finally, C. S. Lewis, having arrived late,** walked into the conference and **asked what all the noise was about.** When told **they were discussing** what it was that set Christianity apart from all other religions, **he said, "That's easy. It's grace."**

My friend, **the thing that sets Christianity apart from every other religion, every cult, every philosophy** in the world is **grace,** the **"unmerited, unearned, undeserved, favor we receive from God."** And I want you to know, **God's grace is not only sufficient, but it is also strengthening.** But, just **what is God's grace** ... study on.

Scripture says when we will simply **draw near to Christ,** He will **draw near to us.** And **by drawing near** to **Him, we** will be **given a fresh supply of strength** daily. That is the **"secret of His presence"** that **David refers** to in Psalm 31.

> **"But grow in grace and in the knowledge of our Lord and Savior Jesus Christ" (II Peter 3:18).**

The word "grace" is found in the New Testament about 150 times. That Greek word is "charis", it is **translated "grace."** It means a **favor bestowed.** It means a **generous benefit freely given.** The sense of it **in the New Testament** is that it **means a favor bestowed by God** through **His power to transform** a person's life starting at salvation and going to the end from there.

The gospel of the grace of God is the message **everyone needs.** The word of **grace is proclaimed** from **every page of the Bible** and **ultimately revealed in Jesus Christ.** The **last verse** of the **Bible summarizes** the message from Genesis to Revelation: "The **grace** of the Lord Jesus be with you all" (Revelation 22:21). **Through Jesus** "we have all **received grace upon grace"** (John 1:16) - the **gratuitous** and undomesticated **grace of God.**

It is by God's grace that we draw every breath. **God wants us** to trust in Him. **By definition grace** is **"unmerited divine assistance** given humans for their **regeneration** or **sanctification."** **God's amazing grace** is what **drew me** to God in the first place, in the midst of my sin, **God's grace** sought me out and **God offered forgiveness** through his grace. **God's grace continues** to draw me to Him. **I am weak** in my own ability to turn away from temptation. **I daily thank God** for His **powerful grace** that is **sufficient** for me. **When I sin God** is there to graciously forgive me.

> **Growing in grace is a deepening realization of our nothingness - it is a heartfelt recognition that we are not worthy of the least of God's mercies.**

God challenges us, in His Word, **to "grow in grace...."** (I Corinthians 3:1). **Everyone who studies the Word of God** with a Holy Spirit enlightened eye **knows** that there is in the Word, such **a doctrine as "growth in grace."** **Peter says expressly,** "Grow in grace, and in the knowledge of our Lord and Savior Jesus Christ" (II Peter 3:18) **The faith of the Thessalonians** was said "to grow exceedingly" (II Thessalonians 1:3). And thus **we read of degrees of faith,** from **"little** faith" (Matthew 6:30), **"weak** faith" (Romans 14:1), **"as a grain** of mustard seed," (Matthew 17:20) **to "great** faith," (Matthew 15:28) **"strong** faith" (Romans 4:20), **"fullness** of faith," (Acts 6:8) and **"full assurance** of faith" (Hebrews 10:22).

"When the scriptures speak of "growth in grace," they are speaking of an **increase** in the degree, size, strength, vigor, and **power of the graces** which the **Holy Spirit plants** in a believer's heart at conversion. I hold that every one **of** those **graces** admits **of growth,** progress, and increase. I hold that repentance, faith, hope, love, humility, zeal, courage, and the like may be little or **great,**

strong or weak, vigorous or feeble, and may vary **greatly** in the same man at different periods **of** his life.

> **"Be strong in the grace that is in Christ Jesus"**
> (II Timothy 2:1) for **"it is good for the heart to be**
> **strengthened by grace"** (Hebrews 13:9 BSB)

Peter was careful to put **growth in grace before growth in knowledge** and **to identify** the **Person** of the **Lord Jesus Christ** as the proper content of **spiritual knowledge.** That one whose **growth in knowledge** precedes a **growth in grace,** and whose growth in **knowledge** consists only of a growing mass of **scriptural facts** becomes divisive, judgmental, and ever smaller in his knowledge of Christ. **Such a** one is **constantly finding "new things"** which he then **injects** into a continually growing mass of knowledge which he feels is **necessary before one can truly be saved.**

But that **one** whose **growth in knowledge** is a **product** of a **growth in grace** understands that the fact that believers do grow **in knowledge is proof** of the fact that complete **knowledge is not necessary** for **justifying faith.**

> **The man who has nothing more than a kind of**
> **Sunday religion - whose Christianity is like his**
> **Sunday clothes put on once a week, and then laid**
> **aside - such a man cannot, of course, be expected**
> **to care about growth in grace** - J.C. Ryle.

"When I speak of a Christian 'growing in grace,' I mean simply this -- that **His sense of sin** is becoming deeper, **His faith** stronger, **His hope** brighter, **His love** more extensive, **His spiritual-mindedness** more marked. **He feels** more **of** the power **of godliness** in his own heart. **He manifests** more **of** it in his life. **He is going** on from **strength** to strength, from **faith** to faith, and from **grace** to grace. **I deem** the **truest** and **best account** of such a **man's condition** is this, he is **growing** in **grace"** - J. C. Ryle.

The very idea of "growth in grace" implies **strengthening, advance, growth, progress, increase. Lambs** grow up into sheep, **vine buds** into vine branches, (John 15:5), small **plants** into trees (Isaiah 17:10; 61:3), **sons** into fathers (1 Timothy 1:18, 5:1). **Christians are not gate-posts,** but palm trees and cedars (Psalm 92:12), **not loungers** but soldiers, **warring** a good warfare;

(1 Timothy 1:18), **not idlers** at home on armchairs and sofas, **but travelers** and **pilgrims** seeking a country; **not careless,** and at ease.

In the last chapter we studied the results of **two words: Redemption** and **Justification** ... and how we received, as Christians, the **release from the slavery** of **Sin** and **Acquittal. To be justified** means to be **acquitted,** to gain a **right standing. Justification frees** the guilty man from paying the just penalty for his sin. **It declares that he is totally exonerated.** All charges are dropped.

This acquittal is absolutely free because it is **based on the unmerited favor (grace) of God.** God decided to **set man free,** arranged **a plan** by which He could **justify the guilty** and still remain a moral being, and then carried it out.

This is so hard for us to believe. We would **prefer to work** for our salvation. But **God's gift of salvation costs us nothing,** even **though it cost his Son everything.**

Jesus paid a debt He did not owe. **I owed a debt** I could not pay. The **Lord now says** to us, **"Take my payment for you by faith!** It's yours for **free. I have paid your debt for you."**

In today's Holy Scripture, (verse 8 above) ... **Paul had just prayed for his thorn** to be removed. The Lord's answer was this: **"My grace is sufficient for thee ..."** The word **"sufficient"** means **"to be possessed of unfailing strength; to be enough to overcome."**

The Lord is telling Paul, **"Paul, I know you have a big task to accomplish. I called you** to that task. **I know you feel weak and inferior** for the need. **But, Paul, you need to know that I have the power you lack. You** will **never** be enough, **but I am always enough!"**

How many times have we **looked at our situation** and said, **"If only this problem was solved** or **this thing** over here was somehow different, **then I could** really serve the Lord!" Or, **"If I could just feel better,** I could do something for Jesus." Or, **"If my husband or wife was only saved,** it would be so much easier for me to serve the Lord." Or, **"Oh, I wish I was younger, or smarter, or more talented,** then I could be used by God."

LISTEN: The problem with that kind of thinking is that it is all **wrapped up in self** and **what self can do!** It says, **"I am all I need** and **if I** could just work out a few little details, then **I could** be so much more." **In truth, we are nothing** and we **can do nothing** without Jesus! **When you are redeemed** and you are **walking in** the **will** of the Lord, then you are **right where He** has put you, problems and all (Psalm 37:23; Psalm 40:2).

What we all need to learn and **understand** is the truth that **we will never be enough,** but **He is** always **more** than enough, (Ephesians 3:20)! **What the Lord says to Paul, He says to us, and we must learn:** "I am in control! I will meet your need and I will take care of you!"

God's Word teaches that "my grace is sufficient". Grace is "the undeserved love and favor of God". For you Christian, He always **gives grace to support** you, **strengthen** you, and **sustain** you regardless of **what you may face** before you get out of this life! **What God did for others,** He will do for you! There will be **grace to stand** for Him, **grace to serve** Him, **grace to live** for Him, **grace to die** for Him, **grace to face** life for Him. **There will be grace,** amazing, matchless, **marvelous grace** for every bump in the road of life!

> **Marvelous, infinite, matchless grace, Freely bestowed**
> **on all who believe; All who are longing to see His face,**
> **Will you this moment His grace receive?** (J. Johnston)

The apostle John says of Jesus: "For of His fullness we have all received, and **grace upon grace** (upon grace)" (John 1:16.NASB). **There is never a shortage of the grace** of God, **the resource** of God.

When the Lord says that His "**strength is made perfect in weakness**", it simply **means that God gets more glory** from using the **weak things** of the world than He does by using the things of greatest strength and power (1 Corinthians 1:27).

All Christians need grace for times of **testing** and **opposition** as well as for **serving.** When such times come, **"He giveth more grace"** (James 4:6). **He gives strengthening grace** and **sufficient grace** for every need.

The word, **"power,"** is in the **third phrase of verse 9. The power of God is expressed** through human weakness, "…for power is perfected in weakness." **This may be hard to understand but** the reality is **God does allow difficulty** into our lives so that in our weakness, **we will learn to depend on His strength,** to be receptive to **what He wants** to give us, His resources. **This is a continuing, life-long process … a part of our sanctification in Christ.**

> **Paul stated: II Corinthians 12: 9, "And He said unto me,**
> **My grace is sufficient for thee: for my strength (power)**
> **is made perfect in weakness"** (II Corinthians 12:9).

What did Paul mean when He said – "My strength is made perfect in weakness?" The word 'strength' means power or ability. **Christ's power and ability is perfect.** Christ is God and therefore everything about Christ is perfect. **How then is His strength made perfect in weakness?** The word 'perfect' as it is used here comes with the thought of **bringing something to 'completion'** ... **'fulfillment'** - if you will. **Christ possesses a perfect strength,** yet His perfect strength cannot be fully realized unless there is a need. **Christ allows needs in our lives,** needs that are beyond our ability to handle, **so that He might demonstrate the glory of His power** and **strength.**

Literally, the phrase is translated, "My power is being **made perfect** in your weakness." **Strength that is confident in itself** to be strong is weakness in God's economy, but **weakness that knows itself to be** weak is actually strength.

> **"As every man hath received the gift, even so minister the same one to another, as good stewards of the manifold grace of God"** (1 Peter 4:10).

The Bible speaks of the **"manifold" grace of God.** What does that mean? **It means** we can **experience God's grace** in many ways. For instance, **there is singing grace.** When **Paul** and **Silas** were **in prison, not knowing what** was going to happen to them. **God gave them grace to sing** (Acts 16:25).

There is speaking grace. Colossians 4:6 says, **"Let your speech** be **always with grace,** seasoned with salt, that ye **may know how ye ought to answer** every man." **God will give you** the **ability to talk** about your troubles **with His grace.**

God also gives us strengthening grace. Young **Timothy** was **often sick** with many **infirmities.** Paul **told him to** "be strong in the grace that is in Christ Jesus" (II Timothy 2:1). **We all need "Strengthening grace!"** Spend time in the **Word of God** today and **extract** from the **manifold grace of God.**

Douglas MacArthur once said, **"You are as young** as your faith, **as old as** your doubts, **as young as** yourself with confidence, **as old as** your fears, **as young as** your hope, **as old as** your despair." **God gives His unfading strength** for His increasing promises.

> **"Life is hard. God is good. Glory is coming. Therefore, stand firm in His grace."** – John Piper

Do you know where one of the **great strengths of a church lies?** In its **seniors** who have **walked with God** for years. With their **reservoir of wisdom**

and **fortress of faith,** they **get hold of God,** and **though their bodies** are wearing a bit, they are as **strong as they ever were** - because **God is their strength.**

By allowing or by making Paul weak, **God could display His power and strength!** This may **sound like a paradox,** but it is true! **God gets far more glory** out of **weaker vessels!**

For example: look at the **disciples.** They **were ordinary,** weak men, but **God used them to alter the world** for His glory! **Look at the church,** ordinary, weak, flesh and blood, but **it is the vehicle God has chosen** to **do His work** in this world. (1 Corinthians 1:26).

> **"You then, my child, be strengthened by the grace
> that is in Christ Jesus"** (II Timothy 2:1, BSB)

Christian, have **you ever had** the **bedeviling sense** that everyone **wants something from you?** Maybe it is **a friend.** Your **boss?** Your **spouse?** Some **friend?** Perhaps you've **dreamed** of cutting off your **phone,** unplugging all **media,** and going) a **vacation** to hibernate. **Maybe then** the **demands** would **stop** and you'd have **time to refresh** and **return** with a **smile in your heart.**

Do you get annoyed continually always **trying** to please others? **The truth is: human beings can't** meet **one another's needs** all the time. **That's God's job.** And **because of** the **loving sacrifice of Jesus,** you're free to **admit your limitations** and **rely on His grace** to adjust **unreasonable expectations.** Although it sounds too good to be true, **God makes no unfair demands** of you. **He just wants your faith** – a grace-filled faith that **He strengthens** as you **release to Him** your **unrealistic need** to do it all.

Therefore, when the Lord allows the thorns (perhaps trials and troubles, unwarranted requests) to **pierce** you and **when He allows the trials and sufferings of life to buffet you,** remember that **He has a plan** and He is getting glory out of your weakness. **You may never know, this side of eternity,** just how the Lord used your pain for His glory! You see, **God has a plan for all you are going through,** or you wouldn't be in it! **Someone is watching,** or **God is working** through it some way for His Own glory!

By mercy and grace, just like **He did with Paul, God** will **allow** this **buffeting** and **suffering** to His **body** to finally **bring us to the place of saying,** "God, we can't do this without you!" To **finally bring us to the place** where we, in humility, go back to **prayer again.**

**"As your days, so shall your strength
be"** (Deuteronomy 33:25)

God says, I have to make you weak first, so you **can be strong** because **your strength** is **not** in yourself! **Your strength is in Me; it's in the power of My Spirit** within your life. But **it only comes** when **we are out of the way.** It's the **ultimate irony** in a sense, **when we become weak,** we **become strong.**

Many Christians know the story of Fanny Crosby - blinded at the **age of five** by a wrong **prescription** given by a doctor. But, **in her 90 years of darkness** she **penned** some **8,000 gospel** hymns. **Her pain has brought more glory** to the **grace** and **mercy** of God than she ever could have imagined! **She had** an **inner joy** that others **couldn't see** from the **outside.**

As Paul closes His thoughts in this passage, he reminds us that the **thorns and buffetings of life** are not in vain. There is **much benefit** to be derived from the pains we endure in life. **Of course, Paul does say, " …for Christ's sake."** The things he endured were **not the result of foolish decisions** on his part. He was suffering for Jesus!

In my Texas transliteration of the Greek, Paul says, "It doesn't make sense, but when I am at my weakest after the flesh, I am the strongest spiritually!"

"…the joy of the Lord is your strength" (Nehemiah 8:10). **Where do** the **saints get their joy?** If we did not **know some Christians well,** we might think from just **observing them** that they have **no burdens** at all to bear. **But we must lift the veil** from our eyes. **The fact that the peace,** light, and **joy of God** is in them is proof that a burden is there as well. **The burden** that **God places** on us **squeezes the grapes** in our lives and **produces the wine,** but most of us **see only the wine** and **not the burden. No** power on earth or in **hell** can **conquer the Spirit of God living within the human spirit;** it creates an **inner invincibility.**

If your life is producing only a whine, instead of the wine, then ruthlessly **kick it out.** It is **definitely a crime for a Christian** to **be weak in God's strength.**

My, what a truth! When **we are broken by the buffetings** of life, we are **brought to a place** where God can move in us, on us and through us in extraordinary ways! **Do you want the power of God to rest upon your life?** Then, **prepare to hurt!** You see, God will not share His glory with another (Exodus 20:5)!

As you read these verses, Paul uses words like **"most gladly, glory, take pleasure".** Paul's sufferings, **had taught him how to praise the Lord.** You see,

Paul was seeing beyond the thorn and beyond the buffeting. He was seeing the power and the glory that was coming because of what he was facing! That is **why he had peace and could praise the Lord** in the middle of his buffeting!

Christian, when we come to the place (and you can), where we can see **our trials** from **God's perspective,** then our whole outlook will be altered. **We will stop seeing our situation** as being hard, harsh and difficult, but we will understand that it is God's perfect plan for our life. **We will see that He is working out His will in us.** We will see that **He is getting glory.** We will **learn to yield** to Him and His will for our lives. When we get to that place, **then the Lord can work through us** and our situation in ways we never imagined!

Paul learned to boast only in "weakness," the third element as shown in the **last phrase** in **verse 9** (above), "Most gladly, therefore, I will rather boast (glory) about my weaknesses, that the power of Christ may dwell in me." **Notice the incredible humility here.**

Let me paraphrase: Paul is saying, "I am going to remind myself of **who I really am in Christ,** the need to **rely on Him** and **His resources.** Then I will understand who I can be and what I can do in life. I am **only going to boast in my weaknesses,** in times of apparent failure, in times when I don't think I do very well. **That is what I want to boast about because** those are the times that the **power** of God and the **glory** of God will be most clearly revealed to people."

Ron Artest, a forward for the LA Lakers, was known as one of the **most aggressive** and **violent players** in the **NBA.** Hoping to **change his reputation,** in 2011, **he legally changed his name to Metta World Peace.** He thought the crowd and the Media would **think better** of him with **a peaceful name. That didn't change his behavior,** though. Just a **few months later** he was **ejected from a game** for **violently elbowing James Harden** in the face. **You can call yourself** world peace, **but unless** you **repent** and take **Jesus as your Lord,** you'll **never find inner peace … no peace** in the **world, without** the **Prince of peace.**

Is it possible to **possess true inner peace?** One **woman wrote:** "My **therapist** told me the **way to achieve** true inner peace **is to finish what I start.** And so far today, I have **finished 2 bags of chips** and a **chocolate cake … And I feel better already.**"

A man was leaving church one Sunday and **said to his pastor,** "Your **message today reminded me** of the peace and mercy of God." **The pastor said,** "Why, thank you." The **man said,** "Don't thank me. It was **like the peace** of God because it passed all understanding, and it was **like the mercy** of God because it seemed to endure forever!"

When bewilderment engulfs you and despair looms at your door, when trials storm the beaches of your life and seems to erode them from you, you may want to ask God, "Why? Why?"

> "He is no fool who gives what he cannot keep, to
> gain that which he cannot lose." - Jim Elliot

Friend, you may never fully understand why things are happening the way they are in your life, but that's not your job. You see, it is not necessary for you to know why. That is God's question. Your response is all that matters. There times when we can't feel His hand, we must trust His heart. Our job is to simply 'trust' and 'obey!' Is there something happening in your life for which you have no explanation, but long for answers? Ask God to give you grace to trust Him ... now!

Christian, are you being buffeted right now? Are the cruel and unkind blows of life landing on you, leaving you bleeding, bruised and battered before the Lord? Are you being pained and grieved by the cruel, sharp thorns of physical, emotional or spiritual affliction? If you are, then just let me remind you that God's promises are still true! "His mercies are new every day," (Lamentations 3:21-22)!

"May grace and peace be multiplied to you ..." (I Peter 1:2). The way to have peace is to have grace; grace is the breeder of peace; the one is the root, the other the flower. Peace is the sweet water which distills from a gracious heart. The order: first grace, then peace; grace has the priority. Grace and peace are two sisters - but grace is the elder sister; and give me permission at this time to prefer the elder before the younger. "May grace be multiplied to you ..." "Grace and peace be multiplied unto you through the knowledge of God, and of Jesus our Lord," (II Peter 1:2, KJV).

> The human spirit fills with hope at the sound
> of the encouraging word of grace!

"With great power the apostles continued to testify to the resurrection of the Lord Jesus, and much grace was upon them all." (Acts 4:33). It wasn't just 'grace,' it was 'much grace.' in other words, a multiplied dimension of Grace. The grace of God was multiplied in their lives and when this happened, lack disappeared from their midst.

Grace here is taken in a genuine and proper sense. "**May grace** be multiplied to you." Let me give you this description: **grace is the infusion of a new and holy principle into the heart, whereby it is changed from what it was - and is made after God's own heart. Grace does not make** a moral change only - **but a sacred one;** it biases the soul heavenward - and **stamps** upon it **the image** and superscription of God.

**Any work that God calls us to, He will
empower us to do it - by his grace.**

Grace has a 'soul-strengthening' Excellency. **Grace enables the Christian to do** that which **exceeds** the power of our own abilities. **Grace teaches us** to **eradicate** (erase) our sins, **to love** our enemies - and **to prefer the glory of Christ** before our own lives. Thus the **three Hebrew children** in Daniel, **by the power of grace, marched** in the face of death; **neither the sound of the music** could allure them—**nor the heat of the furnace frighten them** (Daniel 3:17).

Grace is a Christian's armor, which does more than any other armor can—it **not only defends** him, but **puts courage into him. Grace makes us** not only bear suffering - **but rejoice** in suffering (Romans 5:3). **The Christian who is fortified and enthusiastic with grace,** can tread upon the lion and adder (Psalm 91:13), and **with the monster** can laugh at the shaking of a spear (Job 41:29). Thus does **grace inspire a heroic spirit** and **drive strength** into a man - allowing him to act above the sphere of nature.

God's grace has to cover whatever He calls us to do. Christian, examine yourself: **do any of these words describe your walk with the Lord:** Burdened. Stressed. Heavy laden. Mentally drained. Physically fatigued. **These are the outcomes** whenever we re-double **our fleshly efforts to please God.** They're clear **signs that the law, not God's grace,** is in operation. **Now consider these words:** Obligated. Dutiful. Indebted. Guilty. Ashamed. Condemned. **Do these words describe someone who has been set free?**

The apostle Paul wrote, "The Holy Spirit also **helps** our weakness; for **we do not know how to pray** as we should, but the **Spirit Himself intercedes** for us with **groanings too deep** for words; and **He who searches the hearts knows** what the mind of the Spirit is, because **He intercedes for the saints** according to the will of God" (Romans 8:26-27 NASB).

Do you need to come before Him today **to get grace for your race? Do you need quit worrying** about the marathon, and plan for the sprint. **Do you**

need help for your valley of sorrow? **Do you need to find** that **mental healing** in your pain? If you do, I want you to come before the Lord right now.

Christian, for your spiritual maturity, I want **you to stop asking** Him "**Why?**" I want you to get before Him and **ask Him to show you what He is doing** in your life. I want you to **ask Him for grace** to praise Him "**in**" your buffetings. I want you to **bow before the Lord** and **thank Him for your thorn. You may be tempted** to say, "**I can't do that!**", then you need to come and ask Him to **help you reach** that place.

Listen, none of us have arrived! This is hard for me too, **but part of healing our hurts** is coming to the place where **we yield to God** and **to what He is doing** in our lives. This altar is open; **bring your thorn to Him right now!**

The grace of Christ is thus truly **abounding grace,** for "God is able to make **all grace abound** toward you" (II Corinthians 9:8). **It is even giving grace,** and we should "**abound in this grace** also" (II Corinthians 8:7). Therefore, **we should continually:**

"...**grow in grace,** and in the **knowledge** of our Lord."

When we grow in grace, we **can't pick** and we **don't choose** our areas of obedience. **As children of our Father** we're all **required** to do **what the Lord calls** us to do. **When Jesus says we are to be** born again, **to have** faith, **to study** His Word, **to pray** and **to seek** his face, **to love** our neighbor, **to love** our wife as Christ loves the church, **the answer** to **His** every **command** is "**yes and amen.**"

We notice however, that **some churches** prefer **certain areas of obedience** over others. **They emphasize** evangelism, **or** social justice, **or** political activism, **or** serving the poor, **or** prayer. They may not admit it, but they see other churches' emphases as lesser than theirs.

No Christian, **no** group, and **no church is pleasing** to God when it **runs on one cylinder** instead of the **eight it possesses.** He simply **won't allow us** to ignore certain of his commands. **Notice in Revelation 3** to get a picture of **Jesus displeasure** when we do that. **Any person or church** who **isn't obeying** God's commands is living in disobedience - **no ifs, ands or buts!**

Paul wrote, "**To Titus, mine own son after the common faith: Grace, mercy, and peace, from God the Father and the Lord Jesus Christ our Savior**" (Titus 1:4).

This is **part of a lengthy greeting to Titus by Paul** at the beginning of this very **practical book** which has **many nuggets** contained therein, and it is well worth our study.

Paul greets Titus with "grace, mercy, and peace." Grace is a manifestation of God's love toward **undeserving rebels** (you and me), resulting in forgiveness and blessing. **The Word of God states,** "Being **justified freely by his grace** through the redemption that is in Christ Jesus" (Romans 3:24).

Mercy is the attitude and attribute of God toward those who are in distress. "Let us therefore **come boldly unto the throne of grace,** that we may **obtain mercy,** and **find grace** to help in time of need" (Hebrews 4:16).

Peace comes as a result of the **restoration** of harmony between God and the forgiven one. "Therefore being **justified** by faith, we have **peace** with God **through** our Lord Jesus Christ" (Romans 5:1).

This threefold blessing comes from both "God the Father and the Lord Jesus Christ our Savior." **What a comfort** to recognize both Father and Son as involved in the **bestowing of all aspects of our salvation ... through His grace.**

PRAYER- Help us, O Lord, **to look on the bright side of things;** not on the dark cloud, but **on Your rainbow of covenant mercy;** not on the stormy waters, **on the face of Jesus;** not on what You have taken, or withheld, **on what You have given and are giving.** Lord, **enable us to realize** Your all-sufficiency. In the precious, powerful name of Jesus, **we praise You for hearing** and **answering** our petitions. For Jesus sake, **AMEN!**

> **"The grace of our Lord Jesus Christ be with**
> **you all. Amen."** (Philippians 4:23).

Chapter 6

God Made Me 'SOMEBODY' With His Grace

"HE (GOD) **PREDESTINED** us to **adoption** as sons through Jesus Christ to Himself, according to the kind intention of **His will, to the praise of the glory of His grace** (literally: to His glorious grace), which **He freely bestowed on us in the Beloved.** In Him we have **redemption** through **His blood,** the **forgiveness** of our trespasses, **according to the riches of His grace**" (Ephesians 1:5-7 NASB).

The incredible grace of God is **a gift we don't deserve.** Yet, because of the work of the cross, **it is a gift given to us freely. In it we find** forgiveness, mercy, redemption and love. **Through grace we** have hope, the new birth, eternal life, and the ability to receive God's gifts. **That is the power of grace.**

> "Whereof **I was made a minister,** according to the **gift of the grace of God** given unto me by the effectual working of **His power.** Unto me, who **am less** than the least of all saints is **this grace** given, that I should preach among the **unsearchable riches of Christ**" (Ephesians 3:7-8 ASV).

The incredible grace of God is **a gift we don't deserve.** Yet, because of the work of the cross, **it is a gift given to us freely. In it we find** forgiveness, mercy, redemption and love. **Through grace we** have hope, the new birth, eternal life, and the ability to receive God's gifts. **That is the power of grace.**

> "Marvelous, infinite, matchless grace, Freely bestowed on all who believe; All who are longing to see His face, Will you this moment His grace receive?" (J. Johnston)

The grace of God is peculiarly **illustrated** and **glorified** in the **plan of redemption** by Christ Jesus. **By the giving of the Law, God's justice** and **holiness** were rendered most glorious; **by the giving** of the Gospel, **His grace** and **mercy** are made equally conspicuous. **Grace is the only foundation of hope** for man. If **mankind** were **left to himself,** all the **race would reject God's grace,** and the offers of mercy and grace would perish.

> **"God loves you just as you are, and not as you**
> **should be, because you could never be as you**
> **should be without His grace."** – Glenn Clifton

Bob Dylan sang a song more than **25 years ago** that actually **could have come from this Scripture:** "You gotta serve somebody. It may be the devil or it may be the Lord but you're gonna have to serve somebody." **Christian, you and I were made to serve Somebody ... our Almighty God.** That leads to a couple questions. **Who or what are you serving?** Are you **serving sin or** are you **serving the Savior?** Remember: how we live, and who we serve ... reveals **who our Lord is** because **we are slaves** to the **One we obey.**

In **Verse 1 of Ephesians 3,** Paul tells us that he is "**the prisoner of Jesus Christ."** Remember, **when Paul wrote this,** he **was imprisoned** by the Romans on **charges made** by the **Jews.** Yet, **Paul did not see himself as the prisoner** of either Rome or of Judaism; Paul understood that he was **there by the grace and will of God.** Paul was **the prisoner of Christ.** He was **in prison by the grace of God,** for the **glory of God,** for the good of the church, the body of Christ. **What does this mean,** and **how** do you **reconcile this** with the teachings of our day?

Grace is the most beautiful, picturesque word in the Bible, other than Jesus. Grace is **why God loves us** when there is nothing lovely about us. **We are not loved because we are valuable.** We are valuable only **because we are loved. I John 4:10 says,** "Herein is love, not that we loved God, but that He loved us, and sent his Son to be the propitiation for our sins."

This verse **emphasizes "the Beloved."** He (God) has graciously favored us through the Beloved. **"In the Beloved"** must certainly mean **in Christ,** Who is termed God's beloved Son (Matthew 3:17). **God has chosen us in Him,** and it is **through Him** that **these mercies have** been **conferred on us.**

> **"Your potential is the sum of all the possibilities**
> **God has for your life."** –Charles Stanley

Grace has made me somebody because of God's 'soul-ennobling' excellence. **Grace ennobles** a man. **Grace makes us vessels** of honor; **it sets us above** princes and nobles. **Theodosius the Great** (AD 395), was the **last Roman emperor** to rule over of the Roman Empire. **He thought** it **more dignity to be Christ's servant,** and wear His livery laced with the **silver graces** of the Spirit - **than to be great** and **renowned** in the world. **Isaiah 43:4 states,** "Since you were precious in My sight, you have been honorable."

**We cannot change the past, but God is
changing us for the future** (Anon).

Personally, **I had other plans for my career** (family and financial) **before I received** a personal **"call to preach" or to** be a **"full-time" minister** (teacher, preacher, evangelist, or missionary) **through** the **unction** of **His grace** and the **convicting leadership** of the **Holy Spirit of God.** Therefore, **because of God's Spirit** and through **His written Word,** I can faithfully say **that a true minister of the Word** is one who has **been "made or molded."** I was **not a minister** because I was **ordained by a Church,** or **trained at a Seminary** but 'called' and 'made' by GOD.

**"And I thank Christ Jesus our Lord, who hath
enabled me, for that he counted me faithful,
putting me into the ministry"** (1 Timothy 1:12)

The testimony of a **changed life** is perhaps the **best evidence** that **God is alive** and **active today.** At salvation, **I was a dead slave to sin!** Jesus **quickened me** (gave me life), and **a new nature.** This is the only rational explanation **for one who lives in victory** and **power** after a **lifetime** of **spiritual defeat.**

Let me give you a Biblical example: Do you remember when **the Apostle Paul is first mentioned** in your **Bible?** God first **introduces us** to him **as Saul** at the **stoning of Stephen** (Acts 7:58). Here we see his passion for the **Jewish traditions** and **hatred of Christianity** caused him to **wreak "havoc of the church,** entering into every house, and **hauling off men and women** committed them to **prison,** or to their **execution"** (Acts 8:3).

This was not **just casual opposition,** for he was **"breathing out threatening's** and **slaughter** against the **disciples of the Lord"** (Acts 9:1). **He was a "blasphemer,** and a **persecutor** (not only of Christians, but of Christ Himself - Acts 9:5), and **injurious"** (1 Timothy 1:13).

However, "Christ Jesus came into the world to save sinners; of whom I (Paul) am chief" (1 Timothy 1:15), **Paul said. He** "obtained mercy" (v. 13), **not receiving** the **punishment** he **deserved,** through "the grace of our Lord (Who) was exceeding abundant with His grace, faith** and **love** which is in Christ Jesus" (v. 14), **even though** he was **not even seeking God** (Acts 9:1-5).

Listen: God has worked that **same work of grace** in **my** life **that now belongs to Jesus,** to a **greater or lesser degree.** Paul called himself the **chief of sinners,** but **as I examine myself,** I have **been capable of equally sinful acts. Through His grace, I am not only rescued from** the **addiction to sin,** but **transformed** and **empowered** and **given,** as we see in our text, **missions to accomplish** that are of eternal significance. **Let us "thank Christ Jesus our Lord"** with the **apostle Paul.**

"I do not nullify the grace of God" (Galatians 2:21 NASB).

Let me briefly clarify: **In 1940,** I **lost my footing** as a **little boy** in the **undertow** on the **beach** in Long Beach, California, **I felt** as if I was **being dragged** out to the **middle of the ocean** in an undercurrent. It was **a terrifying thing.** I tried to get my bearings and figure out **which way was up.** But I **couldn't get my feet** on the **sand** and the **current** was **too strong** as I was just learning to swim. **As I came up,** I was screaming, and **my daddy ruined a new suit pulling me out** of the water. (Do I remember this? NO! But, my daddy never let me forget it).

When **I felt my daddy's hand take hold** of my upper arm **like a mighty vice grip,** it was the **sweetest feeling** in the world. I yielded entirely to **being overpowered by his strength.** I reveled in being **picked up at his will. I did not resist.**

It didn't enter my mind that I should try to show that things aren't so bad; **or that I should add my strength** to my **daddy's arm.** All **I thought** was, Yes! I **need you! I thank you! I love your strength!** I love **your initiative!** I love **your grip! In that spirit of yielded affection,** one **cannot boast.** I call that yielded affection **"faith."** And **my daddy** was the **embodiment** of the **future grace** that **I craved** under the water. **This is the faith that magnifies grace.**

In 1956, I had my chest caved in, (ribs separated from my sternum), in a freak **football accident** in Ranger Junior College. Every breath **brought pain** during my week in the Hospital. I've had a few **broken fingers, nose** (twice) in boxing sparing with a friend.

In 1958, I fell down a **two story** flight of **metal stairs** at **Pure Milk Company,** tearing my **heel off my foot,** one afternoon. This was where I was working **after graduation** from Baylor University (paying off my school debt) in Waco, Texas. This was done before leaving in 1958 as a **Church Planter in California.** (We called it **'Pioneer Missions'** in that day).

In 2005, I had open-heart, quadruple by-pass surgery after a **heart attack** while driving home. My wife drove directly into the **Emergency Entrance** at Lawnwood Hospital. A couple of hours later, I was **on the table** for **surgery.**

In 2016, a few months ago, I had a **bleeding cancer tumor removed** from the **inside** back wall of **my stomach.** Doing fine now, except for a few chemo pills. (Read Dedication).

You may be asking yourself, "What's **the point** in these stories?" **First,** you're **never** too old, or **never** too young **to give your life to Jesus,** completely. **Second, you never know** when it is your appointed time to die. **Third,** it's **never too late** to win, **even** when **you are down** in the last of the fourth quarter. **Fourth,** when you **are "in Christ," nothing** can **nullify** that **relationship** with our **Eternal God, who gives us eternal life.**

As we ponder how to **live the Christian life,** the uppermost thought should be: **How can I 'magnify' rather** than 'nullify' the **grace of God?** Paul **answers this question** in Galatians 2:20–21, **"I have been** crucified **with Christ.** It is **no longer I that live,** but **Christ living in me.** And **that life which I now live in** the flesh **I live in the faith the faith which is in** the Son of God, Who **loved** me and gave Himself for me" (ASV). **I do not nullify the grace** of God. **Why does my life** not **nullify** the **grace** of God? Because **I live by faith** in the Son of God. **Faith calls all attention to grace** and **magnifies it, rather** than **nullifying it.**

Let me show you with this Biblical illustration: Indisputably, as the **potter's hands** slowly **fashions a lump of clay** on his **wheel** into a **chosen vessel,** so **a minister** of the Word **is made by the hand of GOD.** By doctrine, reproof and correction furnished for his journey.

This is the **word that came to Jeremiah from the LORD,** "The word which **came to Jeremiah from** the **LORD** saying, **Arise** and **go** down to the **potter's house,** and there I will **announce My words** to you." Then **I went down** to the potter's house, and **there he was, making something** on the **wheel.** But **the vessel** that he was **making of clay was** spoiled in the **hand** of the potter; **so he remade it** into **another vessel,** as it **pleased the potter to make"** (Jeremiah 18:1-6 (NASB).

This is **one of the classic passages** in the Bible where **God reveals how he deals with human lives. God is** the **potter** and we are the **clay. We are the clay on the wheel** and **God is shaping us** into the individual vessels that **He wants us to become. We are** literally **clay** in the Potter's hand. **The clay is completely dependent** on the **potter** to be **fashioned and shaped** as the potter desires. **The potter shapes and molds** the clay; the **clay does not shape** and mold itself. **Clay shaped** by the potter **becomes a useful vessel.** It becomes a **vessel useful** for the **Master's purpose.** The **clay cannot stop the wheel** from spinning and get off. **Everything God does in** our lives, he does to **make us dependent upon Him.**

> **There are no ordinary people, Christians are re-born to be extra-ordinary, "In Christ!"** - G. Clifton

This is a simple, yet profound truth. Just as **the clay is dependent upon the potter** to be shaped, so **also are we dependent upon God** to be shaped. **Romans chapter eight** reveals that we are **being shaped into the image of Jesus.** When we go through a **crisis in life,** God uses it to shape and mold us. Sometimes he **has to pound us into a lump** and start again, but **it is God who is in control.** He desires to **make us** into **vessels useful for His own purposes.**

Much of today's preaching leaves out the fact that "**sin debases and damages** a man." We may not like that, but **Christ tells wicked men** of their **pedigree** in John 8:44: "You are of your father the devil." **An ungracious person** is a vile person. **Nahum 1:14 states,** "You are vile" (NIV). **The Hebrew word for "vile" signifies** to be despicable; **there is nothing so vile** but an **ungracious man** will do it. He is **agreeable** to anything; he is like **wire,** which will be **twisted** any way. He will **snare** his conscience, **stain** his credit, and **run as a slave** after the sinful injunctions of men.

But grace ennobles; and being called of God, he is divinely convicted and inspired, as **he is high born** (1 John 3:1), so he **acts suitable** to his new birth. **He hates whatever is hypocritical** and **sordid. The children of God are called kings and priests** for their **dignity** (Revelation 1:6), **and jewels** for their value (Malachi 3:17).

That, dear friend, is God's amazing grace. We **are justified** freely by His grace **through the redemption that is in Christ** Jesus. **I love Him for His grace.** It is **all Jesus!** It's **not the church.** It's **not good deeds. Amazing grace is in the Lord Jesus Christ.** He **loves** you. He **died** for you. He **arose** from the dead for you. He **reigns** in Heaven for you, **and someday soon** He is **returning** for you! **That's grace freely given you!**

> **Theo' many dangers, toils, and snares, I have**
> **already come, Tis grace brought me safe thus far,**
> **and grace will lead me home.** - (John Newton)

We must remember Paul's life was not controlled by **Rome, or** the **Jews: his life was under the direct, sovereign control of the Lord Jesus Christ.** That is **important information!**

If and **when** you become a **prisoner of the circumstances** and **situations** of your life, **you are going to be miserable. If you allow the actions of other people** to imprison your heart and mind, you are going to have a hard time enjoying your life. However, **when you ever come to the place** where you **fully understand** that **Jesus Christ and Jesus Christ alone** is the controller of your life and destiny, then **you can face any trial,** any **situation,** any **person,** and any **problem with confidence, knowing the Lord is in control.** That is where **Paul was** and where **we need to be** as well.

Paul was given this gift of God's grace to be a servant of the gospel; **elsewhere he tells us that the result** of having that gift. **It was this:** "For if I preach the gospel, I have nothing to glory of: for necessity is laid upon me; for woe is unto me, if I preach not the gospel (1 Corinthians 9:16 ASV)!

This, then, is **the staggering claim every true minister** of the gospel makes. **The God** who made the universe, **the mighty Creator** of the heavens and the earth, **the one who sets** the stars, and **sits among** the stars, those immense galaxies, in space. **Remember that He** has **called** and **gifted Christian men to proclaim his word** to the church and the world, and **that it is by this means God saves** those **whom he has determined shall** spend eternity with him.

Listen to Paul: "**To me,** the very least (deserving) of all saints, **this grace was given** (to me), **to preach** to the Gentiles the unfathomable riches of Christ, and **to bring to light** what is the **administration of the mystery** which for ages has been **hidden in God,** who created all things; **in order that the manifold wisdom of God might now be made known through the church** to the **rulers** and the **authorities** in the heavenly places" (Ephesians 3:8-9, parenthesis mine).

> **"Your potential is the sum of all the possibilities**
> **God has for your life." - Charles Stanley**

Did you remember the **Title** of **this Chapter?** If you do not remember, just turn back a few pages and look. **"God has made me somebody ..."** Listen **Christian,** when you received Jesus as **your Lord** and **Savior, "God made you somebody too!"** You may not ever be a minister, preach the gospel, be a foreign missionary, or a leader in your church ... but **remember,** with God, **you are "always somebody with God and His people."**

Grace has made me somebody because of God's 'soul-raising' Excellency. **Grace is a divine spark** which ascends up to God. **When the heart is** divinely **touched** with the magnet of the Spirit - **it is drawn** up to God. **Proverbs 15:24 states,** "The way of life is above to the wise, that he may depart from hell beneath" (KJV).

Oh friend, **when will we learn** that **grace raises a person above others;** he lives in the **altitudes,** while **others crawl around** on the earth and are **almost buried** in it. **A Spirit-filled Christian,** (listen to this Word), **by the wings of grace, flies aloft;** these **saints mount up** as **eagles** (Isaiah 40:31). **Why is it** that **some** Christians **sour** and **descend,** while **others soar and ascend** through the **heavens** on **quills of strength,** in the **riches of God's grace? A believer is a citizen of heaven;** there he trades by faith ... while he abide on this earth.

God's Grace shoots the heart above the world (Psalm 139:17; Philippians 3:21). **God's grace gives us conformity to Christ** and **communion** with Him. **I John 1:3 states,** "Our fellowship is with the Father - and with His Son Jesus." **A man full of grace has Christ** in his heart and life - **and the world under** his feet! **Grace humbles - yet elevates!**

In our day, **the concept of a man set apart** by the **Mighty One** and the **Holy One to speak out for him** to the church and world **is struggling to survive.** According to the **qualifications** as given in the Bible, **I find most of the men and women occupying the pulpits of the nation** have **never been called by God.** Some reading this may ask, "How dare I stand in such judgment on them like that?" **Simply because the message of the Book of God** they **do not believe** and certainly **do not preach.** Many preach 'about' the Bible, however, they **don't preach "the Bible!"** Since they do **not preach the Word of God,** they **do not preach** the **God** of the **Word.**

A young preacher was called out of a life of sin to **preach** the gospel of Jesus Christ. While **in the pulpit one day,** he received **a note** in which someone **had listed all his past sins.** In addition it read, **"Aren't you ashamed of yourself?** And you're up there **telling people to get right with God!"**

Do you know what the young preacher did? He **read** that note, **bowed** his head **in prayer, stood** up and said, "Ladies and gentleman **I have received**

a note, and **here is what it says.**" Then, **in front** of that **whole crowd, he read every one of those sins.** Then he **said this:** "**Yes,** I am **ashamed of myself** and my **past life,** but I am **not ashamed of my Savior!**" Through **God's grace, and Jesus precious blood,** and **His forgiveness,** I am now what I am, a **new creation** in Christ Jesus, **my Lord and Redeemer** (II Corinthians 5:17).

Why Do Christians Keep Books On Past Sins?

For those reading this: "**What are some past sins** in your life that are **holding you back** from **fully proclaiming** God's power to others?" **Confess** them and **bury them** in the **sea of God's forgetfulness,** and **let Him make you somebody too. Oh, you may remember** all those **awful transgressions ... but my God doesn't.**

> "**As far as the east is from the west, so far hath He removed our transgressions from us**" (Psalm 103:12).

This verse is **a wonderful promise of God.** When we come to Christ, **His forgives us** and **cleanses us** from all sin. **Then why do many Christians** still keep books on themselves? If you have **experienced His salvation through Jesus** ... you need to **recognize** that the **books are closed** on **your account.**

Some Christians I've been around are **always remembering** and **bringing up what God has forgotten.** And on the other hand, **some Christians** are **always forgetting what God wants us to remember.**

Let me **be clear; it's good** for us to **ask God** to **search** our hearts and **to see** if there is any wicked way in us, **according to Psalm 139.** We **need to always** be **transparent with God** and **open** to God, but we **should never keep recording our sins** that **are forgiven and cleansed** by the power of Jesus Christ!

> "**Our** greatest **fear** should **not be of failure, but of succeeding at things in life that don't really matter.**" - Francis Chan

Let me **give you** a **good confession** for you to make **every morning** of your life? When you **have your time with God, make these three confessions.** Say, "**I am forgiven!**", "**I am filled with the Spirit of God,**" and "**I am forever secure in the righteousness of Jesus Christ!**"

Don't let yourself feel guilty for sins
that Christ has already forgiven.

Stop keeping books on your past sins … **sin that has already been forgiven by God. God's Word states, "…and You (God) will cast all our sins** into the **depths** of the **sea"** (Micah 7:19 NASB). **Again, God states,** "For I will **forgive their iniquity,** and their sin **I will remember no more"** (Jeremiah 31:34 NASB). **This is also stated in the New Testament,** "For I will be merciful to their unrighteousness, and their sins and their iniquities will I **remember no more"** (Hebrews 8:12). Isaiah 44:22 **contains the same promise** from God, **"I have blotted out your transgressions** like a cloud and your sins like mist return to me, for I have redeemed you" (ESV). Although **my failing grey matter** remembers - **my God Who has forgiven, forgets! You cannot keep books** on things that the **Almighty has wiped clean and forgotten!**

If God knows all things, how can
He not remember our sins?

The Prophet Isaiah states of God, "I, even **I am He Who blots out your transgressions** for my own sake, and remembers your sins no more (Isaiah 43:25 NIV). The **Hebrew word** for **"blot"** is **"machah"** which can **also be translated as** wipe out, destroy, obliterate. The following verses **also link the verb** with the **blotting out** of sin. **God is able to blot** out, erase and obliterate them so that they are no longer recorded against us. The **Hebrew word** for **"remember"** is **"zakar".** It is used of God **remembering His people** and **His covenants** with His people, Genesis 9:15, "I will remember my covenant …"

God sees the beginning to the end, for He is the
Alpha and Omega, the First and the Last!

May I make a confession here? Although **I believed it,** and often said it, **I now find it perplexing** that some theologians, writers and preachers **say that** God **"forgets"** our sins. **Now here's the question:** How can God **"forget" our sins** when He is **Omniscient** (all-knowing - from the beginning to the end)? He knows **the end from the beginning** and **nothing is hidden Him** in the **past, present or future** (Hebrews 4:13).

Here's the difference, remember: There is a **big difference** between God **"forgetting"** and God **"not remembering".** It **is impossible** for the

Omniscient One to forget anything. I feel it is important to convey that these verses do not say that God "forgets" our sins. It says that He "will not remember" them again. The word 'will' means that God is determined not to remember … not just to forget. Hallelujah to our King!

Hebrews 8:12 states: "For I will forgive their iniquities
and remember their sins no more" (ESV).

God says in the Bible, "I, even I, am the one who wipes out your transgressions for My own sake; and I will not remember your sins" (Isaiah 43:25; 10:17). He chooses never to bring them up again. He doesn't forget because He cannot, but He doesn't remember them either; that is, He will never bring them up again. Why? Because they have been forgiven in His Son Jesus.

We cannot be a Law-man and a Grace-man at the same time. We are fully under grace OR fully under law but not both. To try and live by both will only produce frustration and condemnation.

The main reason why so many Christians are living more of a frustrated, unfulfilled, condemned Christian life is because they are trying to embrace both grace and law and grace and law do not mix any more than oil and water can mix.

Religion engages men into the futile efforts of trying to change himself through self-effort, or by keeping certain laws, but this is not how spiritual change comes. True transformation comes by beholding, believing and resting - in Jesus!

Paul writes: "Moreover the law entered that the offense
might abound. But where sin abounded, grace abounded
much more, so that as sin reigned in death, even so grace
might reign through righteousness to eternal life through
Jesus Christ our Lord" (Romans 5:20-21 WBT).

Grace reigns supreme over law, sin and death. Because God is gracious and the supreme sovereign over His creation, and because He is supreme over law as its Giver and can resurrect whom He chooses, grace is His to give freely as He pleases. Grace is supreme over the others because God has willed it so and gives it to whomsoever He chooses.

One other point: **Jesus told us to forgive** as the **Father has forgiven us** (Ephesians 4:32). If someone **does something wrong against you,** then later **asks for forgiveness** and you **forgive him, you** are **never** supposed to **bring up that offense** again ... ever! Maybe **you won't ever forget** the offense, but then again **you can choose not to remember** it. **This is what real forgiveness means** for those of **us** who have **been forgiven by Jesus.**

What does that mean for us **today?** The devil or **Satan is described** in the New Testament **as "diablos", the accuser.** He will **try to accuse us** or confront us with **former sins that have been forgiven.** Unfortunately, **even some** in the **church may try** to do the same to us. **However God's promise** is that **He chooses not to revisit** those sins again.

Paul did not choose the righteous path through life. In fact, he was a **man of position** and **power, and** of **sin before** he met the Lord Jesus. **When salvation came** to Paul, **along with it came the call** of God to carry the Gospel to the Gentiles.

Paul was called by the **same grace** we are: **Galatians 1:15-16** (NASB) **states,** "But **when God,** who had **set me apart** even from my **mother's womb** and called me **through His grace, was pleased to reveal His Son** in me so that **I might preach Him** among the Gentiles, **I did not** immediately consult with flesh and blood."

In today's verse, (Ephesians 3), **Paul says** that **he "was made a minister"** (Verse 8a WBT). This is the **same Greek word (**Diakonos**)** that is translated "**Deacon**" throughout the New Testament. **It is one who executes the commands of another,** especially of a master, a servant, attendant, minister. **This word always refers** to "**a servant.**" It was **literally used to** describe "**a table waiter.**" What does this mean for you and me?

God made a servant/preacher/teacher out of Paul and sent him out with the Word and the mystery of the Gospel! **It was not Paul's education,** his **family,** his **power,** his **esteem among men,** or **any other thing** that made him a **preacher** of the Gospel. **It was the sovereign grace and will of God!**

Paul acknowledges himself to be "**less than the least of all God's people**" (v.8c, above). **All that Paul was** he owed to the enabling of God. **Like his Savior Paul humbled himself.** **He wasn't the one seeking after God** when he was on the road to Damascus breathing out threats and slaughter against the church.

It was the Lord who came there seeking him, finding him, and **calling** him to spend the rest of his days **serving him, likewise, as we are to serve**

Him. The initiative was all divine. **All the gifts of God** to His children, through the Holy Spirit, **are divine.**

Paul wrote to the church at **Philippi, "for it is God** Who is **at work in you,** both to **will** and to **work** for **His good pleasure"** (2:13 NASB). Because God works and has worked, therefore **man must** and **can work. God producing all,** and **we acting** all. It is **not that God does some,** and we the rest. **God does all,** and **we do all. Let me explain in the long run-on sentence below.**

When God has worked in a man **"to will,"** and not only worked in him "to will," but **also worked in him "to do"** (Philippians 2:13) when he has **made him willing to flee** from the wrath to come (Luke 3:7). Besides **working in him "to will,"** and has **worked in him "to do,"** worked in him **faith** to believe, **hope** whereby **he anchors** in the finished work of Christ, and **love** whereby he **cleaves to him** with purpose of heart; **when all this has been** "with fear and trembling" (Philippians 2:12 KJV).

This great position of the Apostle Paul, the heavenly revelation that came to him, **did not puff him up –did not make him proud** - or as we would say, **"It did not give him the big-head."** But **instead, it humbled his heart.**

"Less than the **least of all God's people"** Those words could come **only from a heart totally** and **entirely possessed by the Holy Spirit** and **surrendered to the will of God.** No other man who ever lived on this earth **was ever more completely surrendered to God's sovereign will** than was the Apostle Paul.

Those words are **by no means atypical** of the New Testament; **Paul elsewhere calls himself the chief of sinners** and **the least of the apostles.** Those words destroy the **insistence of today's popular psychology** that people all need to **enhance their sense of self-worth.**

Today's feel-good, self-esteem, get-rich, never-get-sick, get-a-good-attitude gospel is no Gospel of God. Abraham stated, "I am but dust and ashes." **Jacob stated,** "I am not worthy of the least of all thy mercies." **Job stated,** "Behold I am vile, what shall I answer thee?" **Isaiah stated,** "Woe is me, for I am undone; for I am a man of unclean lips." **The Apostle Peter stated,** "Depart from me for I am a sinful man O Lord." **John the Baptist,** the great **forerunner** of our Savior, **cried out,** "The latchet of his shoes I am not worthy to stoop down and unloose."

Christian, **do you get the point?** While **today's modern psychology** and **positive-minded motivational hype** lead us to **boost our self-esteem, although** it definitely can help you in many ways to increase your goal setting and achievement in today's world ... **self-esteem or self-aggrandizement cannot** and **will not help your spiritual welfare. Why? Self,** in the flesh (selfish), **has a problem** … it is **sin!** And we **must realize** that in ourselves, **in our flesh,** there is **no good thing,** and **we cannot overcome sin by ourselves!**

Unlike many of the pastor/teachers I have been **fortunate** to **know** and **fellowship** with, **the Apostle Paul was not a braggart** and did **not spend time promoting himself.** On that note, **most preachers** I have known, **from time to time,** have **lost their anointing ability and power,** because of **PRIDE.** (I know, because **I have been one).**

When writing to the young preacher, Timothy, Paul declared that he **(Paul)** was **chief of sinners** (I Timothy 1:15b). **Husband and wife** are "**heirs together of the grace of life so that your prayers may not be hindered**" (1 Peter 3:7 KJV).

Christian, please be aware that the **Lord still works** in the lives of His children. **He saves us for a purpose.** He **fashions us to fulfill** that **purpose** for His glory. We need to remember that **God has a will for all of our lives,** and that **everything we face** in life is merely **preparing us to fulfill** the **will** and **plan** of God (Romans 8:28-29).

This is how Paul saw himself. He did **not see** himself **as a man** who was **worthy of honor and esteem.** He saw himself as a **servant of his Lord** and Savior Jesus, and a **servant of the church.** He saw himself as **a man who was under that authority of His Master,** the Lord Jesus Christ.

He understood the truth that were it **not for the grace of God,** he would **still be a lost, a religious Jew.** He **understood that the blood of Jesus,** through the **grace of God,** had **redeemed** him. He was not doing what **he was doing of his own initiative,** but he saw his ministry as "**a gift of the grace of God.**"

As victory came to Paul through God's grace **this same victory comes in our lives** as we learn to focus on the promises of God in His word. Especially as we focus on this promise in Isaiah 43:25, and **as we keep on affirming** that in our minds. Then we are in a position to reject the **accusations of the evil one** by standing on the truth, God's truth found in His word.

What a double blessing to know that God **blots out our transgressions** so **the record** of them is **expunged in His sight,** and that **He chooses not to recall them** or to bring them back against us ever again. With this thought in mind, **every Christian should be prepared for service to our Lord.**

Let me ask you a question, "**What are preachers** and **all servants** of Christ **called** by our God to concentrate on?" **Here is the answer,** "**To preach to the Gentiles the unsearchable riches of Christ**" (v.8d). **Christ has riches** that are "**unsearchable.**" The **book of Job** describes the glories of the heavens and the earth that are **beyond our understanding.**

All the riches of Christ are similar, **too vast to explore,** and **too deep to fathom.** The riches of Christ: they are 'in-explorable,' 'untraceable,' 'unfathomable,' 'inexhaustible,' 'illimitable,' 'inscrutable,' 'infinite' and 'incalculable,' and **beyond any** of our wildest imaginations. **Get the picture? Why** does the **Holy Spirit lead Paul to choose** this word **and why** are Christ's **riches unsearchable?** Answer: **His riches are** unsearchable because of **the spiritual poverty** and **insufficiency** of the vast **multitudes who needed them.**

Let me embellish a bit... The word **"unsearchable"** means **"unfathomable."** That is, **the depths cannot be reached.** Since these riches of Christ are **"unsearchable"** or **"bottomless,"** no one **can fully know or comprehend** all that we have in Him. **A few of the priceless possessions** of the redeemed are **made very clear in** the **Word of God.** You **cannot know them** outside the Word. That is **why we must preach the Gospel in its fullness,** so **that the church** may come to **understand our exalted position** in the Lord Jesus Christ.

Furthermore, **the wisdom, prudence, and knowledge of God are revealed** to us through **His work in us** (I Corinthians 2:9, 10). **All that is necessary** for our "effectual working" (Ephesians 3:7) **is "graced" to us** so that we can "work out (our) salvation" (Philippians 2:12). **We are** "complete in Him" **not the things of flesh** (Colossians 2:10).

Paul said it this way, "But by the grace of God I am what I am: and **His grace which was bestowed upon me** was not in vain; but I labored more abundantly than they all: yet not I, but the grace of God which was with me" (I Corinthians 15:10). Whatever **Paul received** by **grace,** doctrine, reproof, and correction, he obeyed! He went and he did what he was led to do.

Finally, **as Paul says,** even **true Christian leadership is a gift of grace.** "**I was made a minister,** according to the **gift of the grace of God** given unto me by the effectual working of his power. Unto me, who am less than the least of all saints, **is this grace given,** that **I should preach** among the Gentiles the unsearchable riches of Christ" (Ephesians 3:7-8). **We should never forget that all God's blessings come by His grace alone,** and **He gives grace to** the humble, **not** the proud.

Hallelujah! What a blessing! **Hallelujah!** What a great **responsibility for each of us to proclaim** these "unsearchable" riches (blessings) **until He returns** for **His bride,** the **true Church** of Jesus Christ. **Amen!**

Let Us Pray: "Father, I praise you for your Amazing Grace. Father - you are the potter, we are the clay. Mold us and make us after your will, while we are waiting, yielded and still. Jesus, pardon me, **correct** me – but **never leave me** to myself! **Draw** me – or **drive** me; but **never allow me** to live long as a **distance** from you. **O, bring** me to **Your sacred feet,** and let me **wander no more!** I thank you **for giving us Your unlimited grace which** leads us to salvation, **sanctification,** and finally **glorification. In Jesus name ... Amen!"**

"**The Lord Jesus Christ be with your spirit.
Grace be with you. Amen"** (II Timothy 4:22).

hapter 7

God 'SUPPLIES' Me By His Grace

"LET US THEREFORE come boldly unto the **throne** that we may **obtain mercy,** and **find grace** to help **in time of need**" (Hebrews 4:16).

Although **I prefer the KJV,** let me give you **a different translation or transliteration of the Greek,** "Let us draw near **with confidence** to the **throne of grace,** so that **we** may **receive mercy** and **find grace** to help in time of our need."

> "**Wonderful grace of Jesus, Greater than all my sin; How shall my tongue describe it, Where shall its praise begin? Taking away my burden, setting my spirit free, for the wonderful grace of Jesus reaches me**" (H. Lillenas).

As **Christians,** we tend to **think about grace** when it's **connected to our salvation.** But **grace is about much more** than just how we come to Christ. **Our entire Christian walk must be fueled by the grace of God.**

Eternal, uncorrupted, **virtuous grace of our Infinite God united us** by faith to **Grace Incarnate, Jesus,** and **blessed us** in him "with every **spiritual blessing** in the heavenly places" (Ephesians 1:3). **We called in grace** with effect (Galatians 1:6) and given new birth. **Because of grace** unmeasured, boundless, free, now our dead hearts beat and lifeless lungs breathe. Only through **grace do we believe** (Acts 18:27), and **only in grace do we receive** "repentance leading to a knowledge of the truth" (II Timothy 2:25 NASB).

We can do nothing in Him or **for Him** that doesn't ultimately **come from His grace.** The Bible says, "For God is working in you, giving you the desire and the power to do what pleases him" (Philippians 2:13 NLT).

> "**We are all faced with a series of great opportunities brilliantly disguised as impossible situations.**" –Chuck Swindoll

Some years ago a certain poor man spent many years **saving money** to realize his dream of **going on a cruise.** When he **finally saved** the required sum, **he bought a ticket.** Knowing he **could not afford** the extravagant **food on board,** he took what he could afford - **crackers and peanut butter.**

After a few days of observing the other passengers eating **luxurious meals,** his peanut butter crackers became stale and tasteless. **Desperately hungry,** he **begged a porter** to allow him to **work for food.** "Why, sir, didn't you realize **meals are included** with **your ticket? You may eat as much** as you like!"

Unfortunately, lots of Christians live like that man. Not realizing the **unlimited provisions** that are **theirs in Christ,** they munch **on stale scraps.** There's **no need to live like that! Everything we could ever want** or need is **included in the cost of admission** - and the **Savior has already paid it for us!**

There's a single word that encompasses all the riches we find **in Christ:** "grace." What a **magnificent word** it is! **Grace** is used **more than 150 times** in the New Testament **to speak of divine favor bestowed** on **undeserving people. Grace** is the means by which we receive every physical and spiritual benefit. **To fully understand** what God has **done for us** by **His grace,** we must know and **accept the price** that **Jesus paid for our sins. The first time Jesus came** to this earth, **He came as Suffering Servant.**

> "**He was wounded** for our transgressions, **he was bruised** for our iniquities: the **chastisement** of our peace was **upon Him**; and with his stripes we are healed" (Isaiah 53:5 (KJV).

Jesus was acquainted with grief and though **He** Himself **was absolutely sinless,** He died as though He had sinned. **God the Father saw God the Son** as a "sinner" though **Jesus remained free** from His own personal sin. "**For He (the Father) hath made Him (Jesus) to be sin for us, who knew no sin; that we might be made the righteousness of God in Him**" (II Corinthians 5:21 KJV, emphasis mine - GC).

Jesus was completely without sin, but was **seen by God the Father** as if **He had sinned** and **was a sinner,** though **He was not. Jesus came the first time literally to die** on behalf of the world (John 3).

> **God gives His grace, that when we put our cares into His hands, He puts His peace into our hearts.** (G. Clifton)

These outstanding doctrines: God's grace and mercy can be viewed as two sides of the same coin. Grace on one side gives us what we do not deserve; mercy on the other does not give us what we do deserve, and the end result is peace.

"Grace and peace to you from God our father and the Lord Jesus Christ." (Philippians 1:2). Sometimes we read over these words so quickly and glibly, that we miss the meaning. Christian friend, "Eighteen Times" we hear this exact greeting, or some variation of it, in the pages of the New Testament. As you study the Word of God you will often read and hear this greeting ... "Grace and Peace." I caution you not to read to fast you will miss the real meaning of Scripture. Oh, did you know this is the favored greeting ... of the Apostles.

> "The best and most beautiful things in this world cannot be seen or even heard, but must be felt with the heart." -
> Helen Keller

> The Introduction to the last book in your Bible begins, "Grace to you ... and peace from Him Who is and Who was and Who is to come, and from the seven spirits, who are before His throne, and from Jesus Christ, the faithful witness, the firstborn of the dead, and the ruler of the kings of the earth" (Revelation 1:4-5 NASB).

Grace, is often defined as approval we don't deserve or (unmerited favor), is offered freely by God "through the redemption that is in Christ Jesus" (Romans 3:24). It is offered to us only through faith in Christ so that we may clearly understand that it is not obtainable by any adherence or keeping of the law. "For the law was given by Moses, but grace and truth came by Jesus Christ" (John 1:17).

One Sunday a little boy was "acting up" during the morning worship. His parents did their best to maintain some sense of order in the pew but were losing the battle. Finally, the father picked the little boy up and walked sternly up the aisle on his way out. Just before reaching the back door, the little boy called loudly to the congregation, "Please pray for me!" Regardless of what you think about the little boy's theology, he knew he had an immediate need.

The phrase, 'Throne of Grace' is an **oxymoron** of sorts. **Why? To the ancient world,** the 'Throne' of the kingdom was a **forbidding place** of **sovereign authority and judgment.** If you approached a throne and the **king did not** hold out his **scepter** (an ornamental staff of a ruling monarch), you were history! **You definitely would not draw near** to the **throne** for sympathy, especially with a trivial problem. But **here,** under the leadership of the Holy Spirit, **the author calls it the Throne of grace. He makes it clear** that we are **welcome at this Throne.** There **is a reason** for this, that we may **obtain mercy** and **find grace.**

Perhaps, you may be asking, "How can **Almighty God,** who is beyond all the heavens relate to **little old me** and **my problems?"** **The author responds,** "For we do not have a high priest who cannot sympathize with our weaknesses, **but One** who **has been tempted** (tried) in all things as we are, **yet without sin.** (Hebrews 4:15 NAS). **We all need someone** to **sympathize** with our **problems** and **weaknesses without condemning us.**

> "**Our God guarantees to provide everything we need to worship and honor Him with our lives."** - Glenn Clifton

In some degree even unbelievers are fortunate **to benefit** from **God's grace.** Theologians call that "**common grace**" because it is **common to all mankind.** Common grace is **God's continual care** for all **creation, providing for** his creatures' needs. **Through common grace God restrains humanity from** utter debauchery and **maintains order** and **some sense** of beauty, morality, and goodness in society's consciousness.

Christians, however, receive a greater grace (James 4:6). To us **God's grace is inexhaustible** and **boundless,** including all that we have talked in earlier posts about regarding **the all-sufficient provisions of Jesus Christ.**

> "**God has in Himself all power** to defend you, **all wisdom** to direct you, **all mercy** to pardon you, **all grace** to enrich you, **all righteousness** to clothe you, **all goodness** to supply you, and **all happiness** to crown you" - Thomas Brooks

This is one of the **most wonderful statements** about our **Lord** is **that He was "full of grace"** (John 1:14) **and** "of His fullness we have all received, and grace upon grace" (John 1:16 NASB). "Grace upon grace" **speaks of**

accumulated grace - one grace following upon another. **Such grace is ours each day.** It is **supplied, unlimited** and **sufficient** for every need.

Paul **called it** "the abundance of grace" (Romans 5:17), "the riches of (God's) grace" (Ephesians 2:7), **and** "surpassing grace" (2 Corinthians 9:14). **Peter called it the** "manifold" (in Greek, **'poikilos'**, "multifaceted" **or** "multicolored") **grace of God** (I Peter 4:10). He used the **same Greek word in 1 Peter 1:6** with reference to the **various trials believers face.** That's a **wonderful parallel:** God's multifaceted grace **is supplied and sufficient** for **our multifaceted trials.**

Let me illustrate: One day, **a little boy** noticed a sign, **"Puppies for sale."** He asked, **"How much do you want** for the pups, mister?" **"Twenty-five dollars, son."** The boy's **face dropped.** "Well, sir, **could I see them anyway?"**

The man whistled and the **mother dog** came around the corner, followed by **four cute puppies, wagging their tails** and **yipping** happily. Then **lagging behind, another puppy** came around the corner, **dragging one hind leg.**

"What's the matter with that one, sir?" **the boy asked.** "Well, son, that puppy **is crippled.** The **vet took an X-ray** and found that it **doesn't have a hip socket.** It will never be right. The man was surprised when the **boy said,** "That's the one I want. Could I pay you** a **little** each week?" **The owner replied, "But, son,** you don't seem to understand. That **pup will never be able to run** or even **walk right.** He's going to **be a cripple forever. Why would you want** a pup like that?"

The boy reached down and pulled up his pant leg, revealing **a brace.** **"I don't walk too good either mister."** Looking down at the puppy, **the boy continued,** "That puppy is going to need a lot of **love and understanding.** It's **not easy being crippled!" The man, with a tear in his eye, said,** "Here, **you can have** the **puppy for free. I know you'll take good care of him."**

That is a very limited illustration of our **Savior's sympathy (understanding)** for our condition. **When Jesus became a man** and **suffered** all that we experience, **He has compassion** with our weaknesses. **He demonstrated His compassion** many times during His earthly ministry. **His understanding** was not diminished in any way when He ascended into heaven. **We have a completely sympathetic High Priest** at the right hand of God, Whoever **makes intercession for us!** He is **our advocate,** our lawyer, our **go-between** ... between us and our Father in Heaven and ever makes **intercession** for **His children** (Hebrews 7:25).

The natural man (the unsaved non-Christian) **cannot receive** this next statement. **Grace doesn't make demands.** Grace **only gives.** And as I study and understand the Bible, **grace always gives to the wrong person**. What? **We notice** this many times in the Gospels: **Jesus is always giving to the wrong people** - prostitutes, tax collectors, half-breeds, drunkards, adulterers. The **most extravagant sinners of Jesus's day receive his most compassionate welcome**. And, how we ought to rejoice in that!

Grace is a divine offensiveness that stands caution on its head. **Why?** Because it **makes people think**, (if they are willing). It **refuses to play it safe** and lay it up. **Grace is recklessly generous,** uncomfortably uninhibited. **It doesn't keep score.**

Grace works without requiring anything on our part. It's **not expensive.** It's **not even cheap. It's free, even though it cost God a tremendous price - His only Son.**

Grace refuses to be controlled by our natural sense of fairness, reciprocity, and evenhandedness. **Grace defies logic.** It has nothing to do with earning, merit, or deservedness. **It is opposed to what is owed.** It **doesn't expect a return** on investments. **Grace is a liberating contradiction** between **what we deserve** and **what we get.**

> **"Grace is unconditional acceptance given to an undeserving person** by **an unobligated giver."** (Anon)

The gifts of God or the **abilities He gives** His children are **by God's grace.** Romans 12:6 states, "We have different gifts, **according to the grace** given to **each** of **us**" (NIV). **God's grace is everything. We cannot boast** in anything. **In faith,** in who we are, in our gifts, in our good works, in our blessings. **God's grace is incomparable!** How wonderful He is! And **He and His grace are inseparable!**

The question here is: **do you experience His grace in your life?** If so, **give thanks** and show forth **His grace by being gracious to one another.** Think of what He has done for you and give thanks.

Paul was **called by grace.** This is **true of all** who **are called to Christ.** In Galatians 1:6, **Paul told those Christians,** "I marvel that you are so soon removed from him that **called you into the grace of Christ** to another gospel" (AKJV).

All who are called to Christ are called by grace. Did we **deserve to be called? No.** We were by nature 'objects of God's wrath.' **What we deserved** was to be cast into hell. **But God** did not treat us as we deserved. He called us to Christ.

**The grace that saves us from sin, is the same grace
that becomes the power that supplies the saint!**

We must remember, **being called by grace is just the beginning.**
Remember, **God gives to us to supply our needs and carry our loads** from
His unlimited treasure house. **Grace is that unlimited support** and **favor,** His
overflowing abundance of unmerited love, an inexhaustible gift which is freely
accessible through Christ alone. Friend, **if you can trust God to save** you from
hell, **don't you think** you can **cast your burden upon** the Lord right now? God
says, "Cast thy burden upon the Lord, and He shall sustain thee" (Psalm 55:22).

The grace of God makes the new man (new Christian) what he is. We
see this in Romans 8:32, which **speaks of God the Father,** "He (the Father)
who did not spare His own Son (Jesus), but **delivered** (gave) Him (Jesus) up
for us all - how will He (Jesus) not also, along with Him (the Father), freely
give graciously) us **all things?**" (Emphasis mine – G.C.).

The word "delivered" conveys the idea of **God handing over His Son in**
'grace.' He did **not grudgingly give up His Son** but **gave Him** up to die on the
cross. Remember: there is **never any point** at which **we can gain God's favor;**
His **favor** is **solely from Him.** God has **provided all** (in Jesus) **we need for
salvation** by giving His **unique Son.** The **words "freely give"** emphasize His
'grace.' God's **grace** is always **generous** and gracious. **"All things" here** refers
to **glorification** in eternity. **We cannot divorce** this **"all things"** from the **"all
things"** of 8:28. Since **God works** "all things together for good" **of believers,**
everything given to them **turns out to their benefit.** This is **especially true
in glorification** in the eternal state.

God's love to us was the **greatest He could offer.** This is true even with us
being as wretched (sinful) as we are. **God's unadulterated love** toward us gives
us **assurance** of an **eternal future** with Him. **The gift of Christ** encompasses
all other gifts. **We have assurance of salvation** because of **what God did,** not
what we do.

The new man (in Christ) **lives by grace.** When **Paul was struggling
against his thorn in the flesh** and asked God to take it away from him, he
asked God that three times, God said to him (II Corinthians 12:8-9) "My
grace is sufficient for you, for **my strength** is made perfect in weakness."

Question: Having read this far ... **how many attributes of grace can you
list** ... let me share a birds-eye view (list) for you here.

Grace calls us (Galatians 1:15), **regenerates** us (Titus 3:5), **justifies** us
(Romans 3:24), **sanctifies** us (Hebrews 13:20-21), and **preserves** us (I Peter

1:3-5). **We need grace to forgive** us, to **return** us to God, to **heal** our broken hearts, and to **strengthen** us in times of trouble and spiritual warfare. **Only by God's free, sovereign grace** can we have a **saving relationship** with Him. **Only through grace** can we **be called to conversion** (Ephesians 2:8-10), **holiness** (II Peter 3:18), **service** (Philippians 2:12-13), or **suffering** (II Corinthians 1:12).

Grace justifies! Grace keeps **breaking through barriers** and casting away restraints. **A perfect,** impeachable, divinely approved, **righteousness is ours** in this union with Jesus. **We are** "justified by his grace as a gift" (Romans 3:24; Titus 3:7). **Through** this one **man Jesus, we** are **counted among** "those who **receive** the **abundance of grace** and the free gift of righteousness" (Romans 5:17 ESV). And so **we happily say with Paul,** "I do not nullify the grace of God, for if righteousness were through the law, then Christ died for no purpose" (Galatians 2:21 ESV).

Sovereign grace crushes our **pride.** It **shames** us and **humbles** us. **We want** to be the **subjects,** not the objects, **of salvation.** We **want to be active,** not passive, in the process. **We resist the truth** that **God alone** is the **author** and **finisher** of our faith. **By our fleshly nature, we rebel against sovereign grace,** but **God knows** how to **break our rebellion** and **make us friends** of this **grand doctrine.** When **God teaches sinners** that their **very core is depraved,** sovereign **grace becomes** the most **encouraging doctrine possible.**

From election to glorification, grace reigns in splendid isolation. **John 1:16 says we receive** "grace for grace," which **literally means** "grace facing or laminated to grace." **Grace follows grace in our lives as waves follow one another** to the shore.

I am supplied by grace that **is delivered,** fully **furnished**; having a **sufficiency.** Hebrews 4:16 states "Let us therefore come boldly unto the throne of grace that we may obtain mercy, and **find grace** to help in time of need." **We live by grace. We stand** by grace. We **go forward** by grace. We **accomplish things** for God by grace. We **mature** by grace. And, **we will die** by grace.

Let's face it: Most of us, including me, **tend to start off in grace** and, at times **slowly default** to our own ability. **We live as** if **walking** with God is like owning a home: **We ask our parents for help** with a **down payment but then we work** to meet the mortgage payments on our own. **No! Jesus' shed blood isn't a down payment for anything – it is everything!**

> **Our life in Christ begins** in grace, it **continues**
> in grace, and it **will end** in grace.

We "grow in the **grace** and **knowledge** of our Lord and Savior Jesus Christ" (II Peter 3:18), **and live "not under law** but under grace" (Romans 6:14). **Grace abounds not** through **our continuing in sin,** but through our **Spirit-empowered,** ongoing liberation (Romans 6:1). **Grace is too strong** to leave us passive, **too potent** to let us wallow in the mire of sins and weaknesses. **"My grace is sufficient** for you," **says Jesus,** "for my power is made perfect in weakness" (II Corinthians 12:9).

Once we grasp this, our lives will be **marked by freedom,** not bondage; **by joy,** not weariness; **by delight,** not dread. Then it will **no longer seem like a duty** to spend time in God's presence, **but a joyous gift.** After all, **Jesus says,** we are no longer his servants but his friends.

Grace sanctifies! Oh, **when will we realize that God has done for us** all that we could imagine and more, **grace shatters the mold** again. **God's grace too perfect** to let us stay in love with unrighteousness. **Grace is too free to leave us** in slavery to sin. **Grace is too untamed** to let our lusts go unconquered. **Grace's power is too uninhibited** to not unleash us for the happiness of holiness.

None of this negates our responsibility. Of course **there is a time** to set the alarm clock to rise and pray. But don't dare do it **without the oil of God's grace.** And don't dare **study your Bible without grace,** or you'll come away condemned and fearful rather than enlightened and empowered. **Why? It is God's work of grace to show us our inability.** That's the only way we will **ever acknowledge** His ability in us.

Grace rains down on us from the Lord's throne; it **doesn't** rise upward **from us** to him. That's what will draw the world to our lives and testimonies. **When people see real grace raining** down on us, they'll **see the wonders** that it works in us. And **they'll know our hearts** have been won not by our work but by God's. May it be so in your life today!

A man was carrying a heavy load of grain down a country road. A **man in a wagon** being pulled by a horse saw the man walking and said to him, **"Mister, you need a ride?"** And so the **man got in the wagon.** But he **kept the load of grain on his shoulder.** The wagon **driver said, "Man, put that down and relax!"** The rider said, **"Oh no. It's enough** for you to carry me **without having you carry this load too."**

Have you ever done that to the Lord? You say, **"Lord, I'll let You** save me, but **I'll carry my own burdens. I'm going to live my own life,** and **make my own decisions." How foolish we are to do this** with the God who hung the stars and planets.

God gives grace to meet our **present & future needs. He gives mercy to cover our past failures & sins. Remember:** Mercy is **not** getting what you deserve. **We deserve Judgment.** We deserve **to be written off,** but the Almighty, through the work of His Son **Jesus, gives grace & mercy.** These two always go together, and **are found at the Throne of God.**

> **"...much more the grace of God, and the gift by grace, which is by one man, Jesus Christ, hath abounded unto many** (Romans 5:15b KJV).

If you **looked in your mail today** and found a **free gift waiting for you,** it **wouldn't really be free.** Someone **paid for it** at some point. **The same is true of God's grace.** It's totally and **completely free to you,** but **someone paid for it - Jesus. Grace is free,** but **it's not cheap. God's grace cost Jesus his life.**

> **The more grace we have, the less we shall think of ourselves - for grace, like light, reveals our impurity.**

Christian, don't be bashful when you come to God with your needs and problems. **The infinite, immeasurable grace** of God's love is **resting on us,** because of Jesus, and the almighty **grace of His Spirit** working **in us** will ever be found at the throne of Grace. **Jesus is always our provision.**

That's why it is **only through Jesus** that **we can find the grace** of God - because **He's the one** who **paid for the grace** we receive. **The Bible says,** "We believe it is **through the grace** of our **Lord Jesus** that **we are saved"** (Acts 15:11a NIV).

> **Faith brings an empty man to God, that he may be filled with the blessings of God.** (John Calvin)

Listen: nobody else has volunteered to pay for your sins. Nobody else paid the **price** for all the blessings God brings your way. **Romans 5:15 says,** "For the sin of this one man, Adam, brought death to many. But even greater is God's wonderful grace and his gift of forgiveness to many through this other man, Jesus Christ" (NLT).

Because **you receive the grace of God through Christ alone,** the **Lord doesn't look at you** like you think he does. **God's Word says those of us** who have accepted God's grace are "in Christ." That phrase is used more than 120 times in the Bible.

To be "in Christ" means that when God looks at you, he doesn't see all your sins, failures, and rough spots. When you're "in Christ," God just sees Jesus. You see the scars, the mess, and the problems, but God sees perfection in Christ.

That's grace, and it can only be found in Christ. Nothing you can ever do can make God love you any less - or any more. His love for you isn't based on what you do. It's based on who you are "in Christ."

> "And God is able to make all grace abound toward you;
> that ye, always having all sufficiency in all things, may
> abound to every good work" (II Corinthians 9:8).

Christian, the devil wants you to live your life with an empty cup. Satan wants you to think that God's cup of grace has dried up for you. He wants you to be disenchanted with God, unhappy. Most especially, Satan wants you to feel that God is a cosmic killjoy - and non-existent - that God is always thinking of ways to rob you of joy and peace. Satan knows that if you start to feel negatively about God, then he can have his way with you in other areas.

Yes, take courage brothers and sisters! Be strong. Jesus has won the victory for you! Send those lies back to the pit where they came from and claim the promises of God!

> "The Lord will give (you) grace and glory!" (Psalm 84:11)

Corrie Ten Boom, who survived the atrocities of a Nazi prison camp said: "There is no pit so deep that God is not deeper still." So when you find yourself facing a situation that would threaten to rob you of sleep remember this powerful promise from God's word. "Don't worry about anything; instead, pray about everything. Tell God what you need. Thank him for all he has done. Then you will experience God's peace, which exceeds anything we can understand. His peace will guard your hearts and minds as you live in Christ Jesus" (Philippians 4:6-7 NLT).

Dear friend, don't just be a visitor to the throne of God. Learn to live at the throne. Learn to live in the Father's presence. Come to the throne: Realize His grace is sufficient (it is enough), take care of all your needs. As God told Paul, "My grace is sufficient for thee: for My strength is made perfect in weakness. Most gladly therefore **will I rather glory** in my **infirmities,** that the **power of Christ** may rest upon me" (II Corinthians 12:9).

As a child of God, we are to "come boldly (confidently, unflinchingly, with expectancy)," as it states in the first part of this verse. **Why?** Because **we have a High Priest** who is both **omnipotent** and **compassionate** and **sympathetic.** We can **come boldly, with confidence** to His throne, and bring our petitions expecting to receive.

When Martin Luther's puppy happened to be at the table, he **looked for a morsel** from his master, and watched with **open mouth** and **motionless eyes.** Martin **Luther said,** "Oh, if I could **only pray** the way this dog watches the meat! **All his thoughts are concentrated** on the piece of meat. Otherwise he has no thought, wish or hope."

Discouraging us from this access is a **central strategy** of Satan. **The devil sometimes wants us** to **consider Jesus** as **unapproachable** and **distant** from our needs. Sometimes Satan gives us **substitutes,** encouraging us to **come by way** of the **Pastor,** or some particular **Denomination,** or **Mary** or by saying so **many prayers** or **"doing penance"** or by the **saints … instead of Jesus.** **Sometimes the devil wants** us to think of **Jesus as being powerless** to help, **not as one** who sits on a throne in heaven. **Not so!**

> **"God's work done in God's way will never lack God's supplies."** –Hudson Taylor

God always 'supplies' me with His provision – Philippians states, "My God shall **supply** all your **needs** - by Christ Jesus." **(4:19); Matthew 6:25-33.** **Jesus taught** us **not** to **worry** about the **'supplies'** that God will provide His children. **These verses,** and many others, **teach us the great truth** that **God is interested in meeting our needs. Please hear** what the **Lord said:** 'Needs,' not 'Greeds'!

Paul stated, "For I am the **least** of the apostles, **unworthy** to be called an apostle, because **I persecuted** the church of God. But **by the grace of God** I am what I am, and **His grace toward me** was not in vain. On the contrary. **I worked harder** than any of them though it was not I, but **the grace of God** that is with me. (I Corinthians 15:9-10 WBT).

In this verse, Paul says that he **worked hard,** but that it **was not him** in the end, but **the grace of God.** What does that mean? **How do Paul's work** and **God's grace relate** to each other? If you will, look at Galatians 2:20; Ephesians 3:14-17 for **help in finding your answer.**

God has promised to take care of His children, and He will! **God's idea of taking care may be different than ours,** but that is where faith in the trustworthiness of God comes in. **We must come to the place where we are willing to trust the Lord** to take care of us in any way that He sees fit. **Our lives are filled** with **challenges, mistakes** are made. **Hearts** have been broken by cherished love, filling our hearts with **grief** and our eyes with **pain. I challenge you** to make your life an up-hill journey, **forgive** even though you'll never forget, **live** and never regret, **be inspired** by God, His **undying love, and never-ending grace.**

Grace glorifies. Just when we're sure it is done, and certain that some order must be restored and some boundary established, **God's grace not only floods** our future in **this life,** but leaps the divide into the next, and pours out onto the plains of our eternity.

If the Scriptures didn't make plain the story of our glory, we'd be scared to even dream of such grace. Not only will **Jesus be glorified in us,** but **we will be glorified in Him,** "according to the grace of our God and the Lord Jesus Christ" (II Thessalonians 1:12 NIV). **He is "...the God of all grace,** who called you unto his eternal glory in Christ, after that ye have suffered a little while, shall himself perfect, establish, strengthen you" (1 Peter 5:10 ASV). So **Peter tells us to "**Therefore, **with minds** that are **alert** and fully sober, **set your hope** on the **grace** to be **brought to you when** Jesus **Christ is revealed** at his **coming** (1 Peter 1:13 NIV). It will be **indescribably stunning** in the **coming ages** as he **shows "the immeasurable riches** of His grace in kindness toward us in Christ Jesus" (Ephesians 2:7 ESV).

Have you ever noticed that we **buy things** we **don't need** with **money we don't have** to **impress people** we **don't even like?** We try to **keep up** with the **Jones family,** but when we **finally catch up** with them, **they refinance!** Let me exhort you to **get off that comparison treadmill** and onto the **pathway** of **contentment. You are accepted right now in Christ.**

"Grace, like water, flows to the **lowest part"** (Philip Yancey)

God does not change you so He can love you. **He loves you so** He can change you! **God loves you** as much as **He loves Jesus.** That may be a **startling statement** for you, so just **think** about it. **If you are saved,** you are **in Christ,** which **means** you are a **son of your Heavenly Father,** and **as His heir,** you are **a joint heir with Jesus.** Romans 8:16–17 states, "The Spirit Himself bears witness with our spirit that we are children of God, and if children, then heirs - **heirs** of God and **joint heirs** with Christ." And where is He? **He is seated** in the heavenlies. **You are also seated** in those heavenly places" (NKJV). Although you still have an address on planet Earth. **You are enthroned** with Him.

> **The fact we could share anything with Jesus is altogether nothing but the grace of God.**

As a joint heir with Christ Jesus, **you inherit everything** that **He is.** How precious Jesus is to the Father, is **how precious you are to the Father.** The **way the Father loves Jesus**, is the way the **Father loves you!**

You may have heard people say, **"Christianity isn't** a **religion,** it's **a relationship!"** When this truth hits home, it's a **reason** for great rejoicing. **Christianity is not a one-sided proposition.** Christians **don't try to earn God's grace** and **favor** to go to Heaven. **Believers in Jesus** and **what He has done** already **have His grace** and **favor** and wholeheartedly set out to do God's will out of gratefulness. God is in and with His people.

> **"Religion is your seeking** after a god in your own image.
> **Christianity is God's seeking you** and moving **to redeem you by** the **death of His Son"** - James M. Boyce

In this verse, **David says that God gives him counsel.** As a Christian, **you house God's Holy Spirit** (I Corinthians 6:19). **You ask for wisdom** and **He supplies** it (James 1:5). **You, as one of His sheep,** know His voice **and follow Him** (John 10:27). **His Spirit teaches you** and **reminds you** of what Jesus said (John 14:26). **He will guide you** into all truth (John 16:13). **Children of God are led by** the **Holy Spirit** (Romans 8:14). Those who are of God hear God (John 8:47).

Today, right now, **thank the Lord** for the **gift of the Holy Spirit** and pray **that your spiritual ears** will be more sensitive to His voice. **Pray, too, that the leaders and citizens** of the United States will seek, hear and obey His voice. **Read:** John 10:1-15.

As we study the **Word of God,** we **notice the trust** that **Job had** in the Lord. **(Job 13:15)** I am sure that **Job would have chosen** another alternative than **losing his children,** his **health** and his **wealth,** but he is willing to **trust the Lord through times that cannot be understood** and that **make no sense.** What about you and me? **Do we really believe** that the **Lord is absolutely**

faithful? Do we believe that He has **our best interests at heart?** Are we confident of the fact that **God will** indeed **provide** for **our needs?**

If we would be enriched with this jewel of grace - let us **take pains for it.** We are **challenged** to **seek after knowledge,** as a man who searches for a vein of gold or hidden treasure. (Proverbs 2:2-3). **Our salvation cost Christ His blood, His life – it costs us nothing ... except devotion** and **commitment.**

> **"God does not give us everything we want, but He does fulfill His promises, leading us along the best and straightest paths to Himself"** - Dietrich Bonhoeffer

Jesus promised us that **when** we **come to Him by faith,** we will **find all that we need** to meet the need of our heart and life. **He will give us exactly** what we **need.** "Fear not, little flock; for it is your Father's good pleasure to give you the kingdom." **And,** "...my **God** shall **supply all your need** according to His riches in glory by Christ Jesus" (Philippians 4:19 ESV).

We need mercy for the forgiveness of our sins **and grace** with which to meet and overcome our trials. (**Hebrews 4:16**). Thankfully **God's amazing grace overpowers** our magnified sin, as it "super-abounds" above all our sins and transgressions. "But where sin abounded, **grace** did much more abound" (Romans 5:20).

Grace and mercy are glorious gifts from God that should take us to our knees in worship and adoration. We can **bring absolutely nothing to God** except a humble and thankful heart as we trust not in our works, **but solely in the finished work of Jesus Christ at Calvary.** "Not by works of righteousness which we have done, but according to His mercy He has saved us" (Titus 3:5).

Thank God that "His mercy endures forever." (Psalm 136:26). **And Romans 12:6-8 states:** "Since we have **gifts that differ** according to the **grace given to us,** each of us is **to exercise them accordingly:** if prophecy, according to the **proportion of his faith;** if service, in his serving; or he who **teaches,** in his teaching; or he who **exhorts,** in his exhortation; he who **gives,** with liberality; he who **leads,** with diligence; he who **shows mercy,** with cheerfulness (NASB).

One undeniable truth that I find in the Scripture is that **each member of the body of Christ is gifted** in a very unique way. **Some may have** the gift of **prophecy** and are able to proclaim the truth of God with power and conviction. **Some may have** the gift of **serving** ... others **teaching** ... others **exhortation** ... and so on. **The point is** that I am not you and you are not me.

We are different! And God has made us different so that each of us can make a unique contribution to his Kingdom on earth.

God wants you to be **honest with yourself** about what you can contribute to the body of Christ. **He never meant** for you to try and fit a **square peg into a round hole.** So many times **I've seen faithful men and women** of Christ who **aren't content with how God gifted them.** So they **end up getting burned out** in a ministry role that just wasn't for them. So let's not quit praying and asking God to reveal to us how **He has gifted us specifically.** When you begin to **understand that** and are **comfortable with** who you are, your life will make an **even greater impact for Christ!**

> **"But God hath chosen the foolish things of the world to confound the wise; and God hath chosen the weak things of the world to confound the things which are mighty"** (1 Corinthians 1:27).

The people God chooses to do His work are **plain, simple folks.** All you have to do is **look at** the **twelve men Jesus chose** to be His disciples. Fishermen, a tax collector, a "zealot." **What a ragtag bunch!** But they ended up "turning the world upside down" (Acts 17:6). And **those who watched them exclaimed,** "Why, these are ignorant and unlearned men!" (Acts 4:13). Maybe you didn't make the "Who's Who," or worse, the "Who's Not"! That's all right. **God has a plan for you. God knows what He is doing.** He turns the table on the world's idea of success. Wealth, fame, acclaim. **None of these are necessary** for you to be used of God.

What a glorious truth for you to share with **someone today who may be feeling like they're not worth much.** Ask God to lead you to that someone right now. **God always supplies us by His grace.**

Years ago, J. Wilbur Chapman experienced a **great sorrow** that nearly **shook his faith.** In addition, **his finances were almost depleted** just when it was necessary for him to take a long trip to the western United States. **One of the elders of his church** who **was a wealthy banker** came to his home to **offer a word** of comfort and encouragement. **As he left, he slipped a piece of paper into** the **pastor's hand.**

Chapman looked at it and was **surprised** to find that it was a **check made out to him** and **signed** by this rich friend. But the figures to indicate the **amount of the gift were missing.** "Did you really mean to give me a signed blank check?" **he asked.** "Yes," said the man. **"I didn't know how much you'd need, and I wanted to be sure you would have enough."**

Later Chapman commented, "While I **never had to use** that **check,** it gave me **a secure feeling** to know that **thousands of dollars** were literally **at my disposal."** Someone has said, **"God too has given us a signed check** in Philippians 4:19 to **provide** for **every genuine need** that arises in our lives."

Accept the grace that God offers through Jesus, and live!

God's grace is all around us. He wants us to **live forever** and **be happy,** but we have a **choice to make.** We **can accept some of His grace** during this "stay of execution" period and live here on earth for a few years, **or we can accept ALL His grace** and live forever with Him! **God's supply of grace** to you is **limitless!**

A ship was sailing in the southern waters of the **Atlantic,** when **another was sighted** which was making **signals of distress.** They **sailed towards** the **distressed ship,** and hailed them. **"What is the matter?"** "We are dying for want of water,"** was the response. **"Dip it up then,"** was the answer, **"you are in the mouth of the Amazon River."**

Those **sailors were thirsting,** and **suffering,** and fearing death, and **longing intensely** for **water,** and all the while they were **supposing** that there was nothing but the **ocean's brine** around them; when, **in fact,** they had **sailed unconsciously** into the **broad mouth of the mightiest river on the globe,** and **did not know** it: and though to them it seemed that they must perish with thirst, yet **there was at least a hundred miles of fresh water** all around them; and they had **nothing to do** but as they were bidden to **"dip it up."**

Let Us Pray: "Father, we thank Thee again **for the Scriptures** and for the **greatness** of the Son of God, **our great High Priest.** And, Lord, as we continue to study what it means to have such a great High Priest, **give us** understanding, encouragement, and motivation, **to come as priests** to our great High Priest. **Again we give thanks for our supply, our needs,** our **family needs,** the **needs of our friends,** the **needs of our church.** For Jesus' sake. Amen."

"Grace be with you all. Amen" (Hebrews 13:25).

Chapter 8

God 'SATISFIES' Me With His Grace

IN II CORINTHIANS 12:8-9, **For the Christian 'student',** it is **captivating** to note that the **Bible** apparently **predicts more than just one future age. The apostle Paul refers** at least **twice to ages yet to come.** I love especially the **promise above.**

We can safely leave all these **undefined "ages to come"** to God who, **for His own good reasons,** has **not chosen** to tell us about them yet. We do have, however, enough information about that **coming age** in the **holy city in** the **new earth,** with its solid and sure foundations, **to look forward to it** with **great anticipation** and **eternal joy.** Don't miss it! "For here we have no continuing city, but we seek one to come" (Hebrews 13:14).

God's glorious salvation is all about God and all about grace. It is God, and **God alone** who "hath quickened" **(made alive) those** who were "dead in sins." Instead of walking according to the course of this world, **He has made us** "sit together in heavenly places in Christ Jesus" (v.6). **It is not humanistic works** by which we are saved, but by "the **exceeding riches of His grace** in His kindness toward us through Christ Jesus" (v 7).

Jesus Christ, who rose victorious over sin and death and satan. **"Jesus is able also to save them** to the uttermost (completely) that come unto God by (through) Him. **He lives forever to intercede** with God on their (our) behalf" (Hebrews 7:25). **Because He has done all this,** we can enjoy throughout "the ages to come ... the exceeding riches of His grace" (Ephesians 2:7).

> **"God is most glorified in us when we are most satisfied in Him"** –John Piper

The expression "Satisfied" (in this Chapters title above), is **comprehensive** and **weighty term.** When you **look this word up in the dictionary,** it speaks of **being fully pleased** because something desired and anticipated **has been accomplished as desired.** There is an **old song, "I am satisfied with Jesus.**

> **"I am satisfied with Jesus,**
> **He has done so much for me:**
> **He has suffered to redeem me,**
> **He has died to set me free.**
> **I am satisfied, I am satisfied,**
> **I am satisfied with Jesus,**
> **But the question comes to me, as I think of Calvary, Is my**
> **Master satisfied with me?** (B. B. McKinney)

If you want to praise and magnify the supremacy of God the way the Bible magnifies the supremacy of God, you have to **call attention to the lavish overflow of God's grace. Remember, the 'Giver gets the glory.'** So knowing about grace and experiencing grace as the power for all Christian believing and living is **the best way to magnify the supremacy of God.** When you **depend on God** for everything instead of just **thinking of Him** depending on you, **you call attention to the supremacy** of **His fullness and His all-sufficiency.**

Remember: Almighty God is most glorified in us when **we** are **most satisfied in Him.** The **connection** between **God's supremacy and our joy** is that his supremacy is manifest most by **His all-supplying, all-satisfying grace.**

> The **Grace of Almighty God** can **transform**
> your **life** from **insignificant** and **meaningless**
> to **justifying** and **meaningful**!

I opened a small box the other day that the Postman had left, **and found** inside a **small engraved note which said, "Satisfaction Guaranteed!" "If"** for any reason I was not **'completely satisfied,'** I could **return the package for a full refund.**

It is my desire, as a **teacher** of the Word of God, **to present to you the Person of Jesus** unto which **God the Father** looks to find divine perfection; **the One to Whom He can and has eternally said, "**This is my beloved Son, in whom I am well pleased." **The Holy Spirit of God desires** to bring us **face to face with the sole object of God's eternal delight,** so that **we may experience satisfaction** and rest for the soul **as God has defined it** from **before the foundation of the world.**

The go-to-church 'religionist,' who is satisfied with **trying to keep all the rules,** warms **a pew once** or **twice** a month, but **starts feeling uncomfortable** whenever you start talking about **enjoying anything religious!** But **grace sets us free to enjoy** a **relationship rather** than endure **rules.**

The **Westminster Catechism asks the question:** What is the chief end of man? And **the answer is simply:** To **glorify God and enjoy Him forever! Amen!** Are you still **enduring Jesus** or are you **enduring a relationship with God?** Jesus said, "If you love Me, you will obey what I command" (John 14:15). In other words, **grace-filled Christians do** what he says **because they love him, not** because they **want to impress Him.**

As the **Scripture states,** "The **grace of God** that brings salvation hath appeared to all men" (Titus 2:11). **What is** this grace? **OR, Who is** this grace? In the simplest of terms, this **grace is Jesus Christ,** full of truth, mercy, kindness and love. **Again Paul wrote,** "teaching us that denying ungodliness and worldly lusts, that **"we should live** soberly, righteously, and **godly, in this present world."**

> The gospel is all about God's grace through Jesus Christ.
> That's why Paul calls it "the gospel of the grace of God"
> (Acts 20:24), and "the word of his grace" (Acts 14:3).

The gospel of the grace of God is the message everyone needs. The **word of grace** is **decreed** on **every page of the Bible** and ultimately **revealed in Jesus Christ.** The **last verse** of the **Bible summarizes the message** from **Genesis to Revelation:** "The **grace of the Lord Jesus** be with all" (Revelation 22:21). **Through Jesus** "we have all **received grace upon grace"** (John 1:16) - the **unwarranted** and **aggressive grace of God.**

This is the grace of God that brings redemption: Christ paying the price for **us who cannot pay,** by the **ransom of Christ's blood.** It is the removal of the curse of the law. We are sinners guilty under the law.

Did you hear about the new product **called "Disposable Guilt Bags"** appeared in the **marketplace.** It consisted of **a set of ten ordinary brown bags** on which were **printed** the following **instructions:** "Place the bag securely over your mouth, take a deep breath and blow all your guilt out, then dispose of the bag immediately." **The unbelievable brazenness of this is** that the **Associated Press reported** that **2500 kits** had been quickly sold at **$2.50 per kit.** Oh, how I wish we could **dispose of our sin and guilt so easily, and yet, with Jesus we can.**

There is nothing on this earth powerful enough in itself to dispose of our guilt. We cannot fix ourselves, which is what many of us are trying to do. America seems to be fixated on Phycologists, Psychiatrists, Ministers, and Psychics; trying to rid ourselves of sin and guilt. That which makes it possible to be forgiven, to be cleansed, to be healed, that which makes it possible for us to receive our life back again, fresh and clean and new, is the power of God's Grace in the Cross of Jesus Christ, released from the bondage of sin into the freedom of Grace.

A story was told of a wealthy man who felt his son needed to learn gratefulness. So he sent him to stay with a poor farmer's family. After a month, the son returned. The father asked, "Now don't you appreciate what we have?" The boy thought for a moment and said, "The family I stayed with is better off. They harvest what they've planted and enjoy meals together and talk to each other. And they always seem to have time for one another."

This story reminds us that money can't buy everything. Money is a necessary part of living. Without money, we couldn't secure the necessities or luxuries of life. But there are things money cannot buy. Money will buy luxuries, but it will not buy love or spiritual power. Money will buy advancement and preferences, but it will not buy the recognition of God. Money will buy favor and accolades, but it will not buy character. Even though our bodies can live on what money can buy, money itself cannot provide health for our bodies, and can't keep our souls from drying up.

> "God does not give us everything we want, but He
> does fulfill His promises, leading us along the best and
> straightest paths to Himself." - Dietrich Bonhoeffer

Is it possible to buy what truly satisfies without money? Yes, the Prophets in the Old Testament and the Apostles in the New Testament are always pointing to the grace of God. This gift is so infinitely valuable that it has no price tag. The One who offers it, Jesus Christ, has already paid the full price with His death. When we acknowledge our thirst is for God, ask forgiveness for our sins, and accept the finished work of Christ on the cross, we will find spiritual food that satisfies and our soul will live forever!

As a Christian we must always remember that we are living because of God's grace, while we are living in God's grace. We must learn to treasure every moment that we have! Treasure it even more, when you share with someone special, special enough to spend their time with you. Remember that time waits for no one. **Yesterday** is history. **Tomorrow** is a mystery. **Today** is a **gift.** That's **why it's called the present!!!**

> **"In Him we have redemption through His
> blood, the forgiveness of our trespasses,
> according to the riches of His grace, which He
> lavished upon us"** (Ephesians 1:7-8 NASB).

This verse mentions "Riches!" How does one **attempt to describe** "the **unsearchable riches** of Christ?" (2:7). **All words fail us; but** I am sure that **Paul must have had in mind** the **fact that JESUS** was in the beginning **with the Father,** in the bosom of the Father, the most **precious jewel in Heaven, coequal with GOD** the Father, **Creator** of all things. Nothing was made without Him, but by Him all things were made (John 1:1-3; Colossians 1:14-19). **He was worshiped and honored** in Heaven because He was/is Deity, co-equal with the Father.

Where do we get the help to be that kind of person if we by nature are accusing, blaming, and fault-finding? **Hebrews 4:16 gives** the most **crucial answer:** "Let us therefore draw near with **confidence to the throne of grace,** that we may receive mercy and **may find grace to help in time of need"** (NASB).

Grace is God's power enacted in a human life. We **need grace** when we **feel we are going to fail,** when we **experience pain, anger,** and **hurt in a relationship,** or when we **are overwhelmed with guilt.** If you **never** get better, **never** grow, **never** beat back that addiction - **God has, does, and will love you.** If you **overcome it** Jesus will **not love you more. His grace remains constant** - and He will **simply come alongside you** and **empower you to become victorious** in every circumstance. **Millions love and sing** that **hymn** almost every week.

Question: Why Is Grace Amazing? I'll let **God's Word answer that!** "... **God,** who is **rich in mercy,** for his **great love** wherewith he loved us, Even when **we were dead in sins,** hath **quickened** (made us alive) **us together** with Christ, **(by grace ye are saved;)** And hath **raised us up** together, and **made us sit together** in heavenly places **in Christ Jesus:** That in the ages to come he might shew **the exceeding riches of his grace** in his kindness toward us **through Christ Jesus.** For **by grace are ye saved through faith;** and that **not** of **yourselves:** it is the **gift of God: Not** of **works,** lest any man should **boast** (Eph. 2:4-9).

Every follower of Christ should have an **understanding of the word grace** on the tip of their tongue. **Grace is the atmosphere in which** our **relationship** with God **lives.** The followers of Jesus Christ **have been singing** about and **reveling** in the **truth of God's grace** for two thousand years. **Grace** is one of **the crown jewels of Christianity** which is **constantly expounded** in the **Word** of the Living God.

I continue to ask: Do you know **what grace is?** Can you say you **have experienced God's grace?** The apostle **Paul was so excited** about **telling the Ephesians** about **grace** that he **snuck in a hint** (see verse 5) **before he arrived** at his great declaration: For by grace you have been saved through faith. And **this is not your own doing;** it is the **gift of God, not** a result of **works, so** that **no one may boast.**

> While **the Law** defines **righteousness,** only **grace delivers** it. The **Law** was **never intended** to be a **means of obtaining grace;** it **was given** to **demonstrate** to **men** that **grace was desperately needed.** - Bob Deffenbaugh

We in **today's church** haven't even begun to **scratch the surface** of grace. We take **only tiny sips** from the **cup of grace** from time to time in our walk with God **before we begin to rely on our own abilities.**

Brethren, this is **a time of need in our churches.** And **an exciting time of need for** love, for patience, for understanding, for forbearance. **Which means it is a time to go to God for grace. We need** to be **sustained by grace.** And **when we are full** of His **grace, grace** will come **out of our mouths** and **our lives will show it.**

Some churches prefer certain areas of **obedience** over others. They emphasize evangelism, social justice, political activism, serving the poor, or prayer. **But no church is pleasing to God when it runs** on **one cylinder** instead of **eight.** Any person or church that is **not obeying God's commands is** living in **disobedience!** He simply will **not allow us** to **ignore** certain of His commands.

> **God always gives His best to those who leave the choice with Him.** - Jim Elliot

Yet perfect obedience is not totally possible; it isn't within the realm of **our ability.** The **reason** we choose **certain areas** of **obedience** is because they are **easier to fulfill than others.**

Where are you going to get that kind of commitment - that kind of **love?** **II Corinthians 9:8** gives the **essential answer:** "**God** is able to **make all grace** abound to you, so that always having **all sufficiency** in everything, you may have an abundance for every good deed" (NASB). **That is another amazing promise.** Every good deed in reconciliation God has for you to do, **He is willing and able to give you the grace to do.** You don't have to wear out. You don't have to give up. **You don't have to be depleted.** There is all sufficiency in everything for every good work. **Future grace is the gas for tomorrow's obedience.**

Having a life of joy and **victory** does not hinge on whether we constantly **succeed or fail at obeying all God's commands**; it has **everything** to do with how we **go about obeying** His commands. **In the 60's,** when I **was a young preacher** in California, my **Youth Director told me,** "You **can change yourself** so that temptations don't return. **You have the ability to pull yourself out** of anything." **Really?** It doesn't take long to see **how futile that really is.**

We cannot make changes in ourselves by our **own fleshly grit** and **determination** we must **allow God's grace** to empower us and **bring transformation - in ourselves** and in our world.

God says in Genesis 15:1, "Do not be afraid, Abram, I am your shield, your exceedingly great reward" (AKJV). **His reassurance applies to us** as well as to him. **God Himself is the reward of those who seek Him.** "Those who seek Him" **is limited to those God invites** to approach Him **and who believe** enough to take advantage of the opportunity and thus stir themselves up to draw near. **The invitation itself is an aspect of God's grace.**

Romans 4:4 makes it clear that **earning access to God is impossible** because it would put God in man's debt. **No, access to Him is the result of freely given grace.** The **pairing of grace** and **reward is** no more inconsistent than **God's almighty sovereignty and man's responsibility** being linked, **or Jesus being both our Lord and our Servant.** Pay attention and read his next sentence twice. **There would be no reward if God did not first give grace.**

Some would say that **Bill Gates is the richest man in the world.** It would **cost him little** to give away a **million dollars,** or **ten million.** He **wouldn't lose a minute of sleep** tonight with his bank balance going down that much. **There are many like him** who **give from their riches** and it **costs them little** because they have so much more in the bank.

Now think with me what it cost Christ for **us to receive** his riches. **He left the bosom of the Father in Heavenly places** for **our benefit, not His** own. **He who was rich yet for our sakes became poor** (II Corinthians 8:9). He **laid aside** the insignia of his eternal glory and became a child **living in**

a workman's home in an insignificant village without any running water. Surely that was wonderful.

We only occasionally put ourselves to a little bit of inconvenience for others. We give up our own bedrooms for special guests, or we live in a camp and sleep in a dormitory with some young people for a week, or we drive or fly for two days and nights to far-away lands to deliver some materials to a church there and sleep in a sleeping bag on the church floor. Those are little deeds of love, but how paltry compared to His thirty years sentence to Nazareth surrounded by sinners.

**When we put our cares into His hands,
He puts His peace into our hearts.**

"For He has satisfied the thirsty soul, and the hungry soul He has filled with what is good" (Psalm 107:9 NASB). How does God satisfy us through His grace? 2,000 years ago, the Apostle Paul wrote "For you know the grace of our Lord Jesus Christ, that, though He (Jesus) was rich, yet for your sakes He became poor, that you through His poverty might be rich" (II Corinthians 8:9 (NASB)." That's real satisfaction! What do you do when you "are satisfied?"

When pure satisfaction comes to a Christian's life, usually there is thankfulness and praise. Perhaps you've heard of the "street preacher" who was right in the middle of his sermon when a rotten egg flew by his head and hit a deacon who was standing beside him. As the stench of the egg covered the deacon, he started cussing up a storm.

A second egg hit the preacher right in the middle of his forehead, and as it trickled down his face, he began shouting and praising all over the sidewalk. The deacon said, "I don't understand it. When I was hit with the egg, I went to cussing; but when that rotten egg hit you, you went to praising."

The preacher, who stuttered like Moses, gave his reply: "You already had the c-c-c-cuss in you. When that egg hit you, it j-j-j-just knocked the c-c-c-cuss out of you. But when I got hit with a rotten egg, I had p-p-p-praise in me, and it j-j-j-just knocked the p-p-p-praise right out of me."

When we lived in Long Beach, CA in the 1960's where I pastored a downtown Baptist Church, I would take my children from time to time to 'The Pike,' the downtown waterfront Amusement Park. It was a rare treat for a pastor with my small salary to be able to take my children to that park. Many of the rides were a dime-a-ride small rides to a quarter for the double Ferris wheel, which swung and swayed in dizzying loops over the water's edge.

"Oh daddy, please let us ride the Cyclone Racer (the largest Roller Coaster on the West Coast), with its dual tracks, hairpin turns, piercing the salty air. We were strapped in and had a metal bar which came down over us to lock us in and protect us from propelling out or into the ocean. We clung to the safety bar, growing queasier by the minute. The hairpin turns and skeletal frame dangling us temporarily over the ocean, terrifying my 9-year-old daughter Pamela. My boys, staggered every two years after Pam, trying to act tough, were skeeered as well! We lived there for five years, and no one was ever lost.

Grace is a bit like a roller coaster; it makes us scream in terror and laugh uncontrollably at the same time. But there aren't any harnesses on this ride. We are not in the driver's seat, but closely secured in our own, and we did not design the twists and turns. We just get on board the ride of grace. We laugh as the binding law of gravity is suspended, and we scream because it looks like we're going to hurtle off into the ocean or outer space. We sometimes shudder as we witness the mighty power of the experience. And, when this ride is ended, those locked- in all finish to the end, the reward is such a ride as this, brings joy and jubilation.

Grace brings us back into contact with the children we once were (and still are) … children who loved to ride roller coasters, to smile and yell and throw our hands up in the air. Grace, in other words, is terrifyingly fun, and like any ride worth standing in line for, it is worth coming back to again and again. In fact, God's one-way love may be the only ride that never gets old, the only ride we thankfully never outgrow. A source of inexhaustible hope and joy for an exhausted world.

Whatever is in you will come out of you in a time of blessing, in a time of stress, trial, or crisis … as well. Deposit the Word of God in your heart that you will not sin against God (Psalm 119:11). We all need the "riches of Christ" in us, don't we? What are the riches of Christ? Why are God's riches described as unsearchable and unknowable? 1 Corinthians 2:9 states, "But as it is written: Eye has not seen, nor ear heard, Nor has it entered into the heart of man, The things which God has prepared for those who love Him" (NKJV).

His riches are unsearchable because the cost of giving them to us was un-measureable. To understand God's riches, we have to first understand our poverty. Before Jesus Christ, we were lost, undone, barren of all lasting life, spiritually bankrupt, and ruined by sin. In fact, we were dead in our sins. Our sins had separated us from Christ. We had offended the Almighty God who is a "consuming fire". We were destined for an eternity in hell. Then

God came to earth in the flesh. Jesus came, Incarnate. He was willing to step down from Heaven's glory and die in our place.

James 2:5 speaks of being "rich in faith." Faith brings Christ's riches into the soul! Faith entitles the soul to the promises. The promises are full of riches: salvation, adoption, justification, sanctification and glorification; and faith is the key which unlocks this cabinet of the promises and empties their treasure into the soul. The riches of God's grace surpass all other riches. Grace "is more profitable than silver and yields better returns than gold" (Proverbs 3:14 NIV).

These riches of grace make a man wise. Wisdom is the best possession; other riches cannot make one wise. A man may have a full wallet and an empty brain. A rich heir, though he lives until he becomes of age, may never come to years of discretion; but these riches of grace have the power to make a man wise.

> "He is a wise man who does not grieve for the things
> which he has not, but rejoices for those which he has."

Psalm 111:10 states, "The fear of the Lord is the beginning of wisdom." The saints are compared to wise virgins in Matthew 25. Grace makes a man wise to know Satan's devices and subtleties (II Corinthians 2:11); it makes him wise unto salvation (II Timothy 3:15).

These spiritual riches sanctify other riches. Riches without grace are hurtful; they are golden snares; they are the bellows of pride and the fuel of lust. They set open hell's gates for men; they are unblessed blessings.

But grace sanctifies our riches; it corrects the poison; it takes away the curse; it makes other riches beneficial to us. These riches shall be certificates of God's love, wings to lift us up to paradise. Thus grace, by a divine chemistry, extracts heaven out of earth - and gives us not only beef - but the blessing.

Grace satisfies while other riches cannot (Ecclesiastes 5:10). Riches can no more fill the heart - than a triangle can fill a circle; but grace fills up every chink and space of the soul. Grace dilates the heart, and ravishes our affections with joy (Romans 15:13), which joy, as Chrysostom said, "is a foretaste of heaven."

What we do deserve, due to our sin, is everlasting punishment and banishment from God. "But God, who is rich in mercy. . . hath quickened us (made us alive) - raised us up - and made us sit together in heavenly places in Christ Jesus" (Ephesians 2:4-6). "The LORD is merciful and gracious, slow to anger, and plenteous in mercy" (Psalm 103:8).

And just how merciful is He? "For as the heaven is high above the earth, so great is His mercy toward them that fear Him" (Psalm 103:11). **"It is of the LORD'S mercies** that we are not consumed, because His compassions fail not" (Lamentations 3:22). **Every born-again Christian has received what the Bible calls,** "the sure mercies of David" (Acts 13:34). **"Surely goodness and mercy** shall follow me all the days of my life: and I will dwell in the house of the LORD forever" (Psalm 23:6).

Paul writes to the Romans, "He who did not spare His own Son, but delivered Him up for us all, how shall He not with Him also **freely give us all things?"** (Romans 8:32 KJV). Because of this, **we now have direct access** to the Almighty God of the universe. You are **now a child** of God, by a real new birth (John 3).

"Behold, what manner of love the Father hath bestowed upon us, that **we** should be **called the sons of God:** therefore the world knoweth us not, because it knew him not. **Beloved, now are we the sons of God,** and it doth not yet appear what we shall be: but we know that, when he shall appear, **we shall be like him;** for we shall see him as he is" **(I John 3:1-2).**

Just because God has **made us His children,** through faith in Christ, **doesn't mean we** are all **alike.** Many Christians make the **mistake of** "comparison Christianity," thinking we must **all be alike, having** the same experiences, **possessing** the same gifts, and even **liking the same preacher** and/or **music and worship style.** Sometimes **we become critical** of others because **they do not act** or **speak** or **do things** we think **they should.**

One reason for this, is that God **does not bestow upon** all his children the **same gifts,** or the **same natural qualities.** The Creator loves variety, as all his works attest. **No two animals** are precisely alike in every feature; **no two plants** are exactly similar in their structure; **no two human lives** in all the races are identical in all respects; and **divine grace does not** recast all **personalities** in the same mold.

When gold is minted, each individual **coin** of a kind is **stamped** by the **same die;** and a **million coins** of the **same value** will all be **precisely alike.** But **life is not minted as gold** is. **Grace does not** transform **Peter into a John,** nor **Paul into a Barnabas,** nor **Luther into a Calvin.** Regeneration does **not** make busy, bustling **Martha** quiet and reposeful, **like** her **sister Mary.** Nor does grace **change Mary's calm,** restful spirit into the anxious and **distracted activity of Martha.**

This **attitude** and **activity** makes them **both friends of Jesus, devoted** to him in love and **loyalty** and **service;** but it leaves each of them herself **in all** her individual characteristics. It makes them **both like Christ** in **holiness,** in **consecration,** in **heavenly longings;** but it **does not touch** those features which give to **each one her personal identity.**

Paul loves to praise the grace at work in other believers, often getting **very personal** and **specific** (Romans 16:3; Philippians 2:19–23; Philippians 2:25–30; and more). But **he's always praising grace in people,** not people apart from grace. And he's always **pushing the praise** through the person to God.

For Paul, he didn't see the riches of Christ as **something to hoard and protect.** He saw it **as something** to **give away. What a change** has been fashioned in all who have tasted the **unsearchable riches** of Christ. **Before Jesus transformed** our lives, **we lived for** such things as money, and possessions, and bigger cars, and more exotic holidays, and expensive hotels, but **they have lost their charm.** We've been there, done that, and **now, because of Jesus, our desires have changed. We want these lasting treasures** that come from heaven, and so are eternal, unchangeable and **never fail to satisfy.**

Grace is not about man becoming **like each other, or even God** awakening to the notion **that he is a "god."** Grace, as well as **all scriptural terms, must** be seen in the **context of the Cross,** because in its truest **definition grace is,** "I am crucified with Christ: nevertheless I live; yet not I, but Christ lives in me."

Grace is not Christ empowering me to live **for** God **or** to live **like** God, **but grace is "not I, but Christ lives in me"** (Galatians 2:20). That is **the reason Paul, can say** as one that has been **experientially crucified with Christ,** "I do not frustrate the grace of God" (Galatians 2:21). Because the **frustration of the grace of God is our attempting** to live unto God **by the life that He has not given** and therefore does not accept.

"Being justified freely (as a gift) by **His grace"** Romans 3:24, John 15:25), **means that within the sinner** there is **no merit** or **cause** for him to be justified. There is **no effective human persuasion** for **any spiritual change** in his life. The sovereign change here **resides with God.**

Jesus Christ made 'satisfaction' for all the sins of all his people, that he **paid the last penny of debt** they owed to the broken law and injured government of God, and that **in Him they are complete and have full redemption. Christ** by his death **did fully pay the debt** of all his people, and did make a proper, real, and **full satisfaction to his Father's justice** in their behalf."

God is most glorified in us,
when we are most satisfied in Him!

How loving and kind God is to shower upon us **His grace and mercy!** We should **exemplify this by treating others** in the same manner. "Put on therefore - bowels of mercies (feelings of compassion), kindness, humbleness of mind, meekness, long-suffering (patience); Forbearing (patient with) one another" (Colossians 3:12, 13, parenthesis mine - G.C.).

Some of you reading this may **need** to **repent of offending against the Spirit of grace** - perhaps most of us. **Hebrews 10:29 speaks of insulting the Spirit of grace.** And **Ephesians 4:30 speaks of grieving** the Holy Spirit by our un-edifying words. So let's repent and **turn from old patterns of negativism** and **fault-finding,** and learn together **to walk and talk by faith** in future grace. **Never forget** that **our God is able to make all grace abound to you,** that always **having all sufficiency** in everything, you may abound for every good deed.

God the Father planned our salvation **in eternity past.** Our **Almighty, Omniscient God** eons ago **ordained** his **plan** for mankind's **redemption,** before the world was created, even to the point of **His Son, Jesus, would come** and die for you and me "before the foundation of the world" (Revelation 13:8).

What does this verse mean? It means that **Christ was slain from the foundation of the world,** in the sense that, it was so **foreordained in God's mind** from the foundation of the world and, therefore, **so certain** that **He would eventually be slain** that God **declares Him** to be slain **before He actually is.** This notion that what **God has foreordained** in advance being spoken of, or declared to be, **as if it has already taken place** upon its having been foreordained is **not unheard of in scripture.**

For instance, **we read in Romans 4,** "As it is written, **I have made thee [Abraham]** a father of many nations," before him whom he believed, even God, who quickens (makes alive) the dead, and **calls those things which be not as though they were** (Romans 4:17). Remember: **God knows the ending from the beginning!**

God is speaking about Abraham whom He had made **a father of many nations before Abraham actually was.** In fact, at the time in which God said to Abraham that He had made him **a father of many nations** (Genesis 17:5), **Abraham was 99 years old** and his **wife Sarah was 90** years old, and **she had not even yet bore a child.** Furthermore, she and he were then beyond child bearing age. So how could God say that He had made **Abraham a father of many nations** when **he had borne no children** through his wife Sarah? Well, as the story goes, **God worked a miracle** and brought about **a son, Isaac,** through Sarah and Abraham in their old age, and it was **through Isaac that Abraham eventually became a father of many nations.**

God the Son purchased and paid for our **salvation** and the **church** at Calvary. **God the Holy Spirit preserves and protects** our **salvation** and **His people** today and forevermore! And that happened because **Almighty God, the Father premeditated and planned it all.** The Father conceived it, **the Son** achieved it, **the Spirit** enables **you to** believe it **now. Will you** receive it?

Actor Jackie Gleason had it all ... fame and fortune. But I've been told that **on his deathbed** he said, **"I'd trade it all** to know **how to get to heaven!"** You might be **wondering how much** a guy like that **left behind. Let me tell you - All of it!**

The **Father wrought** it, the **Son bought** it, the **Spirit taught** it, the **devil fought** it, and **praise God, I caught it. Have you?**

Christian friend, Jesus has given you freedom. The door **has been unlocked.** You have been **set free to serve Him.** Now **that's a sermon you can say "yes" to!** With that change, **we can be totally satisfied! Hallelujah!**

> **The Almighty is greatly glorified in us, when**
> **we are supremely satisfied in Him!** - G. Clifton

I am surprised by God's grace all the time because of **all that He has promised to the family of God.** Paul wrote in Ephesians 2:7, "That in the **ages to come** he might **show the exceeding riches of his grace** in his kindness **toward us** through Christ Jesus" (NKJV).

Many things in life will fail us. **Friendships** will blossom & then die. **Health** can be an elusive thing. **Riches** will often remain just beyond the reach of your fingertips. **Those we love** will pass from the scene leaving a void in our hearts.

However, **there is one thing that every child of God** possesses that **can never fail.** Never end, never run out, and never run dry. That **we will never be found to be insufficient.** That is **the grace of God!** Yes, **the road** may be long & dreary. **Your days may be filled** with **difficulties & struggles.** Please be **assured** that **there will be grace sufficient** for every need and ever trial. **That is the promise of God.** That is the **hope** of the **saints!**

God gives more grace as our **burdens** grow greater, **He sends more strength** as our labors increase; to added afflictions **He adds His mercy,** to multiplied trials **He multiplies peace** in our times of grief. When **we have exhausted our store of endurance,** when **our strength has** failed before the day is half done, when **we reach the end of our hoarded resources** our Father's full giving is only begun. **His love** has no limits, **His grace** has no measure,

His **power** no boundary known unto men; for **out of His infinite riches in Jesus He gives**, and **gives**, and **gives again**.

> **Hope does not put us to shame, because God's love**
> **has been poured into our hearts through the Holy**
> **Spirit Who has been given to us** (Romans 5:5 NIV).

Why are you encouraged even **when the trials and anxieties** of the day **surround you?** Paul says that, **as a believer**, the **love of God** is **poured** into your heart **in the person of the Holy Spirit.** He reminds you of the hope that lies before you.

Think of it! You are justified before God **through His Son,** Jesus Christ. **The unsaved sinner** is at **war with God;** the saved **believer** has **peace with God** (Romans 5:1). You **also** have **access to the Lord** on a daily, hourly, minute-by-minute basis. Because of that, **you can rejoice** in the **hope** of the glory of God (Romans 5:2).

Listen: the Lord will not disappoint! He **loves you** and **took care of your 'past'** - Jesus died for your sins. He **gives you peace** by caring for the 'present' - you can **draw on** the **inexhaustible riches of His grace** in times of need. **Hope and joy speak** to the **'future'** - **one day** you will **share in His glory. Be encouraged** and **rejoice** as you **pray** for **those you love** and for **those in need** of Christ.

The **altar of God's unlimited grace** is now **open for business.** Salvation, prayer, or just to spend time with the Lord. **As the Bible says** in **Revelation 22:17,** "The Spirit and the bride say, "Come." And let the one who hears say, "Come." And let the one who is thirsty come; let the one who wishes take the water of life without cost" (NASB). A promise from the Lord to all of us. **Please come now ... to Jesus.**

Let us pray ... Father, thank You for this wonderful day. **Lord, thank You** for these great truths, **how thrilling** to **dig into Your Word** to find the path laid out for us. **O God, teach us** to be **generous.** May we **learn** and **experience** what it is to have You pour blessings upon us. **Open** the floodgates, **open** the windows of heaven, **fill up** our hearts and minds so that we can **continue to serve. We pray that You will enable us** by Your Spirit **to be faithful** in this regard in Christ's name, Amen!

> **"Brethren, may the grace of our Jesus Christ be**
> **with your spirit. Amen"** – Galatians 6:18

Chapter 9

God 'SUSTAINS' Me With His Grace

"BEHOLD, GOD THE Lord is the sustainer (upholder) of my soul" (Psalm 54:4 NAS).

Sustaining grace is grace given at **special times of need**, especially **during adversity** or **suffering**. "Let us therefore **draw near** with confidence **to the throne of grace,** that we may receive mercy and may **find grace to help** in time of need" (Hebrews 4:16, NAS). "But He **gives a greater grace.** Therefore it says, "God is opposed to the proud, but **gives grace to the humble**" (James 4:6 NASB).

The **concept** of **receiving sustaining grace** from God is quite **profound for every believer.** Every act of **grace on the part of God retains** the **character** of being **fully undeserved, unmerited,** and **solely derived** from the **faithfulness of God** to **His commitments to His Son,** and so to His own people. **Grace is God's bearing of Himself** toward His children, **always** in the context **of loving favor.**

> Cast your burden (cares) on the Lord, and He shall
> sustain (take care of) you; He shall never permit
> the righteous to be moved (Psalm 55:22 ESV).

A great picture of this word "sustained" is seen in this illustration. **In the 'Twin Cities Marathon' on 1995, one of the wheel chair participants** had a **blowout** near the end of the race. But he **kept going on the rim of his wheel,** until **five blocks** from the finish line the **wheel buckled** and the **chair fell over.** Some **people from the sidelines** ran to him and **held the chair level, running along beside him while he finished the race.** They **sustained him.** They **held him up.** They **enabled him** to do what he needed to do. **That's what grace does for us … sustains and satisfies our needs!**

Perhaps some of these distinctions are a bit random, but the point remains that **grace is manifested in a variety of ways. Grace seeks us** and saves us; **grace keeps us** secure; **grace enables us** to serve and to endure the tests and trials of life. **Grace will bring about our sanctification** in this life and will **ultimately bring us to glory.** From **beginning to end we are the object of divine grace. Hallelujah!**

Sustaining Grace is God's **timely infusion** of **spiritual strength** which **protects His people** from despair and bitterness and often uses suffering to mature them. **Grace sustains and satisfies** everything in the Christian life. **It holds up** the broken chair. **It gives** the upper-body strength. **It prevents** other obstacles from stopping us. **It keeps** his heart beating. **It keeps** his eyes seeing. **Grace satisfies everything in the Christian life.**

There is a magnificent Greek word used **155 times** in the New Testament. **That word is 'charis,'** it is translated **'grace.'** It means a favor bestowed. It means a generous **benefit freely given.** The sense of it **in the New Testament** is that it means a favor bestowed by God through **His power to transform a person's life** starting at salvation and going on from there. Let me say that again. **It means a favor bestowed by God** through His **power to transform** a person's life starting at **salvation** and going on from there **throughout one's spiritual life.**

I know **God's Grace saved** me, and will it **sustain me when life gets hard?** A grace that **"sustains,"** is a "grace that **amazes"** and brings it back to **Titus 2:11.** And **no matter what you've done … God still loves you** and will be with you! **His grace sustains** us in every situation, and **is training us** to live a different life! Shalom!

A Nigerian ship sank to the bottom of the Atlantic several years ago. **Three days later, divers** went down to recover the bodies. **As a diver reached out** to a floating hand, **the hand grabbed him.** A man survived, **thanks to an air pocket** and a bottle of **Coke.** And, **of course, God.** All through his ordeal, **he was praying the Psalm,** texted to him by his wife: "Oh God, by your name, save me. … **The Lord sustains my life.**"

The Bible teaches that God not only **created** the universe but that **He upholds** and **sustains** it day by day, hour by hour. **Scripture says, "The Son is … sustaining** all things by his powerful word" (Hebrews 1:3), and "in Him all things hold together (Colossians 1:17).

Turn in your Bible to I Peter 5:10 and we want to teach again on **"Sustaining Grace."** We will **also** be looking at **Philippians 1:6 that says,**

"**Being confident** of this very thing, that He which hath **begun a good work in you** will perform it until the **day** of **Jesus Christ**" (NASB).

Remember: If you started right, you are going to finish right. If Jesus is **the one** who put you in the race, then you are going to **be there at the end of the race** and you are going to **cross the finish line.** He is **not only the author** of your faith; He is **the finisher** of your faith. And again, we are talking about **not only how His grace** not only saves us and **we are in the family of God by grace through faith,** but how His grace **sustains us** in every part of life.

Perhaps you need to **memorize: I Peter 5:10 & 12** where he says, **but "the God of all grace,"** notice that, **He is called** the "**God of all grace.**" As **we talk about** amazing grace, amazing grace **is possible because our God is the God of all grace.** That **means outside of Him,** there is **no grace,** there is **no mercy. Christianity is the only religious faith** in the world that **has the concept of grace.** All **other religions** have the concept of **working your way to heaven** or working your way to **please God.** Only true **biblical Christianity** says that the **only way to God** is through His grace by faith, so the look at what this passage says.

I Peter 5:10; 12 states, "But the **God of all grace,** who hath **called us** unto **His eternal glory** by Christ Jesus, after that ye have **suffered a while,** make you perfect, stablish, strengthen, settle you. By Silvanus, a faithful brother unto you, as I suppose, I have written to you briefly, exhorting, and testifying that this is the **true grace of God** wherein **ye stand.**"

On the Internet, you can find dozens and **dozens of crafts online** to help you **teach your children** that God is the **Creator.** Many times **we forget to emphasize** to our youth that **He is also our sustainer. God not only created everything** around us, but **He has total control over everything we see.** As Christian adults, we must make this an emphasis to our youth. **In our daily Bible study,** we **must teach them** that it is **God that has given them life, and keeps them alive.**

The God Who created and **makes the sun** come up, and **blesses us with food** for our tables, He is very same **merciful God Who sustains us** each and every day.

> "**You, Lord, in the beginning laid the foundation**
> **of the earth And the heavens are the works**
> **of Your hands**" (Hebrews 1:10 NASB).

Listen: some might say, **"It's so hard to be a Christian!"** Let me tell you right here ... **that is true!** **True especially when you don't rely upon,** and **live for Jesus, In fact, it is impossible!** He is the **one who gives the Christian strength.** He is the **one who gives** the believer **wisdom.** He is the one who will **guide you** and **direct you.** **He is** the **one** who will **give you rest** in the midst of the storms of life. **He gives** you **the power you need** when you need it - **rely** upon Him and **rest in Him.**

God's Sustaining Grace is the power to keep you going even **when you feel like giving up.** Do you ever **feel like throwing in the towel?** Do you feel **like quitting?** Do you ever say, "I've **had enough?"** God's **Sustaining Grace is the power** that **helps you endure** even when you don't think you can.

Sometimes I get tired. At **81 years old,** life can be **exhausting. It requires** a lot of energy. **It requires** a lot of **strength.** Easy things are **not always easy** - are they? Some-times we think something will take little time and little energy - **but easy things sometimes consume most of our day.** Easy things are **not always easy** - and sometimes **we get tired.** It is **at times like this that I need 'God's Sustaining Grace.'**

Remember Christian, that **receiving Jesus Christ** as our Lord and Savior **doesn't guarantee** we will **never again suffer** in this life. **This world is a fallen place,** and **Christians** are **not exempt from adversity.** The **good news** is, **grace enables us** to **face life challenges** with **confidence** and **assurance.** **More than** simply **providing forgiveness, grace** supports and **sustains us through our trials.**

Almighty God sustains all **His people** in a **providential way** in their beings, and **supplies** them with **all the necessaries** of life; and, in a **spiritual way,** maintaining their spiritual life, **supplying them with all grace,** bearing them up **under all trials,** holding up their goings in his ways, and preserving them to the end.

Here is a secret that I have learned: **Life is a marathon** - it is **not a sprint. If this is true,** and it is, **why is it that** so many people treat it as such, **then end up frustrated** at their conclusion. As you **live the Christian life** and **train** for one of the **biggest endurance challenges** you will ever face, it is important to **remember this** ... it is a **marathon. Steady paced consistency is the key,** not just for a week, a month or a year.

Friends, I encourage you to **reflect** how you have been **running your race called life.** It's **never too late** to make necessary adjustments. **Take strides** on purpose and **submit** to the process with **patience.** I know **it's not easy,** but you won't be disappointed! Yes, take strides on purpose and remain!

When we become Christians, we must learn participation, because we are already involved. The author of Hebrews states, "…let us run with patience the race that is set before us" (12:3). Do not be too quick to run after every spiritual fad and charismatic guru you are introduced to.

Focus on the word patience for a moment. The Greek word that underlies it means patience/endurance. The word translated race is a translation of the Greek word 'agona,' from where we get our word 'agony.' The point is once again that the Christian life is a marathon. It is not a spectator sport! Our Lord calls you to run with patience (endurance) the race (even in agony) that is set before us. There's no shortcut!

You may be saying to yourself, "This preacher doesn't know what he is writing about." What are the limits of God's grace? You may know some people so deeply entrenched in wickedness they can't turn to the Lord? Amazingly, the answer is: yes they can! God can transform lives and circumstances no matter what kind of sins they have committed.

Unfortunately, however, even many believers don't have an accurate perception of Who the Lord is, and what He can do. He's not a distant, unloving, figment of the imagination, cruel and hateful judge, but a God of grace.

Are you a Christian? If you are, are you running in the marathon or sitting on the sideline because of some excuse you have? If you are sitting on the sideline you need to get in the race.

I have found that there are three kinds of trouble in this world. There is the kind that blows you away like a tornado. There is the kind that weighs you down like a sack of potatoes. Then there is the kind of trouble that pulls the rug out from under you. But no matter what type of trouble you run into – God will give you His sustaining grace.

We're sustained by grace. God will never ask you to do anything He doesn't give you the ability and the power to do. That power and ability is called grace (Philippians 2:13).

God is The Sustainer - God will never fail those who place their trust in Him, Isaiah 49:23; Romans 10:11. Not a single Word of any of His precious promises will ever fail to be honored by Him, Matthew 5:18; Psalm 119:89-90; Isaiah 40:8. If you come to Him for salvation, He will not send you away lost, John 6:37. If you trust Him and rely on Him for salvation, He will never send you away into Hell (John 10:28). If you look to Him for the needs in your life, you will never be disappointed, Luke 12:32. He will sustain you through this life and into eternity.

In 1992, following five operations, British **runner Derek Redman** was **hoping to win gold** at the **Barcelona Olympics.** Everything seemed to be **going well** for the **400 meter race.** He **had recorded the fastest time** in the quarter-final heat. He was **pumped up - ready to go.** As the **gun sounded** he got off to a clean start. **But at 150 meters** - his **right hamstring muscle ripped** and he **fell** to the ground.

When he **saw the stretcher-bearers** rushing towards him he **jumped up** and **began hobbling** toward the finish line. **Despite** his **pain** he **continued** to move forward. **Soon another person joined him** on the track. **It was his father.** Arm in arm - hand in hand - shoulder to shoulder - they **moved toward** the finish-line together. Just **before the finish line - Derek's dad let go** of his son - so that Derek could **finish the race on his own.** The **crowd of 65,000** stood to **their feet cheering, clapping, urging them Derek to finish the race.** **Heartbreaking** - yes! **Encouraging** - yes! **Emotional** - yes! **We need to finish the race - and finish it well.** He **lost** the **sprint,** but **won the respect of those who witnessed his race** (see-Hebrews 12:1).

God who began a good work in you - wants **you to finish** the race. He **wants you to endure.** He wants you to **be successful.** He wants you to **finish and finish well.** God **does not leave you to run** the race **alone** but **He gives you His Sustaining Grace.**

His grace sustains us in **every situation, suffering and trial** (II Corinthians 12:9). When we **are needy, we are invited** to come to **God's throne of grace** to receive mercy and **find grace to help** in our time of need (Hebrews 4:16). We are told to **fix our hope** completely **on the grace** to be brought to us when Jesus Christ returns (I Peter 1:13). **The very last verse of the Bible reads,** "The grace of the Lord Jesus be with all. Amen" (Revelation 22:21).

Grace is compared to the **sweetest things;** to sweet spices, to wine and milk. **Grace is a sweet flower** of paradise, **a spark** of glory. **Grace is nourished** and **maintained** by that sweet Word, **which is sweeter than the honey** or the honey-comb, **and by sweet union** and **communion with the Father and the Son.**

I love the way the Lord speaks to Paul in his second letter to the Corinthians. He says **"My grace is sufficient** for you, for my power is made perfect in weakness" (II Corinthians 2:9).

Friend, **this is a statement of hope.** This is **a promise** that all believers **can rely upon.** No matter what comes my way - **God's grace is sufficient** to help me **through any** and **every weakness** ... through all **circumstances.**

Seven hundred years before Jesus came to earth, He said, "Fear not, for I am with you; Be not dismayed, for I am your God. **I will strengthen you,** Yes, I will help you, I will uphold you with My righteous right hand" (Isaiah 41:10).

Roger Woodward was wearing a life jacket during a tragic **boating accident in 1960** that threw him into the water and whisked the **seven-year old** over the **largest waterfall** in the world - **Niagara Falls.** While going over the brink, **Roger said he felt like he was floating in a cloud with** no sensation of up or down. Some **called it a miracle;** others said it was the **water cone phenomenon** that gently supported his falling body and allowed Roger to be the **first person to go over the falls accidentally and survive.** Whatever the physical explanation, everyone agrees that **without the life jacket,** he surely would have died.

You may wonder why, if God wanted Roger to live, didn't **He just prevent the boating accident** in the first place? The **Lord's sustaining grace** does **not promise the absence** of distress. **It upholds and floats** those it surrounds through the deadly threats into life and safety.

Did you know that there are over **7,000 promises** in the Bible **waiting to be claimed?** Here are a couple of them:

> **"Let us therefore draw near with confidence to the**
> **throne of grace, that we may receive mercy and may find**
> **grace to help in time of need"** (Hebrews 4:16 AKJV).

He gives a **greater grace.** Therefore it says, "God is opposed to the proud, but **gives grace to the humble" (James 4:6). And,** "**Those who wait on the Lord** shall **renew their strength.** They shall **mount up** (soar) with wings like eagles. They **shall run** and not be weary, they **shall walk** and not faint" (Isaiah 40:31).

As you and I face the battles, burdens, valleys, storms and trials of life, **we must always** remember that **we are His little lambs** and that **He is well able to carry us safely through.** So, **what kind of battles are you** fighting today? Bring them to the Father and trust in His unchanging, unfailing faithfulness.

Christian, **when you're in pain,** in **problems,** and **trouble** seems to be all around you, **and you are searching for peace,** the **first thing to know is that God is there** - and our **Omniscient God** sees and **knows what you're facing.** Right now, **I'm thinking of a great** word for God that we don't use much anymore. It is a word that so **describes God's character** that **our Founding Fathers often used** this word for God and is found in our **founding** documents. They just capitalized it and substituted it for God. It appears in our 'Declaration of Independence.'

This word is such a powerful word that the Baptist preacher, Roger Williams, gave it as the name of a city that is now the capital of our smallest state. It's the word "providence." 'Pro' means "ahead." 'Videre' means, "to see." We get our word "video" from it. When used as a title of God, it means that God not only sees what's happening to us now, He sees what's going to happen ahead. So, listen, no matter what you're going through right now, God has already seen the video of what's going to happen. For Christians, trust me, it's 'Good'!

Paul said that he would not boast except in the cross of Christ which is the ground of grace (Galatians 6:14) and in his weaknesses which show his need for grace (II Corinthians 12:9). And it's why he said in Romans 15:18, I will not presume to speak of anything except what Christ has accomplished through me. So for Paul everything good that he has is a gift of grace, and everything he accomplishes with what he has is a work of grace. And so all boasting is excluded, except boasting in grace.

As strong as I can show you, I mean that everything in this spiritual dynamic is sustained by God's grace. "Treasuring all that God is" is a work of grace in my heart. I would not treasure God without a mighty work of grace in my life (Acts 18:27; Philippians 1:29; Ephesians 2:8f). "Loving all whom he loves" is a work of grace in my heart (I Thessalonians 3:12; 4:9; Philippians 1:9; Galatians 5:22).

> "A man can no more take in a supply of grace for the future
> than he can eat enough for the next six months, or take
> sufficient air into his lungs at one time to sustain life
> for a week. We must draw upon God's boundless store
> of grace from day to day, as we need it." - D.L. Moody

Why has God set it up this way? Because the giver gets the glory. God has established the universe in such a way that it magnifies the glory of His all-sufficiency. You can see this really clearly in 1 Peter 4:11. Whoever serves, let him do so as by the strength which God supplies [that's grace]; so that in all things God may be glorified through Jesus Christ, "to Whom belongs the glory and dominion forever and ever. Amen" (I Peter 5:11). God gets the glory because He gave the grace.

God does not change you so He can love you. **He loves you** so He can change you! God the **Father loves** you as much as He loves Jesus. **If you are saved,** a true child of God, **you are 'in Christ.'** And **where is He?** He is **seated in the heavenlies.**

What does Paul mean when he says, "But **God,** being **rich in mercy,** because of the **great love** with which he loved us, even when we were dead in our trespasses, **made us alive** together with Christ - **by grace** you have been saved - and **raised us up** with him and **seated us** with him in the **heavenly places** in Christ Jesus" (Ephesians 2:4-6, NASB). **You are also seated** in those heavenly places, even though you **still have your address** on planet Earth. You are **enthroned** with Him. **When was the last time you compared yourself** with someone else? It's time to **get yourself unharnessed** from the **comparison yoke and break free** as a **child of the King!**

God is in charge of running everything! **He runs** the whole **Galaxy of Love! Astronomers** estimate that the **observable universe** has more than **100 billion galaxies. Our own Milky Way** is home to **approximately 300 billion stars,** but its size is not representative of **all galaxies** in general. The **Milky Way is a giant** compared to more abundant but faint dwarf galaxies. Yet, **in turn, our Milky Way** seems **insignificant** in comparison to rare giant **elliptical galaxies** that can be **20 times more massive.** By measuring the number and luminosity of observable galaxies, **astronomers estimate** there is a total stellar **population** of roughly **70 billion trillion stars!** We must **remember that nothing is too big or impossible for God.**

That's a lot - yet the **Creator** has placed **each star carefully** into its place in the universe. In fact, **He knows them so well** He has **given each of them a name** (Psalm 147:4). Now **consider: He knows you much more than the stars.** Wherever you go, **God is there.** Whatever you do, **He sees it.** The Lord **knows every hair** on your head and **every thought** before you think it. "How does He do this?" you ask. He is an Omniscient God (knowing everything ... past, present and future. **If He wasn't Omniscient, He couldn't be God.**

Take a moment and look up to the heavens **tonight.** As you **survey** the stars, **thank Him** for **His incredible love** for you. **Pray also** that the hearts of **Americans,** our **leaders, and our neighbors and friends** will come to understand His **galaxy of love for them!**

> **Grace operates** on a totally **different** basis. **Grace does not give men what they deserve,** but what **God delights** to give, **in spite** of their sin. **God is only unjust if** He **withholds**

from men **benefits** which they **rightfully deserve,** but **He is gracious** in **bestowing** upon men **salvation** and **blessings** which **they could never merit**. - Bob Deffinbaugh

Grace is power for Christian living. **Grace is the power** to **treasure** all that **God is for us** in Jesus. **Grace is the power** to **love all** whom God loves. **Grace is the power** to **pray** for all God's purposes. **Grace is the power** to **meditate** on all God's Word. **We are utterly dependent on the grace of Almighty God** ... **OR** ... we are lost - doomed - and damned.

Let me reiterate: grace is **not only a past experience** of pardon, it is a **future experience** of power **to do** what God commands us to do. **This is the reason gratitude for past grace is** not the fuel for today's obedience. **You can't run your car** on gratitude for **yesterday's gas.** You need today's **gas for today's trip.** You and I **need today's grace for today's obedience.** And the **pump is not gratitude** but faith in future grace. The **great challenge** of this **mission statement** is **learning how to live by faith in future grace.**

If you are lost and need to be saved, you can come to Jesus today and He will save your soul. **Christian, if you are walking through a hard place** in life and need help; **God will provide** the **help** you need. **If you are struggling** with the **flesh** and some **besetting sin;** there is **help** for that as well.

Christ has replaced the dreaded door of death with the excellent entrance to eternal life! - G. Clifton

You're not saved by grace and works ... but by **grace alone. Grace is not** God making up the difference in your shortfall. It does **not mean that you pay a little bit** and **then God pays the rest.** That's **not grace!**

In August 2010, the **attention of the world** was focused on a **mine shaft near Copiapó, Chile. Thirty-three miners** huddled in the dark, **trapped 2,300 feet underground.** They had **no idea if help** would ever arrive. After **seventeen days of waiting,** they **heard drilling.** Rescuers produced a **small hole** in the mine shaft ceiling, and that hole was **followed by three more,** establishing a **delivery path for water, food, and medicine.** The miners **depended on those conduits** to the surface **above ground,** where **rescuers had the provisions** they would **need to survive.** On **day sixty-nine,** rescuers **pulled the last miner to safety.**

None of us can survive in this world **apart from provisions** that are outside of ourselves. **God, the Creator** of the universe, is the **one who provides**

us with **everything we need.** Like **the drill holes** for those miners, prayer **connects us to the God above** of all supply.

Jesus encouraged us to pray, "Give us today our daily bread" (Matt. 6:11). **In His day, bread** was the **basic staple** of life and pictured all the **daily needs** of the people. **Jesus was teaching us** to **pray** not only for our **physical needs** but also for **everything we need** - comfort, healing, courage, wisdom.

The grace of God means that you and I come without anything to offer. **We come into the Kingdom helpless and hopeless** and **empty.** Jesus **invites** us there, **not** on the basis of our merit or money, but on the **basis of his grace.**

God's Sustaining Grace is the power to keep you going even **when you feel like giving up.** Do you ever **feel like throwing in the towel?** Do you **feel like quitting? Do you ever say,** "I've had enough?" **God's Sustaining Grace** is the **power** that **helps you endure** even when you **don't think you can.**

Here is a secret that I have learned: Life is a **marathon** – it is **not a sprint. There are valleys and** there are **mountains.** There **are bad times** and there are **good times** and there are times when we could **all use** God's **Sustaining Grace** to keep on - keeping on. **God's Sustaining Grace** is the **power** that God gives to **keep you going.**

WE ARE SAVED, SATISFIED AND SUSTAINED BY GOD'S GRACE ALONE!

So today, **remember that your salvation is a gift** of grace through and through. It doesn't depend on what you do ... it's based entirely on **what Jesus did for you!**

Did you know that there are over **7000 promises** in the **Bible** waiting to be claimed? Here's one about **God's sustaining grace.** "Do you **not know?** Have you **not heard? The Everlasting God, the LORD,** the **Creator** of the ends of the earth, **does not** become **weary** or **tired.** His **understanding** is inscrutable. He **gives strength** to the weary, and to him who lacks might **He increases power.** Though youths **grow weary and tired,** And vigorous young men **stumble badly,** Yet **those who wait for the LORD will gain new strength;** They will **mount up** with **wings** like **eagles,** They **will run** and **not** get tired, They **will walk** and **not** become weary" **(Isaiah 40:28-31 NASB).**

God wants His children to be **successful.** He wants us **to over-come** this world. He wants us to **rely on His strength** and **His promises. God gives us all kinds of promises** in His Word – but it does no good unless we rely upon them. **We must trust** in the Lord - we must **put our faith into action** - we must rely upon the fact that **His promises are true.** Put your **hope in the Lord.** Keep your **eyes focused** on the **hope of heaven.**

Let us Pray ... **Heavenly Father,** we **thank You** for the **sustaining power** we have in You. **Jesus, thank You** for **removing the veil** from our eyes and **empowering us** to live in **Your grace** and **presence.** Because of Your blood, I boldly approach our Father and **desire to be changed** in His presence. **Thank you Lord** for all **Your sustaining love** and **blessings. In the precious Name** of Jesus we pray, AMEN!

> **"My love be with you all in Christ Jesus.**
> **Amen." –** I Corinthians 16:24

Chapter 10

God's Grace Is 'SUFFICIENT' To Meet My Need

GOD'S GRACE IS all-sufficient … It is **sufficient for every trial** that we endure, and it goes so far **beyond God's blessing** in our lives. **We must look at our trials** and **tribulations** in light of the **grace of God** … Question: **What is God trying to teach me** here? **Ask yourself: How is His grace working** through this **in my circumstance?**

Problems, situations, troubles, glitches, setbacks, difficulties, complications, **what kind of thorn do you have?** The **cancer** in the body. The **sorrow** in the heart. The **child** in the rehab center. The **craving for whiskey** in the middle of the day. The **tears** in the middle of the night. The **thorn-in-the-flesh.** "**Take it away,**" you've pleaded. **Not once, twice,** or even **three times,** you've **out-prayed** Paul. And **you** keep **hitting the wall.**

Unfortunately, even for some Christians, sometimes life's journey feels like a **funeral dirge. Mistakes** clothe us in robes of mourning. **Circumstances** bury our dreams and desires. On **those days,** all we can **do is cry** out **for mercy.** But **God gives us more than mercy … He gives us grace.**

And, **what you hear is this:** "**My grace is sufficient** for you." **Sustaining grace.** The **grace that meets** us at **our point of need** and **equips us** with courage, wisdom, and strength. **Sustaining grace!** It **doesn't promise the absence of struggle. It promises the presence of God.**

When life gets hard the **hard-working work harder.** Is it **any wonder we're all so tired?** We do **our best** to do better, **do more,** and **do now.** And, **when we think we can't do it anymore grace says,** "**You** can **rest now. Jesus** already **did it all.**" **Every hurt is followed** by a **choice.** We can get **bent out of shape, or** we can **let our response** be shaped with grace. **Bitterness clouds** the **vision.** It makes us **blind to grace.** But **grace isn't blind.** It **sees the hurt** and **chooses to see God's forgiveness** even more.

Grace changes ... everything! It's **God's answer** to the **mess** of a **sinful, broken life.** And as we all know ... **life does messy. Poor** choices ... **wasted** years ... **guilt** ... **regret. God's response is grace, grace, and more grace.** By **grace He saves** us, **strengthens** us, and **softens** us. The **God kind of sufficient grace shapes our lives.**

Either God's grace is sufficient or God is a liar, and we know **God can not lie.** Praise God **His grace is sufficient!** God **so abundantly supplies us** with **sufficient grace** that we have a place to stand and something great for which to live. **Grace is not simply a one-time gift** we receive. It is a state in which we live. **Life itself is a continuing experience** of God's salvation, an experience made possible by **God's continuing grace. Salvation is never** something we can lay claim to as a **possession earned.** It is always a **gift received in grace!**

How do I know that **God's grace is sufficient** to meet my needs? **He said so!** "Cast your burden upon the LORD - and He will **sustain** you" (Psalm 55:22 ESV). **The promise is not** that the **Lord will remove the load** we cast upon Him, **nor that He will carry it for us** - but that **He will sustain us** so that **we may carry** it. **God does not free us** from the duty - but **He strengthens us** for it. **He does not deliver us** from the conflict - but **He enables us** to overcome. **He does not withhold** or withdraw the trial from us - but **He helps us in trial** to be submissive and victorious, and makes it a blessing to us. **He does not mitigate** the hardness or severity of our circumstances, **taking away the difficult elements,** removing the thorns, making life easy for us - but **He puts Divine grace** into our hearts, **so** that **we can live sweetly** in all the **hard, adverse circumstances.**

> **"My grace is sufficient for you, for My strength is made perfect in weakness"** (II Corinthians 12:9 NIV).

When I was a young boy, I thought that God was like some kind of **'Tooth Fairy'** or **'Santa Claus'** with **beautiful clothes** and a **long beard** sitting up in the clouds up in heaven - having nothing to do but **making a list** and **checking it twice,** trying to find out if **I was naughty or nice.** (You do remember the old fat man don't you?) **Then when my life was over,** I would **face Him** and He would **pull out these massive scales** and **weigh** my **good works** against my bad **to see if I made it into heaven.**

Do you know what this kind of thinking did to me? It made me fearful and terrified that **at the end** of **my life** I would **face this ghastly God** and He would say to me, "**Glenn, I'm sorry, but** according to **My calculations, you didn't make it.**" Then, **I would have to turn and ashamedly walk past family and friends.**

Friend, I don't know **what you believe about this,** but **let me set the record straight: Salvation is not an attainment because of accomplishment. It is an atonement, not an attainment!**

You cannot atone or expiate for your sins. Your **good works cannot do it.** None of **us could produce works good-enough** and **fast enough** to atone for sin. **Don't even try.** We **must learn to rest** in the **finished work of the cross.**

The verse above is not just a hope - it is **a promise!** It begins with the words, **"God is able!" Whatever grace God favors us with,** that is **what He gives to us.** It **can** include **spiritual gifts** or **physical things** that He provides. **By His grace, we have food** to eat every day, we have **clothes** to wear, and we have a **roof** over our heads or **cars** to drive, a **job** to go to, a **family** to love, and **a wonderful Lord** to serve.

> **"When through fiery trials thy pathway shall lie,**
> **My grace all sufficient, shall be thy supply, The**
> **flame shall not hurt thee, I only design, Thy dross**
> **to consume, and thy gold to refine."** -John Rippon

Paul had a problem and was asking God for help. **What did God do** for Paul? **How did God answer** Paul's prayer? **Never forget,** my friend, **God is not interested in just** meeting **your need.** He wants always to **give you more than you need.** That is what the word **"abound" means.** It literally means: **an ever-increasing, super-abundant supply!** In other words, in the spiritual Christian life, **as the battle gets hotter,** God's **grace increases!**

Our God is extravagant in his grace, often **liberally dispensing his favor** without even the least bit of cooperation and preparation on our part. What do I mean by that? **I can flip a switch,** but **I don't provide** the electricity. When I **turn on the overhead light** in the morning, I don't celebrate, "Hey, look what I did! I turned the lights on!" **I didn't provide the power.** An **electrician** wired my house; the **power company** provided the energy; **all I did was flip the switch** that released the flow.

It's similar to turning on a faucet. I didn't put the **plumbing** in. **I'm not with the water company** that supplies the water. I **simply turn on the faucet** and the water flows.

So it is, in a limited sense, for **the Christian** with the **ongoing grace of God.** Remember, **His grace is essential** for our **spiritual lives,** but **we don't control** the supply. **We can't make the grace flow,** but God has given us **routes** to connect and **channels** to open anxiously.

> **"God is able to make all grace abound toward you; that you, always having all-sufficiency in all things, may abound to every good word and work"** (II Corinthians 9:8).

All-sufficiency in all things! Believer! Surely you are "thoroughly furnished!" **Grace is no irrelevant thing,** passed out in frivolous trifle. **It is a glorious treasury,** which the **key of prayer** can always unlock, but never empty. **A fountain,** "full, flowing, ever flowing, over flowing."

> **There is a fountain,** filled with His grace, **coming down** from the Throne above; grace so efficient, grace so divine, fills our life with 'Jesus love!

Ah, my friend - **We are saved by grace** (Ephesians 2:8) and **in grace we stand, we serve** (Romans 5:2). **Grace upholds** our salvation, **grace gives** us **victory** in temptation, and **grace helps** us **endure** suffering and pain. It **helps us understand** the Word and **wisely apply it** to our lives. It **draws us** into communion and prayer and **enables us** to **serve** the Lord effectively. In short, **we exist** and are **firmly fixed** in an **environment** of God's **all-sufficient grace.**

Mark these three ALL'S in this precious promise to the church at Corinth. It is a three-fold **link in a golden chain,** let down from a **throne of grace** by a **God of grace.** "All grace!" - "all-sufficiency!" in "all things!" and these to "abound." Oh! Precious thought! **My spiritual need** cannot **impoverish or bankrupt** that **inexhaustible treasury of grace!** Multitudes are hourly **hanging** on it, and **drawing** from it, and yet there is no decrease - **"Out of that fullness** all **we too** may receive, and poses **grace for grace!"**

All believers must learn that **God's grace is sufficient** or **God is a liar,** and we know God can not lie. Praise God, **His grace is always sufficient!** God so abundantly **supplies us** with **sufficient grace** that we have a place to stand and something great for which to live. **Grace is not simply a one-time gift** we receive. It is a **state in which we live.**

My soul, **do you not love to dwell on that all-abounding grace?** Your own insufficiency in everything, met with an "all-sufficiency in all things!" **Grace** in all **circumstances** and **situations,** in all vicissitudes and changes, in all the varied phases of the Christian's being. **Grace in sunshine** and **storm - in health** and in sickness - **in life** and in death. **Grace for the old believer** and the **young** believer, the **tried** believer, and the **weak** believer, and the **tempted** believer. **Grace for duty,** and grace **in** duty—grace **to carry** the joyous cup with a steady hand, **grace to drink** the bitter cup with an un-murmuring spirit - **grace to have prosperity** sanctified - **grace to say,** through tears, **"Your will be done!"**

As the **Apostle John states** in his first Epistle, "And of His **fullness** (sufficiency) And of His **fullness** (sufficiency) we have all received, and **grace for grace,**" have all we received, and **grace for grace,**" (John 1:16). Ah, dear friend, **we can never exhaust the riches of the grace** of our Lord Jesus Christ. **When we receive Him** as Savior, we receive **"grace for grace"** - that is, **one grace after another,** grace upon grace.

As a **preacher** ... I have always **been accused** of **presenting more** than **was needed to be sufficient.** In other words I presented **to much subject** than **time would afford.** Got it? Or, **do I have too present more to be sufficient?** In other words, **"I was long-winded."** Let me show you what I mean.

A man was leaving church one Sunday and **said to his pastor, "Your message** today **reminded me** of **the peace and mercy** of God." The **pastor said,** "Why, thank you." The **man said,** "Don't thank me. **It was like the peace of God** because **it passed all my understanding,** and it was **like the mercy** of God because it **seemed to endure forever,** and **ever,** and **ever!"**

For the Christian, our spiritual life itself is a continuing experience of God's salvation, an experience made possible **by God's continuing grace.** Salvation **is never something** we can lay claim to as **a possession earned.** It is always a **gift received in grace.**

As weakness comes upon you, **His grace brings strength** on you even greater! And **when your burdens** become heavier, **His power and strength** increase in proportion to your burdens!

God never intended for us to be spiritual paupers, poor in the **things of the Lord.** On the contrary, **the bountiful servant is the one** who enjoys a revelation of **all the great provisions God** has prepared for him! And he goes after this revelation by faith!

Let's look at it again: "And **God is able** to make **all grace abound** toward you, that you, always having **all sufficiency** in all things, may have an abundance for every good work." **Please take the time to notice the imagery** that we have here. **God's grace toward us** is like a **fountain** of **living water.**

Such a fountain has a **never ending source** of water. All those who have a fountain have an **all-sufficient supply** of water.

> **The rain of His grace is always dropping.**
> **The river of His bounty is ever-flowing.**
> **The well-spring of His love is constantly overflowing.**

Our churches should always have this **never ending water supply.** The **churches well** should be tapped into this deep spring. Even during the **driest summers,** we have **never run out** of water (Holy Spirit power). Then from that **fountain of living water** we can do much good. **We quench thirst.**

The fountain that supplies all that we need **is God's grace. What is grace?** As stated elsewhere in this book, **by using an acrostic,** it is God's Riches At Christ's Expense. **God's grace** is the **sum total** of all the **unmerited blessings** and **favors** which **come to us from God through Jesus Christ. God's grace** is the **source** of all of **His blessings.**

God's grace is like that. You can **never exhaust God's grace.** And out of the **all-sufficiency of His grace,** we have all the resources we need **to do every good work.** Ephesians 2:10 states that we are **"created in Christ Jesus for good works…"**

Titus 2:14 says that **Christ redeemed us that we might be "zealous for good works." God does not just demand** that we produce good works; **He enables us** to do good works out of the **resources of His grace.**

Most Christians have not honestly faced the power of these **promises of God!** We've **read them** many times, but they remain as dead-letters to us. **We haven't laid hold** of them and **said, "Lord, reveal** to me what You have prepared! **Open my mind** and **my spirit** to Your resources. **Your Word says** I may know all these things that are freely given to me, **so I can claim them for Your glory!"**

It is important that we **remember** that **God does not dispense strength and encouragement** like a **pharmacist** fills a prescription. **God never says,** "Here, take two of these and call Me in the morning." **He *is* the grace.** He *is* the **strength.** His **presence** *is* the power. **All we need** comes through intimacy with Him. **No matter what we face,** Jesus is the complete answer. **"Sufficient for you is the grace of me."** He doesn't give what we need and then go somewhere else. He comes to stay. **"I am with you always"** (Matthew 28:20 NIV).

Our God is all sufficiency: "God is able to make **all grace abound to you,** so that having **all sufficiency in all things** at all times, you may **abound in every good work**" (II Corinthians 9:8 NIV).

Divine grace is sufficient. In fact, **it is more than sufficient!** What **Paul wishes** us to feel is this - to put it into very plain English - **that the good gifts of the divine grace** will always **be proportioned to our work,** and to **our sufferings too.** We shall feel that we have enough, if we are as we ought to be. **Sufficiency is more** than a man gets anywhere else.

A former Buddhist who **became a Christian** wrote, "One of the **hardest things** to understand was **why I didn't have to work** my way to heaven. **In Buddhism** you must **pray** hard, **burn** incense and **give many offerings.** Even so, **you can't know for sure** if you'll go to heaven."

Christian friend, do you realize that **people outside of Christ** have **no assurance** of salvation?! **But you do!** You **are standing** right smack dab **in the middle of God's sustaining grace!**

Paul experienced God's grace as few others have **because he endured suffering** as few others have. In II Corinthians 12:9 the **Lord gave him one of the most profound** truths in all revelation: "My grace is sufficient for you, **for power is perfected** in weakness." **The power** of this **weakness** is abundantly evident in I Corinthians 2:3-5. **This is not the weakness** of **ignorance** or of **unbelief, but** that of **conscious self-inefficiency** and entire **dependence** on the **offered grace** of **God.**

If God's strength is to be made perfect in weakness, surely here is an **opportunity for all of us.** To be **full of self-confidence is to be empty of the power of God.** God will not give His glory to another for self-display. **Humble yourself,** and **He will exalt** you.

That wonderful promise extends to **every believer,** but its context is one of severe difficulties, distresses, persecutions, and human weaknesses (II Corinthians 12:10). **Glorying in our infirmities** is something nobler than merely submitting to them. It is common for **Christian workers to find gladness in their gifts,** but not so common to find gladness in their infirmities. **Rejoice in the Lord always:** He does all things well.

Paul records many of the hardships and **life-threatening situations** he had endured. Included in his list are great physical trials—imprisonments, beatings, shipwrecks, dangerous rivers, stoning's, robbers, Jewish and Gentile persecutions, sleepless nights, inclement weather, and lack of food and drink

(II Corinthians 11:23–27). **He took pleasure in every trial** and **hardship** that made him feel more keenly the measure of his weakness, knowing that this **only made more room in his life for the grace and power of God.** I wonder what would happen **if we all accepted this gift of grace** in the same way Paul did?

We should glory in tribulation (trouble), knowing that **tribulation works patience, experience, hope** (Romans 5:3). "No chastening for the present seems to be joyous, but grievous, nevertheless afterward it yields peaceable fruit unto them that are exercised thereby" (Hebrews 12:11). **Let this** afterward **strengthen our faith** for the present.

When Peter was facing his own execution, and **he knew God was** aware of his situation. **Question: Are you enjoying** that same kind of peace that Peter had? **Can you sleep like a baby** even **when you are frightened** of what might happen tomorrow?

Peter could sleep not only because he **knew God was there,** and that **God was aware of His situation.** He also **knew God cared. Jesus had been** in the **same Stronghold** where he was imprisoned just a few weeks earlier. He had **been beaten** and **tortured** by Roman soldiers - and **I've often wondered** if these were some of the same soldiers guarding Peter.

> **When the Lord is with us, we have no cause of fear. His eye is upon us, His arm over us, His ear open to our prayer - His grace sufficient, His promise unchangeable.** - John Newton

The greatest pain Paul ever knew, however, **came from some of the people he loved** the most—those to whom he had given his soul and his gospel, but who now had turned against him. **More painful than all** that (in Chapter 11) was the **daily concern** he had for **all the churches** (II Corinthians 11:28).

God's people and **His church** were Paul's greatest passion (Colossians 1:28–29) and **they presented the highest potential for pain and disappointment.** Their rejection, betrayal, criticism, false accusations, and **even hatred cut deep into his heart.** In II Corinthians **he wrote as a man who was unloved,** unappreciated, distrusted, and deeply troubled in his soul.

"My grace is sufficient for you" (II Corinthians 12:9 NIV). **It is my prayer that you realize that these are tremendous words! Believe** them! **Apply** them to yourself. **Let the strength and wisdom** of the Lord come to you as you reflect on these great words. **God is speaking His Word to you.** Whatever is going on in your life, **whatever difficulties** you are facing, **God's Word is still the same:** "My grace is **sufficient for you.**"

God is always sufficient with His grace. Matthew states, "But the boat was now in the **midst** of the **sea, distressed** by the waves; for the **wind was contrary.** And in the fourth watch of the night **He came unto them, walking upon the sea**" (Matthew 14:24-25 ASV). **His grace was sufficient!**

God adapts His grace to the **peculiarities** of each of His **children's necessity.** For rough, flinty paths - **He provides** shoes of iron. **He never sends** anyone to climb steep, sharp, rugged mountainsides - wearing silken slippers. **He always gives sufficient grace.**

As the burdens grow heavier - His strength increases. As the **difficulties thicken -** He draws closer. **As the trials become crosser -** the trusting heart grows calmer.

Jesus always sees His disciples when they **are toiling** in the **waves,** and at the right **moment comes** to **deliver them.** The **sharper the temptations -** the more of **Divine grace** is granted. There is, therefore, **no environment of trial** or **difficulty** or **hardship -** in which we cannot **live beautiful lives** of Christian **devotion** and **holy conduct.**

Do you feel that God will let you down? **Don't believe it -** not even for a moment! It is a **lie of the devil.** It's "as old as the hills." Way back in Genesis 3:1, thousands of years ago, **Satan was spreading doubt:** "Did God say?" **God says,** "My grace is sufficient for you." **Satan comes along and says** "Surely you don't believe that!" **"When the howling storms** of **doubt** and **fear** assail, by the living Word of God I shall prevail." **Did God say that? - Yes!**

In our modern fast-paced civilization, **things go wrong.** Have you ever **had an accident? Wrecked** a car? **Wrecked** a friendship? Maybe you **even feel like you wrecked** your life? **Just as reckless driving** has its **consequences, so does reckless living.** No one **gets through life** with a **clean record -** no one except Jesus. And **He extends His record to you - by grace!**

When God gets us alone through suffering, heartbreak, temptation, disappointment, sickness, or by thwarted desires, a broken friendship, or a new friendship - when He gets us **absolutely alone,** and we are **totally speechless** and totally **helpless,** unable to ask even one question, **then He begins to teach us.**

Remember Jesus **Christ's training** of the **Twelve. It was the disciples, not the crowd** outside, who were confused. **His disciples constantly asked Him** questions, and **He constantly explained** things to them, but **they didn't fully understand until after they received the Holy Spirit** (John 14:26).

When He (Jesus) was alone ... the twelve
asked Him about the parable (Mark 4:10).

Consider our journey with God, the **only thing** He **intends** to **be clear** is the **way He deals with our soul.** The **sorrows** and **difficulties** in the lives of others will be **absolutely confusing** to you. **We think we understand** another **person's struggle until** God reveals the same shortcomings **in our lives.** There are vast **areas of stubbornness** and **ignorance** the **Holy Spirit has to reveal** in each of us, but **changes can only be done when Jesus gets us alone.** Are we **alone with Him** now ... today? **Or** are **we more concerned with our own ideas,** our own ambitions, friendships, and cares for our bodies? **Jesus cannot teach us anything** until **we quiet** all our **intellectual, traditional,** and **emotional questions. We must get alone with Him.**

And this is **where God's sustaining grace comes in. God's grace can sustain us** and keep us going if **we will let Him in.** God's **all-sufficient grace will see us through! How?**

Christ is the very **embodiment** of **all spiritual delights** and **pleasures,** the **very soul and substance of them all. As all the rivers** are **gathered into the ocean,** which is **the meeting-place** of all the **waters in the world, so Christ** is that **ocean** in which **all true delights** and **pleasures meet.**

It's been said that **"when the going gets tough, the tough get going."** There may be **some truth** in that statement, but it's **not the whole truth** for us who are in Christ. **When the going gets tough** (and it does ... or will), **that's when we lean - on** the **grace of God! It is not dumb nor sissy to ask for help,** especially **from God!** It's the **smartest thing** we could do.

Why do so many believers experience weakness, feelings of discouragement, despair and emptiness, as if they can't go on? **Why have so many Christians** backed off from God's promises, and become weary in well-doing? **Why have so many quit the fellowship** of other believers in the church? **Why do most believers neglect the study** of God's Word?

To address those questions, perhaps our neglect is because we are **not being led by God's Holy Spirit.** Perhaps it is because we do **not have this revelation** that the Spirit **gave the Apostles and the New Testament saints -** the **revelation** that **all the provisions** has been made possible for those **who would claim them by faith!**

Listen again to Paul, "To keep me from becoming conceited (exalted or boastful) because of these surpassingly great revelations, **there was given me a thorn in my flesh, a messenger of Satan, to torment me. Three times I**

pleaded with the Lord to take it away from me. "And he said to me, My grace is sufficient for you: for my strength is made perfect in weakness. Most gladly therefore will I rather glory in my infirmities, that the power of Christ may rest on me" (II Corinthians 12:7-9 AKJV). **God often sends a thorn** in the flesh **to those** to whom He gives abundant revelation, **in order to protect their hearts from destructive pride.** The apostle Paul said that he had been **given a "thorn in the flesh" in order that he would not exalt himself.**

For some, **the beauty of God's work in them** is **never** put on a **public stage** and is **seldom noticed,** except by a few. In such cases, those **peoples' lives are perfected** for God's pleasure and the impact on individuals around them. **Sometimes the Holy Spirit works inwardly** for almost a lifetime before that person is given the full platform to release the message. **Still others are called to be proclaimers** of the message. Some have been given an early platform and **are allowed to preach** beyond the **maturing work** of the **Holy Spirit** in their lives.

**God has purposed to work a life
message through each of us.**

Let's take another look at this. God said to Paul, "My grace is **sufficient** for you, for **My strength** is made perfect in (your) weakness." **Paul considered** his **malady,** the "thorn in the flesh" **to be part of God's grace,** a hard thing to say. **How could he say** that an **affliction** that **God allowed** could be **part of His grace** toward him? **Because with an infirmity,** whatever it happened to be, **God balanced out** for **Paul the revelations** that he had received, so **that he would not become big-headed** (proud).

The thorn was given because of revelation. On the other hand, it seems that God gives powerful revelation **because of the testing's that some are about to encounter. Paul received a prophetic vision** instructing him to take his missionary efforts into Macedonia rather than Bithynia. **That decision resulted in Paul and Silas being arrested,** dragged before the magistrate, severely **beaten** with rods, **thrown** into the inner prison, and **secured** in stocks. **Though the thorn can come** because of revelation, so also revelation can come to **prepare us for future testing's.** How greatly will the **saints who are awaiting** the **physical** and **visible return of Jesus Christ** be encouraged by the **undeniable confirmations** of His coming!

Contrary to some of the **modern teaching** today … **sometimes God does not deliver us from our suffering but gives us the grace to endure it.** That can be a **more powerful testimony** of **God at work** in us than if we were to be healed. You probably know **someone that lives with hardship** and yet does so graciously, even helping others. **That says more about the power of God** in their life **than if they were to be healed.** Some insist that all people are to be healed. This case of **Paul shows us that is not always the case.**

The writer of Hebrews says **Jesus, our High Priest,** knows our weaknesses. **He was tempted (tried)** in every way we are tempted, **yet He never sinned. Worry is a sin,** and we know **Jesus was tempted** to worry. **Fear is a sin,** and we know **Jesus was tempted** to be afraid. You should know **Jesus knows exactly how you're feeling** when you are afraid. **Jesus shares the feelings** of **our weaknesses.** And more importantly, in our weakest times, **God cares!** Since God cares for you, He, **through His grace,** can give you **peace in spite of your pain.**

Paul had to have such power from God for his ministry that **only an affliction could keep him from pride.** Paul's response to his situation was to **boast about the weakness** so that the power could rest on him. **He would prefer to have the power of God in his life** and be weak than to be in full health and not be used as mightily by God. **Which would you prefer?** If it came down to a choice, **would you choose health or the power of God on your ministry?**

Jude referred to these stumbling blocks as "faultfinders" (v.16). We have a **responsibility to protect the Lord's people from these.** At the same time, we must **guard our own hearts** against becoming cynical or closed to those the Lord may be seeking to join to us. **The faultfinders and the stumbling blocks** that the enemy sends to cause divisions will show their true natures quickly. **We must remove them,** and **turn away** from them, **or they** will **do great damage** to the **fellowship** of the saints. We must also do this in a way that **does not close our hearts to legitimate correction from the authority** that the Lord has established in His church.

Theologians through the ages have given a **great deal of curiosity to know** what Paul's **"thorn in the flesh"** was. There is not, I suppose, **one adversity which has touched humanity,** which has **not been dignified** and made to **stand in the place of this affliction.** The apostle speaks of it as **a definite affliction.** It had a **specific nature.** He **asked God** that it **might be removed.**

This is the most we know about it. It is **very evident** that whatever the **description of the thorn** was, it in some way **impaired his ministerial and**

personal abilities. It was a hindrance, an obstruction, a limitation. **It was a weakness** in which Christ's power was to be made signally illustrious.

"**My grace** is **sufficient** for you." **That word 'sufficient'** has **great richness** in it. It is **not simply a promise of** help - it is a promise that there **shall be enough help to meet the emergency**. **The power/sovereignty of God has a clear field;** and if, **when His servants are in trouble, God's grace** shall **be adequate** to their **needs** - shall be **sufficient** for them - nothing more can be added or imagined.

> **The Apostle Paul** states in **Romans 4:7-8, "Blessed**
> (happy) are they whose **transgressions** are **forgiven,**
> whose sins are **covered. Blessed** is the **man whose**
> **sin** the Lord will **never count against him."**

Why is it that the Lord will **never count** our sins against us at **death nor the judgment?** It's **because of Jesus!** And it's because we've put **our trust** and our hope in Him and Him alone! **Our sins are covered by His blood!** He **bore our sins** in His body on the tree! **He became sin for us** so that in Him **we might become the righteousness** of God!

Every Christian believes that he may carry his **spiritual troubles** to God. All believe that **under great and pressing afflictions**, men may **resort to God** with them. **In the case of the apostle Paul**, we have an instance of a **trouble that carried him to God**.

God's grace is not **just saving grace. God's grace** is not **just to get you to heaven.** God's **grace is** the source of **victorious Christian living.** When we **need strength** & ability to do good works, **God is able to give** that strength. When we **are facing temptation, God's** grace will provide a way to escape it, or **give us strength to resist it.** When we have a **great or difficult task,** God is able to fully **give us all** that we need to meet the challenge. **Whatever God commands us** to do **He will enable us** to bring it to **total fulfillment.**

It is very significant that the **problem** employed is a 'thorn' - **not** sword, **not** spear - **no instrument** that indicates great breadth of power, **but a thorn.** He was nettled, scratched, pierced. **It was a little thing that he was called to endure.** It was the **annoyance** of a **pungent thorn,** which **brought pain** - but no peril; which worried him and troubled him; **which drew his thoughts away** from higher things, and made his life a **burden to him.**

The great evangelist Dwight L. Moody said on the day **he drew his last breath,** "This **is my coronation day!**" My friend, we can **live today with excitement** because **our coronation day** is coming, too.

Listen, I know **we have a hard time thinking like Paul with this kind of attitude.** We consider **this sort of affliction to be evil,** but **Paul turns that on its head,** by saying, "**No, it is good,** because with this affliction, **I am weak,** and because I am weak, then I don't get the big head. **Then Christ can work** in and through me, and the work gets done." So he was content.

There are many troubles that God brings upon His people, or **permits them** to come upon them - which **He does not care to take away** from them, and which **it is not best** for them to be **removed.** Continued **troubles are not,** therefore, **evidences of God's displeasure.** He distinctly affirms, that **unless we have such troubles, we cannot be His sons,** "You have forgotten the exhortation which speaks unto you as unto children" (Hebrews 12:5).

When any Christian is in trouble, God says to him, "**My son,** you have forgotten that word of encouragement that addresses you as sons." "**My son,** do not make light of the **Lord's discipline,** and do not lose heart when **He rebukes you,** because **the Lord disciplines** those **He loves,** and **He chastens** every one **He accepts** as a son. **Endure hardship** as discipline; God is **treating you as sons.** For **what son is not disciplined** by his father?" (Hebrews 12:5-7, NLT).

This is the **word of God. When your trouble is real** and **painful,** and you **carry it to God** and ask for its removal, if it abides with you, **you are apt to think,** "It must be that God is punishing me for my sins, and that He is hiding His face from me." "**No,**" says the voice of God; "so far from it, **I am dealing with you tenderly,** I am your heavenly Father, I love you, and **the trouble that is God's sustaining grace produces a sense** of our real weakness, which is most **wholesome.** For we **tend naturally to arrogance** when we are in strength.

Prosperity has the **effect to puff us up;** and a **sense of our weakness** is a returning to our reason. **God's grace also cultivates us,** and **causes us to sympathize** with our fellow men. **In the day of prosperity,** we are apt to **feel quite independent** of our fellow men; but **when the day of trouble comes,** we find that we **stand greatly in need** of them. **Blessed are those troubles** that make us feel, **not only our dependence** on God, but **our relations to our fellow-men.**

> "**Not that we are sufficient of ourselves**
> **to think anything as of ourselves; but our**
> **sufficiency is of God**" (II Corinthians 3:5).

God promises in v.8 that God's **grace will abound** to us so that **we will have** "all sufficiency in all things." This means that **we have all that we need,** lacking nothing. **We all know** how the **23rd Psalm begins,** "The Lord is my Shepherd, I shall not want." It is so **liberating to find out** that **we do not live** the Christian life in **our own strength,** relying upon our own **limited resources.**

The Christian should be led by the Holy Spirit of God. The **Word teaches us,** "For if you live according to the flesh, you will die; but if by the Spirit you put to death the deeds of the body, you will live. For all who are led by the Spirit of God are sons of God" (Romans 8:13 - 14 NASB).

In fact, **of all the professors** I had in **college or seminary,** none ever **matched the personal instruction** I have received through the years **from God through the Holy Spirit.** In John 14:26, **Jesus promised the disciples:** "The Helper, **the Holy Spirit,** whom the **Father will send** in My name, **He will teach** you all things, and **bring to** your **remembrance all** that I said to you" (ESV). **Question:** Why do we **forget or disallow this truth** so quickly?

God's abundant grace not only saves us but also **is sufficient** and **trains** us. "For the **grace of God** has appeared, bringing salvation for all people" (Titus 2:11 ESV). **What tremendous news: Paul extols God's glorious grace** which saves us - end of story! **No, that's hardly the end of the story.** Paul quickly adds that this **same grace "train(s) us** to renounce ungodliness" (2:12 ESV). This enables us to abound in every circumstance, good and bad.

Anna Warner, author of the **hymn "Jesus Loves Me,"** constantly **faced financial pressure.** Her father had been a **wealthy power broker** in New York City, but the stock market **crash of 1837 wiped out his finances.** As a result, **Anna faced** overwhelming **debt all her life.** But she **learned to trust God** with her needs. **She said,** "There was a time when I was very perplexed, all bills were unpaid. **I knew that God would supply all my needs** so that we will have sufficient resources for our physical needs. **I just knew that Jesus loves me."**

> I Peter 5:10, **"Now the God of all grace, who called you to His eternal glory in Christ Jesus, will personally restore, establish, strengthen, and support you ..."** (HCSB).

"All grace!" God promises an **abundance of "all grace"** to those who learn the grace of giving and exercise it "cheerfully" (the **Greek word** in II Corinthians 9:7 is that from which we derive **our word "hilarious").** **Reader: please note the frequent use of superlatives** in this verse - **"all** grace," **"always,"**

"all sufficiency," "all things," "every good work," with "abound" occurring twice.

Let us go to God for grace. He is called "the God of all grace" in 1 Peter 5:10. We could lose grace of ourselves - but we cannot find it of ourselves. The sheep can wander from the fold - but cannot return without the help of the shepherd. Go to the God of all grace. He is the first planter, the promoter, and the perfector of grace. God is the Father of lights (James 1:17). He must light up this candle of grace in the soul. Grace is in His gift.

> "...that ye, always having all sufficiency in all things,
> may abound to every good work" (II Corinthians 9:8).

God's grace is more than sufficient for a Christian's every need. Is your relationship with Him deep and trusting enough to draw you to Him during times of difficulty? Are you content to endure weaknesses, insults, distresses, and persecutions for Christ's sake so that you can be spiritually strong even amid physical and emotional weakness?

The story is told of Charles Spurgeon, who was riding home one evening after a heavy day's work, feeling weary and depressed, when the verse came to mind, "My grace is sufficient for you."

In his mind he immediately compared himself to a little fish in the Thames River, apprehensive lest drinking so many pints of water in the river each day he might drink the Thames dry. Then Father Thames says to him, "Drink away, little fish. My stream is sufficient for you."

Next he thought of a little mouse in the granaries of Egypt, worried lest its daily nibbles exhaust the supplies and cause it to starve to death. Then Joseph comes along and says, "Cheer up, little mouse. My granaries are sufficient for you."

Then he thought of a man climbing some high mountain to reach its lofty summit and dreading lest his breathing there might exhaust all the oxygen in the atmosphere. The Creator booms His voice out of heaven, saying, "Breathe away, man, and fill your lungs. My atmosphere is sufficient for you!"

Let us determine to rest in the abundance of God's wonderful grace and the total sufficiency of all His spiritual resources. That's the all-sufficient Savior's legacy to His people.

> **"that ye, always having all sufficiency in all things, may**
> **abound** (sufficiently) **to every good work"** (1 Peter 1:2)!

The **grace of Christ** is thus truly **abounding grace,** for **"God is able** to make **all grace** abound toward you" (II Corinthians 9:8). It is even **giving** grace, and we should "abound in this grace also" (II Corinthians 8:7). Therefore, **we should continually** "grow in grace, and in the **knowledge** of our Lord and Savior Jesus Christ." (II Peter 3:18).

> **Remember: "the kind of grace that does not change**
> **my life - will not save my soul." -** G. Clifton

God's Word teaches that out of pure grace God does **not impute our sins to us,** He nonetheless did not want to do this **until** complete and **ample satisfaction** of **His law** and **His righteousness** had been made. **Since this was impossible for us,** God **ordained for us,** in our place, **One (Jesus)** Who took upon Himself all the punishment we deserve. **He fulfilled the law** for us. **He averted the judgment** of God from us and appeased God's wrath. **Grace, therefore, costs us nothing,** but **it cost Another** (Jesus) much to get it for us. **Grace was purchased** with an incalculable, infinite treasure, the Son of God Himself.

A young employee secretly misappropriated hundreds of **dollars** from the Corporation. The theft was discovered and the young man was summoned to the main office of the firm. **As he walked up the stairs** toward the **administrative office** the young man was heavyhearted. **He knew** without a doubt he would **lose his position** with the firm. He **also feared** there would be **legal action** taken against him. Seemingly **his whole world had collapsed.**

When he arrived at the office of **the executive questioned** the **young man** about the incident. He was asked if the **accusations were true** and he **answered** in the **affirmative.**

Then the executive surprisingly asked this question: **"If I keep you** in your present capacity, **can I trust you** in the future?" The young worker **brightened up and said, "Yes, sir,** you surely can. **I've learned my lesson."**

The executive replied, "I'm **not going to press charges,** and you **can continue** in your present responsibility." **The employer concluded the conversation** with his younger employee by saying, **"I think you ought to know,** however, that you are the **second man in this firm** who **succumbed to temptation** and was shown leniency. **There was a pause,** then the **boss said,**

"**I was the first**. What you have done, I did. **The mercy you** are receiving, **I received. It is only the grace of God that can keep us both.**"

We are saved by grace (Ephesians 2:8) and in **grace we stand** (Romans 5:2). **Grace upholds** our salvation. **Grace gives us victory** in temptation, and **helps us endure** suffering and pain. **Grace helps us,** with the Holy Spirit, **to understand the Word** and wisely apply it to our lives. **Grace draws us into communion** and **prayer** and **enables us** to serve the Lord effectively. In short, **we exist and are firmly fixed** in an environment of **all-sufficient grace.**

The Grace of God is sufficient to meet every area of our life. The situations in our lives keep changing. But we can have the **assurance** that the **grace of God** will be **sufficient** for every situation. **When we are in the valley** the grace of God will help us not to be discouraged. **Whatever be the situation** in our life the grace of God will be sufficient for that situation. **The grace of God is sufficient** for our life. **It helps us** to bear **difficulties** that do not go away. **Apostle Paul** had a **thorn** that did not go away but he **received grace to bear it.** When we face such **situations in our life we need the grace of God** to bear it.

> **Hebrews 4:16 states,** "Let us then **approach the throne of grace with** confidence, so that we may **receive mercy** and **find grace** to help us in our time of need" (NIV).

The grace of God will sustain His people **through it all** when we will let it. When we will let Him! **God doesn't just give grace.** He **lavishes us** with grace. He is **generous to the point** of controversy! **Where grace happens, generosity** happens. **And it can happen in you.**

Let us Pray ... "**Father,** we **thank You** for our **time with You** today, **precious time in Your Word** and the **reminder that Your grace is sufficient.** Our **minds fail us to know the words** to express our gratitude to You for **Your continued goodness and provisions.** For that we bless You with thanksgiving. And, Father, **may I recognize the thorns** that come into **my own life as evidence** that **You** are **testing me, molding me,** and **strengthening** me, and **preparing me** to be ready for Your coming. **Teach me** how to **trust all of Your promises** today. And **with your grace,** I thank you in advance for **giving me victory** in my Christian life. **In Jesus name, Amen.**"

> "**The grace of our Lord Jesus Christ be with you all. Amen**" (Philippians 4:23).

Chapter 11

God 'SANCTIFIES' Me
With His Grace

(Part I)

"Jesus also, that He might sanctify the people through His blood, suffered outside the gate" (Hebrews 13:12 NASB).

"And now **I commit you to God** and **to the word of His grace,** which can **build you up** and give you an inheritance **among all who are sanctified**" (Acts 20:32 NIV).

GOD'S SOVEREIGN GRACE begins when **He calls us** to **accept Jesus as our Lord** and **Savior. God's sovereign grace doesn't end** with our **salvation. This wonderful grace** carries **through** to our **sanctification.** How do I know this? Because the **Bible teaches** us that **God's grace is perfect. Grace is perfect at a level** that we **cannot possibly** fully **comprehend. God grants us grace** that **we may** show **grace to others.**

Unfortunately, **every mature believer knows** that there is **within** our 21st Century **churches** a **nominal Christian faith** that has become a **profound problem.** It is an **important** and **needed study** for **our day.**

We live in a **superficially Christianized culture** where **millions of lost people 'think'** they do **believe in Jesus.** In much of **my witnessing** to unbelievers and nominal Christians, **the command,** "Believe in Jesus and you shall be saved," **is practically meaningless. Drunks** on the street say they do. **Unmarried couples** sleeping together say they do. **Elderly people** who haven't sought worship or fellowship for forty years say they do. **Every kind and shape of world-loving** church attendees say they do. **Oh, I'm an American,** and I believe in God they say. **My parents** had **me baptized** when I **was a baby, so I'm O.K.,** they say.

> "Therefore **by the deeds of the law** there shall
> **no flesh be justified** in His sight: for **by the law**
> is the **knowledge of sin**" (Romans 3:20).

There is nothing mortal sinful man can **do to be just** in the sight of the **Holy God. Paul says,** there is a righteousness of God which is revealed apart from the Law. **It is that righteousness,** which is **by faith** in **all who believe/commit** or **put their faith** and **trust** in Christ. These **receive the righteousness of Christ** as God declares it to their account.

The **supreme example** of this concept is the **patriarch Abraham.** Before the Law was given, **Abraham believed God,** and it was **accounted to him** for **righteousness.** "what does the Scripture say? **"Abraham believed God,** and it was **credited** to him as righteousness" (Romans 4:3 NASB). **Abraham was declared to** be **JUST,** even **though** he had **nothing in himself** that righteousness **could boast of** (Ephesians 2:8, 9).

The gospel manifests the **grace of God** which **He gives to His people.** When a **person is justified** before God, **there is peace with God.** "Therefore being justified by faith, we have peace with God through our Lord Jesus Christ" (Romans 5:1). **The believer has direct access** into the **presence of God.** The **believer also begins a pilgrimage of sanctification, which is needed,** for the **Christian is at the same time, made just,** and sinner.

The good news is that **God does not wait until** we are **completely sanctified before we are acceptable** to Him. God **receives sinful men,** even me with **all my sin. We are made acceptable** to the **Father** by virtue of **our relationship in Christ, by** faith. The **faith that saves** is **not alone.** It is **accompanied by a living faith, demonstrated in good works** which **God has also preordained.** A **saved person** is a **changed person** and brought into **conformity to Christ, despite** an inner **great warfare** which Paul speaks of in Romans 6 - 7. There is a **Christian battle to put to death,** the **works of the flesh.**

In Romans 8, Paul declares the **victory** will be **won in Christ.** God's providential care **assures sanctification (holiness)** of the **soul.** All **things work together to good** for those **who love the Lord** (Philippians 4:13).

In Romans 9, 10, and 11, Paul introduces the **grand theme** of **God's sovereignty,** and the **doctrine of election,** illustrated by Jacob and Esau. **Paul**

quotes **Moses** to **remind** his readers that **God will have mercy** on whom He will have mercy. **Salvation is of the Lord**. It is **the Lord's doing.** The appropriate response to **God's sovereignty** is to **break forth in praise.** "And that he might make known the riches of his glory on the vessels of mercy, which he had afore prepared unto glory" (Romans 9:23).

In simplicity: Sanctification is the experience, beginning with **salvation** (regeneration), by which the **believer is set apart** to **God's purposes** and is **enabled to progress** toward **moral** and **spiritual perfection** through the **presence** and **power of the Holy Spirit living in him. Growth in grace** should **continue** throughout the **regenerate person's life. Glorification** is the **culmination of salvation** and is the **final blessed** and **abiding** state of **the redeemed.**

What is needed, therefore, **is not only a recovery** of the **true nature** of **justifying faith,** but **also** a recovery of the **true doctrine of sanctification.** This Chapter and the next will **examine the doctrine of sanctification.**

Do you remember the "**Lord's Prayer?**" I mean, **the real Lord's Prayer** where **Jesus prayed** to the **Father. He prayed for Himself, His disciples,** and **His church** as recorded in **John 17? Let's look** at few **verses** ... where **Jesus prayed** for **US!**

John 17:15-19, "I do not ask that You take them out of the world, but that You keep them from the evil one. They are not of the world, just as I am not of the world. **Sanctify them in the truth;** Your **word is truth.** As you sent Me into the world, so I have sent them into the world. And for their sake I **consecrate** Myself, **that they** also may **be sanctified in truth** (NASB).

Paul wrote: I Thessalonians 4:2-7, "For you know **what instructions we gave you** through the Lord Jesus. For **this is the will of God, your sanctification:** that you abstain from sexual immorality; that each one of **you know how to control his own body in holiness** and **honor, not** in the **passion** of lust like the Gentiles who do not know God; that **no one transgress** and **wrong his brother** in this matter, because the **Lord is an avenger** in all these things, as we told you beforehand and **solemnly warned you.** For **God has not called us for impurity, but in holiness**" (ESV).

Christians are commanded to be holy, which includes **living a life** that is **holy** and **abstaining** from **things like sexual immorality,** but the **Christian should realize** that this **doesn't save them. We can't assume** that just **because we're told to be holy,** and then strive to **please God,** that this has **anything to do our salvation.** It's **not part** of **our salvation** but a **byproduct** of our salvation. We **seek to please the Father** as Jesus did **because we love Him.**

The Bible is completely sufficient for every new challenge the church faces until Jesus Christ appears.

The Apostle Peter wrote, "You shall **be holy**, for **I am holy**" (I Peter 1:16 ASV), and that was in **the context of being told to "not** be **conformed to the passions** of your former ignorance, but as **He who called you is holy,** you also **be holy in** all your **conduct**" (1st Pet 14-15). **Christians realize** it's **not a part** of their **salvation** but **it comes as a result of** their **salvation.**

Listen: God would not command or **require something** of us **that** we **couldn't do** or something we couldn't have done for us, **so, the command to be holy,** although **it sounds humanly impossible** (which it is), **is not impossible for God** (Matthew 19:26). **When a person is born again,** they **become new creations** in Jesus Christ (II Corinthians 5:17), **which means** they now **have the same righteousness** that **Jesus has.**

One of the most powerful and **profound Bible verses** in **Scripture, the Apostle Paul wrote,** "For our sake He **made him** (Jesus) **to be sin** who knew **no sin,** so that in him **we might become** the **righteousness of God**" (II Corinthians 5:21 ESV).

An angel of God once told the Apostle John, "Let the **evildoer** still do evil, and the **filthy** still be filthy, and the **righteous** still do right, and the **holy still be holy**" (Revelation 22:11 ESV). **According to scripture,** "whoever is **deemed holy by Jesus' atoning work** (II Corinthians 5:21) will be **living a holy life. Not a perfect life** but **one** that is **motivated by love to obey God,** so when **Jesus comes again,** they will still be **endeavoring** to **live** a **holy life ("holy still").** It is **not because Christians are better people** or are **living better lives** so that they **can be saved, but** it is **because they are saved,** they **go-all-out to avoid sin.**

Remember: Holiness is not the **way to Jesus** ... **Jesus is the way to holiness!** Far **too often people say,** "I'm **waiting** to get my **life cleaned** up before I come to God" but **the problem is,** they **can't do anything spiritual without Christ** (John 15:5), and **only through Christ** can we **do anything** (Philippians 4:13). **Today** is the **best day** for you to **be saved** (I Corinthians 6:2), because **tomorrow may never come,** and **all of us are one breath** ... one **heartbeat** ... away **from eternity** ... and **then it will be too late** to **give yourself** to **Jesus** Christ.

Listen Christian friend, 'Holiness' must be of extreme importance to God because it is **mentioned 611 times in Scripture** and the **actual word holiness is found 34 times.** The Book of **Leviticus speaks** about the **holiness** of God **more than any book** in the Bible **(80 times!)** and no other book even comes close to that **so if you truly want to know more about the holiness of God,** read the Book of Leviticus. It has **no equal in the Bible** on the holiness of God just as God has **no equal in** the entire universe **for "Holy, holy, holy** is the Lord of hosts; the whole earth is full of his glory" (Isaiah 6:3)!

Let's review: First you're justified, then you **become sanctified,** and finally **you'll be glorified.** To make **progress as a disciple is to grow in sanctification.** Right? Yes, this is how we talk. And when we talk this way, we know what we're talking about. **The word "sanctification"** points to **a process** of **development, a growing** "in the grace and knowledge of our Lord and Savior Jesus Christ" (II Peter 3:18).

God's definitive action whereby he **declares a person to be holy** before him, and places that person **in a position of holiness ("positional sanctification").** I think it **is especially clear** in the **Old Testament,** where **objects** and **places are sanctified** for God's use.

Paul says that Christ gave himself for the church "that he might **sanctify** and **cleanse it"** (Ephesians 5:26). The **Corinthian Christians are told** "you were **washed,** you were **sanctified, you were justified in** the **name of** the **Lord Jesus Christ"** (I Corinthians 6:11). **Hebrews affirms that Jesus** suffered **"that he might sanctify** the people with **His own blood"** (Hebrews 13:12). In these and many other cases, **the Bible is** using the **word "sanctify"** to point to a **definitive past act,** as well as a **continuing one.**

Paul uses the term "sanctification" in the sense it is used in this second set of texts - to refer **to the ongoing process** by which **believers grow in maturity and holiness.** The term **"sanctification" refers** broadly to a **Christian's growth** and **pursuit** of **Christ-likeness.**

The process of sanctification is something **to be pursued.** This suggests that **not all believers** are being **sanctified at the same rate** and that our **rate of sanctification may vary** throughout our **lifetime** (Hebrews 12:1-3, 12-14).

"Do you not know that **in a race all the runners run,** but only **one receives the prize?** So **run** that **you may obtain it.** Every **athlete exercises self-control** in all things. **They do it** to receive **a perishable wreath,** but we an imperishable (one). So **I do not run aimlessly;** I do not box as one beating the air. But **I discipline my body** and **keep it under control,** lest after preaching to others I **myself should be disqualified** (Corinthians 9:24-27 ESV).

As John Owen famously wrote, "Do you mortify; do you make it your daily work; be always at it whilst you live; cease not a day from this work, be killing sin or it will be killing you." We know, however, that the process of sanctification is never completed in this life. We will always need to grow in holiness since we will always need to mortify remaining sin.

Sanctification is the process by which God has chosen to create a people for himself. Sanctification is a major part of God's redemptive plan and the primary work He does to develop godly character in His people.

Sanctification is a word that has been used in a variety of ways, but biblically speaking, it primarily pertains to Christian conversion and secondarily to growth in the Christian life.

Sanctification is highly Christological, for it is through identification with Jesus that one becomes sanctified and grows in sanctification. But as much as sanctification is Christological, it is also pneumatological (spirit = pneuma), for it is the Spirit Who, at every level, makes identification with Christ both a possibility and a reality for the believer. The Holy Spirit is the primary agent who serves as both the source and the instigator of such activity.

God's grace is all-sufficient. It is sufficient for every trial that we endure, and it goes beyond God's blessing in our lives. We must look at our trials and tribulations in light of the grace of God … Ask yourself: what is God trying to teach me here? How is His grace working through this in my circumstance?

We are saved by grace (Ephesians 2:8) and in grace we stand (Romans 5:2). Grace upholds our salvation, gives us victory in temptation, and helps us endure suffering and pain. Grace helps us understand the Word and wisely apply it to our lives. Grace draws us into communion and prayer and enables us to serve the Lord effectively. In short, we exist and are firmly fixed in an environment of all-sufficient grace.

So, just what does this $1000.00 word mean? 'Sanctification' comes from two Latin words: 'sanctus' which means 'holy', and 'ficare' which means 'make.' So to 'sanctify' means to 'make holy.' But, of course, the word 'holy' isn't much more relevant today than sanctification - what with "holy mackerel" and "holy cow" and "holy buckets" - we've just about ruined one of the highest and most exquisite words in the Bible.

Paul gave us in Romans 15:16 and 18 a definition of sanctification so that it can be a part of our wartime vocabulary. Sanctification is obeying the Commander-in-Chief of the universe. Sanctification is a wartime word. A sanctified person has unswerving commitment to His cause. A

sanctified person has **uncompromising loyalty** to the **Commander** and to his **companions in arms.** So whenever you think of sanctification, **think of wartime missions** and **wartime character.** It was the **goal of Paul's mission strategy,** and it was the **radical obedience to Christ** that **fulfilled that goal** from Jerusalem all the way around to Illyricum (Romans 15:19).

According to Romans 15:15, **God's grace turned Paul into a minister** of Christ. **Moved by this grace,** then, **Paul undertakes the service** of the gospel - **he preaches** the good news that **Christ died for sinners** and **offers eternal joy** to those who believe. **According to verse 16,** then, the **result of this preaching** is that **Gentiles** become **sanctified by the Holy Spirit. Sanctification happens** when the **gospel is preached** and **the Spirit poured out** meet **with power** in the human heart.

There are **progressive steps** to **maturity in Jesus Christ.** These **that few Christians** even **know** about them, much less follow the course where they lead. **The failure to know and follow these steps** is probably **the greatest reason for the defeat** of those **who fail** to **walk in a victorious Christian life.** Our **goal** is to **first see** and **understand** these **steps** to maturity, **conquering ourselves** and the enemy trying to thwart us. **We must grow** in vision, faith, and power which is the **sure result of maturity in Christ.**

Having said that, let me say, **on the path** to **holiness** and **sanctification,** there are **many** who **quickly give excuse** saying **that** "they are too big a sinner," **or that** "they are so unworthy," **or** "they know they can't be pure, and continue to sin," **and since this is so,** "they refuse to be a hypocrite because they still have bad thoughts and actions, etc."

Salvation, although **provided** at the born-again experience, **continues development** and **advancement** until it is **totally complete. What? Why?** Complete **salvation involves justification, sanctification,** and **glorification. By grace,** through faith, **God justifies believers** in **an instantaneous act.** That is to say, **Christ died** for His people **in order that the penalty** for their sins might **be paid** and **His righteousness might be counted** to them. They **are declared just before God** when they believe. **Once justified,** Christ **saves them** from the **power** of their sins through the lifelong **process of sanctification.**

It is clear that God is holy, that **He demands his people be holy** and that **He is the one** who **enables** His people to **become holy** primarily **through** the **agency of his Holy Spirit.** In addition to this, **sanctification primarily denotes a state** in which **believers find themselves** and it can also describe a realm of **human action** in which believers **live in correspondence** with their given holiness. **In short, believers both live and grow in holiness.**

> "**In sanctification,** Christians are **made more** and more
> like Jesus Christ. This **lifelong process never ends,**
> and the **final goal** is **never reached** until **death.** At
> death, **Christians are glorified;** they are **then made**
> **completely perfect** for the **first time.**" - Jay Adams

To the Roman Christians **Paul confirms** our **right standing with God through Christ**: "For if when we **were enemies** we **were reconciled** to God through the death of His Son, much more, **having been reconciled,** we shall **be saved by His life. And not only that,** but **we also rejoice** in God through **our Lord Jesus Christ,** through whom we have **now received** the **reconciliation**" (Romans 5:10-11 NASB).

Though our **hearts condemn us because of present sin,** we are **told by John,** "If anyone sins, **we have an 'advocate'** (lawyer) with the Father, **Jesus Christ** the righteous" (1 John 2:1 NASB).

Remember, the **day before Christ was crucified,** He **washed** His disciples' feet. **He told these** very **imperfect** men, "He who is bathed needs only to wash his feet, but is completely clean: and you are clean, but not all of you" (John 13:10 NASB). **You may wonder:** "How could **Jesus say these disciples** were **clean?**" Any **casual onlooker** at the scene **would have been astonished** by Jesus' statement.

These eleven men (remember: the **traitor** is gone), **He spoke to these wavering, anxious, fearful men** had **already displayed** pride, unbelief, selfishness, unpredictability, ambition, covetousness, inconsistency, vindictiveness, and lack of faith. The fact is, **Christ made** this **statement** about them **because He had 'chosen' them. He** had **put them on the path to holiness.** It was **all by grace! Because** of the **grace of God, He had** 'called' them, **reached down** to each of them, and 'redeemed' them with His everlasting saving blood (Ephesians 1:7).

Jesus also knew what was **in the disciples' hearts despite** their utter imperfection. Moreover, **He saw ahead** to the time of **brokenness** and contriteness they were **about to enter.**

Ready for this: **let's say I asked you** to **list all the sins** that these **disciples had committed.** I believe **I could confidently say that you and I have been guilty** of **all** the **same sins** during certain seasons in our lifetime. **Yet Jesus has the answer** for us all: "Having been justified by faith, **we have peace with God through** our **Lord Jesus Christ**" (Romans 5:1 NASB).

God's sanctifying grace is that **grace which works within** the **true believer in such a way as to bring** growth, maturity, and progress in the **process of becoming Christ-like**: "Now when the meeting of the synagogue had broken up, many of the Jews and of the God-fearing proselytes followed Paul and Barnabas, who, speaking to them, **were urging them to continue in the grace of God**" (Acts 13:43 NASB).

What does the scripture mean by a sanctified man? Sanctification is that **inward, spiritual work that God works in us** by His Holy Spirit **when He calls us** to be a son. **He not only washes us** from **our sins** by Christ's blood, but **also separates us** from our **carnal love** of sin (our carnality), working **into our minds a new motivating principle** of living.

> **As a result of grace,** we have been **saved from sin's 'penalty' (past).** In the meantime we are being **saved from sin's 'power' (present).** One day we **will be saved from sin's 'presence' (future).** - Alistair Begg

Much of this **is done supernaturally** when **we receive His Holy Spirit:** "I will put My law into your mind." He can do that, but **He cannot make a person use it!** It is **when we choose to use it** that it becomes **written in our hearts**—it becomes **part of our nature,** part of our **way of living.** However, this does not occur in the blink of an eye. **It is a process** whose main **element is faith** - **faith in** something **very specific.** It is **not the faith that God is,** but **faith in the teaching of God's Word.** If a person **does not trust** His Word, **he will not obey it,** and if he **does not obey it,** he **will not be sanctified.**

The steamship whose machinery is broken may be **brought into port** and made **fast** (tied) to the dock. **She is safe,** but **not sound. Repairs** may last a long time.

> "**Christ designs** to make us both **safe and sound.
> Justification** gives **the first** – 'safety;' **sanctification**
> gives the **second** - 'soundness'." – John Calvin

The first step toward the **success of any journey** is to **understand** and **be familiar** with **where we are going.** What is our **destination in Christ?** Simply put, it is **to have our intimate relationship with God restored,** to **become like Him,** and **to do the works** that He did. The **goal of redemption** is to **restore man** to his original condition **before the fall of mankind into sin.** (Genesis

1:26-3:24), which is **walking** with God, **obeying** Him, and **fulfilling** His mandate to rule over the earth.

By the **unfathomable riches of God's grace**, He also established that **Christ** would **raise him up** as a glorious "**new creation**" (II Corinthians 5:17). **God walked with Adam** in the garden, but **the new creation man actually has God living in him!** God has actually **made man His temple** and **God now dwells in a redeemed man!** This is **so glorious** that it is **often difficult** even for those who have **tasted the gift of salvation** to fully comprehend.

> "For **I am the Lord your God:** ye shall therefore **sanctify yourselves**, and **ye shall be holy;** for I am holy: **neither** shall ye **defile yourselves** with any manner of creeping thing that creeps upon the earth" (Leviticus 11:44).

God's Word also **urges believers on to holiness** or **sanctification.** It is both a **theological position** in the **finished work of Jesus Christ** and a **call to be Christ-like** in **attitude** and **actions** in daily life. **As salvation is a free gift** and a **cost-everything lifestyle**, so too, is **sanctification.**

Unfortunately, **some people think** that **to be holy means to be odd.** No, we're to **be different.** We have **too many Christians** doing **unbiblical things** who **claim** to be holy when **in reality they are just odd.**

Holiness (sanctification) **is not achieved** by **what we wear**, where we **sleep** and **eat**, or **how many spiritual things we do.** It is **not primarily** a matter of **dress or style of hair.** And we **don't become holy** if we live in a commune, monastery, convent, or college campus. **There is no holiness in a hole.**

The legitimate Biblical testimony of the **Holy Spirit's authority** in a person's life **is not** material **prosperity**, mindless **emotionalism**, or supposed **miracles.** Rather, **it is sanctification!** This is **shown by** the **believer's growth** in **spiritual maturity**, practical **holiness**, and **Christlikeness** through the **authority, control** and leading of the **Holy Spirit** (as **He relates biblical truth** to the hearts of **His children**). A **true work** of the Spirit **convicts** the heart of sin, **combats** worldly lusts, and cultivates spiritual fruit in the lives of **God's people.**

God makes us holy (sanctified) by the **blood of His Son.** And in **return for this great love**, we endeavor **to live holy lives** because **we love Him.** "**Holy**" **is a state of being, not doing.** It is a **God-induced, God-developed character** trait **that grows in us** as **we** grow in **our love relationship** with God.

> The ultimate test of our spirituality is the measure of our
> amazement at the grace of God. - Martyn Lloyd-Jones

When Moses met with God face to face, his face shone with the glory of God. Now, since God dwells inside of us, our whole lives should reflect His glory. This is our calling - to be His temple, the place where His glory is manifested. Our maturity will be reflected by how much of His glory is manifested through our lives.

To be sanctified is to be "set apart." For something or someone to be sanctified means it is set apart for a special use. Synonyms for sanctified are holy, consecrated, and hallowed. The Bible speaks of 'things' being "sanctified," such as Mount Sinai (Exodus 19:23) and gifts to the temple (Matthew 23:17); days, such as the Sabbath (Exodus 20:8); names, such as God's (Matthew 6:9); and people, such as the Israelites (Leviticus 20:7–8) and Christians (Ephesians 5:26).

This word is from the root "holy" (Greek - hagios). The Greek word translated "mature" in Ephesians 4:13 is the Greek word 'teleios'. It is used throughout the New Testament to mean "perfect," "complete," "full-grown," and "mature." What Ephesians 4:13 teaches is that, the more we grow in Christ, the stronger and more unified we will be as a church. The verse does not teach that we will stop sinning.

The Apostle Peter wrote, "You shall be holy, for I am holy" (1 Peter 1:16), and that was in the context of being told to not be conformed to the passions of your former ignorance, but as he (1 Peter 14-15). Christians realize it's not a part of their salvation but it comes as a result of their salvation, so even our trying to be obedient is birthed out of a desire to please God.

Holiness and sanctification has almost become bad words among many Christians in our time. This is usually because it is associated with movements and teachings that are legalistic in their approach to holiness. Even so, not only is holiness fundamental to true Christianity, we are exhorted in Hebrews 12:14: "Pursue peace with all men, and the sanctification (holiness) without which no one will see the Lord" (NASB).

Sanctification is a word that is often interchangeable with holiness, which means to be set-apart, purified, etc. As this Scripture declares, we must be holy if we expect to see the Lord.

Recent studies indicate that there is no longer a measurable difference between the morality of those who claim to be born again Christians and non-Christians. They tell us: Christians are now sliding into debauchery so fast that **soon Christians will,** when measured as a whole, **be less moral,** and **have less integrity than unbelievers!** What is even **more shocking** is that there are **no alarms being sounded** from **every pulpit** and **meeting place** in the land! **Why are they failing** and falling? Many, unfortunately, **joined a church** but **didn't join Jesus** in a full relationship of faith and commitment.

Nevertheless, **the Lord is full of grace and mercy to those** who **humble themselves and repent** of their iniquity. Even when **King Ahab,** one of **Israel's most evil and idolatrous kings, repented** near the end of his life, the **Lord immediately responded to him** with mercy (I Kings 21:20-29). **When we have been caught** in the **snares of evil,** we must **run** to the Lord, **not away** from Him. **He will have mercy and help us.**

Remember again that sanctifying Grace is "the work of the Holy Spirit **moving us on toward perfection** in love and truth." **This stage of grace** has **several** other **names:** Christian Perfection, Perfect Love, Heart Purity, Christian Holiness. **Holiness and sanctification come from the same root** and really **mean the same** although **technically sanctification is "the process of making someone or something holy."**

The Bible challenges us to be holy, but how is that possible with sinful people?

To try and live lives that **please God,** we must **be diligent** in **obeying God's Word,** even though **we're swimming upstream against** the **current** of the world, the **pulls of** our **own flesh,** and our **Enemy. We Christians are commanded** to **be holy,** which includes **living a life** that is **holy** and **abstaining** from things like **sexual immorality,** but the **Christian** should **realize that this doesn't save us.**

So, what is sanctification? Sanctification is the believer leaving the **courtroom where God** has once and for all time **declared him righteous,** and immediately **beginning the process** whereby God's Spirit **enables him to** increasingly **conform to Christ's righteousness, both inwardly** and **outwardly. Sanctification is** the **growth** that necessarily **results from it.** We may say that **sanctification has nothing to do** with **regeneration** or **justification,** and **yet** it **has everything to do** with **demonstrating** that one has **experienced them.**

The believer should be different from the world, and I'd say, **radically different,** and so much **so that it's clear to others** that that person is a believer. **That does not mean** there is any **superiority** in them, but rather the **opposite because believers** are told to **esteem others better** than themselves (Philippians

2:3-8), **whether they are believers or not.** God **never saved us because** we are **better** than others … but **only** because **He loved us** (Romans 5:8).

God would not command or **require something** of us that we **couldn't do** or something we **couldn't have done for us,** so the **command to be holy,** although it sounds **humanly impossible** (which it is), is **not impossible for God** (Matthew 19:26). When a person is **born again,** they become **new creations** in Jesus Christ (II Corinthians 5:17), **which means** they now **have** the **same righteousness that Jesus** has. One of the **most powerful and profound Bible verses** in Scripture, the Apostle **Paul wrote,** the righteousness of God (II Corinthians 5:21).

The **Almighty God is not looking** for **skilled and talented people or** people who **are self-sufficient** (abundantly adequate). He is **looking** for **inadequate people** who will **give their weakness** (limitations and vulnerabilities) to Him and **open** (expose) **themselves** to the **ministry of the Holy Spirit** and the **transforming grace** of the **new covenant** as it is **ministered by Christ Jesus Himself.**

The **Holy Spirit,** Who is the **personification of the holiness** of God **by His very name,** is also the **Helper. God does not require us to do anything** that He will not **also empower us to do by His Holy Spirit.** However, **we must understand** that this is **His name for a reason.** If we **want the fullness of the Holy Spirit in our lives,** we too **must be holy** as the **Scriptures teach.**

On one occasion, **an angel of God told the Apostle John,** "Let the **evildoer still do evil, and** the **filthy still be filthy,** and **the righteous** still do right, and the **holy still be holy**" (Revelation 22:11, ESV), and this **was written** in the context of Jesus' return, beuse in the very next verse, **Jesus says,** "Behold, I am coming soon, bringing my recompense with me, to repay each one for what he has done" (Revelation 22:12 ESV). So **whoever is deemed holy** by Jesus' **atoning work** (II Corinthians 5:21) will be **living a holy life.**

> **"Those** who have **been justified** are now **being sanctified;**
> those who have no experience of **present sanctification** have
> no **reason to suppose** they have been **justified"** - F.F. Bruce

Through God's grace, He provides sanctification. This is **not an instantaneous act. This a process** – the process of **becoming more like Christ, of growing in holiness.** This **process begins** the instant **you are converted** and will **not end until** you **meet Jesus** face-to-face.

Sanctification is about our own choices and **behavior.** It **involves work.** Empowered by the **Holy Spirit,** we endeavor. **We fight sin. We study Scripture** and **pray,** even **when we don't feel like it.** We **flee temptation.** We **press on; we run hard in the pursuit of holiness. And** as we **become** more and **more sanctified,** the **power of the gospel conforms us** more and more closely, with ever-increasing clarity, **to the image of Jesus Christ.**

Regeneration is the new birth, **justification is** God's declaration that a believing **sinner is righteous** because of the **merits of Christ** imputed to him.

The Bible repeatedly **emphasizes** the **legal aspects of justification. God does not make us righteous** in that moment; God **declares us righteous** in **that moment,** just **like** a **judge passes sentence** on the **defendant in his courtroom.**

Through the ministry of the **Holy Spirit,** God will over time **make us more** and **more righteous** in the way we live. **This process is called sanctification.** But we **do not grow** in **sanctification** in order **to be justified.** We **grow in sanctification** because **we are justified.** The **declarative act of justification** is gracious **foundation** out of which **grace-filled** lives **will grow.**

The guarantee that we are placed into His **perfect righteousness, accepted,** and **loved** by our **Father** in heaven is **one of our greatest encouragements** in **the process of sanctification.** We are **free to love God** with all our heart because **we know** that **His love** for us **is completely secure.** We can live as children and not as slaves. - Jay Harvey

Sanctifying Grace is the **work of** the Holy Spirit molding **us into the image of our Lord** and **Savior Jesus Christ making us like Him.** It is the **process** by which **the Holy Spirit** makes us **"holy as God is holy."**

Sanctifying Grace is the **work of the Holy Spirit** in **rooting sin out - moving us** from 'imputed' **righteousness** (what Christ **did for** us) to 'imparted' **righteousness** (what Christ **does in** us). **Impute is** "a heavy, **theological word"** that simply **means "to count, credit, or reckon." God's word declares** in Psalm 14 and Romans 3:10-11: "There is **no one righteous,** not even one; there is **no one who understands,** no one **who seeks for God"** (NASB).

In Sanctifying Grace our hearts are cleansed from the **control of sin,** and we are **liberated from slavery** to it. **The imputed righteousness of Justifying Grace** is God **delivering us** from the **consequences** and **penalty of sin;** the imparted righteousness of **Sanctifying Grace is** God **delivering us** from the **control** and **power of sin** so we are **enabled to live in** the victory of Romans 6:14, "For sin shall no longer be your master, because you are **not under law,**

but **under grace**" (NIV). **The Holy Spirit in 'Sanctifying Grace'** empowers us **victoriously** to **overcome sin.**

> **"And the very God of peace sanctify you wholly;**
> **and I pray God your whole spirit and soul and**
> **body be preserved blameless unto the coming of**
> **our Lord Jesus Christ"** (I Thessalonians 5:23).

Some people get confused about when **salvation happens.** Let me see if I can **shed some light** on this subject. **Salvation can be explained** by using **three verbal tenses** in the English language.

The **moment you repent** and **believe/trust** upon **Jesus** Christ as your **Lord and Savior,** you **are saved from** the 'penalty' of sin. **After that,** you **enter a process of sanctification** where you are being **saved from** the 'power' of sin. **When** you **get to heaven,** you will be **saved from** the actual 'presence' of sin.

What happens when you **enter** into a **saving relationship with Jesus Christ?** You are **justified immediately** in your **spirit.** You are **sanctified progressively** in your **soul.** And you will be **ultimately glorified** in your **body.** Using Psalm 32:7, 41:2, 121:7-8, **praise God** that the **preservation of your salvation is His job** and **not yours.**

In the **grand purpose of our "selection"** into God's family, **two key words** are used: **"Holy"** (Greek **hagios**) **stresses dedication.** A holy man or woman is distinctively God's, **set apart for God's use, separated** from the secular, and **consecrated to** God's service. **All who are "chosen" are chosen to be holy.**

In 1Thessalonians 3:13, **Paul used 'hagiosune'** which is **the state of 'being holy'.** "May He strengthen your hearts so that you will be **blameless** and **holy** in the **presence** of our **God and Father** when our **Lord Jesus** comes with all His saints" (NIV).

There is no holiness in men **naturally;** what is in them **without the grace of God** is **only** a **show; true holiness** is **from** the **Spirit of God.** This is a stable thing in itself, and can **never be removed** or **taken** away It is **fascinating to note** that the most **concentrated use** of the masculine noun **'hagiasmos'** is found here in I Thessalonians 4:1-7 where **we encounter three of the ten** New Testament uses (I Thessalonians 4:3, 4, 7).

The true key to living a holy life is **not** just **determining** that we are **going to stop doing** what we know is **wrong, but to** simply **return to our first love,** God. That is **why the Lord summed up** the **entire Law of Moses** with the two commandments: to love the Lord, and to love our neighbors. **If we love God,**

we will **not worship idols** or do the **things** that **offend Him** because **we are** the **temple of His Holy Spirit** (I Corinthians 6:19-20). **If we love our neighbors,** we **will not** murder, steal, or even envy them. **When we live** a life **devoted to loving God** and **our neighbors,** we will **not do wrong things,** and will **therefore fulfill the Law.** True **holiness is not motivated by fear, but love.**

The true holiness to which the **church is called is not** that of a **bride who is afraid** that **if she is not perfect** her **bridegroom will punish her. True holiness** is that of **a bride who is so passionately in love with her Bridegroom** that **she wants to be perfect for Him** in every way. Therefore, **the first step** in recovering **any spiritual ground** that we have **lost by falling into sin is to pray for God** to have **mercy** on us and **restore to us our first love** (Revelation 24-7). To then **stay on the path** is a **simple devotion** to **growing in love for Him** and our **neighbors.**

It must be noted, that **no man is perfectly holy in this life;** no man is **without sin in himself,** or lives **without the commission** of it; **holiness in the best is imperfect;** no **man, as yet,** is in himself **sanctified wholly;** there is **no un-blamable holiness but in Christ;** and **in Him** the saints are **without spot** and **blemish,** who is **their sanctification** and **their righteousness.** In themselves they are **full of spots** and **stains;** yet through the **grace of God** their **hearts** may be so **established** with **principles of holiness,** and they may be **so assisted** in the acts of it daily, as to give **no just cause of blame to men,** and so to **behave as to approve themselves "before God,"** who **sees the heart,** and **knows** from what principles all actions flow: and this the apostle desires **may be at the coming of our Lord Jesus;** or unto the **coming of Him,** as in I Thessalonians 5:23.

People who are sanctified are **born-again** and therefore part of **God's family** (Hebrews 2:11). They are **reserved (set-aside) for God's use.** They **know "the sanctifying work of the Spirit"** in their lives (I Peter 1:2). **They abstain** from sexual **immorality** (I Thessalonians 4:3). **They understand** they have been **"called to be his holy people"** (I Corinthians 1:2 NIV).

Under the Old Testament Law, the **blood of a sacrifice** was required to **set things apart** unto God: **"In fact, the law requires** that nearly everything be cleansed with blood" (Hebrews 9:22, NIV). **Blood** was sprinkled on **tabernacle furniture,** on **priestly clothing,** and on **people. Nothing was considered sanctified** until it had come in contact with the **blood.** This was a vivid and **beautiful picture** of the **spiritual application of Christ's blood** for our salvation - **we are** "sprinkled with his blood" (1 Peter 1:2). Just as the temple of old was sanctified for God's use, **our bodies,** which are now **temples of the Holy Spirit,** are **set apart** for **God's holy purposes** (1 Corinthians 6:19).

The New Testament proclaims that when **sinners turn to Jesus** in **repentance** and **faith** (Mark 1:15; Acts 3:16, 19; 20:21), they are **instantaneously justified** and **sanctified.** This **is their new position in Christ.** The **righteousness of Christ** has been **imputed to them** (Genesis 15:6; Romans 4). **They are declared right** and **holy** (a forensic act of God). To **be sanctified** means that **God's Word** has had an effect on us. **It is "through the word"** that God **cleanses us** and **makes us holy** (Ephesians 5:26; John 17:17).

> **What God has joined together - justification and**
> **sanctification - let no one separate.** - John Calvin

As a Christian, Jesus is within (our) spirit, which has been **regenerated by the Holy Spirit;** but in too many cases He is limited to a very **small corner** of our nature, and exercises but a limited power over our life. **There needs to be an anointing,** an **enthroning,** a **determination** that **He shall exercise His power over the entire Temple** of our Being; the spirit, which stands for the Holy of Holies; the soul, **for the Holy Place; the body,** for the outer court.

Holiness or **Sanctification** is **not a quality** or **attribute** which can be **attributed to us** apart from the **indwelling** of the **Holy Spirit. If we would be holy,** we must be **indwelt by Him Who is holy.** If we would have holiness, **we must be infilled by the Holy One.** But there must **be no limiting** of His power, **no barrier** to His control, **no veiling** or curtaining of His light. **The veil,** if such there be, **must be 'rent in twain'** from the top to the bottom.

Does living the Christian life seem like an **impossible** task to you? **Yes!** It **is impossible** - when we depend solely **on self. The motivating force behind our service to God** is our **loyalty, love, and 'sold-out' commitment** to Jesus. When our **attitude, gratitude and appreciation for Jesus is lacking,** then so will our **dedicated service** in the kingdom of God. **Jesus pointed out** that the **result of our loving Him,** is **serving** Him, and **keeping** of His commands (John 14:15, 21; I John 5:2, 3).

The Apostle Paul said it this way: "For through the Law **I died** to the Law, that I **might live unto God.** I have **been crucified with Christ,** and it is **no longer I who live,** but Christ lives in me; and **the life which I now live in the flesh** I live by faith in the Son of God, **Who loved me** and **delivered Himself up** for me" (Galatians 2:19-20).

We know we need grace. Without it we'd **never come to Christ** in the first place, but **being a Christian** is **more** than just coming to Christ. It's **about growing and becoming** more like Jesus - it's about pursuing holiness. **The pursuit of holiness** is hard work, and **that's where** we turn from grace to discipline - and often make a big mistake. **Remember that your worst days are never** so bad that you are **beyond the reach of God's grace,** nor are your **best days** ever so good that you are **beyond the need of it.**

Someone once said, **"Growth begins in sanctification when we start to accept our own weakness - humility."**

Grace is every bit as important for growing as a Christian as it is for **becoming a Christian.** The **journey of consecration and holiness,** must be **anchored in the grace of God;** otherwise it is doomed to **failure." Grace is at the heart** of the gospel, and without a **clear understanding** of the gospel and **grace, we can easily slip** into a **performance-based** (legalistic) **lifestyle** that bears **little resemblance** to what the gospel offers us.

Unfortunately, **many Christians don't have a good grasp** of what the **gospel message is.** We must never forget that **the same grace** that **brings us to faith** in Christ also **disciplines us** in Christ, and how we **learn to discipline ourselves** in the **areas** of commitment, conviction, choices, watchfulness, and adversity.

If you've ever struggled with what **your role** is and what role God takes in your growth as a Christian, the information in this book **should help comfort and challenge you** as you learn to **rest in Christ** while vigorously pursuing **a life of holiness.**

This life, **Paul realized,** was his only hope. **Seeing the need** to "live in the flesh … by faith in the Son of God" **does not nullify the grace of God.** Unfortunately, there are still some that say that **being saved by grace** means we are **saved no matter how we walk,** but the **Bible does not teach that** (II Corinthians 5:10). **Grace does not nullify** the need to "live by faith." **Grace does not take away** the need to love, trust and obedience to Jesus.

Strange doctrines have **originated and were rearing their ugly spiritual heads** in the **early church** … just **as they have in our day.** Some of the **false teachings** were on this **subject of sanctification.** Some appear to **confound and even combine** it with **justification. Other groups** just **squander** it away to nothing, under the **pretense of zeal for free grace.**

The grace that brings us to salvation, is **also** the grace that **gives us responsibilities.** As those responsibilities are met, we **are living by faith.** There is quite simply **no other path to God; and if** there is, the "Christ died needlessly" (Galatians 2:21). But there is not. **His death was an absolute necessity,** and there is **no other way** to the Father but by Him (John 14:6).

Sanctification is an inward and upward spiritual work which the Lord Jesus **Christ works** in a person **by the Holy Spirit,** when He **calls him to be a true believer. Jesus not only washes him from his sins** in His own blood, but **He also separates him** from his **natural love of sin** and the world, puts a new principle in his heart, and makes him practically godly in life. **The instrument by which the Spirit** effects this work is generally the **Word of God** ... and **prayer! The subject of this work of Christ** by His Spirit **is called in Scripture a "sanctified" man.**

The Word of God states, "May the God of peace himself **sanctify you wholly** (entirely), and may **your spirit** and **soul** and **body** be kept sound and **blameless** (without blame) at the coming of our Lord Jesus Christ. **He who called you and saved you** is faithful, and **He will do it** (I Thessalonians 5:23-24 ESV). **Holiness is not** the way to Christ; **Christ is the way to holiness.** Better still, **Christ IS our holiness.**

Paul prayed that believers be **sanctified** and **preserved** by God. This shows **sanctification is both a gift** at salvation and a **continuing task.** "And the **very God of peace sanctify you** wholly (completely)" (I Thessalonians 5:23, I Thessalonians 5:24 KJV). **When we pray to be sanctified, are we prepared to face** the **standard** of these verses? **We take the term sanctification much too lightly** (or not at all). Are we prepared for **what sanctification will cost?** Remember the words of Jesus, when He told His disciples that they must, take up their cross and follow Him (Matthew 16:24). It will **cost an intense narrowing** of all our **interests on earth,** and an **immense broadening** of all our interests in God.

> **Doctrine is the framework of life - the skeleton**
> **of truth, to be clothed and rounded out by the**
> **living grace of a holy life.** - Adoniram Gordon

Sanctification means to be intensely **focused** on **God's point of view.** It means to **secure and to keep** all the strength of our body, soul, and spirit **for God's purpose alone.** Are we really **prepared for God to perform** in us **everything for which He separated us?** And after He has done His work, **are**

we then prepared to separate ourselves to God just as Jesus did? "For their sakes I sanctify Myself ..." (John 17:19 KJV).

The reason some Christians have not entered into the 'experience' of sanctification is that we have not fully realized the meaning of sanctification - from God's perspective. Sanctification means being made one with Jesus so that the nature that controlled Him will control us. Are we really prepared for what that will cost? It will cost absolutely everything in us which is not of God.

Are we prepared to be caught up into the full meaning of Paul's prayer in this verse? Are we prepared to say, "Lord, make me, a sinner saved by grace, as holy as You can"? Jesus prayed that we might be one with Him, just as He is one with the Father (John 17:21-23). The resounding evidence of the Holy Spirit in a person's life is the unmistakable family likeness to Jesus Christ, and the freedom from everything which is not like Him. Are we prepared to set ourselves apart for the Holy Spirit's work in us?

Have you ever looked at the requirements of the Christian life and felt inadequate? Do words like "holiness, sanctification, perfection, blameless, or pure" scare you? It will be a great day for you when you admit in and of yourself you are totally incapable of living the Christian life. When you admit that, you are ready to experience the wonderful liberation of God's grace.

Change for most is a difficult process. Here's the good news. Sanctification and transformation come from beholding - not from striving! Part of the Christian world has dived headlong into a never-ending cycle of recovery, self-help, and how-to-do-it sermons, books, and tapes, etc.

Transformation comes from beholding the glory and splendor of Jesus, who is a real person. Unless God changes our hearts with His presence, we will remain inadequate and unable and will never change. We may drag ourselves into the prayer room on a regular basis, but only God can change the heart. It happens by His grace working in us, not us working to receive His grace. There is never anything inadequate about the grace of God.

Ephesians 4:13 says that the spiritual gifts are given to build up the body of Christ "until we all reach unity in the faith and in the knowledge of the Son of God and become mature, attaining to the whole measure of the fullness of Christ." Some translations say that we will become "perfect" (instead of "mature"), and from this some people have mistakenly thought that we can reach sinless perfection in this life. The Bible teaches that, while we are in the flesh, we will **always struggle with a sin nature** (Romans 7:14–24). **No one will be "perfect" (sinless) until we reach heaven.**

Another passage that people **sometimes get confused** about is **Colossians 1:28,** which says, in some translations, **that Paul wants to** "present every man perfect in Christ Jesus." Also, in Colossians 4:12 **Paul prays that we would** "stand **perfect** and **complete** in all the will of God" (KJV). In both verses, the **Greek word for perfect or complete** should be understood to **mean "mature"** or "full-grown," **not "having no sin.**

"Without blame" refers to our **reputations.** This **character** will only be **fully realized in heaven** (1 Corinthians 1:8), but there is a **present responsibility** to **"present your bodies** a living sacrifice" … (Romans 12:1-2 ESV).

The character of holiness and **a pure walk** with God will become the cause of a **lifestyle of blamelessness. Christians, we are to be the** "sons of God, without rebuke, in the midst of a crooked and perverse nation, among whom ye shine as lights in the world" (Philippians 2:15).

This holy and blameless condition will result in "the praise of the glory of his grace" (Ephesians 1:6), **where God will someday** "gather together in one all things in Christ" (v. 10).

What a magnificent thought! The **purpose** for which we have been chosen, predestined, redeemed, and forgiven **is to be holy in character** and **blameless** in reputation, so that when God **gathers us all together in Christ,** we will be the praise of the glorious grace of God.

Do you remember the **story of Jacob's ladder** in Genesis 28? **Jacob's ladder** (a Type of Christ) is the **everyday name** for a **bridge** between the **earth** and **heaven** that the biblical **Patriarch Jacob dreams about** during his **flight from** his brother **Esau,** as described in the Book of Genesis. This address how "**Jacob's Ladder" is Jesus Himself,** as we see in John 1:47-50. **We are called to be the messengers** who **ascend** on Him into the heavenly realm.

The **rungs on this 'Ladder'** are the **progressive revelations** of who Jesus is. **We go up as we see Him as** our Savior. **We go higher** as we come to **know Him as** our **Lord. We go up** when we **see Him** as the **Good Shepherd,** and we go higher when we **know Him** as the **"Apostle and High Priest." We go higher** when we **see Jesus** as the **Creator** and the **reason** for the **creation,** as the Apostles John and Paul wrote.

"Therefore leaving the elementary teaching about
the Christ, **let us press on to maturity,** not laying

again a foundation of repentance from dead works
and of faith toward God" (Hebrews 6:1 NAS).

We are to "**leave the elementary (simple) teachings about Christ**" to **go on to maturity.** This does **not mean** we **leave** the **teachings about Christ,** but rather the **basic** ones so that **we can go on to more advanced (intensified) teachings about Him.** It is **all about Jesus.** We will **never stop seeking to know** Him better and **abide in Him more fully.** As **members of His body,** we **ascend with Him** and **sit with Him** on His throne in the heavenly places.

Conversion is not regeneration only. This is a **neglected fact** in our **preaching today.** When a person is **born again, he knows** that it **is because** he has **received something** as a **gift from Almighty God** and not because of **his own decision.** People may **make vows and promises,** sign membership **cards, pray** the "sinner's prayer," and be **determined** to follow through, **but none of this is salvation.**

Salvation means that we are **brought to the place spiritually,** where we are **able to see ourselves in sin** and **place our life completely** in the **finished work of Jesus,** and to **receive something from God** on the **authority of Jesus** Christ, **namely, forgiveness of sins.** This is **because of God's amazing grace, but it doesn't end here.**

> "God's lavish grace and His abundant, never-ending love
> means our sanctification is a never-ending account in His
> glorious eternal kingdom yet to come" - Glenn Clifton

This is followed by God's a mighty work of grace: "And now, **brethren, I commend you to God,** and to the **Word of his grace,** which is able to **build you up,** and to **give you an inheritance** among all **them which are sanctified**" (Acts 20:32). **In sanctification,** the one who has been born again, **deliberately gives up his right to himself to Jesus Christ,** and **identifies himself** entirely with **God's ministry to others.**

The sanctified are, because of **that experience, heirs** of God and **joint-heirs** with Jesus Christ (Romans 8:17). "For both **He that sanctifies** and **they who are sanctified** are all of one: for which reason he is not ashamed **to call them brethren**" (Hebrews 2:11). The **experience of Sanctification** makes us **one with Christ,** standing on an equal basis with Him **in the sight of God** with respect to **this particular inheritance.**

In this world human beings **are bound under Adam's nature** in this. No matter **how hard we try** not to, in this flesh, **we will still sin against God**. This holds **true for everyone**. The apostle Paul rebuked Peter for showing favoritism (Galatians 2:11–13). **Late in his ministry, Paul calls himself the chief of sinners** (1 Timothy 1:15). **Peter, James, John, and Paul all admitted that they were imperfect.** How could you or I claim anything different?

True perfection will not come until the rapture of the church, when we **rise to meet Jesus** in the air (1 Thessalonians 4:17). At that time the dead in Christ will be resurrected, and the **bodies of the living will be changed** (Philippians 3:20, 21; 1 Corinthians 15:54). We will **stand before the Judgment Seat of Christ** (II Corinthians 5:10) **where our works** will be judged and rewards will be given (1 Corinthians 3:9–15). **Our redemption will be complete, and our sin will be gone forever.** We will **live and reign with Christ in sinless perfection forever.**

Sanctification means that we are "**made holy**" and **can now understand with intense concentration on God's point of view.** It **means every power** of body, soul and spirit chained and kept for God's purpose only. **Are we prepared for God to** do **in us** all that He separated us for? And then after His work is done in us, **are we prepared to separate ourselves** to God even as Jesus did? **Jesus prayed,** "For their sakes I sanctify Myself." (John 17:19).

"**God saves believers by imputing** (crediting) **to them** the merit of **Christ's perfect righteousness** - **not** in any sense because of their own righteousness. **God accepts believers in Christ. He declares** them **perfectly righteous** because of Christ. **Their sins have been imputed to Christ,** who has paid the full penalty. **His righteousness is now imputed to them,** and they receive the **full merit** for it. **That is what justification by faith means**" - (John MacArthur).

The **reason some of us have not entered** into the **experience of sanctification** is that **we have not realized the meaning** of **sanctification** from God's standpoint. **Sanctification means being made one with Jesus** so that the disposition that ruled Him will rule us. Are we prepared for what that will cost? **It will cost everything that is not of God in us.**

When Jesus commands us to be perfect as our Father in heaven is perfect (Matthew 5:48), this **simply shows that God's own absolute moral purity** is the **standard** toward which **we are to aim** and the **standard** for which **God holds us accountable.** The fact **that we are unable** to attain that standard **does not mean** that it **will be lowered; rather,** it means that **we need God's grace** and **forgiveness** to overcome our remaining sin. Similarly, **when Paul**

commands the **Corinthians** to make **holiness perfect** in the **fear** of the Lord (II Corinthians 7:1), or prays that **God would sanctify** the Thessalonians wholly (I Thessalonians 5:23), he is **pointing to the goal** that he desires **them to reach.** He does **not imply** that any reach it, but only that this **is the high moral standard** toward which God wants all believers to aspire.

This phrase, "sanctify you entirely" has a **depth of meaning** that I want you to understand. **In this sentence,** two Greek **words,** "entire" and "complete," **combined** with three **nouns,** "spirit, soul, and body," underscore **the completeness of our person. Paul stated,** "I am sure that God, who **began the good work within you, will continue** His work **until it is finally completed** on that day when Christ Jesus comes back again." (Philippians 1:6, NASB).

Sanctification is by faith, not works! It is **wrong to assume** that the **Christian life proceeds on a different** basis than the **one by which it began ... faith.** Some have **erroneously thought** since **salvation is by faith,** and it is a **free gift** from God, **sanctification must be by human effort.** The reason for this **assumption is the idea that by making sanctification a legal works issue,** a category is thereby created in which to put many **verses in the New Testament that teach obedience.**

The notion is that we get to heaven based on Christ's finished work, **but we grow in the Christian life** by **obedience** to God's moral law (our works). **The problem with this** view is that it **creates a false dilemma.** It is **supposed** by many that **faith and obedience are** somehow at **odds with one another. Not true!**

The truth is that **obedience is the result of real faith,** and that any legitimate **obedience that is pleasing to God** is obedience that comes out of a **relationship** of hope and **trust** in the Lord. **We know God and love Him,** therefore we **obey Him.** This is **not legalism,** it is a **relationship with God by faith.**

> **"The further you go in obedience, the more you see of God's plan. God doesn't often tell us the end from the beginning. He prefers to lead us on step-by-step in dependence upon Him."** - Iain Duguid

Consider how Paul described the purpose of his ministry: "...Through whom we have **received grace** and **apostleship** to **bring about the obedience**

of faith among all the Gentiles, for His name's sake" (Romans 1:5, NAS). **The inner work of the Holy Spirit** in the life of the believer brings forth obedience.

This is not "works righteousness" but a practical expression of the righteousness of **Christ which was first imputed** and then **progressively** and **practically imparted. Those who have come to Christ by grace through faith** can be **confused** or **misled** by those **who claim** that following certain **regulations,** ceremonial **laws, rules,** etc., are necessary for the Christian life. **This false approach is corrected in the Book of Galatians.** But **it is not the case that the freedom** we have in Christ is best expressed through licentiousness (decadence) Galatians 5:13. **The walk of faith in the power of the Spirit** is a **walk of love** for God and **one's neighbor.** Such **love cannot** be expressed through **breaking** the **moral law of God.**

We see this in Luke 1:46-47, where the parallelism shows that **soul and spirit are synonymous.** We need to remember that **humans do not have a soul - they are a soul** (Genesis 2:7). This phrase **emphasizes a believers' call to holiness** in every area of **their lives** (Matthew 5:48; Ephesians 1:4).

The Word states, "You are witnesses, and God also, how holy and just and **un-blamable** (without blame) was our behavior among you that believe ..." (I Thessalonians 2:10, ESV). **Notice the word, "without blame."** This term **is only found here in the New Testament.** It has been **found in inscriptions** at Thessalonica. **It means "free from blame or accusations,"** therefore, "**morally pure."** It **reflects** the OT term **"blameless"** that **meant free of defects** and, therefore, **available for sacrifice.** (1 Thessalonians 2:10). **Accept it!** Because of **His Grace, it is yours!**

God's immense flood of grace not only **sees us as holy in Christ,** but also progressively **produces holy desires** in us. It is **grace to be forgiven** of sinful acts, and **grace to be supplied** the heart for righteous ones. **It is grace** that we are increasingly "conformed to the image of his Son" (Romans 8:29), **and grace that he doesn't leave us** in the misery of our sin **but pledges to bring to completion** the good work he has begun in us (Philippians 1:6).

Christ will be master of the heart - and **sin must be mortified (**put to death/crush/put down). **If your life is unholy** - then your heart is unchanged, and **you are an unsaved person.** The Savior **will sanctify His people, renew** them, **give them** a hatred of sin, and a love of holiness. **The grace that does not make a man better than others** - is a **worthless counterfeit. Christ saves His people, not in** their sins, **but from their sins.** Without holiness, no one shall see the Lord (Hebrews 12:14 NIV).

No one experiences complete sanctification without going **through a "death," a "funeral"** - the **burial of the old life.** If there has never been this crucial moment of **change through death, sanctification will never** be more than an elusive **dream.** There must be a "funeral," **a death** with only **one resurrection** - a **resurrection into the** life, as a **new creation,** of Jesus Christ. **Nothing can defeat** a life like this. **This new life** has **oneness with God** for only one purpose - to **be a witness for Him.**

God has given us a beautiful **picture** of conversion and obedience with the Greek word **"baptizo" of those** coming to Jesus as Lord. Although a **person's sins are forgiven,** based on **faith in Jesus** alone, **baptism is** an **important symbol** of **death** to our **old way** and **resurrection** living of a new beginning in Christ. **Acts 8 shares** the **story of the Ethiopian Eunuch who**

Have you really come to your last days? You have often come to them in your mind, but have you **really experienced** them? **You cannot die** or go to **your funeral** in a **mood of excitement. Death means** you stop being. You **must agree with God** and **stop** being the intensely **striving kind** of Christian you have been. **We avoid the cemetery** and continually **refuse our own death.** It will **not happen** by striving, **but by committing and yielding** to death. It is **dying** - being "baptized into His death" (Romans 6:3).

Again: have you **had your "funeral,"** or are you **piously deceiving your own soul?** Has there been **a point in your life** which you now **mark as your last day?** Is there a place in your life **in which** you **had your funeral (spiritually),** that you allowed God to have your life completely?

"This **is** the **will** of **God,** your **sanctification."** (I Thessalonians 4:3 NASB). **Once** you truly **realize** this is **God's will,** you will **enter** into the **process of sanctification** as a natural response. Are you **willing to experience** that "funeral" **now?** Will you agree with Him that **this is your last day** on earth spiritually? **The moment** of **agreement depends on you.**

Warning: For **many believers,** this is a **"hard study." I understand that!** Just like there are **some things** that **I cannot fully understand or explain, I simply accept the teaching** of God's Word. According to the **Scriptures,** all **true believers** are **positionally** and **spiritually declared "right," "blameless," "righteous,"** and **"just"** by the **work of Christ.**

What many believers simply **don't understand** or **accept** is: when they come to Christ, they are **placed "in Christ"** (II Corinthians 5:17), and are **to possess** their **new position.** They are to **possess** their **profession** in Christ. **Scripture states** that **we are to:** "Walk in the light as He is in the light" (I John 1:7). **We must:** "Walk worthily of the calling" (Ephesians 4:1 ASV).

Too many Christians live their entire lives in a spiritual comfort zone unwilling to make a full commitment to God and His will for us.

It is past time for us, as **Christians**, to **face up to our responsibility** for holiness. Too often we say we are **"defeated"** by this or that sin. **No, we are not defeated;** we are **simply disobedient.** It might be well if we **stopped using the terms like victory and defeat** to describe our **progress in holiness.** Rather we should use the **terms obedience and disobedience.**

Faith, holiness and sanctification are inextricably **linked. Obeying the commands** of God usually **involves believing the promises** of **God**....most we **don't know** about, **because** we **refuse to immerse** ourselves (study) the **Word of God.**

Grace is the mother and nurse of holiness - and not the apologist of sin! - (Spurgeon)

Sin is the **antithesis** (opposite) of **holiness,** it befits all who would desire to pursue His holiness to **pay real attention** to **J. H. Jowett's** sobering **description of sin:** "Sin is a blasting presence, and every fine power shrinks and withers in the destructive heat. **Every spiritual delicacy succumbs** to its malignant touch ... **Sin impairs the sight,** and works toward blindness. **Sin deadens** the hearing and tends to make men deaf. **Sin perverts** the taste, causing men to confound the sweet with the bitter, and the bitter with the sweet. **Sin hardens** the touch, and **eventually renders** a man 'past feeling."

All these are Scriptural analogies, and their common significance appears to be this--**sin blocks and chokes** the fine senses of the spirit; **by sin we are desensitized,** rendered imperceptive, and the range of our correspondence is diminished. **Sin creates** callosity. **It hoofs** (stomps on) the Spirit, and so reduces the area of our exposure to pain."

F. B. Meyer was visiting in a Scottish home. It was **washday,** and the **clothes** were on the line. **It began to snow,** and soon the clothes did not look **so white against the background of the snow.** When Meyer remarked about it, the old **Scottish landlady cried,** "Mon, **what can stand** against **God Almighty's white?" When Isaiah saw the Lord in His holiness,** he saw himself in **his sinfulness** and the people in their wickedness. **A sense of God brought a strong sense of sin.**

It is quite true to say, "I can't live a holy life," **but you must decide to let Jesus make you holy.** The destined end of man is **not happiness,** nor **health,** but **holiness.** Remember: **God's one aim is the production of saints. He is not an eternal blessing machine** for men; **Jesus did not come to save men out of pity. He came to save men** because he had **created them to be holy.** The **holy man** is the **most humble man** you will ever meet.

It is well that we remember that **there is no holiness without regeneration.** It is "the new man which is created in true holiness" (Ephesians 4:24). And **no heaven without holiness;** for "without holiness no man shall see the Lord," (Hebrews 12:14). **None will be transported** into the **paradise above** - but **out of the nursery of grace below.** If you **are unholy** while in **this world,** you **will be forever miserable** in the world to come.

C. H. Spurgeon had much to say about **holiness** … "Though you **have struggled** in vain **against** your **evil habits,** though you **have wrestled** with them sternly, and **resolved,** and **re-resolved,** only to **be defeated by your giant sins** and your **terrible passions,** there is **One who can conquer** all your sins for you.

There is One who is stronger than Hercules, **who can strangle the hydra** of your lust, **kill the lion** of your passions, and **cleanse the horse stable** of your evil nature by turning the great rivers of blood and water of his atoning sacrifice right through your soul. **He can make and keep you pure within.** Oh, look to him!"

A baptism of holiness, a demonstration **of godly living** is the crying need of our day. **The holiest person is one who is most conscious of what sin is.** Holiness **does not consist** in mystic speculations, enthusiastic fervors, or un-commanded severities; **it consists in thinking as God thinks,** and willing as God wills.

Jesus has restored the image of God in His creations, through grace. Intimate fellowship is now possible, but **remember God wants a people** who **reflect His character,** as His Son did, to a lost world (the nations). **We are called to nothing less than holiness and purity.** (Matthew 5:20, 48; Ephesians 1:4; I Peter 1:13-16). **God's holiness,** not only legally, **but existentially** (things that exist and experienced)!

Biblical holiness extends to every part of our person, **fills up** our being, **spreads** over our life, **influences everything we are,** or **do,** or **think,** or **speak,** or **plan,** small or **great,** outward or inward, negative or **positive, our loving,** our **hating,** our **sorrowing,** our **rejoicing,** our **recreations,** our **business,** our **friendships,** our **relationships,** our **silence,** our **speech,** our **reading,**

our **writing,** our **going out** and our **coming in** - **our whole man in every movement of spirit, soul, and body.**

Also be aware of, the coming of our Lord. This has **been the theological focus** of the **entire letter** to the Thessalonians, **the Second Coming** (I Thessalonians 1:10; 2:19; 3:13; 4:13-15:11; 5:23). **Paul reminds** you again that **Jesus will return.**

These verses show that "sanctifying grace" is that **grace** which works **within the true believer** in such a way as **to bring growth, maturity, and progress** in the **process** of becoming **Christ-like ... sanctified.**

Paul wrote in Titus 2:11-12 "For the **grace of God** that brings salvation has appeared to all men. **It teaches us to say 'No,'** to ungodliness and worldly passions, and to live self-controlled, upright and godly lives in this present age."

Initial sanctification occurs instantly at the **moment of salvation** when we are delivered from the kingdom of darkness and brought into the Kingdom of Christ (Colossians 1:13).

Progressive sanctification continues over time until we go to be with the Lord. **Initial sanctification is entirely** the work of God the **Holy Spirit who imparts** to us the very life of Christ. **Progressive sanctification is also the work** of the **Holy Spirit,** but it **involves a response** on our part so that we as believers are actively involved in the process." - Jerry Bridges

The grace of God sanctifies us. As noted, sanctification is the **act of becoming holy** and **godly. And this process should start** when we **come in contact with God's grace** and **surrender** our lives to Jesus Christ. **The grace of God should motivate us** to live right. **Grace** should be a **controlling power** in our lives.

Without grace, there would be **no Holy Spirit conviction** of sin, no **calling,** no **salvation,** no **justification,** and no **sanctification** - let alone, **glorification.** I could **go as far as to say** that there would be **no creation!** In short, in terms of our salvation, **grace is the key element in God's entire purpose.**

I once read of a missionary who had **in his garden a shrub** that bore **poisonous leaves.** At that time he **had a child** who was prone to put anything **within reach into his mouth. Naturally he dug the shrub out and threw it away.** The **shrub's roots,** however, were very deep. Soon the **shrub sprouted again.** Repeatedly the missionary **had to dig it out.** There was no solution but to **inspect the ground every day,** and to **dig up the shrub every time it surfaced.** Indwelling sin is like that shrub. **It needs constant uprooting,**

gathering and burning. **Listen: our hearts** need **constant mortification** (a daily defeat or killing of sin in our lives.

We must be exercising 'mortification' every day, and in every duty. **Sin will not die,** unless it be constantly weakened. **Spare it,** and it will **heal** its wounds, and **recover** its strength. **We must continually watch** against the **operations of this principle of sin:** in our duties, in our calling, in conversation, in retirement, in our straits, in our enjoyments, and **in all that we do.** When we **are negligent** on any occasion, we **shall suffer** by it; every mistake, **every neglect is perilous.**

Leonard Ravenhill once said, "The **greatest miracle** that God can do today is to **take an unholy man** out of an **unholy world,** and make that **man holy** and **put him back** into that **unholy world** and **keep him holy** in it." The **biblical process** of **sanctification** is a **continual thing.**

> "For **the grace of God** has **appeared, bringing salvation**
> to all men, **instructing us** to **deny** ungodliness and
> worldly desires and to **live sensibly, righteously** and
> **godly** in the **present age**" (Titus 2:11-12 (NASB).

The grace of God should sanctify us. **Sanctification is the act** of **becoming holy** and **godly.** And this **process should start** when we **come in contact with God's grace** and **surrender our lives to Jesus Christ. The grace of God** should **motivate us** to **live right.** Grace should be a **controlling power** in our lives.

One time a man came into a **village** and asked **an old man** living there, **"Any great men born here?"** The old man **said, "No, just babies." Great men are not born;** great men **are made, investing** in the lives of others, **sharing** God's love, and **showing** His mercies.

There is not a **magic formula** that **instantly makes us sanctified. Sanctification** is a **continual process (as my brother in Christ, Sal said, "It's a marathon, not a sprint").** Our calling is to be **poured out into the lives** of others for **His glory. Pray about it** and **then watch** how **God provides!**

God invites us sinners to come to Him **"just as we are" in repentance, and receive** His mercy, redemption, forgiveness, and sanctification. **When we are saved, the Holy Spirit begins** His **amazing work** of **transforming us** into the **image** and **likeness of Christ. To be sanctified means** that God **loves us too much** to let us stay the same.

The apostle's prayer is for **all believers, everywhere:** "May God himself, the God of peace, **sanctify you** through and through. **May your whole spirit,**

soul and body be **kept blameless** at the coming of our Lord Jesus Christ" (I Thessalonians 5:23 NIV).

> **Grace does not permit a Christian a green light to**
> **continue living in the flesh; but grace does provide us**
> **to be alive and triumph in the Spirit.** - G. Clifton

We, as children of God by the new-birth (John I and 3), **must learn quickly** that **sanctification is not what we can do or have done, but what Jesus has done** and **is doing in us.** The **Christians job** is simply to **have confidence** and **commit ourselves** to Him. We **can live a holy life,** but **not in our own strength.** True **sanctification is Jesus' life in us.**

We must learn that God is holy. If we are to experience the manifest presence of God's glory, **we must repent.** When **Isaiah saw the glory of God** in the **Temple,** he was driven to brokenness, confession, and repentance. **Too many in this modern world** desire to know the manifest love of God **without the manifest holiness of God.** We **have lost the message of repentance, cleansing and holiness.** Now **the church** in our country is a **sleeping Giant.** The church in the East sends a strong message: **The "repenters" must repent!**

Many so-called Christians have attached themselves to the church **without becoming "repenters."** We have **preached a gospel without a distinct call for repentance.** But throughout the **Scriptures we are admonished to repent** and **believe.** John the Baptist **preached and baptized** with a "**baptism of repentance" prior** to the ministry of **reconciliation** of Jesus.

It is a **question of the utmost importance** to our souls. **If the Bible be true,** it is certain that **unless we are "sanctified,"** we shall not be saved. Study on …

The character of a person is expressed in his **will;** therefore, **since God is holy,** He can **desire only holiness for His children,** "but like the Holy One who called you, be holy yourselves also in all your behavior because it is written, **'YOU SHALL BE HOLY, FOR I AM HOLY'"** (I Peter 1:15 NASB).

When you apply that **definition of holiness** to **God** Himself, something **interesting happens. God is holy** in that **He is set apart from all that is evil** and **defective** and **impure. He is absolutely free** from any **taint of evil** or **deficiency.**

Also, God's holiness is **His set-apartness** for God. Now we have to **be careful here** lest we **wipe out** all the **biblical distinctions** between the **holiness of God** and the **glory of God** and the **righteousness of God.** I'll try to give you a **simplified picture** of the **relationship** between these **three for you to test** as you **study** the **Scriptures.**

The **holiness of God** is the **reality** that **God is utterly unique** and in a **class by himself** - that's **His set-apartness** - none compares with him. There is **no other Creator**, no other **sustainer**, no other **final measure** of good and evil.

> "**There is no one holy like the Lord, indeed,**
> **there is no one besides thee, nor is there any**
> **rock like our God**" (1 Samuel 2:2).

He is utterly set apart in a class by Himself, unequaled, unrivaled, totally underived, unchangeable, and **perfect in His being** and perfection, **without** beginning or ending or improvement. **In a word, His holiness** is the **supremacy** of his **infinite worth** among all that is.

The **glory of God** is the **radiance** or the **outward expression** of that **perfection** and value. As **you might say** that **light is the glory of the sun,** and **fire is its holiness. "Holy, holy, holy is the Lord** of hosts, the **whole earth** is **full of his glory**" (Isaiah 6:3 ESV).

We must remember the Scriptures where we are **taught that all men by nature follow the desires** of the flesh and of the mind, "**Among them we** too all **formerly lived in the lusts** of our flesh, indulging the **desires of the flesh** and of the **mind,** and were by nature **children of wrath,** even as the rest" (Ephesians 2:3), **and are thus** in chronic **opposition to the will of God,** "those who are in the flesh cannot please God" (Rom. 8:8 ESV).

> "**The natural man does not** perceive (accept) the things of
> the **Spirit of God;** for they are **foolishness** to him; neither
> **can he understand** them because they are **spiritually**
> **discerned** (unregenerate)" (I Corinthians 2:14).

And **the righteousness of God** is **His faithfulness** or **commitment** to **act always in accord** with the **beauty** of **His glory** and the **value of His holiness. His righteousness is His allegiance** to **uphold** and **magnify** the glory and the **holiness of Himself** (Psalm 143:11). **If God were ever** to **act** as if **His glory** were not the **supreme value** in the universe, **He would be unrighteous.** His action would be untrue.

Scriptures tell us as believers in **Jesus, to build our lives** on the **righteousness of God** and the **glory of God.** But in this context **Peter here**

focuses on the **holiness of God**. So we want to ask, **"How does** the **holiness** of God **make its proper impact** on our lives? **Paul wrote,** "For whom he did foreknow, he also did predestinate to be conformed to the image of his Son, that he might be the firstborn among many brethren. Moreover whom he did predestinate, them he also called: and whom he called, them he also justified: and whom he justified, them he also glorified" (Romans 8:29–30). This call is the **effect of God's life-giving word** that **brings us out of agitation** and **aggravation** into the **submissive attitude of faith.**

The **beautiful picture** of the **'The Potter and the Clay' shows** the **idea of sanctification** is that **something or someone is set aside** for the use **intended by the designer.** For example, a **fountain pen** is "set aside" or "sanctified" for the **purpose of writing.** A **pair of glasses** is "sanctified" and set aside for **use in improving one's sight.** In short, **as used in the Bible,** things **are sanctified** when they are used **for the purpose God intended.** The **clay** (mud) **being molded** is **always in the Potter's hand,** even though the **wheel** is **spinning, mud flying,** as the **shaping** and **reshaping takes place.**

A **human being is sanctified,** therefore, **when he or she lives according to God's design and purpose,** walking in a manner which **is pleasing** to His and **worthy of His great Name.**

> **If we give God service** it must be **because**
> He gives us grace. We work **for** Him because
> **He works in us**. - C.H. Spurgeon

As previously stated, 'sanctification' means to "make holy." In the **Old Testament, vessels of silver and gold** are said to be **sanctified. Vessels and other things** for the **use of the worship of God in** Tabernacle and Temple **were to be sanctified to God** in the **first sense** of that word, **as they were set apart** from profane and ordinary to sacred uses. **A golden cup** may be used for common purposes of drinking, or it may be **set apart** to be used only **in the celebration** of the **Supper of the Lord.** In this case it is **separated to holy uses.**

When, therefore, Paul tells us, "This is the will of God, **even your sanctification,"** he means that both in **our bodies and in our minds** we should **be separated,** not only from the particular evil spoken of by the Epistle, but, in the full meaning of the word, from all evil. **As Christians, we are to be set apart** from all that is profane, wicked, and ungodly, and **to wear the "white flower of a blameless life."**

**Our Eternal God states, "I am the Lord your God,
which brought you out of the land of Egypt, to be your
God: I am the Lord your God"** (Numbers 15:41 NIV).

God divided light from darkness, **water** from dry land, and the **heavens** from the earth. **He called Abraham** to **separate** himself from his former life. In all His determined transactions with Israel, **He identified Himself** as the **Lord** who had brought them out of bondage and **set them apart** (1 Kings 8:53).

When we **enter a covenant relationship with God,** we must also **separate ourselves** from **our past** and from **our ungodly associations.** The **call to separate yourself unto God** is **not a punishment** but an **exciting divine privilege.**

Another separation will take place **in heaven,** when **those who have entered His covenant** will eternally **be divided** from those **who have chosen to live apart** from it. (Matthew 25:32).

There are three things which, **according** to the **Bible,** are absolutely **necessary to the salvation** of every man and woman in Christendom. **These three are, regeneration, justification,** and **sanctification.** He that lacks any one of these three things, will **never find himself in heaven** when he dies. Where, then, is the harm of asking, **"Are we sanctified?"**

Someone once said, "What **health** is to the heart, that **holiness** is to the soul." **Holiness is not exemption** from conflict, **but victory** through conflict. **Holiness is not freedom from temptation,** but power to **overcome** temptation. **Holiness is not the end of progress,** but deliverance from standing still. **There is no holiness without a warfare.** I believe the holier a man becomes, the more he **mourns over the un-holiness** which remains in him … **because he sees himself** as he really is. **The closer he** gets **to the light,** the more **imperfections and filth** is exposed. **Victory over evil** tendencies, strong **tempers,** and **evil habits, He will gladly grant,** and we ought **not to remain it sin.**

**"A man is not saved against his will, but he is made
willing by the operation of the Holy Ghost. A
mighty grace which he does not wish to resist enters
into the man, disarms him, makes a new creature
of him, and he is saved."** - C.H. Spurgeon

It is God's will, the great **purpose** that **He has at heart concerning men,** that they should be holy. **"Sanctify them through Thy truth:** Thy word is truth." **Pardon and all other blessings** are a means to this great end. **The Great Sculptor** would **think** and **plan** and **labor** only for a **torso**, in **preparation** of **a statue**. Without this; **the Great Builder would never see the top stone** on His **chosen temple** without it; and **the Great Husbandman would never taste** of the **fruit** of His **vineyard** without it.

Now, **if our sanctification** - our **growing holiness** here and our **perfected holiness hereafter** - is God's will, then **holiness does not consist** in mystic speculations, enthusiastic fervors, or un-commanded austerities; **it consists in thinking as God thinks, and willing as God wills."**

Paul wrote, "This is the **will of God,** even **your sanctification**" (I Thessalonians 4:3). There is no article in the original, therefore, **this is one of many of God's wills. For example:** "Therefore do **not** be **foolish,** but **understand what the will of the Lord** is" (Ephesians 5:17 NIV). **And after salvation,** "And **this is the will of Him who sent Me,** that everyone who sees the Son and believes in Him may have everlasting life; and I will raise him up at the last day" (John 6:40 AKJV).

Compared with the miracle of the forgiveness of sin, the experience of sanctification is small. **Sanctification is simply the wonderful** expression or **evidence** of the forgiveness of sins in a human life. But the thing that awakens the **deepest fountain of gratitude** in a human being **is that God has forgiven his sin.** Paul never got away from this. Once you realize **all that it cost God to forgive you,** you will be held as in a vise, **constrained by the love of God.**

> **"But grow in the grace and knowledge of our Lord and**
> **Savior Jesus Christ. To him be the glory, both now and**
> **to the day of eternity. Amen"** (II Peter 3:18 ESV).

It is God's purpose for Christians that **they should be holy, as He is holy** (1 Peter 1:15-16). **As soon as a person believes in the Lord Jesus,** he or she belongs to God. Then they should do what He wants. **That is what being holy means.** That person **should now live for God.** A **process has begun** in which the **new life** that God gives **replaces** the **old manner of life. Christians should be changing** in this process to **become what God wants them to be. Being sanctified means to,** as **we grow** in **grace** and **knowledge, make Jesus Lord** (boss) of **our lives.**

Vance Havner once **told the story** about **Dr. Clyde Turner** who was the **pastor** of the First Baptist Church of **Greensboro, KY. A youngster** in the **Sunday School** was a **terror** and nobody knew what to do with him. Finally, he **stopped coming** to Sunday School. **Dr. Turner said,** "I am ashamed to say it, but I think we were all glad of it." **Nobody made any special effort to get him back.**

They were having a little **meeting** and **here came that boy running down the aisle** with a **musical instrument** case under his arm. **"Dr. Turner,"** he **said,** "they gave me a fiddle for being good." **"In the first place," Dr. Turner said,** "I could imagine nobody giving him a fiddle; and in the second place, certainly not for being good."

The boy sensed the wonder on the pastor's face and said, "You see, **preacher, because of Jesus, I am 'gooder' than I used to be."** Dr. Turner said, **"As the boy scampered** down the hall, **I thought,** "Yes, thank God, **by the grace of God** a **lot of us** are 'gooder' than we used to be."

Thank God for His wonderful, amazing grace! Because it is by **surrendering to His powerful grace** that we **all can become 'gooder'** than we used to be!

Holiness is not the way to Jesus … Jesus is the way to holiness. Far too **often people say,** "I'm waiting to get my life cleaned up before I come to God" but the **problem is,** they **can't do** anything without Christ (John 15:5) and only through Christ can we **do anything** (Philippians 4:13), so it's sort of **like saying,** "I'm going to drive the car but I'm waiting for it to be fixed." **The worst thing an unbeliever** can do is **wait and think,** "someday," but **that day** may **not come** before **Jesus returns** or the **person dies,** and by then, it's **too late** (Hebrews 9:27) so **procrastination** can be **deadly. Today** is the best day for you to be saved (I Corinthians 6:2), because **tomorrow may not come,** and **all of us** are **one breath** … one **heartbeat** … away from **eternity** … and that will be **too late** to make a **commitment** for Christ.

A magnificent example of the inherent **idea of separation** that is found in the **word holiness** comes **from the world of nature … In the forests of northern Europe** and **Asia** lives **little animal** called the **ermine,** known for his **snow-white fur** in winter. He instinctively **protects his white coat against anything that would soil it.**

Fur **hunters take advantage** of this unusual trait of the **ermine.** They **don't set a snare to catch him,** but instead they **find his home,** which is usually a cleft in a rock or a hollow in an old tree. **They smear the entrance and interior with mud and grime.** The hunters **let their dogs loose** to find and **chase the ermine.**

The **frightened animal flees** toward home but **doesn't enter because of the filth.** Rather than **stain** his white coat, **he is trapped** by the dogs and is **captured** while **preserving his purity. For the ermine, purity is more precious than life. Perhaps** we have **set our bar of excellence to low.**

Let us Pray: … Father, we thank You very much for our calling, for **Your grace,** Your **kindness,** and Your **care for our lives,** helping us. **Lord Jesus, show me** by Your Holy Spirit the **things I need to come away** from. **I ask Your blessing** on the **study today.** Help me **understand it** and **apply it** to my life. And Father, **to understand our purpose here,** and **teach me** in this **period of human experience** when there is such **spiritual darkness all around. Since I have entered a covenant relationship** with You, **I leave the darkness** behind and **come joyfully into Your marvelous light that I might grow** into the **person You would have me to be.** In the **precious, powerful name of Jesus, I ask this, Amen.**

"The grace of our Lord Jesus Christ and the love of God, and the communion of the Holy Spirit Spirit be with you all. Amen" II Corinthians 13:1 (NASB).

hapter 12

God 'SANCTIFIES' Me By His Grace

(Part II)

God "called us to a holy calling ... because of His own
purpose and grace" (II Timothy 1:9 ESV).

"For this is the **will of God, your sanctification**"
(I Thessalonians 4:3 ESV).

SANCTIFICATION TO BE explicit, is God's **will in your life!** (I Thessalonians 4:3). **It is the will of God** in general that **we should be holy,** because **He that called us is holy,** and because **we are chosen** unto salvation **through the sanctification of the Spirit. Not only** does God **require** holiness **in the heart,** but also **purity in our bodies,** and that we should cleanse ourselves from all filthiness both of flesh and spirit (II Corinthians 7:1).

Whenever the body is, as it ought to be, **devoted** to God, and **dedicated** and **set apart** for Him, it **should be kept clean** and **pure** for his service; and, **as chastity** is one branch of our sanctification, so this is one thing which **God commands** in his Word, and what his **grace effects in all true believers.** Question, **how is all this** completed?"

Vine's Expository Dictionary says the word **"sanctification" is** used of **"(a) separation** to God, I Corinthians 1:30; II Thessalonians 2:13; I Peter 1:2; **(b)** the **course of life** befitting those so separated, I Thessalonians 4:34,7; Romans 6:19,22; I Timothy 2:15; Hebrews 12:14." **He also says, The Holy Spirit** is the **Agent in sanctification (Romans 15:16**; II Thessalonians 2:13; I Peter 1:2; I Corinthians 6: 11).

As we examine the scriptures, let's **review the purpose** for which the **Apostle Paul wrote this letter.** In Colossians 1:6 **we read,** "This **gospel** will

bear fruit and **grow if you truly believed,** just as it has been doing **among you since the** day you **heard** it and **understood the grace of God** in truth" (ESV).

Remember that the verb form "sanctify" means "to set apart" or **"to make holy."** In **Old Testament** Scripture, days, houses, fields, feasts, altars, people, and **many other things were sanctified.** Today, all **Christians are to be sanctified.** This means that they are **to be set apart for the Lord** and **consecrated for his uses** and **purposes.** As our subject affirms, the **Holy Spirit has a work in this sanctification.**

The Bible teaches that the **Holy Spirit works through** the **Word** in the **conviction** and **conversion** of the alien. We affirm that **He continues His work** of **sanctifying the Christian** through the same means. **Jesus prayed,** "Sanctify them in the truth: Thy word is truth" (John 17:17 ASV).

As we live by faith and **do** what the **Bible clearly tells us to do,** we can be sure **the Lord will lead us through the difficult decisions** when the options may not be clear. Above all else, **God's will is that we submit to Him** and be willing to **follow wherever He leads. Holy** has the **same root as wholly,** it means **complete.** Now **please be attentive to this.** According to the Word of God, **a man is not complete in spiritual stature if all his mind, heart, soul, and strength are not given to God.**

"Gradual growth in grace, growth in **knowledge,** growth in **faith,** growth in **love,** growth in **holiness,** growth in **humility,** growth in **spiritual-mindedness** – all this I see **clearly taught** and **urged in Scripture,** and clearly **exemplified in the lives** of many of **God's saints.** But **sudden, instantaneous leaps** from **conversion** to **consecration** I fail to see in **the Bible"** - J.C. Ryle

The nature of sanctification is sinful man changed and **raised** into the image of **Eternal Purity!** And **the transformation is** thorough. **It takes place in the soul,** and **can be seen by God only;** it is then **exhibited in the life,** that it may be **seen of angels and men. Someone has said, "Holiness** has **love** for its essence, **humility** for its clothing, the **good** of others as its employment, **and the honor of God** as its end."

God's will in this verse is "your sanctification" This word shares the **same root word** wi.th **"holy"** and **"saints." Sanctification,** like **justification,** is **an initial instantaneous act of grace** (I Corinthians 1:2, 30; 6:11). **Positionally, believers are 'in Christ.'** However, it should develop into lifestyle character, **progressive sanctification** (I Thessalonians 4:7; 3:13; Romans 6:19-23). **God's will** for **every Christian is Christlikeness!!** We **cannot separate justification** from **sanctification,** though they are **different works** of the **Grace of God!**

> "Grace is free sovereign favor to the ill-deserving." - B.B. Warfield

Christians and the church cannot set their sail as to how the wind may blow. **We must set our sail according to the will of God,** which may mean that we sail against the prevailing winds of opinion. **We want to sail in the same direction God is going.** Before we can do the will of God, **we must be willing to do His will** no matter what the cost. **The Christian who is willing to open himself to God's will unconditionally is the Christian God will use.**

The Scriptures constitute: "the Word of Life" **in written form.** Jesus Christ is "the Word of life" in human form (I John 1:1). **The Scriptures are also called** "the word of **His grace**" (Acts 20:32); "the word of the **kingdom**" (Matthew 13:19); "the word of **promise**" (Romans 9:9); "the word of **faith**" (Romans 10:8); "the word of **reconciliation**" (II Corinthians 5:19); "the word of **truth**" (Ephesians 1:13); "the word of **exhortation**" (Hebrews 13:22); and other such marvelous titles.

What does the Bible mean when it speaks of a **"sanctified" man?** Sanctification is that **inward spiritual work** which the **Lord Jesus Christ works** in a man **by the Holy Ghost,** when He **calls him** to be a true believer, **separates him** from his natural love of sin and the world, **puts a new principle** in his heart, and **makes him** practically godly in life.

> **A holy life will make the deepest impression. Lighthouses blow no horns, they just shine** - D. L. Moody

It is a great deal better to **live a holy life** than to **talk about it.** We are told to **let our light shine,** and **if it does we won't need to tell anybody** it does. The **light will be its own witness. Lighthouses don't ring bells** and **fire cannons** to call attention to their shining - **they just shine.**

The instrument by which **God's Spirit effects the continued work of sanctification** is generally the **Word of 'God,** though **He sometimes uses afflictions** and **providential visitations'** "without the Word." **The subject of this work** of Christ, by His Spirit, is **called in Scripture a "sanctified" man.**

To repeat: sanctification means the impartation of the **holy qualities** of **Jesus Christ to His children.** It is the **gift** of His patience, love, holiness, faith, purity, and godliness that is **exhibited in and through every sanctified soul.** Sanctification is not drawing from Jesus the power to be holy - it is **drawing**

from Jesus the **very holiness** that was exhibited in Him, and that He now exhibits in me.

And what a start God gives us in His **full forgiveness through Christ!** He thereby e to "Mortify therefore your members which are upon the earth; fornication, uncleanness, inordinate affection, evil concupiscence, and covetousness, which is idolatry" (Colossians 3:5, (ASV). Do you realize what that verse says? **Read it again** ... slowly ... First, **you must know** what **mortify means. Mortify means, 'Put to Death.'**

I want you to understand the on-going process of sanctification. Sanctification, **like** Salvation, **is wholly the work of God in us;** but unlike Salvation, **Sanctification requires a certain amount of effort** on our part. No, it is **not our effort** which accomplishes Sanctification (**we can in no way make ourselves holy**), but we are called **to mortify,** literally, **to put to death the sin that we practice**.

It is possible to **stand perfect** and **complete in all the will** of **God.** "Epaphras, who is one of you and a **servant of Christ Jesus,** sends greetings. He is always **wrestling in prayer** for you, that you may **stand firm** in all the will of God, **mature** and fully **assured**" (Colossians 4:12, NIV). **Jesus Himself prayed for His disciples,** "Sanctify them through Thy truth." (John 17:17). **The word sanctification signifies to consecrate** and **set apart** to a holy use: thus **they are sanctified people** who are **separated** from the world, and **set apart for** God's service. Sanctification has a privative and a positive part.

> **Christian, we are never nearer Christ than when**
> **we find ourselves lost in a holy amazement at His**
> **unspeakable love, provided by His Divine Grace!**

As stated at the top of this Chapter ... **Acts 20:32 states,** "And now, brethren, I commend you to God, **and to the word of his grace,** which is able to build you up, and to give you an inheritance among all **them which are sanctified**" (KJV). **"Sanctify:"** This word is from the root **"holy"** (**Greek - hagios**). This can **mean a couple of things.**

In its New Testament, believers are called to **Christlikeness** (John 17:19; Romans 8:28-29; II Corinthians 3:18; 7:1; Galatians 4:19; Ephesians 1:4; 4:13; I Thessalonians 3:13; 4:3, 7; 5:23; I Peter 1:15). **This can only happen** through **knowledge of the truth, which is both living word** (Jesus in John 1:1-14) **and written word** (John 15:3).

Peter goes on to tell us to grow in our lives **and increase** in the true knowledge of Jesus Christ (II Peter 1:5-8). But **what if we are not growing or changing?** Does this suggest we need something more like **therapy based** on **human wisdom? No! Peter tells us of the problem if we do not grow:** "For he who **lacks** these qualities **is blind** or **short-sighted,** having forgotten his **purification from** his former sins" (II Peter 1:9, NASB).

The problem is that we **forgot what God did for us** in Christ. **The means of grace** make sure that we remember. Sanctification is through **what God has done for us** and what **He has promised to do** as we walk in faith. It is not about what great things we imagine that we are going to do for God.

Remember, "Sanctify," biblically **means "to set apart for God's service."** John 17:18 clarifies **the purpose** for them **"being sanctified."** This is **seen in Jesus' life of obedience and service,** even to the point of death (II Corinthians 5:14-15; Galatians 2:20; I John 3:16), **sets the pattern for His followers** (John 17:19). **He will send them** into the **lost world on mission** just **as He was sent in** John 20:21. They must **engage** the world, not **retreat** from it.

It is quite possible that John has the **disciples "sanctified"** for **God's service** as an **analogy** of the **Old Testament priests set apart** for **God's service.** They **served as mediators** of the OT sacrifices, but **the disciples' served as the revealers** of the NT **perfect, once-for-all sacrifice, Christ.**

What does the scripture mean by a sanctified man? Sanctification is **that inward, spiritual work that God works in us** by His Holy Spirit when He calls us to be a son. **He not only washes us** from our sins **by Christ's blood,** but **also separates us** from our **carnal love** of sin (our carnality), working **into our minds a new motivating principle** of living.

Much of this **is done supernaturally** when we receive His Holy Spirit: I will put My law into your mind. He can do that, but **He cannot make a person use it!** It is **when we choose to use it** that it becomes **written in our hearts** - it becomes **part of our nature,** part of our **way of living.** However, this does not occur in the blink of an eye. **It is a process** whose main **element is faith** - faith in something very specific. It is **not the faith that God is,** but **faith in the teaching of God's Word.** If a person **does not trust** His Word, **he will not obey it,** and if he **does not obey it,** he **will not be sanctified.**

God's work of grace in the elect begins **when they are born again** by the **quickening (being made alive) operation of the Holy Spirit.** From that moment on **this work of grace** is **continued** throughout our remaining life on this earth. **It is true** that this **total perfection of grace** is **not completely attained in this earthly life.**

Nevertheless, **we are to diligently seek** that **holy** life (Philippians 3:12-13; II Peter 1:5-7). **Because of God's grace** we **cannot rest satisfied** in our present spiritual progress. Indeed, it is the **realization that God has** turned away His wrath, and **has only thoughts of grace toward us** that motivates us to live a life pleasing to Him in thought and action. We need to pray **for a constant supply of sanctifying grace** that we might **please Him** in our daily life.

What Really Is Sanctification?

"For there are **certain men crept** in (slipped in) unawares (unnoticed), who were before of old ordained to this condemnation, **ungodly** men, **turning** (perverting) **the grace of our God** into lasciviousness (to immorality, sensuality, or license), and **denying** the only **Lord God,** and **our Lord Jesus Christ**" (Jude 1:4 KJV, parenthesis and emphasis mine - G.C).

Christians are called out of the world, from the **evil spirit** and **temper** of it; called **to live above** the world, **to higher** and better things, to heaven, things unseen and eternal; **called from sin to Christ,** from **vanity to seriousness,** from **uncleanness to holiness;** and this according to the **Divine purpose and grace** of God. **If sanctified** and glorified, **all the honor and glory must be ascribed to God,** and to him alone. As **it is God who begins the work of grace** in the souls of men, **so it is he who carries it on,** and perfects it. Let us not trust in ourselves, nor in our stock of grace already received, **but in Him,** and in **Him alone.**

G. Campbell Morgan was right when he said that: "the
church did the most for the world when the **church** was the
least like the world."
Salvation to Sanctification

Conversion is not only regeneration. This is a **neglected fact** in our **preaching today.** When a person is **born again, he knows** that it is because he has **received something** as a **gift from Almighty God** and not because of **his own decision.** People may **make vows and promises,** and may be **determined** to follow through, **but none of this is salvation.** Salvation **means** that we are **brought to the place** where we are **able to see ourselves in sin** and **place our life completely** in the **finished work of Jesus,** and to **receive something from God** on the **authority of Jesus** Christ, namely, **forgiveness of sins.**

This is followed by God's a mighty work of grace: "And now, **brethren, I commend you to God**, and to the **Word of his grace**, which is able to build you up, and to **give you an inheritance** among all **them which are sanctified**" (Acts 20:32, KJV). **In sanctification,** the one who has been born again, **deliberately gives up his right to himself to Jesus Christ,** and **identifies himself** entirely with **God's ministry to others.**

The sanctified are, because of **that experience, heirs** of God and **joint-heirs** with Jesus Christ. "For both **He that sanctifies** and **they who are sanctified** are all of one: for which cause He is not ashamed **to call them brethren.**" The **experience of sanctification makes us** one with Christ, standing on an equal basis with Him **in the sight of God** with respect to **this specific inheritance** (Hebrews 2:11 NASB).

> **Sin's shadows disappear when the light of Jesus is publicized to transgressors!** - G. Clifton

Sanctification is the Spiritual **process of Almighty God** taking **sinful men** from **where they've been, to where they are,** and to where **they're going to be.** The holy man is **not** one who **cannot sin.** A **holy man** is one who **will not sin.**

Holiness is the way **God is. To be holy** he does **not conform** to a **standard. God Himself is that standard.** He is **absolutely holy** with an infinite, incomprehensible **fullness of purity** that his characteristic, qualities and traits are holy; that is, whatever we think of as **belonging to God** must be thought of as holy. **Justification starts the sanctification process** through the **ministry of the Holy Spirit** who is our **Comforter promised to the Church** at the Last Supper. **Faith is never alone** but with regards to **faith that brings salvation** it is **apart from works.**

We must remember that **grace is not a one-time happening,** and **does not stop** once we are saved. **Salvation** and **God's favor** are **only a part** of what we gain when we receive God's grace. **We receive justification** before our Holy God (Romans 3:24; Ephesians 1:7; Titus 3:7). **Grace provides us access** to God to **communicate** with Him and **fellowship** with Him (Ephesians 1:5–6; Hebrews 4:16). **Grace opens the door** in our hearts for new levels of **intimacy** with God (Exodus 33:17), and **grace also disciplines us** to live in a way that honors God (Titus 2:11–14; 2 Corinthians 8:1–7).

"**This is crucial** ... that we **not confuse** or **combine**
justification and **sanctification**. **Confusing them** will,
in the end, **undermine** the gospel, and **turn justification**
by **faith** into **justification** by **performance**" - John Piper

We receive enormous spiritual riches (Proverbs 10:22; Ephesians
2:7), **such as** comfort, encouragement, and strength (2 Corinthians 13:14;
2 Thessalonians 2:16–17; 2 Timothy 2:1). **Grace helps us in our every need**
because God is continuously close to us (Hebrews 4:16), and **grace is the reason
behind** our very deliverance (Psalm 44:3–8; Hebrews 4:16).

The true Christian ideal is not to be **happy but** to be **holy.** The **whole
purpose of God** in redemption is to **make us holy** and to **restore us to the
image of God.** To accomplish this **He disengages us** from earthly aspirations
and **draws us away** from the **cheap and unworthy prizes** that worldly men set
their hearts upon.

**The sovereign electing grace of God chooses us to
repentance, to faith and afterwards to holiness of
living, to Christian service, to zeal, and to devotion.**

As stated, according to the Word of God, **the true Christian ideal** is **not
to be happy** but to **be holy.** No man should desire to be happy who is not at the
same time holy. **He should spend his efforts in seeking to know** and **do the
will of God,** leaving to Christ the matter of **how happy he shall be.**

Speak to God and have an understanding. **Tell Him** that it is your **desire
to be holy** at any cost and then ask Him never to give you more happiness than
holiness. **When your holiness becomes tarnished,** let your joy become dim.
And **ask Him to make you holy** whether you are **happy or not.** Be assured that
in the end you will **be as happy as you are holy;** but for the time being let your
whole **ambition be to serve God and be Christ-like.**

Sanctification: Just to add a theological note, **grace is not permissive or
a license** to **sin.** Grace justifies in order to sanctify ... and **sanctification
brings holiness** in our living, which brings a holy, stable, committed **desire
not to sin.**

God asks you this question through the Apostle Paul, "What shall we
say, then? **Shall** we go on sinning so that grace may increase? **By no means!
We are those** who have died to sin; how can we live in it any longer? **Or don't
you know** that all of us who were baptized into Christ Jesus were baptized into

his death? **We were therefore buried** with him through **baptism into death** in order that, just as **Christ was raised** from the dead through the glory of the Father, **we too** may live a new life" (Romans 6:1-4 NIV).

In endeavoring to understand how **Paul thinks** of those he addresses in **1 Corinthians Three,** we must bear in mind **the designation he gives to them in Chapter One.** He says they are "sanctified in Christ Jesus," they are **recipients of "the grace of God,"** enriched by Christ **"in all utterance, and in all knowledge"** (1:2-5 KJV). **They are rebuked** in Chapter 3, **not for** failing to attain to privileges which some Christians attain to, **but for acting,** despite their privileges, **like babes** and **like the unregenerate** in one area of their lives.

As stated, grace is not a one-time occurrence and does **not stop** once we are saved. **Salvation and God's favor** are only a part of what we gain when we receive God's grace. **We receive justification** before a holy God (Romans 3:24; Ephesians 1:7; Titus 3:7). **Grace provides us access to God** to communicate with Him and fellowship with Him (Ephesians 1:5–6; Hebrews 4:16). **Grace opens the door in our hearts for** new levels of intimacy with God (Exodus 33:17). **Grace** also **disciplines** us to **live** in a way that honors God (Titus 2:11–14; II Corinthians 8:1-7).

> **"What shall we say, then? Shall we go on sinning**
> **so that grace may increase?"** (Romans 6:1 NIV).

When God calls you into **His covenant,** He **calls** you **to separate yourself from everything that hinders** you from **fulfilling His purpose** for your life. **God instructed Abraham,** who came from a **long line of idol-worshippers,** to **leave** his home and **go into an unknown land.** God's call to Abraham **required both obedience** and **personal commitment to Him** in order to receive all that He promised.

To receive all God promised, Abraham had to **leave all** his past security. **He had to come out of relying** on what he **could see** and **begin trusting** what he **could not see.** "For we walk by faith, not by sight" (II Corinthians 5:7).

Because of Abraham's **faithful obedience,** He **became the father** of the **entire Jewish nation,** which **included the Savior** of all mankind. **All these blessings ensued** from that moment **when God said, "Come out,"** and **Abraham replied, "Yes."**

When God calls you into **His covenant of salvation,** He **calls** you **to separate yourself** from **everything that hinders** you from **fulfilling His**

purpose for your life. **Lay aside your idols** of **power, prestige**, and **position**; say **"Yes" to God** and **walk under the blessing** of God's covenant with mankind!

Grace also provides enormous **spiritual riches** (Proverbs 10:22; Ephesians 2:7), such **as comfort, encouragement, and strength** (II Corinthians 13:14; II Thessalonians 2:16–17; II Timothy 2:1). **Grace helps us in our every need** because God is continuously close to us (Hebrews 4:16), and it **is the reason** behind **our very deliverance** (Psalm 44:3–8; Hebrews 4:16). **We can interact with grace** (much like love and forgiveness) because **grace is actively and continually working** in the lives of God's people.

Someone put it like this ... To be **"In Christ,"** is the **source** of the Christian's **life**. To be **"Like Christ,"** is the **sum** of the Christian's **excellence**. To be **"With Christ,"** is the total **summation** of the Christian's **joy**. **Dear Christian, remember** and **do** what you have just read and **live** so that **the preacher** can **tell the truth at your funeral!**

All the prophets testified about Him that everyone who "believes in Him receives forgiveness of sins through his name. While Peter was still speaking these words, the Holy Spirit came on all who heard the message" (Acts 10:43 - 44 NIV).

Faith is an **act of obedience** to **God's grace** and **calling** (John 7:38; Acts 16:31). This is the **specific act of faith** by which a **sinner is justified** before God (Romans 3:22, 25; Galatians 2:16; Philippians 3:9; John 3:16-36; Acts 10:43; 16:31). **What is more, we see in** this passage directly ties **the reception of the Holy Spirit** with **receiving the Holy Spirit which is the seal that guarantees** our inheritance till the redemption of the purchased possession (Ephesians 1:13). **Grace saves**, grace **sanctifies** and grace **works** to **produce** peaceable **fruits of righteousness** (works).

The **Scriptures nowhere teach** us that **faith sanctifies us** in the **same sense** and in the **same manner that faith justifies us! Justifying faith** is a **grace that "works not,"** but simply trusts, rests, and **leans on Christ** (Romans 4:5). **Sanctifying faith is a grace** of which the very life is action: it **"works by love,"** and, like a **mainspring, moves** the man (Galatians 5:6) - J.C. Ryle

The Lord Jesus has undertaken everything that His people's souls require; **not only to deliver them** from the guilt of their Sins by His atoning death, but from **the dominion of their sins**, by **placing in their hearts the Holy Spirit; not only to justify them, but also to sanctify them.**

Hear what the Bible says: Jesus said, "For their sakes **I sanctify myself,** that they also **might be sanctified." "Christ loved** the Church, and **gave Himself** for it; that He might **sanctify** and **cleanse it." "Christ gave** Himself for us, that He might redeem us from all iniquity **and purify unto Himself a peculiar people,** zealous of good works." "**Christ bore our sins** in His own, body on the tree, that we, being dead to sins, should **live unto righteousness.**" "**Christ has reconciled** (you) in the body of His flesh through death, to **present you holy** and **un-blame-able** and **un-reprove-able** in His sight." (John 19; Ephesians 5:25; Titus 2:14; I Peter 2:24; Colossians 1:22).

Let the meaning of these five scriptures be cautiously pondered. If words mean anything, **they teach that Christ undertakes** the **sanctification,** no less than the **justification,** of His believing people. **Both are** alike **provided for** in that "everlasting covenant ordered in all things and sure," of which **the Mediator is Christ.** In fact, **Christ in one place is called "He that sanctifies,"** and His people, "**they who are sanctified**" (Hebrews 2:11).

Sanctification, is the **outcome** and **inseparable consequence of regeneration.** He that is **born again** and made a **new creation,** receives a **new nature** and a **new principle,** and **always lives a new life.** Caution: **A regeneration** which a man can have, and **yet live purposely and carelessly** in **sin** and/or **worldliness,** is a regeneration **never mentioned in Scripture.**

Sanctification is the certain evidence of that **indwelling of the Holy Spirit** which is **essential to salvation.** "If any man have not the Spirit of Christ he is none of His." (Romans 8:9). The **Spirit never lies dormant and idle** within the soul: He always **makes His presence known** by the **fruit** He causes to be borne in heart, character, and life. "The fruit of the Spirit," **says Paul,** "is love, joy, peace, long-suffering, gentleness, goodness, faith, meekness, temperance," **and such like** (Galatians 5:22). **Where these things are to be found,** there is the Spirit: where these things are missing, **men are spiritually dead** before God.

Sanctification, again, **is a thing** that will always be seen. **Like the Great Head** of the Church, **from whom it springs, it "cannot be hidden."** "**Every tree is known** by his own fruit." (Luke 6:44.) **A truly sanctified person** may be so clothed with humility, that **he can see in himself nothing** but infirmity and defects.

Through Sanctifying Grace the **Holy Spirit empowers us to love as God loves. Another term for Sanctification is Perfect Love.** Our **Lord gives us the two greatest commandments** in Mark 12:29-31, "'**The most important one,**' answered Jesus, is this: '**Hear, O Israel, the Lord our God, the Lord is one. Love the Lord your God** with all your heart and with all your soul and with all your mind and with all your strength' (NIV). The **second is this:**

'Love your neighbor as yourself.' There is no commandment greater than these."

We possess sanctification by the Spirit. Jesus prayed, "Sanctify them in the truth: thy word is truth" (John 17:17). Jesus promised to send the Holy Spirit to guide the apostles into all truth. He said, "Howbeit when He, the Spirit of truth, is come, he shall guide you into all the truth" (John 16:13). If Jesus did what he promised, the inspired New Testament writers received, by the Holy Spirit, everything that pertains to life and godliness (II Peter 1:3). All was revealed, including all that pertains to our sanctification. He has given complete instructions and guidance in the inspired written revelation. The Holy Spirit is God's agent in the work of sanctification but the means used by the Spirit is the word of truth.

Holiness is not the way to Jesus ...
Jesus is the way to holiness.

The apostle Paul said, "And such were some of you: but ye were washed, but ye were sanctified, but ye were justified in the name of the Lord Jesus Christ, and in the Spirit of our God" (I Corinthians 6:11). In speaking of his work among the Gentiles, he said, "Ministering the gospel of God, that the offering up of the Gentiles might be made acceptable, being sanctified by the Holy Spirit" (Romans 15:16 ERV).

We are saved by faith, and sanctification by the Spirit; and living by law where it perpetrates falling from grace, (not our salvation). Being saved by faith and walking in the Spirit - produces fruit of the Spirit. The method of sanctification is by the Holy Spirit. We see the Spirit versus the flesh. Either it is a do-it-yourself Christian life OR somebody else will have to do it through you. His method is doing it through you. Christians have a responsibility in their own sanctification.

Peter wrote, "Be ye yourselves also holy in all
manner of living" (I Peter 1:15 ASV).

All Christians must realize holiness is not a part of their salvation but it comes as a result of their salvation, so even our trying to be obedient is birthed out of a desire to please God. At least it should.

Sanctification is not something imposed by the Holy Spirit apart from the obedient will and action of the Christian. The individual must act, as a new creation, in **separating himself from sin** and he must live in being holy. **The Holy Spirit in the written Word** has **told us how** it is to be done. **Our part is to give diligence** to **present ourselves approved** unto God (II Timothy 2:15), and to be **doers of the word,** and **not hearers only** (James 1:22).

Let me state again, justification is by faith; **sanctification** is by the Spirit of God. **Scripture tells us,** however, that **the Lord Jesus Christ** has been **made unto us sanctification** - that is, **God sees us complete in Him.** Regardless of **how good** you become, you will **never meet His standard.** You **will never be completely like Christ in this flesh – in this life.** Christ is the **only One** about whom **God said,** "…This is my beloved Son, in whom I am well pleased" (Matthew 3:17). **But the body** of believers, **the church,** has been **put "in Christ."** He is the **Head of the body;** those of us who are **believers are His body** in the world today - and **we should represent Him,** by the way.

The **idea of someone being** "sanctified," while **no holiness can be seen in his life, is flat rubbish and mis-application** of words. **Light may be very dim;** but, if there is only a **spark** in a dark room, it will be seen. **Life may be very feeble;** but, if the pulse only beats a little, it will be felt. It is just the **same with a sanctified man:** his **sanctification** will be something **felt and seen,** though **he himself may not understand it. A "saint"** in whom **nothing can be seen** but **worldliness or sin,** is a kind of **monster not recognized in the Bible.**

Sanctification is **a spiritual phenomenon** for which **every believer is responsible.** In saying this I would not be mistaken. **I hold as strongly** as any one that **every man on earth is accountable to God,** and that all **the lost** will be **speechless** and **without excuse** at the last day. **Whose fault is it if they are not holy,** but **their own?** On whom can they throw **the blame if they are not sanctified,** but themselves? **God,** who **has given them grace,** and a **new heart,** and a **new nature,** has **divested them** of **all excuse if** they **do not live for His praise.**

If the Savior of sinners gives us **renewing grace,** and **calls us by His Spirit, we** may be sure that **He expects us** to **use our grace,** and not to go to sleep. **It is forgetfulness of this** which **causes many believers to "grieve the Holy Spirit,"** and makes them **very useless** and **uncomfortable Christians.**

God chose you as the firstfruits to be saved, through sanctification by the Spirit (II Thessalonians 2:13 ESV).

Dozens of **passages in the Bible** speak of **our final salvation** as **conditional** upon a **changed heart and life.** The question arises then, **how can I have** the assurance I will **persevere in faith** and in the **holiness necessary** for **inheriting eternal life?**

Election secures that "those **whom (God) justified** He also **glorified**" (Romans 8:30), so that **all the conditions** laid down **for glorification** will be met **by the power of God's grace. Election is** the final **ground of assurance** because, since it is **God's commitment to save,** it is **also God's commitment** to **enable all** that is **necessary for salvation.**

> **"I will put my Spirit within** you, and cause you **to walk** in my statutes" (Ezekiel 36:27 ESV). **This is the meaning** of the **new covenant: God does not** merely **command obedience. He gives it!**

The answer is that assurance is **rooted in our election** (II Peter 1:10). **Divine election** is the **guarantee that God** will undertake to **complete by sanctifying grace** what His **electing grace has begun.**

Sanctification is a **progressive spiritual happening** that **does not prevent a man** from having a great deal of **inward spiritual conflict.** By conflict I **mean a struggle** within the heart between the **old nature and the new,** the flesh and the spirit, which are to be found together in every believer.

> **"Grace is love that cares and stoops and rescues."** - John Stott

The Apostle Paul said about "**walking in the Spirit,**" "**I say then:** Walk in the Spirit, and **you shall not fulfill the lust** of the flesh. For **the flesh lusts against the Spirit, and the Spirit against the flesh;** and these are contrary to one another, so that you do **not** do the things that you wish. But if you are led by the Spirit, you are **not** under the law" (Galatians 5:17 NIV).

A deep sense of that **struggle,** and a vast amount of **mental discomfort** from it, **are no proof** that a man is **not sanctified. A true Christian** is one who has not only **peace of conscience,** but war **within.** He may be **known by his warfare** as well as by **his peace.**

The heart of the **best Christian,** even at his best, is a field occupied by **two rival camps,** and the "**company of two armies.**" "**Although born-again** and baptized in Christ, **we offend** in many things; and **if we say** that we **have no sin, we deceive ourselves,** and the **truth is not** in us."

Sanctification is an **act of God** which **cannot justify a man,** and **yet it pleases God.** This may seem wonderful, and yet it is true. **The holiest actions of the holiest saint** who ever lived are, all more or less, **full of defects** and **imperfections.**

Paul writing to the church at Rome stated: "By **deeds** of the law shall **no** flesh **be justified."** - "We conclude that a man is **justified by faith** without the deeds of the law." (Romans 3:20-28.) **The only righteousness** in which we can appear before God is the **righteousness of another,** - even the **perfect righteousness** of **our Substitute** and Representative **Jesus Christ the Lord.** His work, and **not our work** is our **only title to heaven.**

Authentic Biblical sanctification will **show** itself **in habitual attention to** the **active graces** which **our Lord** so beautifully **exemplified,** and especially to the **grace of love. Jesus** said, "A **new commandment** I give unto you, that ye **love one another;** as I have loved you, that ye also **love one another.** By this shall all men know that ye are **my disciples,** if ye have love one to another" (John 13:34, 35 KJV).

A sanctified man will try to do 'good' in the world, and to **lessen the sorrow** and increase the happiness of all around him. **He will aim** to be **like his Master,** full of kindness and love to every one; and this not in word only, by calling people "dear," but **by deeds and actions** and **self-denying work,** according as he has opportunity.

The self-serving Christian professor, who wraps himself up in his **own conceit of superior knowledge,** and seems to **care nothing** whether others sink or swim, **go to heaven or hell,** so long as he **walks to church** in his **Sunday best,** and is called a "faithful member," - **such a man knows nothing of sanctification.** He may **think himself a Christian** on earth, but he will **not be a saint in heaven.** Christ will **never** be found the **savior of those who know nothing** of following His example. **Saving faith** and real **converting grace** will always produce some conformity to the image of Jesus (Colossians 2:10).

The Christian's spiritual progress in growth is **not** constant and undisturbed. **There are many hills and valleys** in the process of sanctification; and there are **many stumbling's,** falls and crooked steps in the **process of growth in grace. There are examples** in the Bible of **grievous falls** and **carnality** in the lives of true believers. Thus **we have the warnings and the promises of temporal judgment** and of **chastisement** by our heavenly Father.

Paul writes, "Of Him are ye in Christ Jesus, who of **God is made unto us - sanctification"** (1 Corinthians 1:30 KJV).

Or, my transliteration ...
"**Because of Him** you are united in Christ Jesus, **Who
has become** for us **wisdom** from God - that is, our
righteousness, holiness and redemption, freed from
sin - **sanctification.**"

The mystery of sanctification is that the **perfections of Jesus Christ**
are **imparted** to me, not gradually, **but instantly** when **by faith** I enter into
the **understanding** and **realization** that **Jesus Christ is made unto me
sanctification. Sanctification does not mean anything less** than the **holiness
of Jesus** being **made mine** manifestly.

The one marvelous secret of a **holy life** lies **not** in **imitating Jesus,** but
in **letting** the **perfections of Jesus** manifest themselves **in my mortal flesh.
Sanctification is "Christ in you, the hope of glory"** (Colossians 1:17). It is
His wonderful life that is **imparted to me in sanctification, and imparted
by faith** as a **sovereign gift** of **God's grace.** Am I willing for God to **make
sanctification as real in me** as **it is in His word?**

**Tell me not of your justification, unless you have also some
marks of sanctification. Boast not of Christ's work for you,
unless you can show us the Spirit's work in you.** (Anon)

**Christian, how much do you know about the difference between
justification and sanctification?** "**Justification is** being declared righteous.
Sanctification is being made righteous. **Justification is objective** and a
unilateral act of God; it relates to our position before God. **Sanctification is
subjective** and a process in which we are daily involved; it relates to our practice
before God. **Justification is complete,** total, and immediate at the moment
of conversion. **Sanctification is progressive,** beginning at the moment we are
converted and continuing until the moment we go to be with the Lord. **These
two doctrines are distinct,** yet inseparable, **for God never justifies without
also sanctifying.**" - C.J. Mahaney

Sanctification means the **impartation** of the **Holy qualities of Jesus
Christ.** It is **His patience,** His **love,** His **holiness,** His **faith,** His **purity,**
His **godliness,** that is manifested **in** and **through every sanctified soul.
Sanctification is an impartation, not an imitation. In Jesus Christ is the
perfection of everything,** and the **mystery of sanctification** is that all the
perfections of Jesus are at my disposal, and slowly and surely **I begin to live**

a life of **inexpressible order** and **sanity** and **holiness**. We are "**kept by the power of God.**"

Likewise grace is not a substitute for a changed life, but is the **agent of** such change. **For example,** consider **Paul's description of the activity of God's grace:** Paul stated, "For the **grace of God has** appeared, bringing salvation to all men, instructing us to deny ungodliness and worldly desires and to live sensibly, righteously and godly in the present age, looking for the blessed hope and the appearing of the glory of our great God and Savior, Christ Jesus" (Titus 2:11-13 NASB).

Like the passage considered earlier in I John 3, this passage shows that the hope that **we have of eternal life with Christ** is a hope that motivates present change. **Grace "teaches" something practical** about what kind of people we should be. **Those who truly** have **faith in God** and are **empowered by the Holy Spirit** must and will respond to this teaching and **God will change** their lives.

**Paul again writes ... "This is the will of God,
your sanctification"** (1 Thessalonians 4:3)

Sanctification is not a question of whether God is willing to sanctify me - is it my will? **Am I willing to let God do in me** everything that **has been made possible through** the **atonement** of the Cross of Christ? **Am I willing to let Jesus become sanctification to me,** and to **let His life** be exhibited **in my** human flesh? (1 Corinthians 1:30). **Beware of saying, "Oh, I am longing to be sanctified." No, you are not.** Recognize your need, but **stop longing** and make it a matter of action. **Receive Jesus Christ to become sanctification for you by absolute, unquestioning faith,** and the **great miracle** of the **atonement** of Jesus **will become real** in you.

Realize that all Jesus made possible becomes yours **through the free and loving gift of God** on the basis of what Christ accomplished on the cross. **And my attitude as a saved and sanctified soul** is that of profound, **humble holiness** (there is no such thing as proud holiness). **It is a holiness based on agonizing repentance,** a sense of inexpressible shame and degradation, and also on the **amazing realization** that the love of God demonstrated itself to me **while I cared nothing about Him** (Romans 5:8). **He completed everything for my salvation** and **sanctification.** No wonder **Paul said** that **nothing "shall be able to separate us** from the love of God which is in Christ Jesus our Lord" (Romans 8:39).

Realize also that **sanctification makes you one** with **Jesus Christ,** and **in Him one with God,** and it is accomplished only through the **magnificent atonement** of Christ. **Never confuse the effect with the cause.** The **effect in you** is obedience, service, and prayer, and is **the outcome** of inexpressible thanks and adoration for the **miraculous sanctification** that has been **brought about in you** because of **the atonement through** the **Cross of Christ.**

Sanctification requires our coming to the **place of death. There is always a tremendous battle before sanctification is fully realized** - something **within us pushing** with resentment **against the demands** of Christ. **When the Holy Spirit begins** to show us **what sanctification means,** the struggle starts immediately. **Jesus said,** "If anyone comes to Me and does not hate ... his own life ... he cannot be My disciple" (Luke 14:26 NASB). It becomes matter of **putting Jesus first!**

In the process of sanctification, the Spirit of God will strip you down until there is nothing left but yourself. **Am I willing to be myself** and nothing more? **Am I willing** to have no friends, no father, no brother, and no self-interest - simply to be ready for death? That is the **condition required** for sanctification. **No wonder Jesus said,** "I did not come to bring peace but a sword" (Matthew 10:34 NASB). **This is where the battle comes,** and where so many of us falter. **We refuse to be identified** with the **death of Jesus Christ** on this point. **We say,** "But this is so strict. Surely He does not require that of me." **Our Lord is strict,** and **He does require** that of us.

Am I willing to **reduce myself down to simply "me"? Am I determined enough** to strip myself of all that my friends think of me, and all that I think of myself? **Am I willing and determined** to hand over my simple naked self to God? **Once I am, He will** immediately **sanctify me** completely, and **my life** will **be free** from being determined and persistent toward anything except God (I Thessalonians 5:23-24).

When you pray, "Lord, show me what sanctification means for me," He **will show** you. It means being made one with Jesus. **Sanctification is not something Jesus puts in you** - it is **Himself in you** (I Corinthians 1:30). **We cannot do anything pleasing to God** unless we deliberately **build on the foundation of the atonement by** the Cross of Christ.

> **"...present - your members** (your body) **as instruments (weapons) of righteousness to God"** (Romans 6:13 NASB).

I cannot save or sanctify myself; I cannot make atonement for sin**; I cannot redeem** the world; **I cannot right what** is wrong, **purify** what is impure, **or make holy** what is unholy. **That is all the sovereign work of God.** Do I have faith in what Jesus Christ has done? **He has made the perfect atonement** for sin. **Am I in the habit** of constantly realizing it? **The greatest need** we have is **not to do** things, but to **believe** things.

> **"And whosoever doth not bear his cross, and come after Me, cannot be My disciple"** (Luke 14:27).

The cross not only saves us, but it continues **to sanctify us.** Have you read where **Jesus said,** "Whosoever will come after Me, let him **deny himself,** and **take up his cross,** and **follow Me"** (Mark 8:34b).

Many people think that this means that **our "cross" is a sickness,** an **unsaved spouse,** or a **cruel boss,** or some other incident that has attacked us. However, a cross **is not something** that is **forced upon you,** over which you have **no choice.** A cross **is something you willingly take up. Jesus willingly** laid down His life. **He calls us** to do the same. **Your cross** is when **you willingly die to yourself.** You do this by **saying no to sin** and **self,** and **yes to Christ.**

> **The last time you heard a challenging sermon on your personal holiness was when?**

The of Christ is **not an experience, it is the great act of God which He has performed through Christ,** and I have to build my faith on it. **If I construct my faith on my own experience,** I produce the most **unscriptural** kind of life— an isolated life, with my eyes focused solely **on my own holiness. Beware of that human holiness** that is not based on the atonement of the Lord. It has no value for anything except a life of isolation— **it is useless to God** and a nuisance to man. **Measure every kind of experience** you have by **our Lord Himself.** We cannot do anything pleasing to God unless we deliberately **build on the foundation of the atonement by the Cross of Christ.**

Let me repeat, you may be asking, "how do we become holy?" By the **sanctification of the Spirit. The Spirit of God** is named the **Holy Spirit** because **He makes us holy.** He **reveals** and **glorifies Christ in us. Through Him, Christ dwells** in us, and **His holy power works** in us. **Through this Holy Spirit, the workings of the flesh are mortified,** and God works in us both the will and the accomplishment. Here are **two scriptures** to study and meditate upon …

> "But as **He which has called you is holy, so be you holy** in all manner of conversation: because it is written, **Be holy; for I am holy**" (I Peter 1:15, 16).

> "**God has** from the beginning **chosen you** unto **salvation** through **sanctification of the Spirit** and **belief of the truth**" (II Thessalonians 2:13b).

Not only has God chosen and called us for salvation, but **also for holiness** - salvation in holiness. **The goal of the young Christian must not only be safety in Christ,** but **also holiness** in Christ. **Safety and salvation are,** in the long run, found **only in holiness.** The **Christian who thinks** that his **salvation consists merely** in **safety** and **not** Christian, listen to the Word of God - Be ye holy.

And why must I be holy? Because **He who called you is holy** and **summons you to holiness.** How **can anyone be saved in God** when he **does not have** the same **disposition** as God?

> "But of Him **are ye in Christ Jesus,** who of God is **made unto us - sanctification**" (1 Corinthians 1:30).

Grace, which is of more worth than we can imagine (II Corinthians 9:15), **is the reason** for our **salvation** and **new life** in Christ. **Without grace we can do nothing** (John 15:5), and it is **a continual reminder** of God's love and work in our lives. **Followers of Christ** should **be gracious** with others because of **their own inherited** grace (I Peter 4:10).

God's holiness is His highest glory. In His holiness, **His righteousness and His love are united. This is how He keeps Himself free from sin,** and in love makes others also free from it. **It is as the Holy One of Israel** that He is the **Redeemer,** and that **He lives** in the midst of His people. **Redemption is given to bring us to Himself** and to the **fellowship of His holiness.** We cannot possibly take part in the love and salvation of God if we are not holy as He is holy. **Young Christians, make up your mind, be holy!**

And what is this holiness that I must have? **Christ is your sanctification.** The life of Christ in you is your holiness. In Christ you are sanctified--**you are holy.** In Christ you **must continually be sanctified.** The glory of Christ must penetrate **your whole life.**

Holiness is more than purity. In Scripture we see that **cleansing precedes holiness. Cleansing** is the **taking away** of that **which is wrong** - liberation from sin. **Holiness is the filling** with that which is good and divine - the disposition of Jesus. Holiness is conformity to Him. **Holiness is separation** from the **spirit of the world and being filled with the presence of the Holy God.**

Paul wrote: "Flee from sexual immorality. Every other sin a man can commit is outside his body, but he who sins sexually sins against his own body. **Do you not know that your body is a temple of the Holy Spirit who is in you,** Whom you have **received** from God? You are not your own; you were **bought with a price.** Therefore glorify God with your body. ..." (I Corinthians 6:18-20 BSB).

The Scripture teaches that an **individual IS** as his **thoughts ARE.** Each person **has control** over his thoughts. **You cannot know** a person merely by **listening** to his **words** or watching his **actions.** There is always more, and often better, in men than comes into expression. **The claims of God reach** beyond right **action, and demand right thought.** The **Omniscience of God** searches the **secret intents** of the heart, **and sees** our sin.

God's redemption that is **provided includes** in its **doctrine:** the **sanctification** of our **very thoughts.** All **sin is** represented as **springing up out of,** and finding **expression for,** lust in the subject **of our thoughts.** Show, by appeal to Christian experience, the **difficulty found** in the **restraining of thought.** In the **un-restrained-ness of thought** often **comes to us** the feeling and the **mastery of sin.**

A teacher asked a **little boy** to **finish this proverb:** "Cleanliness is next to...." And **he said,** "Cleanliness is next to ... **impossible.**" Well, **friend** that **little boy wasn't that far wrong,** was he?

It's amazing what people do to **try** and **purify themselves** - fast, pray, kneel, walk, self-flagellate, hibernate, isolate. **Sadly, they discover** that **human efforts are NOT** the **pathway** to **purity** because they **keep doing** what the late **Zig Ziglar** called "**stinkin-thinkin.**" **Before we can hope** to have a **life of purity, we must have** a **clean thought life,** as the **Word of God teaches.**

God works from the inside out. He knows that **you cannot purify the water** by **painting the pump! Remember** the words of Jesus as he **warned the Pharisees,** that **they** were **merely cleaning the outside** of the **dishes,** while leaving the **inside** with all the **repugnant leftovers.**

Question: When was the last time you **memorized** a **verse** of **Scripture?** It's **easier to stay away** from 'stinkin-thinkin' when **your mind** is focused on the **written Word of God** that tells us of **Jesus** the **living Word of God.** Here's one you can **start with …** if you have an **unclean mind. Start working** on **memorizing** this passage **today.**

> "**Restore** unto me **the joy** of **Thy salvation** and
> **uphold me** with Thy free Spirit. Then **will I**
> **teach** transgressors Thy ways, and **sinners shall**
> **be converted** unto Thee" - **Psalm 51:13**

Remember, the **tabernacle was holy** because God lived there. **We** are **holy,** as **God's temple,** after we have **God living** and **working** within us. **Christ's life** in us is our **holiness, our purity.**

Christians: "Wherefore Jesus also, **that he might sanctify** the **people** through **his** own **blood,** suffered without the gate" (Hebrews 13:12 ASV). **Yes; it is He who sanctifies His people.** "Let us go forth unto him." **Let us trust** Him to make known to us the power of the blood. **Let us yield ourselves** wholly to its blessed efficacy. **That blood, through which He sanctified Himself,** has entered heaven to open it **for us.** It can make our **hearts also a throne of God** that the grace and glory of God may dwell in us.

Our Christian life can be **described** in its **multi-faceted treasure.** We must remember that **as Christians, we are Christ's** servants, believers, ambassadors, soldiers, members of His kingdom, priests, disciples, saints, and called out ones. More can be said, **the New Testament is rich** with **various analogies** and **descriptions of the Christian life.** We must know **that nothing** about this Christian life **is optional,** but **every aspect of it is a gift of God's grace.**

Let us Pray! … We implore you **Father, the God** of our Lord Jesus Christ, **the Father** of **glory,** that you **impute** to us the **spirit of wisdom** and **revelation** in the **knowledge of Him. May the eyes of our understanding** be enlightened; that **we may know** what "**is the hope of our calling?" Help us** to **understand** what is the "**riches** of the **glory of His inheritance"** in the saints, His people? And **what is the** "**exceeding** greatness of **His power** to toward us who believe, **according to the working** of His mighty power?" **In Jesus name, I pray. Amen!**

> "**My love be with you all in Christ Jesus.**
> **Amen."** – I Corinthians 16:24

hapter 13

God's Grace Is "<u>SOVEREIGN</u>" Over All

"(GOD) WHO HAS **saved us,** and **called us** with a holy calling, not according to our works, but **according to His own purpose and grace**, which was **given us in Christ Jesus before the world began**" (II Timothy 1:9).

> "**Before I formed you** in your mother's womb **I chose you; Before you were born,** I set you apart (sanctified); **I appointed** (consecrated) **you** to be a **prophet** to the nations" (Jeremiah 1:5 NET).

I DID NOT CHOOSE GOD.
HALLELUJAH! GOD CHOSE ME!

Out of the millions in this world, **God chose me to be His child.** God chose **to dwell in me** through His **Holy Spirit.** The Apostle **Paul asked,** "Do you not know that **your body** is a temple of **the Holy Spirit** who is in you, **whom you have received from God?** You are **not your own;** you were **bought** at a price. Therefore glorify God with your body" (I Corinthians 6:19 NASB).

Yes, God chose me - a weak, foolish, despised and depraved sinner that I am! **I say these words** - 'despised', 'depraved' - but **I learned that truth only** in my long and continued walk with Jesus. **He has shown me** the **depravity** (decadence) of my own heart (**Jeremiah 17:9**). **Yet in His infinite mercy, He chose me.** And **His choosing me means** that He has a great purpose for me. For **He has chosen me** to be the **recipient of His grace** and the **inheritor of His glory.** That means there is a **great responsibility thrust on me. How** or why does **He do all that?**

Jesus said to his disciples, "**Ye** have **not chosen** Me, but **I have chosen you,** and ordained you, that ye should go and bring forth fruit, and that your fruit should remain: that whatsoever ye shall ask of the Father in My Name, He may give it you" (John 15:16).

Every true Christian desires to be a **fruit-bearing Christian, not** one who is "**barren**" and "**unfruitful**" (II Peter 1:8). He or she also **earnestly desires** that the fruit—whether that of a godly character (Galatians 5:22-23) or that of **others won to Christ** (Romans 1:13) - **will not wither** but **remain strong and healthy** before the Lord.

The promise of Christ in our text is that **our fruit will remain, if He has chosen us** and we **go** forth **praying** in His name and seeking sincerely to **bear fruit** for His name's sake. It is significant that the **Greek** word translated "**remain**" (that is, **meno**) is also commonly translated "**abide,**" as well as "**continue.**" In fact, it **occurs no less than 12 times** in John 15:4-16, the last being in our text verse above.

Jesus also has said, "If ye continue in my word, then are ye **abide** in you, **ye shall ask** what ye will, and it shall **be done unto you**" (John 15:7). **See the progression.** He says, "**Abide** in me, and I in you" (v. 4). This **means** He says that "**my words abide** in you," and also we are to "**continue in my love,**" which **implies** that "**ye keep my commandments**" (v. 9). It follows, then, that **as we** "**continue**" in His Word, we shall "**bring forth fruit**" that **will "remain"**!

It's Time We Plunge Your Mind into the Depths of the Ocean of God's Grace and Sovereignty!

Sovereign grace is the 'preeminence' of the '**divine- personality**' of our **Triune God** which is **exercised only toward the elect.** In the **Old Covenant** and the **New,** the **grace of God** is **never mentioned** in association with **mankind generally,** and **never** with lower orders of **His creatures. We must also remember that** "**grace**" **is distinguished** from "**mercy,**" for the **mercy of God** is over all His works (Psalm 145:9).

What God's Sovereignty Truly Means....

Sovereignty means that **God, as the Ruler of the Universe,** is free and **has the right to do whatever He wants.** He is **not bound** or limited by the **dictates** of his **created beings.** Further, **He is in complete control** over **everything** that happens here on Earth. **God's will is the final cause** of all things.

Have you ever heard someone say, "God is in control." How do they know that? Some cannot tell you why. Let me share! It is because God is Sovereign! What does that mean? ... Keep reading. God is sovereign in creation, providence, redemption, life, the afterlife, and judgment.

The Sovereignty of God is a dominant essential declaration of Christian belief in Biblical Theology. God is King and Lord of all! To put this another way: categorically nothing happens without God's willing it to happen, willing it to happen before it happens, and willing it to happen in the way that it happens. Put this way, it seems to say something that is expressly in doctrine. But at its heart, it is saying nothing different from the assertion of the Nicene Creed: "I believe in God, the Father Almighty." Now, to be honest, I am not a big follower of creeds. To say that God is sovereign is to express His Infinite Almightiness in every area.

A basic Biblical description of God's sovereignty is His Kingship, His Rule, and the fact that He has the Final Authority in everything. Sovereignty means that from the highest king to the smallest atom, everything bows, ultimately, to His power (Romans 14:11, 11:36). The proof, as they say, is in the pudding! A life that is touched and changed by Jesus will be a life that lives a new kind of life. If there is no change, there has been no conversion! When Jesus moves into a life, everything changes!

> "When I am full of myself, have my own fleshly desires,
> demands, and personal ambitions; then when I come to
> the end of myself, I immediately find the beginning of
> God, His will in my life and then... I can have the mind
> of Christ leading me." (Philippians 2:5) - Glenn Clifton

Historical theism insists that God is omnipotent (all powerful), omniscient (all knowing), and omnipresent (present everywhere) - all at the same time! Each declaration is a deviation of God's holy sovereignty. His power, knowledge, and presence ensure that His goals are met, that His designs are fulfilled, and that His superintendence of all events is in His hands. God's power ensures that He can do all that is logically possible for Him to will to do. "He cannot deny himself" for example (II Timothy 2:13).

> I John 4:8 states, "The one who does not love does
> not know God, for God is love" (NASB).

Every thought, every **word,** every **act of God** is **expressive** of **love. God is sovereign,** and He has **the right to do** whatever He wants. **This would be tyranny except** for **one** simple **fact: Everything God does,** whether seemingly arbitrary or not, **is motivated by love.** Even **our trials** are **supreme acts** of love as **Hebrews 12:5-11** and **Job's experience** show. The **natural man** will **never comprehend** or accept this. **As the scripture states,** "**I Corinthians 2:14,** The person without **the** Spirit does **not** accept the things that come from the Spirit of God but **considers them foolishness,** and **cannot understand** them because they are **discerned** only through the Spirit."

Stranger than we can think, if this is **true of the universe,** how **much more** should we expect it **to be true of God Himself?** The **extraordinary preeminence of God** is **hard to understand. Our finite thinking never** comprehends the **infinite Creator** and **Lord! Our brains struggle** trying to **reconcile** how **a particle** can pass **through two separate openings** at the same time **without dividing.** How can it be that **we are surprised** that we **struggle to reconcile** the **co-existence** of **God's sovereignty** and **human accountability?**

> **Oh, the depth of the riches and wisdom and knowledge**
> **of God! How unsearchable are His judgments and**
> **how inscrutable His ways! "For who has known the**
> **mind of the Lord"** (Romans 11:33–34 ASV)?

The Word of God discloses and **exposes** some things **we find** extraordinarily **hard to understand** - **unfathomable things** that **perplex, confound,** and **even disturb us. As nature reveals traces** of the **Master Designer.** When we run up against **enigmas that show us** the **limits** of our academic capacities, **we don't need** to follow **cynical doubts.** But **like Paul, our limits can lead us to awe-filled worship.**

It's surprising how easily **we forget** that with God, we're **dealing with an Omniscient Entity** Whose **intelligence, power,** and **complexity** so far **exceed all our understanding** that we have **no comparison** or **superlative** that can even remotely do him justice. **With patience** we should **expect perplexing mysteries.** And if we're **paying attention, we can see** in these **dramatic mysteries** the **same marks of genius** that are present in our Christian puzzles and perplexities. **They are revealing God's** eternal power and divine nature (Romans 1:20).

> "I rejoice in the sovereignty of God because
> He wields it in all things to preserve Himself
> as my greatest treasure." - John Piper

Sovereignty is often expressed in the language and actions of kingship: God rules and reigns over the entire Universe. He cannot be opposed. He is Lord of heaven and earth. He is enthroned, and His throne is a symbol of His sovereignty. God's will is supreme.

The sovereignty of God is supported by countless verses in the Bible, among them: Isaiah 46:9–11 states, "I am God, and there is no other; I am God, and there is none like me. I make known the end from the beginning, from ancient times, what is still to come. I say, 'My purpose will stand, and I will do all that I please.' What I have said, that I will bring about; what I have planned, that I will do" (NIV).

> Psalm 115:3 states, "Our God is in heaven;
> He does whatever pleases Him" (NIV).

> Daniel 4:35 states, "All the peoples of the earth are
> regarded as nothing. He does as he pleases with the
> powers of heaven and the peoples of the earth. No one can
> hold back his hand or say to him: What have you done?"
> (NIV).

Grace is the sole source from which flows the kindness, generosity, love, and salvation of God unto His chosen people. Grace is the unending, supreme, and perfect free favor of God, demonstrated in the imparting of spiritual and perpetual blessings to the guilty and the unworthy."

I have learned that I cannot take the sovereign grace of God lightly or for granted. I cannot be casual about the salvation and redemption that He bought with His own blood and gave me. There is an 'eternal purpose' behind the sovereign grace of God. Oh, how great is this grace of God! God doesn't choose in a whimsical fashion and for trivial reasons. Behind His sovereign grace is His eternal salvation, eternal redemption, eternal kingdom, eternal glory, and, above all, His eternal presence (I will see Him face to face!) throughout eternity.

"**Patience** is a vibrant and virile **Christian virtue,** which
is **deeply rooted** in the Christian's absolute confidence
in the sovereignty of God and in **God's promise** to
bring all things **to completion** in a way that most
fully **demonstrates His glory**" - Albert Mohler

I'd like to begin by **writing** about the **problem of "spiritual indigestion."** That's a **brand-new term** (for me), that I **recently learned.** This **phrase came from** a **preacher friend** of mine … who **quoted Dr. J. Grant Howard.** I would like to **give you some highlights** from his teaching. **Dr. Howard says,** "**Spiritual Indigestion**" happens **when we take in more** than **we understand.** It's a **common problem** in many **churches** where we often measure **growth by knowledge.** We **read books,** we listen to **tapes** and to Christian **radio** and **TV,** go to **Bible studies,** Bible **Conferences,** and we **love** to listen to **good** preaching. We are **overfed** and **undernourished** at the **same time.**

What happens when we get a case of **spiritual indigestion?** The **pressure builds** up and we **sound forth** with a **doctrinal burp!** That's the **sudden release** of a lot of **hot air surrounded** by **noxious fumes.** It **happens when we take** in but **don't digest** the **truth,** when **we listen** but **never let the truth change** our lives.

"**Our God is in the heavens: He has done whatever
He has pleased**" (Psalm 115:3 AKJV).

Being God, He discusses and **consults with no one;** yet being **omniscient** and **infinitely holy,** He **does only** that which **is good** and **right.** We are **finite creatures;** yes, **fallen creatures,** and **sin** has **darkened our understanding.** Therefore **we** are quite **incompetent** to gauge or **grasp God's ways;** and to **criticize** or **murmur** against them is the height of **ungodliness** and **wickedness:** "No but, O **man, who are you** that reply against God? **Shall the thing formed** say to **Him that formed it, Why** have **You made me thus** (this way)" (Romans 9:20 AKJV)?

God's Sovereignty is a truth that **touches all of life.** It is a **truth meant** to be **digested** so it becomes **a part of our very being.** We begin with **the word itself.** The word "sovereign" is **both a noun and verb.** As a **verb it means "to rule,"** and as a **noun it means "king"** or "**master**" or "**absolute ruler.**" To say that God is sovereign means **God is in Charge** of the "**Entire Universe All**

the Time." In the words of the Westminster Confession of Faith, **"He ordains whatsoever comes to pass."**

> **"For I am confident of this very thing, that He (Jesus),**
> **Who began a good work in you will perfect it until**
> **the day of Christ Jesus"** (Philippians 1:6 NASB).

There are many churches these days **that avoid** talking about repentance, sin, salvation, sanctification under God's sovereignty. **Sound doctrine** is **not** a **"feel good" topic.** But **sin is a critical topic** if we want to be **effective servants** of Christ and to **grow spiritually.**

One of the **big questions** the **church** has **before them today** is this: **People often ask me,** "Can some **sin cause me** to **lose my salvation?"** And I'll tell you what I've said, **"Absolutely not!" You cannot sin your salvation away. (Remember: It is not your salvation anyway. It is God's salvation in you!)** Remember, **when you asked Jesus** to **forgive** your sin and **made Him Lord** of your life, **He began a "good work"** in you. **He promised** to **complete** that work **within you!**

> **"Whatever the Lord pleases, He does, in heaven and on**
> **earth, in the seas and all deeps"** (Psalm 135:6 NASB).

Beyond salvation, God is **also at work to help you deal** with the **issue of sin** in your life on a **daily basis.** You and I desperately **need** this **because sin** will **remain** a **reality** in our **lives this side of heaven.** But **we can overcome.**

We see this clearly in some of **God's choicest saints.** Men like **Simon Peter** and **Paul admitted** to the **sin in** their lives. But **listen, sin was not a pattern** in their lives! And **that's the difference** that **Christ made in their lives! Will you let Jesus** do the **same for you?** He wants to! **Let Jesus break the sinful patterns** and **habits** in your life!

Sovereignty: Let's **begin** by **acknowledging** that this is **not a popular doctrine.** You **don't hear many sermons** on this subject in most churches. And **most of us** would **rather hear about love, happiness and grace.**

Some people object to the **idea** that **God knows all events in advance** of their **happening.** Such a **view, some insist,** deprives mankind of its **essential freedom.** Open **theists** or **free-will theists,** for example, insist that **the future** (at least in its specific details) is in some **fashion "open."** They say that **even God does not know all** that is to come. **He may make predictions** like some cosmic poker player, but He cannot know absolutely. This explains, open theists suggest, why God appears to change His mind: God is adjusting His plan based on the new information of unforeseeable events (see Genesis 6:6–7; I Samuel 15:11). No event happens that is a surprise to God. To us it is luck or chance, but to God it is part of His decree. "The lot is cast into the lap, but its every decision is from the Lord" (Proverbs 16:33 NIV). Language of God changing His mind in Scripture is an accommodation to us and our way of speaking, not a description of a true change in God's mind.

God is the "first cause" of all things, but evil is a product of "second causes." In the words of John Calvin, "First, it must be observed that the will of God is the cause of all things that happen in the world: and yet God is not the author of evil," adding, "for the proximate cause is one thing, and the remote cause another." In other words, God Himself cannot do evil and cannot be blamed for evil even though it is part of His sovereign decree.

Sovereignty also a very "Humbling Doctrine." Sovereignty reminds us that God is God and we are not. When we think we're ready to advise God on how to run the universe, He just looks at us and says, "How many stripes do you have on your sleeve?" God's Eternal Sovereignty puts us in the place where we feel free to say nothing about the way God runs the universe.

> "The Most High is sovereign over the kingdoms of men,
> and gives them to whomever he will" (Daniel 4:25 AKJV).

What does the sovereignty of God mean to you? God is sovereign over all events, and tragedy should not surprise us, but it does! Why can't we take Psalm 46 to heart, "Therefore we will not fear, though the earth give way and though the mountains fall into the heart of the sea. The Lord Almighty is with us." God is 'our refuge and strength, a very present help in trouble" (Psalm 46:1-7 various verses NASB)."

And, there's more we must consider. Paul wanted to visit the church in Thessalonica and encourage them in the joy of the gospel. He said we tried again and again to come to you, but Satan prevented us (1 Thessalonians 2:18). Paul believed in the sovereignty of God, but he also knew we're in a spiritual war. He wrote, "For we wrestle not against flesh and blood, but against principalities, against powers, against the rulers of the darkness of this world, against spiritual wickedness in high places" (Ephesians 6:12. He took comfort in always relying upon total commitment to the God of his Authority.

Sovereignty is an 'Exalting Doctrine" because it shows us and gives us a very big God. It reminds me of a book J. B. Phillips wrote years ago, "Your God Is Too Small." That's where the title told the whole story. Many have a problem because our God is too small. But when you ever understand that God is sovereign over the entire universe, even us, you'll never have a small God again.

It is not possible for a finite creature (man) to fully grasp the inspired complexities of God's infinite will (Romans 11:33-36). Bible students have been discussing free will and sovereignty for ages and will continue to do so. It's good to think about it, to study the Bible, and to ask for wisdom to understand it. Yet, in the meantime, we must not forget that He has given us commands to follow. We are to take the gospel to the whole world (Matthew 28:18-20; Acts 1:8). We are to turn away from sin and follow Him, forsaking this world. We are to love Him and love our neighbors, our brothers, and our enemies in emulation of Christ.

"Grace calls us (Galatians 1:15), regenerates us (Titus 3:5), justifies us (Romans 3:24), sanctifies us (Hebrews 13:20-21), and preserves us (I Peter 1:3-5). We need grace to forgive us, to return us to God, to heal our broken hearts, and to strengthen us in times of trouble and spiritual warfare. Only by God's free, sovereign grace can we have a saving relationship with Him. Only through grace can we be called to conversion (Ephesians 2:8-10), holiness (II Peter 3:18), service (Philippians 2:12-13), or suffering (II Corinthians 1:12)" - Joel Beeke

This world owes its existence to the creating power of God, and that He established its laws, and put it's every wheel in motion - is a truth so evident, that it has wrested the consent of all mankind. We were at first the creatures of his power - we are still the subjects of his government - He still supports and rules the world which he made.

> Someone once said, "In every undertaking it is expedient and necessary to implore the blessing and protection of Almighty God."

Question: If Almighty God does not govern the universe and this world, and order all the affairs of men according to His sovereign pleasure, then where is the expediency or necessity of imploring his blessing and protection?

As you read and study this doctrine, there is a powerful and treacherous enemy is making inroads upon our territories, our Bibles, churches and belief systems, and our liberty, our property, our lives; and everything sacred or dear to us is in danger! We must be ready to make a defense; and our most gracious King has been pleased to send the Holy Spirit to assure us that all is well with our souls," and that we can have confidence that He will oppose the unjustifiable attempts of our enemies.

This is also a marvelous, yet mysterious doctrine because it brings us face to face with the problem of evil and free will. If God is sovereign, why is there evil in the universe? If man has free will, how can God be sovereign? Christians have debated these questions for centuries. Is it sufficient to say that God is sovereign, and you and I are truly responsible for all the choices we make? Often we can't understand how they work together, but they do.

Sovereignty is a "Clarifying Doctrine." It teaches us that there is no such thing as luck, chance, fate or coincidence. You can have God or chance, but you can't have both.

I suppose you've heard about the cowboy applied for health insurance, the agent routinely asked if he had had any accidents during the previous year. The cowboy replied, "No. But I was bitten by a rattlesnake, and a horse kicked me in the ribs. That laid me up for a while." The agent said, "Weren't those accidents?" "No," replied the cowboy, "They did it on purpose." The cowboy realized that there are no such things as 'accidents.'

How about you, Christian? Do you believe that some things catch God by surprise? In the words of a good friend, "God is too sovereign to be lucky." Sovereignty is an "Empowering doctrine." If you believe God is sovereign, no mere human can intimidate you. You'll respect authority but you won't cringe before it.

What gave David the courage to go down into the Elah Valley and face that giant Goliath? He said, "I come to you in the name of the God of Israel, the Lord of hosts?" David had a God so big that Goliath was like a midget to him.

> "Grace is love that cares and stoops
> and rescues." - John Stott

Sovereign divine love and grace is the saving favor of God exercised in the giving of blessings upon those who have no merit or value in them and for which no reward is demanded from them. The sovereign grace of God can **neither be bought, earned,** nor **won** by **any person.** If it could be, it **would cease to be grace.** When a thing is **said to be of "grace,"** we mean that **the recipient has no claim upon it,** that it was in **nowise due him.** It comes to him **as pure charity.**

> **"According as He hath chosen us in Him before the foundation of the world, that we should be holy and without blame before Him in love"** (Ephesians 1:4 KJV).

The **inspired, authoritative Word of God teaches us that we have been chosen** in Christ **before the foundation** of the world. God **knew me** even **before I was born.** Why are **some Christians bothered** and **upset** with this teaching? Listen: **If we believe** that God is **Omnipotent** (Almighty/ all-powerful), and **Omniscient** (all-knowing/wise), and that **"all things** are **possible with Him,"** why **do we hesitate** to give Him **acknowledgement** for **Who He is - an Almighty, all-wise God?**

Sovereign grace crushes our **pride.** It **shames** us and **humbles** us. **We want** to be the **subjects,** not the objects, **of salvation.** We **want to be active,** not passive, in the process. **We resist the truth** that **God alone is** the **author** and **finisher** of our faith. **By our fleshly nature,** we **rebel against sovereign grace,** but **God knows** how to **break our rebellion** and **make us friends** of this **grand doctrine.** When **God teaches sinners** that their **very core is depraved,** sovereign **grace becomes** the most **encouraging doctrine possible.**

> **"If you believe in a God who controls the big things, you have to believe in a God who controls the little things. It is we, of course, to whom things look 'little' or 'big'."** - Elisabeth Elliot

Did you realize, before you read that verse, God chose you before He laid the foundations of the earth? You **talk about "old time religion"!** Well, friend, **you can't get much older** than that! **Before there were any** trees, mountains, birds, and bees, **God chose you** to be **one of His children.**

Charles Haddon Spurgeon said, "God certainly must have chosen me before I came into this world because He never would never have chosen me afterward." **That means you and I cannot take credit** for God's salvation. **First John 4:19 says,** "We love Him, because He first loved us" (AKJV).

One day, somebody asked a little boy, "Have you found the Lord?" **And the little boy said,** "I didn't know He was lost." **How miraculous that God has chosen us.** When **left alone** to ourselves, **we would never have chosen Him.**

Though His love for us is a **divine mystery,** it **can bring great assurance to a believer's heart** to know "He first loved us." **Allow God's Word to teach you** further **what it means to be chosen.** (Matthew 20:16, 24:22; Luke 10:20; John 6:37-39; Romans 8:28-39; I Corinthians 1:26-31; Ephesians 1:9-11; II Timothy 1:9).

Although there are a **multitude of scriptures** about the **Sovereignty** of our **LORD GOD,** I would **like to, again, give you** just **one paragraph from God's Word** here about some of the **characteristics** of **our Sovereign God.**

Psalm 139 contains **insight** into **the nature** and **character of God. In verses 1-6** we see that **God is 'omniscient,'** which means **He is "all knowing."** This knowledge is "wonderful" and too high to attain to. **In verses 7-12** we are challenged to consider the **'omnipresence' of God** - that **He is always everywhere.** This God deserves the worship of a creation bound by the limitations of time and space. **In verses 13-18** the song teaches of God's **'omnipotence'** - that He is **all-powerful.** His power is seen in His ability to create us (v. 13), **His 'sovereign rule'** over creation (v. 16), and **His 'constant care'** (vv. 17-18). Since God is fully **aware of everything** in your life, what about that **makes you thankful?** What causes **concern?** Do you feel **comforted** or **threatened** by God's **never-leaving presence?** What impact does **God's all-powerful character** have on **how you view life's challenges?**

The **mystery of God's ways,** the mystery of **God's sovereign grace** is beyond our **wildest imaginations. Paul says,** He **called me by His grace.** (Galatians 1.6). **He chooses,** He **calls,** He **saves,** He **satisfies,** He **secures,** He **sanctifies ...** because **He is sovereign!** Sometimes **we think and believe** that when we have **made a 'decision'** for Christ, **or that 'we have chosen Him.'** But, **actually it is His Spirit** working in us to **bring us** to the Savior. Otherwise, **we would never** have come to God or Christ. **We were 'lost' in sin** - utterly **cut off from God. God sent Christ** into this world, and He **sent Christ to me,** that lost sheep! **I didn't even have the strength** to come to Him. **He came** into **the wilderness** of the **world.**

"Therefore, leaving the discussion of the **elementary principles (teachings) of** Christ, let us **go on to maturity,** not laying again the foundation of repentance from dead works and of faith toward God" (Hebrews 6:1 NASB).

Jesus found me and He **carried me** on His shoulders, **like a Shepherd** holding a small lamb. (Luke 15.4-6) **What did the Lord Jesus tell** His disciples? "You have **not** chosen Me, but **I have chosen you**" (John 15.16 KJV). **What does God say there?** "I will have mercy on whom I will have mercy; and I will have compassion on whom I will have compassion." **Again God says,** "Jacob I have loved, but Esau I have hated" (Romans 9:13).

> **"(Grace) is God reaching downward to people who are in rebellion against Him."** - Jerry Bridges

We are unable to understand all the **inscrutable ways** of God. He **is,** after all, a **supernatural, awe-inspiring God.** His **thoughts** are **far higher** than our thoughts. But in I Corinthians 1:27-28c (NIV). **He tells us** whom He has chosen - the **weak,** the **foolish,** the **despised!** The **Word of God states,** "God has chosen the **foolish** things of the world ... God has chosen the **weak** things of the world ... **God has chosen** the **base** things of the world, and the things which are **despised** ... the things which are not!"

I pray you understand what God is saying here. Often **we deceive and mislead ourselves** by **thinking** that because we are 'far better' than others, **we have been chosen by God.** But if we have been **truly called, chosen and saved** by God, **we will realize** that we are 'no better' than others; perhaps we are worse! **The Bible instructs us** and the **Christian life shows us** how **wretched,** how **mean,** how **selfish** we are - deep within ourselves. **It is past time** we learn that there is **nothing good in us!** (Romans 3:10; 7.18). **I can boast of nothing** in myself. **I have no merit,** I am **not worthy.** It is **by the sheer sovereign grace of God** that **I was chosen!** I was **called!** I was **saved!**

For centuries many have **twisted** and **perverted** the **teaching** of the **sovereign grace of God.** Nobody can fathom it. But **I praise God for knowing one thing,** His **choosing me** means that He has **brought me** into **His glorious purpose,** and by His **amazing** and **abounding grace.** He will fulfil that purpose in me. (Philippians 1:6) **But, I must surrender** to Him, **submit** to Him; for **He is the sovereign God,** the **sovereign Lord** of heaven and earth.

> **Grace is God's favor shown** to people who **do not deserve** any **favor** at all ... **We deserve** nothing but **hell.** If you **think you deserve heaven,** take it from me, **you are not a Christian.** - Martyn Lloyd-Jones

Every knee shall bow to Him in the **here and now,** or in the **hereafter! If you have been chosen to enjoy the grace of God,** tremble! The **Almighty God has no time** for haughty fools who think they are a **superior and privileged class** of the predestinated 'elect'. **The Word of God says grace is given to the humble.** And the **lesson of humility takes a lifetime to learn!**

God's sovereign grace is 'eternal' because **our sovereign God is eternal.** This **'grace' was 'planned'** before it was **revealed,** and was **'purposed'** before it was **conveyed. God planned us** and **knew our name** before we **were even born,** He **knows everything from** the **beginning.** This is true, **even in the Old Testament.** Then the **Word of the LORD came to me (Jeremiah),** saying: "**Before I formed you** in your mother's **womb I knew** you; **before you were born I sanctified you; I ordained you** a **prophet** to the nations."

> **"(Grace is) free sovereign favor to the ill-deserving." - B.B. Warfield**

There are **so many characteristics** and **attributes** that are all **about Almighty God** and so many things **He has done** for us that are **awe-inspiring.** In **Psalm 139,** we see **David's praises** for **four of God's awesome characteristics:** His knowledge, presence, power, and judgment.

Let's face it, **we live in a very technical, skeptical and scientific world,** it seems **we have abandoned** or **forsaken** our childlike **sense of wonder** and **reverence** for the **characteristics of God. We fail to notice the daily miracles** surrounding us. **Jesus warned us,** "Anyone who will not receive the kingdom of God like a little child will never enter it" (Mark 10:15 NIV).

Jesus told us to call upon God with the **wonder** and **amazement** of a child. **He calls us to believe in Him** with the trusting nature of a child. **God wants to see our excitement** every time we seek His presence. Let me ask you, **have you lost your wonder** and **amazement** of God? **Do you take** the **sophistications and specifics** of His creation for granted? **Spend some time reflecting** on the **awe-inspiring work of God** and recapture the wonder of a child.

When we think of God's sovereignty, we often **associate it** with **His power, knowledge** of the big, eternal picture, yet **He** also **knows** the very deepest **little corners** of our **hearts. Almighty God knows us inside and out**--better than we know ourselves. He knows **what we're going to say** even **before we say it** (Psalm 139:1–4). **Because our God is sovereign,** He is **able to create life itself** (Psalm 139:13–14). **How amazing** is **our God who designed**

everything from the **tiniest cell** in our bodies to the **grandest star** in the universe!

God is sovereign, and **His grace likewise** is **sovereign.** Just what does that mean? **God exercises grace toward** and **bestows it upon** whom **He pleases:** "Even so might grace reign," **Paul wrote** in Romans 5:21. **If grace "reigns"** then it is **on the throne,** and the **occupant** of the throne is sovereign. Consequently, "the throne of grace," in **Hebrews 4:16 states,** "Let us therefore come boldly to the **throne of grace** that we may obtain mercy **and find grace** to help in time of need" (NIV).

"Marvelous grace of our loving Lord,
Grace that exceeds our sin and our guilt!
Yonder on Calvary's mount outpoured, There
where the blood of the Lamb was spilled." (J. Johnson)

Marvelous grace is the **sovereign** and **saving favor** of God **exercised** in the **bestowment of blessings upon those** who have **no merit** in them and for which **no compensation** is demanded from them. **Grace can neither be** bought, earned, nor won by the creature. **If it could be,** it would **cease to be grace.** When a **thing is said to be of** "grace," we mean that **the recipient has no claim upon it,** that it was in **nowise due him.** It comes to him **as pure love,** and, **at first, unasked and undesired.**

Because of God's sovereign, gracious dealings with
us, we should praise Him, obey Him, and make Him
known to others through our faithful witness.

Let me **write this again** ... **God's grace is sovereign!** Since **we have no claim on God's grace** and **cannot contribute anything to it,** then grace must be **sovereignly bestowed upon His children.** As **God said to Moses,** "I will have mercy on whom I have mercy, and I will have compassion on whom I have compassion" (Exodus 33:19 NIV).

Some Christians, less-studied in the Scriptures may **become greatly troubled** by the **fact that grace is bestowed sovereignly.** Let me **ask you a question** ... what **other basis** is there for **its distribution?** In Romans 9:14 **Paul asks** the question: **Can God be just** when **grace is given to some** but **not to others?** He **answers his own question** by **reminding** the reader that **justice**

can only condemn all men, for all have sinned. We dare not plead for justice with God, for justice can only be satisfied by our condemnation.

God is sovereign in the exercise of His grace. Grace, in its broadest biblical sense, is favor shown to the undeserving. It is the antithesis of justice. Justice demands the impartial enforcement of law, requiring each to receive his legitimate due. It bestows no favor and is no respecter of persons, thus it knows neither pity nor mercy.

> Nothing whatever pertaining to godliness and real
> holiness can be accomplished without grace. - Augustine

While the Law is the 'standard' of righteousness, grace is the 'source' of righteousness. The Law defines righteousness, only Grace delivers it. The Law was never intended to be a means of obtaining grace; it was given to demonstrate to men that grace was desperately needed.

Whatever the Law says, it speaks to those who are under the Law, that every mouth may be closed, and all the world may become accountable to God; because by the works of the Law no flesh will be justified in His sight; for through the Law comes the knowledge of sin. But now apart from the Law the righteousness of God has been manifested, being witnessed by the Law and the Prophets (Romans 3:19-21).

Grace operates on a totally different basis. Grace does not give men what they deserve, but what God delights to give, in spite of their sin. God is only unjust if He withholds from men benefits which they rightfully deserve, but He is gracious in bestowing upon men salvation and blessings which they could never merit.

> "Grace is unconditional love toward a person
> who does not deserve it" (Paul Zahl).

Someone has written, "Grace reigns!" I like that, although sometimes I don't always totally understand it. Grace reigns everywhere and over all things grace reigns, then it reigns from a throne. And the One who sits upon the throne is sovereign. The throne of the sovereign God is called, "the throne of grace" (Hebrews 4:16).

Grace is a perfection of the divine character which is exercised only toward the elect. Grace is the sole source of all spiritual blessings of God.

It is the eternal and absolute free favor of God, displayed in the bequeathal of spiritual and eternal blessings to the guilty and the unworthy.

Each time the Bible declares that grace is sovereign it is declaring that God is gracious to whom He will be gracious (Romans 9:11-18). Salvation and eternal life is the gift of God (Romans 6:23). If it is a gift, it cannot be claimed as a right. If it is a gift, it cannot be earned by works. If it is a gift, the Giver is free to bestow it upon whom He will - those who will receive.

On most occasions, as stated, this is a hard truth, so hard that the natural man (unsaved), and the carnal man (babes in Christ) cannot receive it. In fact, on most occasions, nothing more riles the natural man, and brings to the surface his inborn and habitual hostility and animosity against God and his Christian friends, than to press upon him the eternality, the freeness, and the absolute sovereignty of divine grace.

He reasons, that God should have formed His purpose from everlasting, without in any way consulting this fleshly little creature, is too abasing for the unbroken shallow heart. That grace cannot be earned or won by any efforts of man is too self-emptying for self-righteousness. And that grace singles out whom it pleases to be its favored object arouses hot protests from haughty rebels. The clay rises up against the Potter and asks, "Why have You made me like this?" A lawless insurrectionist dares to call into question the justice and wisdom of divine sovereignty.

> "I rejoice in the sovereignty of God because
> He wields it in all things to preserve Himself
> as my greatest treasure." - John Piper

The grace of God is shown in and by and through the Lord Jesus Christ. "The law was given by Moses, but grace and truth came by Jesus Christ" (John 1:17). This does not mean that God never exercised grace toward any before His Son became incarnate; (Genesis 6:8, Exodus 33:19), clearly show otherwise. Grace and truth were fully revealed and perfectly exemplified when the Redeemer came to this earth, and died for His people upon the cross.

It is through Christ, the Mediator alone, that the grace of God flows to His elect. Paul writes, "Much more the grace of God, and the gift of grace, which is by one man, Jesus Christ, much more those who receive abundance of grace, and of the gift of righteousness, shall reign in life by one, Jesus

Christ, so might grace reign through righteousness unto eternal life by Jesus Christ our Lord" (Romans 5:15,17,21).

Let me continue: the Grace of God is asserted in the Bible, (Acts 20:24), which is to the self-righteous Jew a "stumbling block," and to the conceited and philosophizing Greek (Gentile), "foolishness." It's because there is nothing whatever that can be credited to the gratifying of the ego and pride of man. It proclaims that unless we come to God under God's terms and are saved by grace, we cannot be saved at all.

The Word of God declares in no uncertain terms, that apart from Christ, the indescribable and unspeakable Gift of God's grace, the state of every man is lost, desperate, irredeemable, and hopeless. The Gospel addresses men as guilty, condemned, perishing criminals. The Word declares that the most virtuous moralist is in the same terrible plight as is the most pitiful lawbreaker; and the most passionate confessor, with all his religious pretending, is no better off than the most profane infidel.

> Grace is sovereign. As God said to Moses, "I will have
> mercy on whom I have mercy, and I will have compassion
> on whom I have compassion" (Exodus 33:19 NIV).

Many, through the years, have been greatly troubled by the fact that grace is bestowed sovereignly, but what other basis is there for its distribution?

God's sovereignty is not an easy issue, is it? It's a subject that raises lots of questions and I want to ask you some of those questions today to make you think. I want your help in finding biblical answers.

Many people throw around the idea, "Well, God is sovereign, and He is in 'Control' of everything." And they struggle for an answer to that. So I think this will help a lot of people if we can get a biblical handle on how to understand the sovereignty of Almighty God.

The sovereignty of God is a stumbling block for atheists and unbelievers, who demand that, if God is in total control, why doesn't He answer questions that the human mind cannot grasp? Like, "why does God allow evil?" Instead, we are called to have faith in God's goodness and love.

This theological puzzle is also raised by the phrase 'sovereignty of God.' If God truly controls everything, how can humans have free will? It is obvious from Scripture and from life that people do have free will in many areas of their life. We make both good and bad choices. However, it is the Holy Spirit Who prompts the human heart to choose God, a good choice.

In the **examples** of **King David** and the **Apostle Paul**, for example, **God also works** with **man's bad choices** to **turn lives around … theirs or others!**

The ugly truth is that **sinful humans deserve** 'nothing' from **a holy God. We cannot manipulate God** in prayer. We cannot **expect a rich, pain-free life**, as touted by the **prosperity gospel.** Neither can we **expect to reach heaven because** we are a **"good person."** Jesus Christ has **provided Himself** to us as **the way** to eternal life and heaven (John 14:6).

Part of God's sovereignty is that **despite our unworthiness, God chooses to love** and **save us anyway.** He gives everyone the **freedom to accept** or **reject** His **love.**

God says, **"For my thoughts are not your thoughts, neither are your ways my ways, declares the Lord. For as the heavens are higher than the earth, so are my ways higher than your ways, and my thoughts than your thoughts"** (Isaiah 55:8-9 NASB).

God's thoughts far **surpass** the **human** capacity for thinking. **He doesn't** always **operate** in **a way that makes sense to us. Isaiah's words remind us** that the **Lord is sovereign** - even in **our pain,** even in **our troubles.** Through it all, **His love is transforming** us, **perfecting** us, and **completing** us. Remember, **Almighty God is Infinite,** while **humans** are **finite.**

"God's sovereignty is first painful, then slowly **powerful,** and over much time seen to be **profitable.** It is **to be studied** with **great sensitivity** for the **experiences of others** and **deep reverence** for the **One who controls** the outcomes of **every matter in the universe."**

Grace operates on a totally **different basis. Grace does** not give **men what they deserve,** but **what God delights to give,** in spite of their sin. **God is only unjust** if He **withholds** from men **benefits which they rightfully deserve,** but He **is gracious** in **bestowing** upon men **salvation** and **blessings** which they **could never merit.**

Grace does not look for good men whom it **may approve,** for it is **not grace but mere justice** to approve goodness. **God is looking for condemned,** guilty, speechless, sinful and **helpless men** that **He may save, justify, sanctify and glorify.**

Again … What is sovereign grace?

It is our **Sovereign God's richness in grace** which provided the **plan** for **deliverance** (salvation) from disobedience, sin and death. **Paul gave that truth a prominent place** in **Ephesians** for our **close consideration.**

Paul's epistle to the saints (Christians) **at Ephesians** is an incredible book, **affluent** in the **doctrines of God** that gives us **hope, assurance,** and the **protection** we'll need as we live in this age. **It teaches** that **the enemy** is out there **trying to destroy our faith in Christ** and **abolish our testimony.** That's **why** every Christian needs to **armor up** and **be prepared** for a **spiritual battle** that we're **already in and** for the **battles yet to come.**

> **"He predestined us** to **adoption** as **sons** through Jesus
> Christ to Himself according to the kind **intention**
> **of His will,** to the praise of the **glory of His grace,**
> which He freely bestowed on us in the Beloved. **In**
> **Him** we have **redemption** through **His blood,** the
> **forgiveness** of our trespasses, **according to the riches**
> **of His (God's) grace"** (Ephesians 1:5-7 NASB).

Paul emphasized again to the **Ephesians God's promised riches of grace** to the redeemed. "In order that in the **ages to come** He might **show** the **surpassing riches** of **His grace** in kindness toward us in Christ Jesus" (Ephesians 2:7 NASB).

Paul also used the delightful **phrase, "the grace of God" early** in **Colossians.** And again it seems to be **another direct reference to Jesus.** "You previously heard **in the word of truth,** the **gospel,** which has come to you, just as in all the world also it is constantly bearing fruit and increasing, even as it has been doing in you also since the day you **heard of it and understood the grace of God in truth"** (Colossians 1:5, 6 NASB).

> **"Grace is the free and sovereign work of God**
> **to do for us what we cannot do for ourselves,**
> **even though we don't deserve it."**

The sovereign grace of God combines **two of God's attributes, His sovereignty** and **His graciousness.** Both **characteristics of God** are **so all-encompassing** that **many volumes have been written** about each. The **doctrine** of **sovereign grace** is the merging of the two into a **thrilling truth** that **gives us a glimpse into the mind and heart of our great God.**

The sovereignty of God is His total control of all things past, present, and future. Nothing happens beyond His knowledge and control. All things are either caused by Him or allowed by Him for His own purposes and in accordance with His perfect will and timing (Romans 11:36; I Corinthians 8:6). He is the only absolute and omnipotent ruler of the universe and is sovereign in creation, providence, and redemption.

The Word of God states, "We are His workmanship, created in Christ Jesus unto good works; which God hath before ordained (or prepared before) that we should walk in them …" (Ephesians 2:10). Our effectual calling depends not upon our goodness or pious religious acts, but upon God's purpose and grace. This grace was given to us in Christ Jesus before the world began (II Timothy 1:9).

The apostle Paul admits that he was a servant of God only by grace and it was by grace that he labored effectively for the cause of Christ (1 Corinthians 15:10). Sovereign grace chose to save Paul on the Damascus Road, and sovereign grace showered him with untold blessings.

As Christians we benefit from God's sovereign grace. "For by grace are you saved through faith" (Ephesians 2:8). Our very salvation and position in Christ is due to His grace through the faith that He gives us (Hebrews 12:2). Even those who hate God receive His grace. Every breath God allows them to take is a product of His common grace to all creation: "He makes His sun to rise on the evil and on the good, and sends rain on the just and on the unjust" (Matthew 5:45 ASV). Even the atheist enjoys the effects of God's sovereign grace through God's beautiful creation and His provision of the resources necessary for food, clothing, and housing. God doesn't owe these things to us, but He sovereignly provides them to exhibit His grace.

The sovereignty of God is His total control of all things past, present, and future. Nothing happens beyond His knowledge and control. All things are either caused by Him or allowed by Him for His own purposes and in accordance with His perfect will and timing (Romans 11:36; I Corinthians 8:6). He is the only absolute and omnipotent ruler of the universe and is sovereign in creation, providence, and redemption.

"The key to Christian living is a thirst and hunger for God. And one of the main reasons people do not understand or experience the sovereignty of grace and the way it works through the

> awakening of sovereign joy is that their hunger
> and thirst for God is too small" - John Piper

The apostle Paul admits that he **was a servant of God 'only' by grace.** and it **was by grace** that **he labored effectively** for the cause of Christ (1 Corinthians 15:10). **Sovereign grace chose** to **save Paul** on the Damascus Road, and **sovereign grace showered** him with **untold troubles** and **blessings.**

The sovereign grace of God is **noted** most often by theologians in the matter of election. **We see it best explained** in Ephesians 1:5–6: "**He predestined us** to be **adopted** as his sons through Jesus Christ, in accordance with **His pleasure** and **will** - to the **praise of his glorious grace,** which he has freely given us in the One he loves." Here, **in the same sentence,** we have a reference **to predestination** (God's sovereignty) and **God's glorious grace** - sovereign grace..."according to the **purpose of His will"** (Ephesians 1:5-6) **by purpose,** which He set forth in Christ" (Ephesians 1:9 ESV).

With the **inspiration of God,** Paul wanted the Ephesian **church** readers **to know** that is was **only because** of the **mercies of God** that **we are saved by grace through faith** and that faith is in Jesus Christ but **even that faith** is a **gift from above.** Even more, **Paul wanted to prepare the Christian** for their **walk with God** and to **know that we** "**we do not wrestle against** flesh and blood, but against the rulers, against the authorities, against the cosmic powers over this present darkness, against the spiritual forces of evil in the heavenly places" (Ephesians 6:12 ESV), so they will **need to put on the full armor of God** so that they "may be **able to withstand in the evil day** (Ephesians 6:13), and the **evil one and his demons.**

God sovereignly chose those He would save **through His gracious act** of sending His **Son to die** on the cross for their salvation. **Sinners were unable to save themselves** or, **like Mary, to merit God's favor** because of their **transgression** (disobedience) of **His Law.**

> "But **where sin** abounded, **grace did much more abound"** (Romans 5:20).

If someone reading this doesn't believe in predestination or **election,** then **my question is; what do you do** with the first chapter of **Ephesians?** What about **Paul writing that God** "**chose** us in Him **before** the foundation of the world, that we should be holy and blameless before him." In love **He predestined** us for **adoption as sons** through Jesus Christ.

God was the 'initiator' of our calling (Ephesians 1) and not we ourselves and it is He Who provided the way through Jesus Christ (Acts 4:12) to make possible our work-free salvation. This should keep us humble because we can look at the lost and say "there we go except for the grace of God." He also wants to prepare the Christian for a spiritual battle that is too much for us; not too much for us if we put on the armor of God but even with that, He provides for us (Ephesians 6:10-17).

We have been chosen in Christ before the foundation of the world (Ephesians 1.4). God knew me even before I was born (Jeremiah 1:5). The mystery of God's ways, the mystery of God's sovereign grace. Paul says, He called me by His grace. (Galatians 1.6). He chooses, He calls. Sometimes we think that when we have made a decision for Christ, that we have chosen Him. But actually it is His Spirit working in us. Otherwise, we would never have come to God or Christ.

We were 'lost' in our own wickedness – utterly cut off from God. The Father sent Christ into this world, and He sent Christ to me, that lost sheep! I didn't even have the spiritual strength or knowhow to come to Him. He came into the wilderness of the world, He found me and He carried me on His shoulders, like a Shepherd holding a small lamb (Luke 15:4-6).

Therefore, Christians are "justified freely by His grace through the redemption that is in Christ Jesus" (Romans 3:24). God in His sovereign grace has chosen to save those on whom He has set His love (Romans 9:8–13). They are picked out of the stream of helpless men and women cascading into hell. This is a humbling truth and should result in immense gratitude on our part.

Why did God grant His sovereign grace on believers? Not because we deserve salvation but to demonstrate "the riches of His glory" (Romans 9:14–23). Our only proper response is to proclaim, "Blessed be the God and Father of our Lord Jesus Christ, who has blessed us with every spiritual blessing in the heavenly places in Christ" (Ephesians 1:3 NASB).

> "For whom he did foreknow, he also did predestinate to be conformed to the image of his Son, that he might be the firstborn among many brethren" (Romans 8:29).

> Remember: that Scripture NEVER speaks of repentance and faith as being foreseen or foreknown by God!

Note: that **Romans 8:29, 30** - "For **Whom (not what, but Whom)** He **foreknew,** He also **predestined** to become **conformed** to the **image** of His Son, that He might be the **first-born** among many brethren; and WHOM He predestined, **THESE** He also called; and **WHOM** He called, **THESE** He also justified; and **WHOM** He justified, **THESE He also glorified.**"

As John wrote, "Beloved, **now we are the sons of God,** and it doth **not yet appear** what we shall be: **but we know that, when He shall appear,** we shall be like him, for **we shall see him as he is**" (1 John 3:2). But of **this we may be sure,** that there will always **be an essential** and unapproachable **distinction between** the **glory of Christ's humanity and theirs.** His **humanity,** being in **eternal union with his Deity,** derives a **glory** which is **distinct** from all other, and to which there **can be no approach,** and with which there can be no comparison. **The glory of the moon never** can be the glory **of the sun,** though **she shines with his reflected light.**

He will change our vile body that it may "**be fashioned like unto his glorious body,** according **to the working** whereby **He is able** even to **subdue all things** unto **Himself**" (Philippians 3:21), but **though alike, it will not be the same.** It will be the **saints' eternal happiness** to **see Him as He is,** and to **be made like unto Him;** but it will be their everlasting joy that he should **ever have that pre-eminence of glory** which is **his birthright,** and **to adore** which will ever be their **supreme delight.**

To have a body free from all sin, sickness, and **sorrow,** filled to its **utmost capacity** of **holiness** and **happiness,** able **to see Him** as He is **without dying** under the sight, and to **be re-united** to its once suffering but now **equally glorified companion,** an **immortal soul,** expanded to its **fullest powers of joy** and **bliss -** if this be not sufficient, **what more can God give?** - J.C. Philpot

> **There can be no grace when there is no sovereignty.**
> **Deny God's right** to choose whom He will and you deny
> His right to save whom He will. **Deny His right to save**
> **whom He will** and you deny that **salvation is of grace. If**
> **salvation is made** to hinge upon **any merit** or **fitness** in
> man, seen or foreseen, **grace is at an end.** - Horatius Bonar

There was a time with each of us, as with the **Colossian Christians,** when we **did not know** "the grace of God in truth." They, perhaps as we, may have **only heard of Jesus,** knowing **little** about Him, His origin, His purpose, and the hope of the life that centers in Him. **But a time came** when **we did know** about **God's great grace.** Such was the **happy experience** of those **Colossians.**

Paul took their minds back to the time - when they heard, knew, and **believed as truth the words** about "the grace of God." "In the word of truth, the gospel" ... "since the day ye heard, and knew the grace of God in truth." **He mixed, merged and repeated** words that pertain to salvation ... truth, gospel, the grace of God, hearing. **Again Paul intentionally put in focus** the important aspects of salvation **which are supplied through God's riches by Christ Jesus** our **Lord,** the **living example of divine grace.**

Salvation to Sovereign Sanctification

Conversion is not just regeneration. This is a **neglected fact** in our **preaching today.** When a person is **born again, he knows** that it is because he has **received something** as a **gift from Almighty God** and **not** because of **his own decision.** People may **make vows and promises,** and may be **determined** to follow through, **but none of this is salvation.** Salvation **means** that we are **brought to the place** where we are **able to see ourselves in sin** and **place our life completely** in the **finished work of Jesus,** and to **receive something from God** on the **authority of Jesus** Christ, **namely, forgiveness of sins.**

This is followed by God's a mighty work of grace: "And now, **brethren,** I **commend you to God,** and to the **Word of his grace,** which is **able to build you up,** and to **give you an inheritance** among all **them which are sanctified**" (Acts 20:32). **In sanctification,** the one who has been **born again, deliberately gives up his right to himself to Jesus Christ,** and **identifies himself** entirely with **God's ministry to others.**

> **For Christians, the Apostle Peter challenged us with, "He who called you is holy,** you also **be holy** in **all** your **conduct,** since **it is written,** "You shall be holy, for I am holy."
> And **if you call on him as Father** who judges impartially according to each one's deeds, **conduct yourselves** with fear **throughout the time of your exile, knowing** that **you were ransomed** from the futile ways inherited from your forefathers, not with perishable things such as silver or gold, but **with the precious blood of Christ,** like that of a **lamb** without **blemish** or **spot** (I Peter 1:15-19).

I want to **focus your attention on the phrase,** "throughout the time of your exile" in this passage. It's an **important insight** that can **directly impact how you live** your life here on earth as a follower of Christ. **The Bible calls us strangers or "aliens" in this world** because our **affections** and ambitions are to be focused on **things beyond this life.** Like **Abraham,** who lived in tents and kept on moving through the Promised Land, **we are merely travelers through this life.**

As believers today we need **to live** in our **spiritual "tents,"** not getting **too attached** to the stuff of this world. Do you remember the old song, **"This world is not my home, I'm 'just- a-passin' through,** my treasures are laid up, somewhere beyond the blue." We're only here **temporarily!** Unfortunately, far too many of us **get too attached to our "stuff."** We labor, fret and worry about all the 'stuff' we are **accumulating here** on this **earth,** when all along, **we know** we **cannot take it with us.** Our **God** has **promised** that "He would supply all our needs," not our 'greeds.'

Have you ever noticed that we **buy things** we **don't need** with **money we don't have** to **impress people** we **don't even like?** We try to **keep up** with the **Jones family,** but when we **finally catch up** with them, **they refinance!** (Chapter 7 above),

In this present 'world system,' we are **in exile from heaven,** which is our **true home.** And since **our true citizenship is in heaven** and not on earth, we must **detach ourselves** from the things of this world, and **attach ourselves to eternal things.**

When you live like an alien and stranger who **is** in **exile here** on earth, other **people may wonder** about you a little bit. But that's fine. Just **be ready to fold your spiritual "tent",** because you're **moving onward and upward one day!**

Live your life as a citizen of heaven who is
temporarily exiled here on Earth.

The sanctified are, because of **that experience, heirs** of God and **joint-heirs** with Jesus Christ. "For both **He that sanctifies and they who are sanctified are** all of one: for which cause he is not ashamed **to call them brethren"** (Hebrews 2:11). The **experience of Sanctification makes us** one with Christ, standing on an equal basis with Him **in the sight of God** with respect to **this particular inheritance.**

As Christians we, too, **benefit** from God's **sovereign grace.** "For by grace are you saved through faith" (Ephesians 2:8). **Our very salvation** and

position in Christ is **due** to His **grace** through the faith that **He gives us** (Hebrews 12:2).

Listen, even those **who hate God receive His grace.** Every **breath** God allows them to take **is a product of His** common **grace to all creation:** "He makes His sun to rise on the evil and on the good, and sends rain on the just and on the unjust" (Matthew 5:45). **Even the atheist enjoys** the **effects** of God's **sovereign grace** through **God's beautiful creation** and His **provision** of the **resources** necessary for food, clothing, and housing. **God doesn't owe** these things to us, **but He sovereignly provides** them to exhibit His grace.

God is sovereign in creation, providence, redemption, and judgment. That is a **central assertion of Christian doctrine. This means,** among other things, **that God is King and Lord of all.** To put this another way: **nothing happens without God's willing it to happen, willing it** to happen **before it happens,** and willing it to happen **in the way that it happens.** But at its heart, it is **saying nothing different** from the assertion of the Nicene Creed: "I believe in God, the Father Almighty." **To say that God is sovereign** is to express **His almightiness** in every area.

The sovereign grace of God is noted most often by **theologians** in the matter of **election.** We see it best **explained in Ephesians 1:4–6:** "For **He chose us** in Him **before** the **foundation** of the **world** to be holy and blameless in His presence. **In love He predestined us** for **adoption as His sons** through Jesus Christ, according to the good pleasure of His will, to the **praise of His glorious grace,** which He has **freely given** us **in the Beloved One**" (BSB). **We see** here **in the same sentence,** we have a **reference** to **predestination** (God's sovereignty) and **God's glorious grace - sovereign grace.**

Election is the gracious purpose of God, according **to which He regenerates, sanctifies, and glorifies sinners.** It is consistent with the **free agency of man** and comprehends all the means in connection with the end. **It is a glorious display of God's sovereign goodness,** and is infinitely wise, holy, and unchangeable. **It excludes boasting and promotes humility.**

All true believers endure to the end. Those **whom God has accepted in Christ,** and **sanctified by His Spirit,** will **never fall away from the state of grace** but shall **persevere to the end.** Believers **may fall into sin** through **neglect** and **temptation,** whereby **they grieve** the Spirit, **impair their graces** and comforts, **bring reproach** on the cause of Christ, and **temporal judgments** on themselves; yet **they shall be kept by the power of God** through **faith unto salvation.**

God sovereignly chose those He would save through **His gracious act of sending His Son to die** on the cross for their salvation. **Sinners** were **unable** to **save themselves** or, like Mary, **to merit God's favor** because of their **transgression of His Law.** "But where sin abounded, grace did much more abound" (Romans 5:20). **Therefore, Christians are "justified freely by His grace** through the redemption that is in Christ Jesus" (Romans 3:24).

As we study the sovereignty of God we notice that it is a very humbling doctrine. Why? Because our **stubborn flesh** wants to be **in control** of every situation.3

Sovereignty reminds us that **'God is God'** and **'we are not!'** Listen, **understanding God's sovereignty** causes us to **focus on Him,** not ourselves. **Our response** should be to **fall at His feet** and to **give Him** everything we are and everything we own. **Pride is not** the sole possession of the powerful, the rich, or the famous. **Pride controls each of us** if we're not careful, and **keeps us from** not yielding to Him.

> **"The Lord** has **established His throne in heaven,**
> **and His kingdom rules over all"** - Psalm 103:19

These verses, 19-21, **plainly assert that God is sovereign** over the universe...that **He rules all things. His throne** is settled and established. **It cannot be shaken** by the affairs of men. **His kingdom rules over all.**

In the abstract, most have **no problem** with this doctrine. It **is not hard** for us to believe that the **Almighty orders the path** of the stars in the skies. **We** can't say **how He does it,** only that He does it, and if He didn't do it **the stars would cease** Way shine. He put the **Milky Way** in its place and all the galaxies beyond. That's **not hard to believe.** After all, **somebody's got to create** and take care of the stars. **God does! We accept that.**

Our problems begin when **sovereignty becomes personal.** To speak of the **stars** is one thing. **That's God's designation,** but to say **God is in charge of all** that happens **to me,** the **good** and the bad, the **positive** and the negative, and that **God is working out His plan**...that somehow **includes everything** that happens **to me**...to suppose that He works out the **details of my life** and **gives me what is best** for me every day, **that's another story!**

Question: If the **Man** in charge, **our Almighty, Eternal, Omnipotent God,** isn't running the show, please tell me, **who is?** A. W. Pink once wrote, "To say that **God is Sovereign** is to say that **'God is God'.**" And I add again, that **"we are not!"**

Consider this: **In the beginning**, there was **only one will - God's!** When there was only one will – the **world was filled** with **peace** and **harmony.** Next comes **man, Satan** and **sin.** Yet, from **our limited, finite,** human point of view, this is **seemingly not fair. Get a grip! Accept** the **infallible Word of God** for what it **says, change your beliefs,** or **get out of church work,** because **you** will **never be happy spiritually outside His Word and His will.**

God in His sovereign grace has **chosen** to save those on whom **He has set His love** (Romans 9:8–13). They are picked out of the **stream of helpless men and women plummeting** into hell as of a result of their transgressions. **This is a humbling truth** and **should result in immense gratitude** on our part. **Why did God bestow** His **sovereign grace** on believers? **Not because we deserve salvation** but to **demonstrate** "the riches of His glory" (Romans 9:14–23). **Our** only **proper response is to proclaim,** "Blessed be the God and Father of our Lord Jesus Christ, who has blessed us with **every spiritual blessing** in the heavenly places in Christ" (Ephesians 1:3).

"**The Spirit of the Sovereign LORD** is on me, because the **LORD** has **anointed me** to proclaim good news to the poor. **He has sent me** to bind up the brokenhearted, **to proclaim freedom** for the captives **and release** from darkness for the prisoners!" (Isaiah 61:1 NIV).

In closing, let me ask you: **What can arise** from the **infusion of divine relationship** with the **human heart?** What happens when a person **runs out of themselves** and desperately **hangs onto** an **invisible thread of faith** energized by **personal relationship** with the **Son of God?**

This is **not a call** to **unattainable greatness.** This is **not a teaching** on **doctrinal secrets** that **must be unlocked** in order **to experience the extraordinary.** This **book is about** what can **happen when normal, ordinary** people **truly meet Jesus** and **surrender** their **lives to Him.**

It **doesn't matter** what **stage of spiritual maturity** you **find yourself** in right **now.** If **you will engage** with **Jesus** on a **regular basis,** in **Bible Study** and your **fellowship with the Lord,** He will **astound you** with **what He does** both **in you** and **through you!** When you **allow these teachings** into your daily life … '**Be ready to be challenged!'**

> "**Soli Deo gloria**" "**God is sovereign,** and in His sovereignty **He displays** His **majestic glory.** Without it, we would have **no being, no salvation,** and no hope. - Derek Thomas

This is the mission of Christianity in the world - **to help** men to be victorious, **to whisper** hope wherever there is despair, **to give cheer** wherever there is discouragement. **It goes forth** to **open** prisons, to **unbind** chains, and **to bring out** captives. Its **symbol** is not **only a cross.** We know **what that means.** It **tells of** life, **not** of **death;** of life **victorious over death.** We must **not suppose** that its promise is only for the final resurrection; it is for **resurrection every day,** every **hour,** over **all death. It means** unconquerable, unquenchable, indestructible, immortal life - at every point **where death seems to have won a victory!**

Let us pray ... Dear Father, as I have studied today **I ask Your blessing,** and Your **guidance** in every way upon what is accomplished in me, **that it would honor** and **please** You, **glorify Your name and Your Son.** I commit myself into Your hands, asking Your blessing, not only now, **and for those** who will be **reading this study** at a later date, **that Your Word written here,** taught, would **have a positive impact** in the lives of **all** who **seek You. Lord, You are the One** who **never changes,** and You are **so good** to us. **Calm our hearts** today with the **grace and peace** that come only from You. **I pray** and **ask all** of this, and **commit it into Your hands** in the **name of Jesus Christ, and for His sake. Amen!**

"The grace of our Lord Jesus Christ be with you all ... Amen" (Romans 16:24).

Printed in the United States
By Bookmasters